Economics
for AS

Economics
for AS

edited by
Colin Bamford

CAMBRIDGE
UNIVERSITY PRESS

PUBLISHED BY THE PRESS SYNDICATE OF THE UNIVERSITY OF CAMBRIDGE
The Pitt Building, Trumpington Street, Cambridge, United Kingdom

CAMBRIDGE UNIVERSITY PRESS
The Edinburgh Building, Cambridge CB2 2RU, UK
40 West 20th Street, New York, NY 10011-4211, USA
10 Stamford Road, Oakleigh, VIC 3166, Australia
Ruiz de Alarcón 13, 28014 Madrid, Spain
Dock House, The Waterfront, Cape Town 8001, South Africa

http://www.cambridge.org

First published 2000
Reprinted 2000

Printed in the United Kingdom at the University Press, Cambridge

Typeface Minion   *System* Apple Macintosh Quark® 4.04

A catalogue record for this book is available from the British Library

ISBN 0 521 77728 3 paperback

Cover photo by courtesy of Gettyone Stone

Every effort has been made to reach copyright holders of material in this book previously published elsewhere. The publisher would be pleased to hear from anyone whose rights they have unwittingly infringed.

Contents

Contributors

Colin Bamford is Professor and Head of Transport and Logistics at the University of Huddersfield. He has written various applied Economics textbooks and more specialist articles in his field of transport economics. Currently Chief Examiner in Economics with OCR, he has almost 30 years experience of examining at A Level.

Keith Brunskill was formerly Head of Economics at Greenhead College, Huddersfield. He is currently a part-time member of staff at Huddersfield University Business School. An experienced A Level examiner with various examination boards, including OCR, he has written a wide range of articles on topical areas of Economics.

Gordon Cain is a Sector Manager in Administration, Management and Business at Bury College. He has taught A Level Economics in a range of schools and colleges. He is a Principal Examiner with OCR, with over 20 years experience of examining at A Level.

Richard Crum was a Lecturer in Economics at the University of East Anglia until his early retirement. He still teaches at the University, in particular on courses in Economics for mature students. He has had extensive A Level examining experience, including for many years Chief Examiner in Economics with the Oxford Delegacy.

Susan Grant is a Lecturer in Economics at West Oxfordshire College. She is an experienced examiner and written various text books and articles on Economics. She is a Principal Examiner with OCR and has a specialist area of interest in macroeconomic policies.

Stephen Munday is an Assistant Head at Saffron Walden County High School. An experienced A Level teacher, he has produced a recent textbook on Current Developments in Economics. He is a question paper setter and teacher moderator with OCR.

Steve Tidball is Head of Economics and Business at Ipswich School. He has written extensively for A Level students and is a regular contributor to *Economics Today*. He is a Principal Examiner with OCR, with a specialist interest in labour economics.

Stephen Walton is Head of Economics at the Kings School Chester, having previously taught in Surrey. He is a Principal Examiner with OCR and has a specialism in aspects of Economics of Europe.

Tony Westaway is a Senior Lecturer in Economics at Loughborough University. He is a Principal Examiner with OCR and has 25 years experience of examining at A Level. His specialist areas of interest are in welfare economics and the economics of sport and leisure.

Preface

This book has been specifically produced for OCR's new AS/A Level specification in Economics, which has been approved by the Qualifications and Curriculum Authority (QCA) for teaching from September 2000.

Its main purpose, as the title indicates, is to provide a self-contained text for the new AS Level. This in itself is a recognised qualification as well as the first stage of the new A Level qualification.

Certain aspects of the book provide an appropriate underpinning for the full A Level – the Introduction and elements of units 1–3 provide material which extends the students' knowledge of the AS specification and, in unit 4, there is comprehensive material to underpin OCR's terminal synoptic module.

The book has been produced by nine authors all of whom have substantial teaching experience and who currently have senior examining roles with OCR. All have also been involved in the development of OCR's specification.

The book has various distinctive features:

- The subject content is arranged in sections and units, each of which is fully compatible with the OCR specification
- The Introduction provides students with the skills they will need to succeed in the AS examination; the section on Preparing for Examinations provides specific advice on how these skills and the subject concepts will be examined by OCR, and includes specimen question papers for each AS module.
- There are Self-assessment tasks included in each section. These are designed for student-centred activity and can also be used by teachers in class situations. A small number of answers to these tasks are also provided.
- Each section highlights key economic concepts as they occur in OCR's specification. These are systematically defined in a glossary at the end of the book.

Although the book has been specifically produced for OCR's examinations, the content of Units 1–3 matches the subject criteria published by the QCA. It is therefore of value to students and teachers who are registered with the other two main awarding bodies. The content of Unit 4, the synoptic module, will also be of value to all students of A Level Economics.

Finally, could I record my thanks to the various people who have made the production of this text possible. In particular to,

- My fellow contributors who have responded positively so that the book will be available for use in schools from September 2000.
- My good friend and OCR colleague, Ian Wilson of the King's School, Macclesfield, for his comments on the draft text.
- Anne Rix for her prodding, prompting and dedication in managing the project.
- Karen Brooke for word processing certain sections of the text; also Suzanne Scott for her work on some of the early material.
- My wife Elisabeth and daughters Emily and Alice for their understanding and patience during the many hours I spent working on the manuscript.

My sincere hope, and that of my colleagues, is that this book will be well-received by students and teachers of Economics. The new specification represents an opportunity for Economics teaching to receive a welcome boost in schools and colleges. If this book helps to achieve this outcome than all the late nights spent on the PC will have been most worthwhile.

Colin G. Bamford
Head, Transport and Logistics, University of Huddersfield
Chief Examiner, OCR Economics

January 2000

Introduction

The economist's 'tool kit' and the OCR examination

On completion of this unit you should:

➤ have a broad idea of what is meant by Economics
➤ know how economists seek to explain economic phenomena
➤ be aware of the 'tool kit' of skills required at AS level
➤ be aware of the structure of the OCR AS/A Level Economics specification

What is Economics?

There are almost as many definitions of Economics as there are economists! Although a definition of the subject is to be expected, it is probably more useful at this stage to set out a few examples of the sort of issues which concern professional economists. These topics occur in an introductory form in the OCR AS specification.

Let us take yourself first of all. Most teenagers find that they want to lead an exciting and full life but unfortunately do not always have the money necessary to do everything they would like to do. So, choices have to be made or, as an economist would say, individuals have to decide:

How to allocate scarce resources in the most effective way?

A body of economic principles and concepts has been developed to explain how people and also businesses, react in this situation. This is a typical example of what an economist would refer to as 'microeconomics'.

It is not only individuals and firms who are faced with having to make choices. Governments face many such problems. For example, how does our government decide how much to spend on the National Health Service and how much should go into providing Social Security benefits? This is the same type of problem facing all of us in our daily lives but on a different scale.

The UK government also has extensive responsibilities in looking after the well-being of our national economy. The Chancellor of the Exchequer, for example, prepares an annual Budget for the economy, in which taxation and government expenditure plans are reviewed. It is also an opportunity to 'manage the economy', by seeking to ensure that policy objectives are being met. As the economist would say, the Chancellor has to decide:

'How to keep the rate of change of prices under control' or, alternatively, 'how to reflate the economy to increase the number of jobs which are available'.

These are typical topics which come under the broad heading of 'macroeconomics' since they relate to the economy as a whole.

As you progress through this text you will come across many other economic problems and issues of both a micro and macro nature. You may now find it useful to complete the following Self-assessment task.

Self-assessment tasks

1 Make a list, in your own words, of some of the economic decisions that:
   ◆ you are facing;
   ◆ your family has to take;
   ◆ the country has to take.
2 Pick up any quality newspaper. Look through it systematically and make a note of the various:
   ◆ microeconomic,
   ◆ macroeconomic,
   problems and issues you find.
   Have you found it easy to classify problems in this way?

Source: Photo by Ann Doherty, *Sunday Times*, London.

The last part of the task is designed to get you to appreciate that many economic problems and issues cannot be satisfactorily classified as micro or macro. In other words, such problems encompass both of the main branches of Economics. For example, an increase in prescription charges may reduce the demand for prescriptions from patients – depending on the extent of this there is an effect on the income of individuals and the government and, in turn, this affects the economy as a whole. So, there can be complex inter-relationships coming into play. In many respects this makes Economics an interesting subject to study.

As you progress through this text, you will be introduced to concepts, theories and simple models which are used by economists to explain the many economic problems and issues which come within the scope of Economics. In time, you will build up a portfolio of such techniques, from a micro- and macroeconomic perspective. Virtually all have their origin in some sort of empirical investigation, that is a study of real economic phenomena. Some concepts have their origin 200 years ago, others are much more contemporary or may have been refined and revised in the light of the growing complexity of the present-day global economy. Again, this serves to enhance the interesting nature of the subject.

Regardless of what you may think about Economics and economists at this stage of your AS studies, few would deny that Economics is a logical subject and that the advice provided by economists is derived from a set of well established principles relating to the operation of the market economy. Many of these are set out in unit 1 of this text. Figure 1 shows in simple terms how economists think and how they seek to explain real problems and issues like those you will have come across in the Self-assessment task above.

At this stage, bear the process shown in figure 1 in mind and return to it whenever you are learning new concepts as it will help you understand how economists think and operate.

To conclude, therefore, it is appropriate to give a clear definition of 'What is Economics?' For a start,

'The child born on a run down housing estate should have the same chance to be healthy and well educated as the child born in the leafy suburbs'

Tony Blair, 18 March 1999

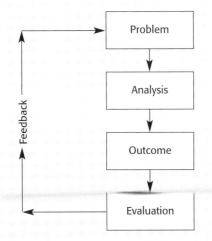

Problem	Statement of a particular economic problem or issue.
Analysis	Application of concepts and techniques of Economics.
Outcome	The result of economic analysis.
Evaluation	An appraisal of the extent to which the outcome is acceptable for individuals or groups.

Figure 1 The road to economic explanation

Self-assessment task

Think again about what you have found out in completing the first Self-assessment task. Now read the article from *The Economist* on the so-called puzzling failure of Economics. Do you agree at this early stage of your studies with what the author is saying? Why might you not yet be in a position to make a proper evaluation?

The puzzling failure of economics

If the world were run by economists, would it be a better place? You might expect economists, not to mention a newspaper called *The Economist*, to think so. After all, many of the policies that people fight over have economics at their core – jobs, wages, investment, growth. Economists, professional and otherwise, are forever criticising those who do run the world for making such a mess of it, and are keen to change the way people think so that things will be run more to their liking. As one Nobel laureate put it, 'I don't care who writes a nation's laws ... if I can write its economics textbooks.'

Paul Samuelson, the author of that remark, has seen his wish fulfilled. His 'Economics', first published in 1948, has sold millions of copies and is still, with its 16th edition in preparation, doing well. Down the editions, the book's views on policy have changed, as have those of the profession at large. These shifting ideas have in turn influenced policy, and to a degree that would make other social scientists drool. Lately the results have been good. During the past decade, some of the worst economic incompetence has ended: central planning has given way to 'transition economics' in Eastern Europe and the former Soviet Union; many developing countries have opened their economies to the outside world; every week another state-run company is put up for sale. Textbook wisdom seems to prevail.

The message and the messenger

But don't praise the dismal scientists too much. Who designed those earlier policies, which failed so disastrously? Economists. Where were those theories of planning, of demand management, of industrial dirigisme and public ownership that did such harm in the third world so persuasively set out? In economics textbooks.

These days, it is true, the advice is better – but it often gets dangerously garbled in transmission. Trade is the best example. By pitting exporters against importers, successive rounds of trade negotiations have encouraged politicians in many countries to lower trade barriers. Yet this effort is based on a false premise: that freeing trade is good for you only if other countries do the same. This basic misunderstanding, left unattended, may one day lead governments to turn back the clock on liberal trade.

Other good policies have likewise been founded on bad economics. Privatisation, for instance, has more often been seen as a way to raise revenue than as a way to promote competition; and deregulation is often portrayed by governments as something that global markets have forced upon them, rather than as a way of raising living standards. As for bad policies based on bad economics, these remain too numerous to mention, despite Mr Samuelson's prodigious efforts.

Why has economics not done better? Economists tend to blame others for being too lazy or too stupid to understand their textbooks. There is doubtless something in this. Economics is hard to teach well. To the uninitiated, its basic principles often seem surprising or odd. And whereas most people will admit their ignorance of physics or biology, the armchair economist is convinced that he knows exactly what he is talking about.

But the economics profession itself also deserves much of the blame. Crucial ideas about the role of prices and markets, the basic principles of microeconomics, are uncontroversial among economists. These are the first ideas that politicians and the public need to grasp if they are to think intelligently about public policy, and the fact is that they are not widely understood. Yet because economists take these essential ideas for granted, they spend their time arguing about much more contentious notions, developed in one disputed way or another from those common underlying principles. The public and their politicians are treated to perpetual squabbles about the exact effects of raising interest rates or of cutting the capital-gains tax or whatever – and conclude that economists disagree about everything and understand nothing. As long as economists choose to talk loudest about the things they understand least well and to remain silent about the underlying ideas that unite them, this is unlikely to change.

And economists must shoulder a further portion of the blame for quite another reason. The biggest economic-policy mistake of the past 50 years, in rich and poor countries alike, has been and still is to expect too much of government. Statism has always found all the support it needs among mainstream economists. They are unfailingly quick to point out various species of market failure; they are usually much slower to ask whether the supposed remedy of government intervention might not, in practice, be worse.

This is not a failure of economics, in fact, but of modern (one might say Samuelsonian) economics. The classical economists viewed the market economy with a kind of awe. Amazing, it truly is, that all these workers, firms and households, acting without visible co-ordination and guided mainly by self-interest, manage to produce such extraordinarily beneficial results. Smith's 'Wealth of Nations' conveyed this sense that the market, for all its 'failures', is a marvel. Today precious few textbooks even try to guide their readers to any such inspiration. Implicitly, at least, their message is too often quite the opposite: that markets aren't perfect and governments (advised by economists) can be. Dismal is the word.

Source: *The Economist*, 23 August 1997.

Economics is a social science – it adopts a scientific framework but is particularly concerned with studying human behaviour, as consumers, in business or in taking decisions about the economy as a whole. More specifically:

Economics is the study of how scarce resources are or should be allocated.

All of the problems and issues you will come across fit into this broad definition.

The economist's 'tool kit'

The economist has a varied 'tool kit', the term that can be used to describe the skills and techniques available for the analysis of economic problems. Two of particular relevance in the AS examinations are:

- the ability to interpret and use data;
- the ability to write in a clear and effective way.

Each of these will now be considered. *You may find it helpful to return to these parts intermittently when you are undertaking some of the Self-assessment tasks in the main units of the book. You should also refer back to this part before you take any of the OCR AS or A2 examinations.*

Data skills

Five main skills are required in the AS specification – they will be further examined at the A2 stage. These skills are:

- the ability to pick out the main trends and features in economic data;
- a knowledge of fractions, percentages, proportions and the rate of change in a set of time-series data;
- a working knowledge of index numbers;
- how to calculate a simple average and know what it means;
- how to understand economic information produced in visual form.

In addition, you will find it useful to know:

- how to plan an investigation into economic problems;
- what is meant by a forecast.

Each of the above will now be looked at. It is important that you feel confident in handling data – these simple skills will help you. You will also gain confidence as you become more familiar with economic data and complete the various self-assessment tasks in each section.

Economic data generally are of two main types. These are:

Time-series data – as the name suggests, the same information is recorded over a period of time, namely a period of years, for months in a year, days in a week and so on.

Cross-sectional data – the easiest way to imagine this type of data is in terms of a 'snapshot', that is a picture taken at a given time.

Another important introductory point concerns the nature of the data itself. Again two types can be recognised, namely:

Discrete data – the simplest way to imagine these is in terms of values which are shown as whole numbers, for example the number of people or number of cars.

Continuous data – such values can usually be measured in a precise way and are not confined to whole numbers, for example income, hours of work or economic growth.

So, when you are confronted with economic data for the first time, ask yourself:

- Is the data shown time-series or cross-sectional data?
- Are the values of the data discrete or continuous?

Data skill 1 – How to pick out the main trends and features in economic data

Look more carefully at the data in table 1. (You will find specific reference to unemployment statistics in section 7.)

Year	Number (in '000's)	Rate[2]	Annual charge
1989	2,075	7.2	
1990	1,974	6.8	−
1991	2,414	8.4	+
1992	2,769	9.7	+
1993	2,936	10.3	+
1994	2,736	9.6	−
1995	2,454	8.6	−
1996	2,334	8.2	−
1997	2,034	7.1	−
1998	1,766	6.1	−

Table 1 UK Unemployment 1989–1998[1]
Notes
[1] Measured in Spring of each year.
[2] Total unemployment as a percentage of all economically active persons.
Source: Annual Abstract of Statistics, 1999, Office for National Statistics.

Introduction

The very first skill you need to develop is what is known as 'eyeballing'. All this means is looking down a column of data or going across rows of data very quickly. In examinations you should do this before you start answering the questions. For time-series data, like that in table 1, you might find it useful to very quickly write a '+' or a '−' between each year so you can see how the data changes over time. This is shown in the final column of the table. You can now tell from this that broadly speaking:

- unemployment fell at the beginning of the time period;
- it then increased for three years;
- it then fell consistently for the remaining years.

You can also get an overview of the data by comparing the end points in a time series, in this case 1989 and 1998. What is useful is to know how much the variable (in this case unemployment) fell over the period. To do this, you need to compare the total fall with the original level. The best way to do this is to calculate the *percentage change*. Using a calculator, this is

$$\frac{(2075 - 1766)}{2075} = 14.9\% \text{ (fall)}$$

In other words, there has been a fall in unemployment of around 15 per cent over the period shown.

Looking at the cross-sectional data in table 2, you might find it useful to stand back and pick out the main patterns in these data. For example, you could look at the highest and lowest values and the difference between them. This is sometimes called the range. You could also see how each observation compares with the average. When you do this, you will find that:

- there is a difference of 3.9 per cent between the highest and the lowest;
- the average has relatively little regional significance – it is clear though that some regions, for example South East and East Midlands, are doing better than others;
- the peripheral regions in the UK, for example Scotland and the North West, have the highest unemployment rates;
- the rate for London is very high, particularly when compared with the South East.

Both of these techniques are simple to apply – between them they give you a very useful insight into cross-sectional economic data.

Data skill 2 – Fractions, percentages, proportions and the rate of change

The simple calculations required to work with fractions, percentages and proportions should be well known to students with GCSE mathematics. (The use of percentage change over a period of time has already been referred to earlier.) Fractions, percentages and proportions are not far removed from each other – they are the same thing but with different names.

Let us stay with unemployment. Suppose a town has an economically active population of 50,000 and of these, 5,000 are unemployed. The unemployment rate is therefore 1 in 10 or 1/10 as a fraction, 0.10 as a proportion and 10 per cent as a percentage. The mathematical relationship is that a fraction can be converted into a proportion by dividing the bottom number or denominator into the upper number or numerator. By multiplying this by 100, a percentage can be obtained. Knowing these relatively straightforward links helps in understanding economic data.

The idea of *rate of change* is rather more difficult to grasp. It is a very relevant mathematical tool widely used and applied in Economics. Referring back to table 1, if we look at the period 1993–8, unemployment has fallen from 2.936m to 1.766m. In other words, it has fallen by 1.170m or 1,170,000 people over a period of five years. In turn, this represents a percentage fall of

Region	%	
North East	6.1	
North West	8.2	
Yorkshire and Humberside	7.0	
East Midlands	4.9	
West Midlands	6.3	UK average 6.1%
Eastern	5.0	
London	8.1	
South East	4.3	
South West	4.5	
Scotland	7.4	
Wales	6.7	
Northern Ireland	7.3	

Table 2 UK regional unemployment rates 1998[1]
Note: [1] Seasonally adjusted.
Sources: As table 1.

1.17/2.936 × 100%, that is approximately 40 per cent over this time. Averaged out, this is an 8 per cent fall per year or a rate of change of 8 per cent per annum.

Looking at table 1, we can also see that the rate of change varied over the years in question. For example, there was a particularly steep fall between 1996 and 1997 (12.9 per cent) and a modest fall from 1995 to 1996 (4.9 per cent). The figures in brackets, which are rates of change per annum, when looked at over a shorter period of time, do vary from the 8 per cent over a five year period. So, when using a rate of change, be very careful to always specify the time period you are working with.

A final word of warning. Often, with economic data, absolute totals for a variable might increase but this increase might be at a slower rate of change than in the past. Going back to table 1, if we look at the period 1990 to 1993, then unemployment increased from 1.974m to 2.936m. It increased in absolute terms for each year within this time window. However, the rate of change or increase varied quite dramatically from just over 22 per cent between 1990 and 1991 to 6 per cent between 1992 and 1993. If you are faced with these rates of change in isolation, you might be led to conclude that unemployment fell between 1992 and 1993, which is clearly not the case. Unemployment continued to increase – it was, though, growing at a slower rate during the period. So, once again, be careful when looking at data where rates of change are being used.

Data skill 3 – A working knowledge of index numbers

Table 3 contains a very familiar and useful set of data for economists (see section 7 for more details). Very simply the 'Index of Retail Prices' attempts to measure the underlying inflation rate, that is the annual price change for a wide basket of goods and services which are purchased by consumers. Not only is this series an index in itself, it is usual to represent it in terms of a *base year*. So, 1985 is the base year and it is given an index of 100. What this means is that the value for 1985 acts as the base value. Subsequent values are calculated in terms of the percentage change from this initial figure. For example, between 1985 and 1986, the 'Index of Retail Prices' rose 3.4 per cent. If the typical basket of shopping in 1985 had cost £20, in 1986, it would have

1986	103.4
1987	107.7
1988	113.0
1989	121.8
1990	133.3
1991	141.8
1992	146.4
1993	148.7
1994	152.4
1995	157.1
1996	161.0
1997	165.9
1998	171.0

Table 3 'Index of Retail Prices' in the UK, 1985–1997 (1985 = 100)
Source: *Economic Trends*, 1998, Office for National Statistics.

cost £20.68. Although this is a gross simplification it illustrates how index numbers can be compiled.

So to construct an index number:

◆ choose a base value or a value for a base year and assign this an index of 100;
◆ divide it by 100;
◆ divide every subsequent value by this amount to calculate the index number for that value or year.

A crude 'eyeballing' of these data indicates that:

◆ retail prices have persistently increased on a year-on-year basis over the whole period;
◆ the annual rate of change has been more variable – it was particularly high between 1989 and 1990;
◆ there has been some relative slowing down in the rate of increase towards the end of the period.

Data skill 4 – How to calculate a simple average and know what it means

The *average* is a measure which is often used to summarise a particular set of data. Most of you will have come across it in GCSE mathematics, more specifically through being able to calculate various measures of average, such as the mean, median and mode. These different measures have their strengths and weaknesses from a mathematical standpoint. For the economist, usually through an arithmetic mean or weighted average, individual comparisons can be made in relation to the average for the population group as a whole. A good illustration of this is shown in table 4

Introduction

Luxembourg	37,381
Denmark	35,073
Sweden	28,312
Germany	27,418
Austria	27,347
Belgium	25,445
France	25,425
Finland	25,364
Netherlands	25,159
UK	23,478
Ireland	22,537	← EU average
Italy	21,685
Spain	15,032
Portugal	11,846
Greece	11,739

Table 4 GDP per head in the EU in 1999 (US$)

when the living standards of the 15 EU (European Union) member states are compared with the average for the EU as a whole.

Section 7 explains why the indicator shown in table 4, GDP per head, is a good measure of living standards. To see what is not so obvious is why the data in the table have to be looked at more critically.

Self-assessment task

Study the data in table 4.
(a) What can you deduce about relative living standards in the EU?
(b) What relevance might these data have for an economist employed by the European Commission?

Averages are also used by economists in the compilation of statistics. For example, the average weekly earnings of employed people in the UK would need to be calculated using a structured sample of all types of employee, that is male/female, professional/manual, salaried/hourly paid and so on. Its use is to give the economist a sound estimate in order to be able to make comparisons and possibly point to areas of potential poverty.

Data skills 5 – How to understand economic information produced in visual form

So far in this section all of the data used have been presented in tabular format. This might give a false impression because economists do use a much wider variety of visual means to present economic information. Charts of one form or another are a very good way of showing the main trends in data or emphasising a particular economic issue. Also, when economists produce business reports or write newspaper articles, various forms of data presentation are often used.

Figures 2 and 3 are typical examples of two such forms namely a *bar chart* and a *pie chart*. Both represent the rather tedious data of table 5 in a more effective manner. In particular it is relatively easy to see:
◆ the rank order of importance of government spending;
◆ how government expenditure in one area compares with that in another.

The basic principle behind the bar chart is that the particular economic variables (in this case social security, defence and so on) are represented by a series of bars or blocks, each of equal width. The bars though are of variable height, indicating their relative importance as measured on the vertical scale. In the pie chart, each slice of pie indicates the proportion or percentage of the total taken up by any one of the items. On figure 3, the respective percentages are indicated – this is not always the case. Students familiar with spreadsheets, such as Excel, will know that a very wide range of bar charts and pie charts can be easily produced from this software.

	% of Total
Defence	7
Health and social services	17
Transport	6
Debt interest	7
Social security	32
Education	12
Law and order	6
Other	13
	100

Table 5 Government spending in 1996/7

8

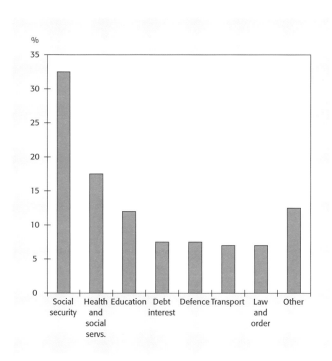

Figure 2 Government spending in 1996/1997

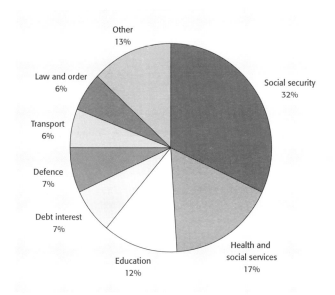

Figure 3 Government spending in 1996/1997

When confronted with any chart, it is very important to look carefully at the vertical scale. In particular, see whether it has been modified to make small changes look bigger. You should also check to see if the section immediately above the origin is shown as a set of short straight cross lines. Again, this can indicate that the degree of change shown should be carefully considered.

Increasingly in newspapers, economic information is being represented in a highly attractive way in the form of inter-related graphs, charts, pictures and diagrams. A very good example of this is shown in figure 4, which contains a lot of economic information on many aspects of Premier League football including:

◆ sources of revenue for clubs;
◆ how clubs make profits or, in some cases, losses;
◆ the growing power of the Premier League clubs in football;
◆ the socio-economic profile of football spectators;
◆ the change in ticket prices and how this varies between the Premier League and other leagues.

All of the above concepts are covered in Unit 1 of the book.

Self-assessment task

Study the information provided in figure 4. (You should be able to answer the following questions when you have completed unit 1.)

(a) Describe the cost structure and composition of revenue for a typical English professional football club. Why do many clubs run at a loss?

(b) Compare the revenue breakdown of Manchester United, Leeds United and Tottenham Hotspur. Do the variations shown have any economic implications for the respective clubs?

(c) In 1995/6 the rate of inflation was about 3 per cent. What might you deduce about the price elasticity of demand for football tickets?

(d) What might you deduce about the income elasticity of demand for watching football at Premier League clubs?

How to plan an investigation into economic problems

So far in this introduction it has been assumed that the data being used by the economist are readily available and meet the particular need in hand. This is often the case – economists often use published data to support their views and theories. There are, though, many occasions where this is not possible and the economist has to carry out a specific investigation in order to obtain the data needed to make meaningful conclusions. This process in practice can be costly and time consuming.

Within the AS specification, some basic knowledge of 'how to plan an investigation into economic problems'

But clubs still lose out

Some clubs make big profits, but in total the 92 professional English clubs spent more than they made in 1995/96

Income £517m

million	
TV	£75
Gate receipts/season-ticket income	£218
Commercial and other income	£224

Spending £578m

million	
Transfer fees to non-English clubs	£93
Other operating costs	£187
Wages and salaries	£298

TV revenue is increasingly important

Year	BSkyB, £m	BBC, £m
1995/96	39.5	4.5
1996/97	89.5	4.5
1997/98	135.0	17.0
1998/99	145.0	17.5
1999/00	160.0	18.5
2000/01	180.0	20.0

Earning power

Percentage of fans earning more than £30,000

Club	%
Wimbledon	23.6
Chelsea	19.4
West Ham	18.6
Southampton	16.8
Crystal Palace	15.9
Arsenal	14.9
Spurs	13.8
Man Utd	13.6
Coventry City	13
Leicester City	12.4
Blackburn	12.3
Newcastle Utd	12.1
Liverpool	10.3
Everton	9.9
Aston Villa	9.6
Sheff Wed	9.4
Leeds Utd	6.3

Going up
Average ticket prices

England	1996 (£)	1997 (£)	% increase
Premier	13.25	15.45	16.6
First	11.43	12.19	6.0
Second	10.25	10.60	3.4
Third	8.61	9.00	4.5

Scotland	1996 (£)	1997 (£)	% increase
Premier	10.56	11.78	11.5
First	9.63	10.25	6.4

How a typical Premier League club makes its money

These are estimates based on a model which takes 1995/96 as a total of 100. Gate receipts are rising – but proportionately other sources of income are rising more steeply, from a much lower base.

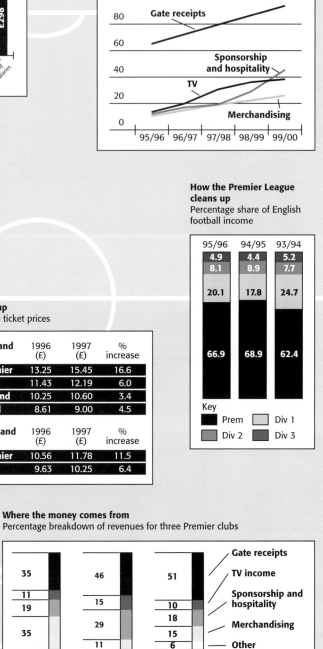

How the Premier League cleans up

Percentage share of English football income

	95/96	94/95	93/94
Div 3	4.9	4.4	5.2
Div 2	8.1	8.9	7.7
Div 1	20.1	17.8	24.7
Prem	66.9	68.9	62.4

Key
Prem Div 1
Div 2 Div 3

Where the money comes from

Percentage breakdown of revenues for three Premier clubs

	Manchester United	Leeds United	Tottenham Hotspur
Gate receipts	35	46	51
TV income	11	15	10
Sponsorship and hospitality	19		18
Merchandising		29	15
Other	35	11	6

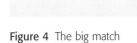

Figure 4 The big match

is required. Note that the emphasis is on 'how to plan' rather than going as far as actually carrying out the investigation. This skill covers two main aspects:

1 The design of an economic investigation, that is how it might be carried out and how the information might be collected.

2 The information to be collected in order to investigate a particular economic issue, that is what data are needed in order to be able to make some conclusions or calculations.

Mastering this skill is not easy for students of AS Economics. It does though fit more into place once the economic concepts involved have been studied and understood. Some typical examples (all of which are likely to be asked in examination questions) are:

♦ how to plan an investigation into the price, income or cross elasticity of demand for the product or products of a business (see section 2);

♦ how to plan an investigation into the benefits of economies of scale for a particular firm (see section 3);

♦ how to plan an investigation into the respective costs and benefits of a particular project (see section 6).

There are others which can be added to this list, not least as most economic concepts have developed as a consequence of economists undertaking investigations.

In general, there are two main sources of original data. These are:

1 The internal information or records of a business or organisation. For example, data on fixed and variable costs could be compiled in this way as might information on the benefits gained from economies of scale. Often, though, in practice data are not always available in the specific form required by economists.

2 A particular investigation to obtain information. Often in such cases the data required are not available or have never been collected. For example, this is likely to be the case with most cost–benefit studies or for businesses looking to estimate their price elasticity of demand for a given product or service. Some sort of survey needs to be carried out to provide the first-hand data that are required.

Many investigations require a *sample survey* to be undertaken. This is intended to be representative of the population from which it is drawn and, if properly carried out, permits the economist to make statements about the population's characteristics. Various types of survey methodology (for example random, stratified or quota) are used in practice to obtain the information that is required.

Each has their strengths and weaknesses:

1 A *simple random sample* is one where respondents have the same chance of being selected. To be able to achieve this it is usual for the population to be listed on some sort of sampling frame, such as a listing of customers or households.

2 A *stratified sample* can produce more accurate and robust estimates, mainly because the population to be sampled is split into strata on the basis of variables such as income level, sex or occupation.

3 A *quota sample* is widely used by commercial market research businesses. In such cases, a sampling frame is unlikely to be available.
The quota is intended to be a 'footprint' of the population, normally in terms of some fundamental characteristic such as age, car availability and similar variables.

It is also interesting and relevant to note that most government statistics are obtained through sample surveys. A good example is the 'Index of Retail Prices' which was referred to earlier (see table 3). Other sample surveys are the *Family Expenditure Survey* and the *National Travel Survey*. All in all, these often provide valuable information – their accuracy, though, is not always understood by those using their results.

Self-assessment task

Your local 'take-away' has asked you to plan an investigation into how the sales of its products might change with variations in price. It is also considering whether to charge a discounted price on certain quiet mid-week evenings when demand is low. (You should be able to answer the following questions when you have completed unit 1.)

Explain:

(a) How you would collect the information required to investigate these two problems.

(b) What information you need to collect.

How and why economists make forecasts

One of the most important tasks of the professional economist, whether in government or private sector employment, is to be able to forecast future economic phenomena. For example, many economic variables are heavily dependant upon the state of the economy. Forecasts of economic growth in particular are widely used by economists for all sorts of reasons related to economic policy and business well-being.

For AS, no more than a general understanding of what is meant by a forecast is needed. For A2 modules though students should be familiar with the material which follows.

Economists use various types of forecasting method. The three main ones are:

◆ statistical forecasts based on simple or complex future extrapolation techniques;

◆ using models to produce a range of forecasts – this is particularly true of models of the economy such as the one developed by the Treasury;

◆ forecasts based on intuition, experience or even guesswork, that is not involving statistical methods.

Two examples of forecasts are:

Macroeconomic forecasts – the Chancellor of the Exchequer and other government departments find it essential to have estimates of projected variables, such as the unemployment rate, inflation rate, balance of payments position and economic growth rate (see figures 5 and 6 for a typical example). These are required on a short-term basis (1 year or less) or over a longer period of time. Take the case of the unemployment rate – the importance of forecasting is shown below in figure 7.

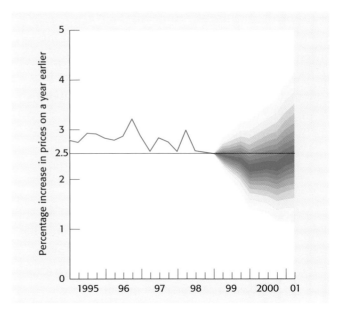

Figure 6 Current RPIX inflation projection based on constant nominal interest rates

This seems quite simple. In practice, though, the process is much more difficult to set out and at stages 3 and 4 requires further assumptions to be made with regard to other sources of revenue and taxation.

Microeconomic forecasts – these are not quite as obvious but one which develops out of section 7 is the need to be able to forecast tax revenue from wine consumption, which has a positive income elasticity of demand. This process is shown in a simplified way in figure 8.

How to write in a clear and effective way

It is really beyond the scope of this book to include a lot of material on this part of the 'tool kit'. But having said this, much of the work of economists is communicated in a written manner, in books and newspaper articles especially. For students, examinations in Economics (OCR included) require you to communicate your ideas in a written form. The section on Examination skills gives you very specific advice on how to impress examiners.

From a more general standpoint, you must always think about what you are writing and how you might improve your writing skills. You can enhance these skills by reading a good newspaper, particularly if you read material which supports your AS/A level studies.

For the time being, you might like to think about the following 'Ten tips for budding writers' (based on work by John Hart at the University of Huddersfield):

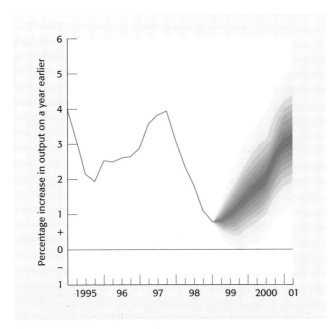

Figure 5 Current GDP projection based on constant nominal interest rates

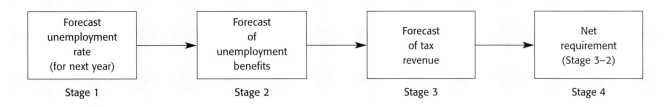

Figure 7 Use of unemployment forecasts

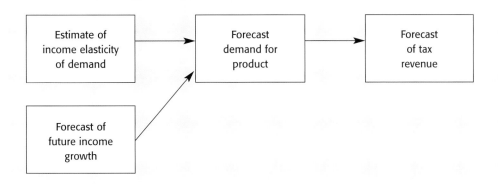

Figure 8 Use of income elasticity estimate

1 *Be clear and precise in your writing* – use words you understand and when using technical terms be specific, not least because Economics has many terms which are very similar.

2 *Remember to match your writing to your audience* – in most cases this will be your teacher or an OCR examiner. They are likely to be older than yourself and will be looking to read material from you which is written in a relevant way.

3 *Write impersonally* – in other words, do not use 'I' or 'we' in your written essays and examination answers. This particularly applies when you are asked to make an evaluation of an economic issue or argument.

4 *Think carefully about what tense you are writing in* – try and be consistent.

5 *Take care with sentences and punctuation* – in general, try to write short sentences, to the point and which contain words you understand and know how to use.

6 *Use one idea per paragraph and develop your ideas* – this makes it relatively easy for someone reading your work to know what your answer is about and to see how your idea has been developed.

7 *Support your arguments* – in other words, never make rash statements you cannot back up. Always try to elaborate or develop your statements and arguments.

8 *Avoid humour* – if in any doubt, leave humour and wit out of your written answers. Many economists do have a sense of humour – examinations and essays are not the place for it to be demonstrated.

9 *Be professional* – do not insult or offend even if you do not agree with what you might have read or with the examination question. There are other ways in which you can make your opinions known.

10 *Keep working at your writing* – never be satisfied and keep thinking about how you can write in a clear, relevant, authoritative and positive way.

An outline of the OCR structure

It is useful from the outset for you to know the structure of the OCR Economics specification. This is shown in figure 9. The AS stage consists of three units, as does the A2 stage.

This book provides the subject content and skills you need to succeed at AS level. (The final unit of the book contains material to underpin the final 'synoptic' module if you go on to the A2 stage.)

AS

THE MARKET SYSTEM	MARKET FAILURE AND GOVERNMENT INTERVENTION	THE NATIONAL AND INTERNATIONAL ECONOMY
Unit 1	Unit 2	Unit 3

Weight	AS	30%	30%	40%
	A level	15%	15%	20%

Method of Assessment: Short unseen case study examination drawn from real material which may also contain quantitative information.

Time Allowed: All units – $1\frac{1}{2}$ hours

A2

OPTION 1	OPTION 2	ECONOMICS IN A EUROPEAN CONTEXT (SYNOPTIC)
Unit 4 or Unit 5	Unit 6 or Unit 7	Unit 8

Weight	A level	15%	15%	20%

Method of Assessment: Options: Data Response question

One structured essay from choice of three

Pre-issued case study

Time Allowed: $1\frac{1}{2}$ hours

$1\frac{3}{4}$ hours

Options:

Unit 4   Economics of Work and Leisure
Unit 5   Transport Economics
Unit 6   Economics of Development
Unit 7   The UK Economy

Figure 9 OCR's economics specification

Three important new terms are now introduced:
Module – this is the term used to denote a block of subject content from a teaching and learning standpoint.
Unit – this is the term used to describe the subject content of a module and its associated means of assessment; it is the smallest part of the qualification.
Stage – this is the term used to describe the two parts of the specification, that is the AS and the A2. The AS is in itself a recognised qualification and some students may decide to terminate their studies on completion of this stage. Others will use their AS studies as the basis for completion of the A2 stage and, if successful, obtain an A level award.

The OCR specification can be taken by you in a variety of ways to best suit your own needs and progress in studying Economics. (Don't worry too much about this as your teachers will know what is best for you.) The important thing to note is the *flexibility*. The following approaches are possible:

◆ *Staged assessment* – an arrangement whereby you can take the various units throughout your course. For example, you can take unit 1 in January of year 12, followed by units 2 and 3 in June. This cycle can be repeated in year 13 for the A2 units. Alternatively, you may prefer to take three units in June.

◆ *Linear assessment* – this is the traditional way in which many students have taken A levels. It will involve you taking all six units in June of year 13.

You are allowed to **re-sit** any unit for one further time, the best mark being the one credited to you. This opportunity, though, can only really be realised if you study the specification in a staged manner by

14

sitting units throughout the period of your course. Again, don't worry about this. The important things for you to be aware of are the flexible study and examination possibilities.

The appendix to the section on Examination skills shows you some examples of specimen OCR examination papers. As you work through the units, and the content of this book, you will become increasingly familiar with the subject matter in these examination papers. You will also become familiar with the assessment methods which OCR use.

So, good luck and welcome to OCR Economics!

Summary

In this introduction we have established that:

- Economics is a social science concerned with how scarce resources are or should be allocated – it is often split into principles and concepts of microeconomics and macroeconomics.

- Economists have a varied 'tool-kit' to enable them to analyse economic problems and issues. Interpreting data and using data are particularly important – economists use many of the basic statistical skills for this purpose.

- It is also important that economists know what information they might need and how they can collect it. There are occasions when economists need to make forecasts.

- Economists must be able to express their ideas in a clear, relevant manner so that they can be easily understood.

- The above skills will be assessed in OCR's Economics examinations at AS and at the A2 stage of the GCE A Level examination.

- OCR's examination consists of three AS and three A2 units which can be taken in various possible ways to best suit individual needs.

Unit 1

The market system

1 Managing scarce resources: the reasons for choice and its consequences

On completion of this section you should be able to:

➤ describe what economists mean by the 'economic problem'

➤ understand the factors of production as economic resources

➤ explain the concept of specialisation and the economic benefits it offers

➤ explain the concept of opportunity cost and the nature of trade-offs

➤ explain the principles underlying production possibility curves and how opportunity cost can be used to analyse production decisions which have to be taken in an economy

➤ understand the importance of money and exchange in an economy

➤ understand the role of markets

One economic problem or many?

Economists have to deal with a whole range of **economic problems**. You may have seen TV programmes about the misery of unemployment and poverty; you may have read about the difficulties caused by inflation or heard politicians discuss exchange rate crises on the evening news. You may also be aware of debates surrounding issues such as the United Kingdom's future relationship with the European Union, the problems of global warming and the population explosion in the Third World. Despite this extensive range of issues which economists are trained to consider, they often talk about *the* economic problem. This is the fundamental problem from which all others arise. This is the fact that we have scarce **resources** to satisfy our unlimited **wants**. As a result of this problem, which is sometimes called the problem of **scarcity**, we have to make **choices**, and it is the task of the economist to explain and analyse the nature of choice facing economic agents, such as consumers, producers and governments.

The economic problem is

SCARCE RESOURCES IN RELATION
TO UNLIMITED WANTS

Because the basic economic problem exists, societies need to confront three interrelated questions. These are:

1 *What to produce?*

Because we cannot produce everything, we need to decide what to produce and in what quantities. We have to choose, for example, whether to produce lots of goods and services, such as food, clothing and leisure pursuits, to improve our standard of living, or whether we need to produce lots of military hardware to improve our defences.

2 *How to produce?*

This question arises from the basic economic problem that, since resources are scarce in relation to unlimited wants, we need to consider how resources are used so that the best outcome arises. We need to consider how we can get the maximum use out of the resources available to us. It should be noted, however, that other issues besides purely economic concerns should be considered when deciding how to produce. It may be true, for example, that through slavery or forced labour we could produce more goods and services in an economy, but there is a moral objection to such arrangements. Similarly crop yields could well be increased through the introduction of genetically modified plants but this may lead to damage to the ecosystem. The decision to maximise output and satisfy more wants would need to consider the full impact on the environment and any potential long-term health risks.

3 *For whom to produce?*

Because we cannot satisfy all the wants of all the population, decisions have to be taken concerning how many of each person's wants are to be satisfied. On a broad level we need to decide whether everyone is going to have more or less an equal share of what is produced or whether some will have more than others. In some economies there are deliberate attempts to create a more egalitarian society through policies that re-distribute wealth and income from the rich to the poor. This could be through the adoption of progressive taxation systems. In other economies there are no such policies and inequalities of wealth and income, usually based upon inheritance, remain extreme. In answering this question, moral aspects of decision making again become important.

Self-assessment task

Read the article below and then answer the questions that follow.

Survey On The Economics of Ageing: The luxury of longer life

In the world's rich countries, when you retire at 65 you can expect to live, on average, for another 15 or 20 years. A hundred years ago you would, on average, have been already dead. The late 20th century has brought to many the ultimate gift: the luxury of ageing. But like any luxury, ageing is expensive. Governments are fretting about the cost already, but they also know that far worse is to come. Over the next 30 or 40 years, the demographic changes of longer lives and fewer births will force most countries to rethink in fundamental ways their arrangements for paying for and looking after older people.

In 1990 18% of people in OECD countries were aged over 60. By 2030 that figure will have risen to over 30%. The share of the 'oldest old' (those over 80), now around 3%, is set to double. The vast majority of these older people will be consumers, not producers. Thanks to state transfers, being old in developed countries mostly no longer means being poor. The old people will expect decent pensions to live on; they will make heavy demands on medical services; and some will need expensive nursing care. Yet while their numbers are expanding fast, numbers of people at work – who will have to foot the bill – will stay much the same, so each worker will have to carry a much heavier burden.

Mass survival to a ripe old age will not be confined to rich countries. Most developing countries, whose populations are now much younger than the developed world's, are starting to age fast. In Latin America and most of Asia, the share of over-60s is set to double between now and 2030, to 14%. In China, it will increase from less than 10% now to around 22% in 2030, thanks partly to the government's stringent population-control measures. Only Africa is likely to remain exuberantly young right through to the middle of the next century, though AIDS may reduce population growth in some countries.

Already the numbers of old people in poor countries are beginning to dwarf those in the rich world. By 2000, there will be 400m people over 60 in

Elderly people enjoy a supervised game of cards at Britain's first Granny Creche at Peugeot's car plant in Coventry
Source: Popperfoto Reuters.

developing countries, twice as many as in the developed. In many places, the ageing process is being compressed from the four or five generations that it took in rich countries to just one or two.

A new twist to getting old

This will produce a historical first: countries with big old populations that are also poor. All the other permutations are familiar: old and rich (most of the industrial world), young and poor (most of the developing world for now) and, less common, young and rich (Australia, New Zealand, Ireland; up to a point, America, though not for much longer). Eastern Europe is something of an odd case out, being old but, thanks to its communist past, not as rich as it should be; and in Russia life expectancy for men, against the trend elsewhere, is falling rather than rising.

The new combination of age and poverty in several countries in Latin America and Asia will create many problems that are already familiar to industrial countries, but with far fewer resources to tackle them. Ethical dilemmas over the use of scarce resources will be magnified. Financing of health care and pensions could be a nightmare.

When demographers first started drawing attention to the coming age bulge, the discovery was hailed as that rare thing in the affairs of nations, a foreseeable problem. Forewarned would, surely, mean forearmed. Even the tag invented for it, 'the demographic time-bomb', seemed to imply that the bomb could be defused. The demographic facts were inescapable because the people concerned had already been born. The same baby boomers who crowded the nurseries after 1945 would be packing the nursing homes of the 2030s. Yet so far there has been more talk than action.

The trouble has been that the demographic problems ahead, however predictable, are still not imminent enough to create any real sense of urgency. Modern democracies with electoral cycles of four or five years are not designed to solve problems that impose short-term costs to reap long-term benefits.

In many countries, older people are still too few in number, and for the most part too politically passive, to act as an effective pressure group for long-term policies to further their own interests (perhaps to the detriment of other groups). But that is changing as their numbers increase, and they learn to flex their political muscles. By 2030, it would be a bold politician who neglected one voter in three – especially as older people in general turn out to vote in much bigger numbers than others.

Source: Barbara Beck, *The Economist*, 27 January 1996.

1 Summarise the trends in world population structure identified in the article.

2 Discuss the significance of the changes for decisions concerning:
   ◆ what to produce;
   ◆ how to produce;
   ◆ for whom to produce.

Limited resources

In Economics we categorise the resources available to us into four types. These are known as **factors of production**:

1 **Land** This is the natural resource. It includes the surface of the earth, lakes, rivers and forests. It also includes mineral deposits below the earth and the climate above.

2 **Labour** This is the human resource, the basic determinant of which is the nation's population. Not all of the population are available to work however, because some are above or below the working population age and some choose not to work.

3 **Capital goods** These are any man-made aids to production. In this category we would include a simple spade and a complex car assembly plant. Capital goods help land and labour produce more units of output. They improve the output from land and labour.

These three factors are organised into units of production by firms.

4 **Enterprise** *(or entrepreneurship)* This factor carries out two functions. Firstly, the factor enterprise organises the other three factors of production. Secondly, enterprise involves taking the **risk** of production, which exists in a free enterprise economy. Some firms are small with few resources. The functions of enterprise are undertaken by a single individual. In larger, more complex firms the functions are divided, with salaried managers organising the other factors and shareholders taking the risk.

Some economies have a large quantity of high-quality factors at their disposal. They can create lots of goods and services to satisfy the wants of their population. They are said to have a good **factor endowment**. Some economies lack sufficient quantities of one or more of the factors. Developing countries, for example, might have large quantities of land and labour but lack sufficient capital and enterprise. The former economies of Eastern Europe, such as Poland, have found it difficult to develop because they have few people with entrepreneurial experience. As you may see in unit 4 these economies have to make some difficult choices if they are to develop.

Production and consumption

Resources are combined in the process of **production** to create goods and services. Goods and services have the capacity to satisfy wants. The process through which individuals use up goods and services to satisfy wants is known as **consumption**. Some goods, such as a chocolate bar, are quickly used up to satisfy our wants. Others satisfy wants over a longer period of time. These are called consumer durables. Examples of consumer durables include television sets and washing machines.

Unlimited wants

If we were asked we could all identify certain basic wants which must be satisfied if we are to stay alive. These include the obvious essentials of food, shelter and clothing. We might also identify those wants which are clearly less essential but which we think improve our quality of life. Some might include television sets, cars, trips to the cinema and so on. These are sometimes called luxuries but it is important to remember that what might be a luxury for one individual may be considered an essential for others. This is because we all have a **scale of preference** with our more urgent wants at the top and the less urgent ones at the bottom. Each individual's scale of preference is a product of a complex set of influences, involving our culture, upbringing and life experiences. These together influence our likes and dislikes. Unsurprisingly, since we all have different experiences, there is bound to be great variation between any two individuals' scales of preferences. You may find it interesting to conduct a class exercise in which everyone makes a list of ten wants in descending order of priority. When you compare results you may be surprised to find that, although there may be broad agreement on the first few choices, there is likely to be considerable variation as you compare people's choices over the full list. You may also consider how your list would compare to lists compiled by others with very different life experiences, such as your teacher, your grandparents or even a student of Economics in another country, such as in Africa. A further point to consider is whether you could imagine any end to your list if you were not limited to ten choices. It is important to remember that our wants are continually expanding, developing and changing. Some wants expand as we grow up, marry and raise a family. Imagine how our housing needs change as we

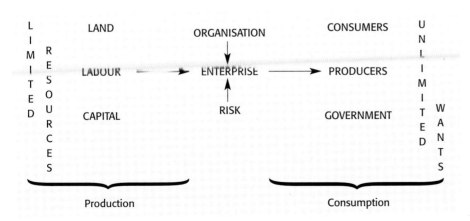

Figure 1.1 Elements of the economic problem

go through this process or how we change from wanting a small car with two doors to wanting a large family saloon with four doors. Some of our wants develop and expand when we see others enjoying goods and services around us and we feel the need to keep up. Sometimes our wants change as we have new experiences, for example we might become vegetarian because we have seen a TV programme on the health risks of eating meat.

All of this points to the fact that we can never imagine a time when all our wants are satisfied. Our wants are continually expanding and changing. Despite the fact that we are continually finding new, more efficient ways to produce more and more goods and services with the resources available to us, we are still faced with the basic economic problem that we have limited resources and unlimited wants. This is sometimes called the problem of **scarcity**. As a result we have to make choices.

Self-assessment task

Read the case study below and answer the questions that follow.

Rich and miserable … or poor and happy?

It's often said that those who say that money can't buy you happiness simply don't know where to shop. So when you've finished leafing through the Guardian, the odds are that you'll be off to the mall, armed with your plastic for a bit of conspicuous consumption.

After all, Christmas is only five weeks away and spending money makes you happy, right? Wrong. According to economists it's a myth that the more we spend, the better we feel.

The evidence – to be published in this month's edition of The Economic Journal – that the link between happiness and income/consumption is tenuous – is quite compelling.

The West is much richer than it was 50 years ago but:
  ◆ in the USA, reported 'happiness' has gone up only fractionally over this period;
  ◆ in Europe, 'satisfaction with life' is actually lower than it was 20 years ago.
This is evidenced in a number of ways. For example:
  ◆ in rich countries, male suicide rates have gone up;
  ◆ unemployment rates have increased – unhappiness is far more prevalent amongst the jobless.
According to Professor Andrew Oswald of Warwick University, money is to blame for this state of affairs. He

argues that it buys very little well-being, yet everyone wants more of it. He says it is akin to the spectator who stands up at a football match to get a better view; by the time all of his neighbours are standing up, everybody is no better off than before.

Other economists agree:
  ◆ Yew Kwang Ng, a Chinese economist, has argued that production and consumption, 'to keep up with the Joneses, continue to impose substantial environmental costs, making economic growth happiness decreasing.
  ◆ Robert Frank, an American economist, argues that we would be better off if we all agreed to consume less. We could work less, meet other people more regularly and cut down on workplace commuting.

But what can we do to change?
Frank's solution is a progressive consumption tax, levied on a family's income minus its savings. A large standard deduction would ease the burden on poor families with low levels of consumption. For everyone else, the resulting real increase in consumption would encourage greater savings and permit a transfer of resources into the things that really make us happy – better education, good health and a decent environment.

Source: The Guardian, 22 November 1997 (adapted).

This article expresses the view that, through economic growth, people may actually be worse off.

1 What other examples can you think of which might support the views of these economists?
2 Do you see any conflict between these views and your understanding of the 'economic problem'?

Specialisation and exchange

One of the ways in which more goods and services can be produced in the economy is through the process of specialisation. This refers to a situation where individuals and firms, regions and nations concentrate upon producing some goods and services rather than others. This can be clearly illustrated at the individual level. Within the family there may be some specialisation in the performance of household tasks, with one person doing the ironing and gardening while another does the shopping and cooking. At the workplace, of course, the fact that some people are computer programmers while others are accountants is also a reflection of specialisation. At this level, specialisation allows individuals to concentrate upon what they are best at and thus more goods and services will be produced. With such specialisation, however, although more is produced no-one is self-sufficient. It becomes necessary to exchange goods and services. As an individual specialises they will produce a surplus beyond their needs, which they can exchange for the surpluses of others.

In very early economies, exchange took place through a barter system in which goods were exchanged for others. This was very inefficient, however, and inhibited trade. As a result money arose as a medium of exchange. This had several advantages and allowed for expansion in specialisation, exchange and trade. Markets developed in which buyers and sellers came together to exchange surpluses using the medium of money.

With the expansion of the use of money and the development of markets, the benefits of regional and national specialisation became apparent. Surpluses produced by regions and countries were bought and sold, allowing world living standards to rise. Just as individuals concentrated on what they were best at, so did regions and countries.

Specialisation has clearly resulted in a massive expansion in world living standards, but there are dangers in specialisation. Given the pace of technological change in modern society, there is always the possibility that the specialist skills and accumulated experience, which any individual has acquired, may become redundant as the economy develops. Individuals need to be flexible and multi-skilled and be able to move between occupations. At regional and national levels, changes in consumers' wants can sometimes mean that the goods and services produced in a region or country are no longer required in the same quantity and unemployment can result. Policies then have to be adopted to deal with the economic and social problems that will arise. This issue will be looked at in depth in section 9 of unit 3.

The division of labour

With the technical advances of the last few hundred years, production of goods and services has taken place on a much bigger scale. The concentration of large numbers of workers within very large production units allowed the process of production to be broken down into a series of tasks. This is called the division of labour. For example, Adam Smith, writing at the end of the eighteenth century, showed how the production of pins would benefit from the application of the division of labour in a factory. He suggested that pin-making could be divided into 18 distinct operations and that, if each employee undertook only one of the operations, production would rise to 5,000 pins per employee per day. This was compared to his estimate that each employee would be able to produce only a few dozen each day if they produced pins individually.

Although the division of labour raised output, it often created dissatisfaction in the work force, who became bored with the monotonous nature of their task. The process was taken a stage further in the 1920s when conveyor belt production was introduced in the United States car industry by Henry Ford. Ford's method of car production provided the model for much of manufacturing production in the twentieth century. In more recent times the de-humanising impact of production techniques, such as those using a conveyor belt, have been recognised and alternative methods of production have been introduced.

Choice and opportunity cost

Given limited resources and unlimited wants we have to choose which wants to satisfy. The true cost of any choice we make between alternatives is expressed by economists through the notion of opportunity cost. This looks at the cost of our choice in terms of the next best alternative foregone. For example, suppose you were given a £15.00 gift voucher for your birthday. You could either buy a new compact disc which cost £15.00

or two paperback books for £7.50 each. It is clear that you could not have the CD *and* the books. The opportunity cost of the CD, therefore, is the two paperback books. The value of the concept of opportunity cost is that it brings home to us the real cost of our choices. It can be applied in a variety of contexts in Economics and is helpful for economic decision makers, such as households, firms and governments.

Production possibility curves

How many goods and services an economy is capable of producing is determined by the quantity and quality of resources available to it, together with the state of technical knowledge. These factors determine an economy's production possibilities.

Example: An imaginary economy, given its available resources can either produce military goods or consumer goods or a combination of each. The various possibilities are shown on the following production possibility schedule.

Military goods	Consumer goods
10,000	0
8,000	4,000
6,000	8,000
4,000	12,000
2,000	16,000
0	20,000

It is sometimes useful to illustrate the choices open to an economy by considering the production possibility curve. From the above schedule we can produce a production possibility curve with military goods plotted on the vertical axis and consumer goods on the horizontal axis.

Figure 1.2 shows all possible combinations of military goods and consumer goods which could be produced given the existing quantity and quality of resources in our imaginary economy and the existing state of technical knowledge. At point a, only military goods are produced, and, at point d, only consumer goods are produced, but between these two extremes lie all the other possibilities. The term production possibility curve emphasises that this shows what levels of output an economy can achieve with its existing resources. It

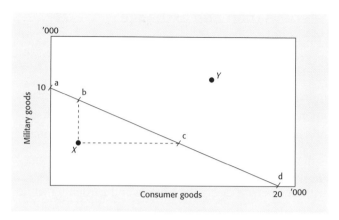

Figure 1.2 A production possibility curve

can also be used to show what the economy is *not* able to achieve. Point Y on the graph represents a combination of military and consumer goods which it is not possible to achieve. It is beyond our production possibilities. Sometimes the curve is called a **production frontier** because it draws the boundary between what can and cannot be achieved.

This diagram is also useful in illustrating the real cost to society of unemployed resources. The point *X* on the diagram represents a production of 4,000 military goods and 2,500 consumer goods. This is possible to achieve because it is within the production frontier, but it represents a point where some resources are unemployed or not employed effectively. The economy is capable of moving to point b with more military goods and the same number of consumer goods or to point c, which would bring more consumer goods and the same quantity of military goods. Alternatively at point c the economy can have more of both types of goods. Looking at the diagram in this way illustrates the waste from unemployed resources. We are not satisfying as many of our wants as possible.

A further alternative name for the production possibility curve is the **product transformation curve**. This emphasises a further use for the concept in introductory Economics. As the economy moves along the curve from point a through to point d then a different combination of goods is being chosen. More consumer goods are being produced and fewer military goods. This emphasises that the cost of producing more consumer goods is the military goods which have to be sacrificed. Given the figures, we can calculate the opportunity cost of consumer goods in terms of military goods. A move from b to c on the graph leads to a gain of 4,000 consumer goods but we sacrifice 2,000 military goods. The opportunity cost of one consumer good is therefore half of a military good. This is equivalent to one military good having an opportunity cost of two consumer goods. As we move along the curve the composition of our output is being transformed. We should also note that for this to happen we need to switch our resources from one use to another. Resources have to be switched from producing military goods to producing consumer goods and vice versa. This is known as the **reallocation of resources** and in the real world, as we decide to change the composition of our output, we need to consider the costs of reallocating resources between uses. These include the costs of re-training our work force in the skills required to produce different types of goods and services. This might take a considerable period of time and might only be possible as new entrants to the labour force are trained in new skills. The extent to which resources can be reallocated from one line of production to another is known as **factor mobility** and, if we want resources to be swiftly allocated to the use we choose, we have to ensure that factors are as mobile as possible.

It should be noted that, in our example, the opportunity cost of military goods in terms of consumer goods has not changed as we have chosen different combinations of the two goods. This is in fact quite unrealistic. A more likely outcome is that the production possibility curve will illustrate increasing costs. Consider the production possibility schedule in table 1.1, which shows the quantities of agricultural goods and manufactured goods that can be produced in an economy given existing resources and state of technology.

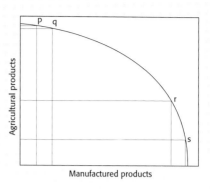

Figure 1.3 A production possibility curve with increasing costs

Assume that initially the economy is producing at point p with 660 agricultural products and 100 manufactured products (Figure 1.3). Then assume that it is decided to move to point q to gain an extra 100 units of manufactured products. Clearly resources need to be reallocated from agricultural use to manufacturing. At first the least fertile land will be reallocated and only 60 units of agricultural produce will be sacrificed. This means that each extra consumer good has cost 0.6 of an agricultural good. Now compare this with a movement from r to s, to gain an extra 100 manufactured goods we have to sacrifice 200 agricultural goods. This means that one extra manufactured good has cost 2 agricultural goods. The cost has increased as we have reallocated our resources. This is because at this stage we are switching the more fertile land into manufactured good production so that agricultural output is going to be affected to a much greater extent. This diagram illustrates a production possibility curve with increasing costs.

Shifts in production possibility curve

A production possibility curve is drawn on the assumption that the quantity and quality of resources and the state of technology are fixed. Through time, of course, economies can gain or lose resources, the quality of resources and the state of technical knowledge can change. Such changes will shift the production possibility curve to a new position. Figure 1.4 illustrates the outcomes of changes in the quantity and quality of resources and changes in technology.

Figure 1.4(a) shows a situation in which the production possibilities available to an economy have expanded. This is known as **economic growth**. This

Agricultural products	Manufactured products
700	0
660	100
600	200
500	300
300	400
0	500

Table 1.1 A production possibility schedule

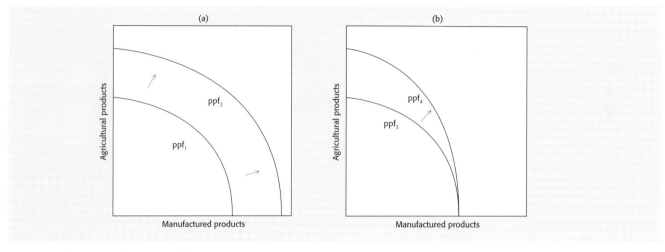

Figure 1.4 Shifts in production possibility curves

could be due to an increase in the quantity and/or the quality of resources available to the economy or an improvement in the state of technology. Here the changes have improved the economy's ability to produce both agricultural and manufactured products. In Figure 1.4 (b) however only our ability to produce agricultural products has been improved. This could perhaps be because there has been a technological breakthrough in producing agricultural products, which does not apply to the production of manufactured products. Nevertheless, this economy's production possibilities have improved and the curve has shifted outwards from the origin.

The production possibilities could also have declined. This could be because in some way the resources available to the economy have declined. Perhaps some of the economy's natural resources have become exhausted or the working population is falling. It might also be because the technology available to us has changed. An example might be the impact of controls on global emissions, which will affect our production possibilities as controls become more rigorous.

Applications of production possibility curves

We can use production possibility curves to illustrate some of the issues facing economic decision makers in the real world.

Jam today or more jam tomorrow? As stated previously, the production possibilities open to an economy are determined by the quantity and quality of resources available. In the process of production, resources are used up and they need to be replaced if production possibilities are to be maintained. The term **capital consumption** or **depreciation** describes the using up of capital goods during the process of production. Some resources need to be devoted to the production of capital goods if production possibilities are to be maintained. The creation of capital goods in the process of production is known as **investment**. This can be defined as *any production not for current consumption*. A choice has to be made therefore between producing consumer goods and services or producing capital goods through the process of investment. The more consumer goods and services produced, the higher the standard of living in the current time period, but the standard of living might fall in the future if there is a failure to produce enough capital goods to replace those worn out in the process of production. In addition, the quality of an economy's capital goods will not be improved and the full benefits of new technology will not be enjoyed if there is a failure to devote sufficient resources to investment.

Figure 1.5 shows the production possibilities between capital goods and consumer goods. These possibilities are determined by the quantity and quality of resources in the economy, which include the capital goods that have been produced in the past. If we assume that the quantity of capital goods which are wearing out in each time period is shown at a, then we can see the consequences of our choices. If we fail to produce the quantity at a then our capital stock will decline. Our production possibilities will diminish and the curve will shift to the left.

We use the term gross investment to describe the total quantity of capital goods produced. If we deduct

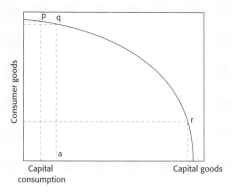

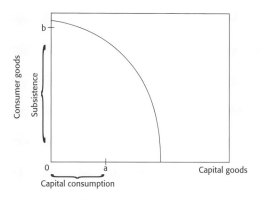

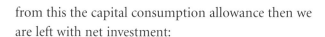

Figure 1.5 The choice between consumer goods and capital goods

Figure 1.6 Capital consumption in a developing economy

from this the capital consumption allowance then we are left with net investment:

Gross investment minus capital consumption = Net investment

Self-assessment task

Use the terms gross investment, capital consumption and net investment to analyse the effect of economic decision makers choosing each of points p, q and r in figure 1.5. Explain the choices in terms of the present and future standard of living in the economy.

Hard choices for developing economies Developing economies are characterised by low standards of living. If they are to grow then they need to increase their capital stock. Like all economies they need to divert resources from current consumption to investment. Some resources must be devoted to consumption, however, to keep their expanding populations alive. We refer to this as the subsistence level of consumption. The difficulty they face is that in the poorest developing economies almost all their production possibilities need to be devoted to subsistence.

In figure 1.6 0a represents the capital consumption in a developing economy and 0b represents the consumer goods required for the subsistence of the population.

Self-assessment task

Explain the choices facing decision makers in this developing economy. Discuss the difficulties they face and suggest any solutions to their problems.

Summary

In this section we have recognised that:

● All economies face the so-called economic problem of limited resources and unlimited wants.

● Choice is necessary in order to decide what to produce, how to produce and for whom to produce.

● Factors of production (land, labour, capital and enterprise) are essential for the production process.

● Specialisation allows more goods and services to be produced.

● The true cost of choices we have to make is known as opportunity cost.

● A production possibility curve is a representation of what can be produced in an economy and the trade-offs involved in making choices.

Key words

Definitions of Key words can be found in the Glossary on page 240.

capital consumption	money
capital goods	opportunity cost
choice	production
consumption	production frontier
developing economy	production possibility
division of labour	curve
economic growth	product transformation
economic problem	curve
enterprise	resources
factor endowment	reallocation of resources
factor mobility	risk
investment	scale of preference
labour	scarcity
land	specialisation
medium of exchange	wants

2 Competitive markets and how they work

On completion of this section you should be able to:

➤ understand what is meant by a competitive market

➤ explain the role of markets in allocating resources

➤ understand the different objectives of consumers and producers in markets

➤ understand what is meant by individual demand, market demand, effective demand and consumer surplus

➤ explain how demand is influenced by price, income, the prices of other goods and taste

➤ analyse the difference between shifts in demand and movements along a demand curve

➤ explain what is meant by the concepts of price, income and cross elasticity of demand and how they can be calculated

➤ evaluate the business relevance of these elasticity estimates

➤ explain what is meant by individual supply, market supply and producer surplus

➤ understand the range of factors influencing supply

➤ analyse the difference between shifts in supply and movement along a supply curve

➤ explain the concept of elasticity of supply, how it can be calculated and its economic relevance

➤ analyse how equilibrium price and quantity are determined

➤ analyse how and why the equilibrium position changes

➤ apply the analysis of demand and supply to the labour market and to the money market

Markets

'Oil prices fall to $10 per barrel – consumers everywhere will rejoice at the prospect of cheap, plentiful oil for the foreseeable future' *Economist*, 6 March 1999

'Cheap mortgages fuel boom in house prices' *Sunday Times*, 28 March 1999

'Personal computers are now more affordable than ever bringing the power and convenience of modern technology within the reach of most people' *Daily Mail*, 25 March 1999

'Rent one of our new widescreen TVs and you can get a Nicam stereo video for only £5 per month extra' Advert in *East Anglian Daily Times*, 11 March 1999

'Fly with us to Singapore for £355 return and get quality accommodation from only £20 per night' Advert in *Independent on Sunday*, 28 March 1999

To many people a market is something that happens in the town or city centre once or twice a week. It is characterised by a large number of traders setting up stalls that sell a whole range of products: food – such as fruit, vegetables, fish – clothes and a wide selection of other items. Economists, however, take a broader view of the word market. The essence of any market is trade – somebody has something to sell and somebody else wants to buy the product that is being offered. So, whenever people come together for the purposes of exchange or trade, we have a market.

For example, economists talk about the housing market, where people buy and sell houses; look in the newspapers or estate agents and you will see evidence of this market. They also refer to the labour market, where individuals' labour power is 'bought and sold' – if any of you have jobs part time or full time, then you have participated in the labour market as a seller of labour.

The television news often makes reference to the stock market, where shares are bought and sold, and the foreign exchange market, where currencies are bought and sold. Think about what happened when you last went on holiday overseas – if you at any time bought foreign currency you influenced the foreign exchange market in a small way, although you probably didn't realise it!

These examples indicate that to an economist a market does not have to have a clearly defined physical presence as the typical town or street market might have. It is simply a term used to describe the process through which products that are fairly similar are bought and sold.

Self-assessment task

How do you participate in the following markets:
◆ the personal computer market?
◆ the fast food market?
◆ the telecommunications market?
◆ the transport market?

Sub-markets

You might, however, begin to feel a bit uneasy at this point. Whilst it is clear that houses, labour, personal computers (PCs) and fast food may be fairly similar, it is also clear that there are significant differences within each market – the types of houses, PCs, transport services that are traded are not identical. So a good question to ask is: 'How valid is it to lump all the different types of computer together into one single market?'

Whenever we break an investigation down into smaller sections of the overall market, we are looking at sub-markets. So, if we want to look at the sub-markets of the computer industry, we might want to look at the various types of computer: memory, speed, features, PCs and laptops, the various brands and so on. We may need to consult (or become!) specialists in the economics of particular industries.

Demand

Let us first of all look at the buying side of the market – this is referred to as the demand side of the market. To an economist:

demand refers to the *quantities* of a *product* that *purchasers* are *willing and able* to buy at *various prices* per *period of time, other things remaining the same.*

Self-assessment tasks

1 What are the various sub-markets that we could identify if we wanted to look in more detail at the following products:
◆ alcoholic drinks?
◆ leisure equipment?
◆ holidays?
◆ personal computers?

2 Why do you think it is often important for companies to look more at sub-market issues? How could we break the market down even further to find out about an individual consumer's demand for a particular product?

3 Find out about the last big equipment order placed by your school or college – see if you can find out what factors influenced the decisions of the person who made the choices.

Definitions are of critical importance in Economics, so let us break this definition down to understand in some depth what this means.

◆ *Quantities* – economists often deal with numerical values and very often try to represent information in a quantitative way. This point is reinforced by the use of the term 'prices'.

◆ *Product* – this is a general term that simply refers to the item that is being traded. It can be used for goods or services. We could also stretch this to include tradable items like money or other financial assets such as shares.

◆ *Purchasers* – these are the buyers of the product and are often referred to as 'consumers', although they may simply be intermediaries in the production–consumption chain, for example Nestlé purchasing large amounts of cocoa to be used in the production of chocolate for sale to the final consumer. We could look at an individual purchaser's demand for a product or, more usefully, we can aggregate this to look at the demand of an overall market or sub-market.

◆ *Willing to buy* – clearly purchasers must want a product if they are going to enter into the market to buy it. Economists use the terms 'satisfaction' or 'utility' to describe the benefit or pleasure that the final consumer derives from the product.

◆ *Able to buy* – to an economist, the **notional demand** for a product, which emerges from wanting it, must be backed by purchasing power if the demand is to become **effective**. Companies are only willing to sell a product if the purchaser has monetary ability to pay for the product – the world is full of wishful thinkers who would love to own a Ferrari sports car or the most sophisticated music or computer system. It is, however, effective demand that is of real importance for economists.

◆ *Various prices* – prices are crucial to the functioning of a market. Although demand for a product is influenced by many things, it is at the moment of purchase, when we have to hand over our money and pay the price, that we really judge whether the product is value for money, that is, whether we really are willing and able to buy it. As the price goes up, and provided no other changes have occurred, more and more people will judge the product to be less worthwhile.

◆ *Per period of time* – demand must be time related. It is of no use to say that the local McDonalds sold 20 Big Macs to consumers unless you specify the time period over which the sales occurred. If that was per minute then demand is probably quite high, but if that was per week then clearly there is little demand for Big Macs in this sub-market.

◆ *Other things being equal* – we will see shortly that there are numerous potential influences on the demand for a product. Analysing the connections between the various elements is very difficult if lots of these elements are changing simultaneously. The process is similar to that of a scientist who, when conducting an experiment, will control the general conditions except for the two elements that he/she wishes to investigate. So, for simplicity, we start with the assumption that all the other factors are constant and analyse the response of purchasers on the basis that price alone changes. We will relax this assumption as we progress. Economists often use a Latin phrase, **ceteris paribus**, to indicate this assumption – this simply means '*other things being equal*'.

The innovative quick service restaurant concept pioneered by Dick and Mac McDonald in California has grown into the worlds largest food service organisation, serving millions of customers every day.
Source: McDonald's Corporation.

The demand curve

Let us now take this definition and represent it diagrammatically to construct what is known as a **demand curve**. We will make up an example based on the overall market demand for personal computers to illustrate the point. Let us make an assumption that we can identify and therefore analyse a typical personal computer, that is one with a set of standard specifications. Remember we can break the analysis into sub-markets later if we want to become more detailed. Let us also assume that we have collected statistical data about people's preferences and that the quantity of PCs that people are willing and able to buy at various prices per period of time, ceteris paribus, can be represented by table 2.1. This is known as a **demand schedule**. We can now plot the **market demand** schedule on a graph to see how the quantity demanded of PCs relates to variations in price. Figure 2.1 shows the demand curve for the data in table 2.1.

Price of a 'standard' PC (£)	Quantity demanded per week – demand curve D_0
2,000	1,000
1,800	2,000
1,600	3,000
1,400	4,000
1,200	5,000
1,000	6,000
800	7,000

Table 2.1 Market demand schedule

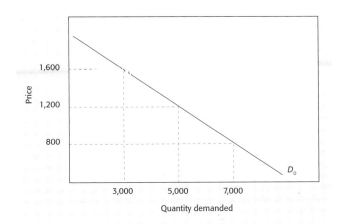

Figure 2.1 The market demand curve for PCs

Points to note:

◆ An inverse or negative quantitative relationship between price and quantity demanded. When price goes up, there is a **decrease** in **quantity demanded**. When price goes down, there is an **increase** in **quantity demanded**. Notice the language that is being used here – changes in price cause changes in quantity demanded and we illustrate this by movements up and down the demand curve.

◆ A causal relationship – we are saying that changes in price cause changes in quantity demanded.

◆ A linear relationship – this demand curve has been drawn again for simplicity as a straight line. However, it is perfectly acceptable for price and quantity demanded to be related in a non-linear manner.

◆ A continuous relationship – we could look at the diagram and find out at what price consumers would be willing and able to buy 1,259 PCs.

◆ A time-based relationship – the time period here is weekly.

Note that we are also assuming ceteris paribus – you should briefly review what this means.

Notice how important it is to label diagrams – the price axis, the quantity demanded axis, the demand curve and the P and Q_D reference points on each axis.

Self-assessment tasks

1 How many PCs per week are people willing and able to buy if the price is £1,100?

2 What price will persuade people to buy 1,350 PCs per week?

3 What assumptions are you making when you answer these questions?

Figure 2.1 is a very useful diagram since it allows us to visualise a quite complex relationship – simple pictures are usually easier to understand and remember than a large number of words. It also allows us to estimate how much consumers may spend when buying PCs, or conversely how much revenue companies may receive from selling PCs. If the price of PCs is £1,800 and the above information is accurate then consumers will buy 2,000 units and their total spending will be equal to £3,600,000, which, of course, will be the revenue that companies receive from selling this quantity of the product. (Note that, since we do not know the firms' production and distribution costs, we are as yet unable to say anything about profit.)

Self-assessment task

Explain how the area under the demand curve could be used to illustrate total consumer expenditure/total revenue of the firms selling PCs.

Consumer surplus

The underlying principles behind the demand curve are relatively simple to understand. They are also ones which many of us follow in our daily lives. For instance, when a product is on 'special offer' in a local shop, and its price has been reduced, more will be demanded and purchased.

For any good or service, though, there are always some people who are prepared to pay above the given price to obtain it. Two of the best examples where this happens are in the cases of tickets to popular rock concerts or to watch premier league football clubs, such as Manchester United or Newcastle United or even tennis at Wimbledon. The stated price of tickets may well be £20 per ticket, but there will always be some people who are willing to pay over £20 to obtain a

ticket. Another example might be the case of a chocoholic who is prepared to pay over the odds to get a bar of his or her favourite chocolate. To the economist, such situations introduce the concept of consumer surplus.

Consumer surplus arises because consumers would be willing to pay more than the given price for all but the last unit they buy. This can be illustrated in figure 2.2(a) where consumer surplus is the shaded area under the demand curve and above the price line. More specifically, it is the difference between the total value consumers place on all the units consumed and the payments they need to make in order to actually purchase that commodity.

If the market price changes then so does consumer surplus. For example, if the price increases then consumer surplus is reduced as some consumers are unwilling to pay the higher price. This reduction is shown in figure 2.2(b). The loss of consumer surplus is shown by the area $P_1P_2E'E$.

How much is a Wimbledon ticket worth to you?
Source: Popperfoto Reuters.

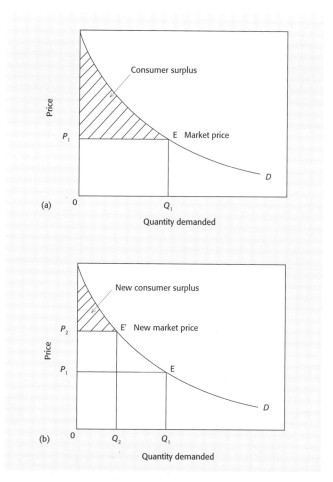

Figure 2.2 Consumer surplus

Shifts in the demand curve

Whilst the above analysis is useful, it is clearly limited because the price of a PC is not the only, or in many cases not the most important, factor influencing demand for it – other things play a part and are not always constant. Changes in these 'ceteris paribus' factors can be illustrated by shifts in the demand curve. A rightward shift indicates an increase in demand; a leftward shift indicates a decrease in demand. Notice how the language changes here when we are talking about a shift in the whole curve rather than simply a movement along it – a change in demand rather than quantity demanded (see table 2.2 and figure 2.3).

Price of a 'standard' PC (£)	Quantity demanded per week – demand curve D_2
2,000	2,000
1,800	3,000
1,600	4,000
1,400	5,000
1,200	6,000
1,000	7,000
800	8,000

Table 2.2 Shifts in the demand curve

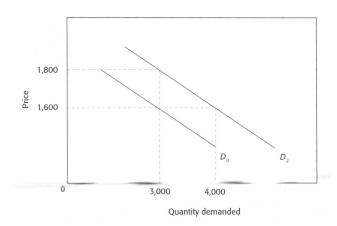

Figure 2.3 A shift to the right in the market demand curve for PCs

Points to note:
- *Explanation in terms of the horizontal shift* – consumers are now willing and able to buy more PCs at each and every price. So, whereas previously they had only been prepared to buy 3,000 units per week at £1,600, now they are prepared to buy 4,000.
- *Explanation in terms of the vertical shift* – consumers previously were prepared to pay £1,600 for 3,000 PCs, now they are prepared to pay £1,800 for that quantity.

Self-assessment task

Use the information below to draw a demand curve and explain what has happened to that demand curve – remember you are showing a decrease in demand. Draw in demand curve D_0 as well so that you can use it as the basis for your comparison.

Price of a 'standard' PC (£)	Quantity demanded per week – demand curve D_1
2,000	0
1,800	1,000
1,600	2,000
1,400	3,000
1,200	4,000
1,000	5,000
800	6,000

Causes of shifts in the demand curve

Individuals may differ widely in their attitudes towards products. We could therefore spend a lot of time constructing a very long list of non-price influences. This might be useful in certain circumstances but not in all cases; remember the ideas of simplification and generalisation. Fortunately, economists have identified that there are three key non-price categories that can be used to describe and analyse the factors that influence the demand for most products. They are:

(a) the financial ability to pay for the product;
(b) our attitudes towards the product itself;
(c) the price, availability and attractiveness of related products.

Let us look at each in turn.

The financial ability to pay

We have already noted the importance of effective demand. So what influences someone's ability to pay for a product?

- the purchasing power of their income after taxation;

♦ the availability of loans/credit and the interest rate that must be paid on loans or credit card balances. In general we would expect a positive relationship between the financial ability to pay and the demand for a product. So an increase in purchasers' financial ability to pay generally leads to an increase in demand, and this would be represented by a rightward shift in the demand curve from D_0 to D_2 in figure 2.3. A decrease in the ability to pay would lead to a decrease in demand, and this would be represented by a leftward shift in the demand curve from D_2 to D_0.

Self-assessment task

Draw diagrams and briefly explain how you expect changes in the following to influence the position of the demand curve for PCs:

♦ an increase in interest rates;

♦ a large increase in unemployment;

♦ a sustained rise in earnings from work;

♦ a reduction in income tax.

There is an important qualification to this general rule. The single most important influence on people's financial ability to pay for goods and services is generally considered to be income. In most cases there is a positive relationship between income and product demand, that is, as income rises, normally the demand for the majority of goods and services also increases; as income falls, so does the demand for most products. Such products that are characterised by such a relationship are labelled **normal goods**.

However, there are some products that are characterised by a negative relationship between income and demand. As income rises the demand for dated types of PC, such as 366 and 486MHz speed PCs, will fall; as income rises people tend to choose UK-based holidays less often. Products that are characterised by such a relationship are referred to as **inferior goods**.

Attitudes towards the products

We all buy products for a reason, that is our behaviour is purposefully motivated, at least at the time of purchase! Economists usually consider our behaviour to be a reflection of our tastes and preferences towards different types of goods and services. For example, you may buy a PC to play computer games or to help with

Self-assessment task

Would you classify the following products as normal goods or inferior goods. In each case draw a diagram to explain how a decrease in income will shift the demand curve. Explain your reasoning. What difficulties did you have in deciding? What information would you need to resolve these difficulties?

♦ Premium brand lager beers   Supermarket own label beers

♦ Holidays in Malaysia   Holidays in Blackpool

♦ Black and white TV sets   Nicam stereo, digital TVs

school work or to get access to the internet. You may buy a particular type or brand of PC because of its reputation for reliability. You may buy a pair of branded name trainers because you want to play sport and you genuinely believe them to be of better quality or you may buy them simply because they are fashionable and you want to look cool.

Detailed understanding of the psychological motives that determine our behaviour are beyond our scope here, but clearly we are influenced by our own individual likes and dislikes, by peer pressure and by advertising and the marketing images that surround us. Nowhere of course is this more evident than in markets for clothing and recorded music, where tastes and preferences can be extremely volatile.

Self-assessment tasks

1 What, at present, is the dominant brand of sports clothing? Why do you think it is dominant? Is it because it is of genuinely superior quality or is there another explanation?

2 Think of a successful advertising campaign that is running on the TV at present. Why is it successful and what impact would you expect it to have on sales over the next six months?

The price, availability and attractiveness of related products

Economists classify types of related products into two categories: **substitutes and complements**.

♦ *Substitute products* are alternatives – products that satisfy essentially the same wants or needs. The range of substitutability can be fairly narrow, for example in terms of different product brands: IBM and Dell computers, Casio and Accurist watches and Ford and Vauxhall cars. Or the range of substitutability can be broad, in terms of product groups, for example different types of transport – rail, buses and cars; different types of alcoholic drinks – beer, wine, spirits, alcopops. Changes in the price or attractiveness of one of these products will have an impact on the demand for all substitutes.

◆ *Complements* are products that enhance the satisfaction we derive from another product. Common examples are fish and chips, TVs and video recorders, airline flights and hotel accommodation, PCs and modems or software. In some cases, without the complement the main product would be useless. Examples here include: cars and fuel; video recorders and video tapes. Once again changes in price or attractiveness of one of these products will have an impact on the demand for the complementary product.

Self-assessment tasks

1 What would you expect to happen to the demand for Dell PCs if IBM cut their prices?
2 What would you expect to happen to the demand for all PCs if the price of software and printers came down sharply?
Use a diagram to help explain your answers.

Other demand-influencing factors

Clearly this is not an exhaustive list of the factors that influence demand. Each product will have some factors that are peculiar to it, for example the weather may influence the demand for ice cream. Expectations of the future can be important in determining the demand for certain products. If house prices or share prices are expected to rise, this can be a major influence in boosting demand. If unemployment or interest rates are expected to go up, this can have a dampening effect on the demand for some products. The skill of the economist is to use the categories above and knowledge or intuition to identify the key influences on demand, in any particular market, to explain past behaviour or to try to predict future behaviour.

Supply

We must now turn our attention to the other side of the market and consider the meaning of and influences on supply. To an economist:

> **supply** refers to the *quantities* of a *product* that *suppliers* are *willing and able* to *sell* at *various prices* per *period of time, other things remaining the same.*

Note the similarities below with the definition of demand:

◆ *'Quantities'* – once again we must emphasise that economists often deal with numerical values and very often try to represent information in a quantitative way.

◆ *Product* – as with demand we are using the term to refer to any item that is being traded. It can be used for goods or services. We could also stretch this to include tradable items like money or other financial assets such as shares.

◆ *Suppliers* – these are the sellers of the product and are often referred to as 'producers', although they may not be manufacturers of the product but again may simply be an intermediary in the production–consumption chain or they may be selling services. We could look at an individual company's supply of a product or, more usefully, we can aggregate this to look at the supply for an overall market or sub-market.

◆ *Willing and able to sell at various prices* – clearly, in a market economy, companies must gain from selling their products. The ability to earn profits is likely to be a major (but probably not the only) influence on company behaviour – the higher the price, ceteris paribus, the more profit companies are likely to make. However, as companies produce more, they may find that **costs** start to go up (because of something called diminishing returns or capacity constraints), so they may need to sell at higher prices to convince them to produce more of the product.

◆ *Per period of time* – supply must also be time related. It is of no use to say that IBM supplied 200 computers unless you specify the relevant time period. Clearly this needs to be consistent with the time period being used for demand.

◆ *Other things being equal* (ceteris paribus) – we will see shortly that there are numerous potential influences on the supply of a product. Analysing the connections between the various elements is very difficult if lots of these elements are changing simultaneously.

The supply curve

We need to take this definition and represent it diagrammatically to construct what is known as a **supply curve**. We could do this for an individual firm selling PCs or, by aggregating each separate company's supply curve, we could get the industry or market supply curve for PCs. Assume again that we have collected statistical data about companies' selling intentions and that these plans can be represented by table 2.3 (this is known as a **supply schedule**). We can now plot this supply schedule to see how the quantity of PCs supplied relates to variations in price. Figure 2.4 shows the supply curve (S_0) for the data in the table.

Price of a 'standard' PC (£)	Quantity supplied per week – supply curve S_0
800	1,000
1,000	2,000
1,200	3,000
1,400	4,000
1,600	5,000
1,800	6,000
2,000	7,000

Table 2.3 Market supply schedule

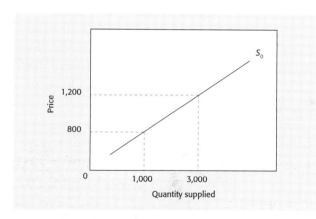

Figure 2.4 The market supply curve for PCs

Points to note:
- A positive or direct relationship between price and quantity supplied.

When price goes up there is an **increase** in **quantity supplied**.
When price goes down there is a **decrease** in **quantity supplied**.

- Again notice the language that is being used – changes in price cause changes in quantity supplied and we illustrate this by movements up and down the supply curve (again some economists prefer to use the terms extension of supply for a movement up the supply curve and a contraction of supply for a movement down the curve).
- A causal relationship – we are saying that price changes cause the change in quantity supplied.
- A linear relationship – the supply curve has been drawn for simplicity as a straight line, but of course there is no reason why the supply curve should not be represented in a non-linear way.
- A continuous relationship – we could look at the curve to find out how many PCs companies would plan to supply at a price of £1,150.
- A time-based relationship – the time period again is weekly.

Note we are also assuming ceteris paribus – any other supply influencing factor is assumed to be unchanged.

Self-assessment tasks

1 How many PCs per week are companies planning to supply if the price is £1,100?
2 What price would persuade companies to supply 1,350 PCs?
3 What assumptions are you making when you answer these questions?
4 What might be the advantages and disadvantages of using a diagrammatic form such as in figure 2.4 to represent supply?

Producer surplus

This is a similar concept to that of consumer surplus introduced above, but, as its name indicates, it is looked at from the perspective of the supply of a product. A very brief outline of the concept follows.

Looking at figure 2.5, the total value of the output supplied can be represented by the area $0P_1EQ_1$, that is the market price multiplied by the quantity supplied. Below this price, producers are still willing to supply the market but not at the same quantity as when price is P_1.

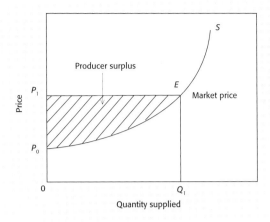

Figure 2.5 Producer surplus

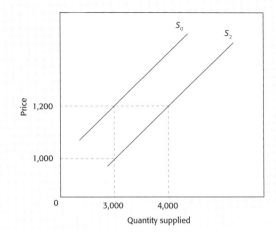

Figure 2.6 A shift to the right in the market supply curve for PCs

So as price falls towards P_0, where no units will be supplied, producers are less and less willing to supply.

Producer surplus is the shaded area above the supply curve and below the price line. It occurs because units of a firm's output are sold at the same market price P_1 – all except for the last unit are produced at less than the market price. The area P_0P_1E, therefore, are surplus earnings for the firm.

Shifts in the market supply curve

Whilst the above is useful, one of the limitations is that companies' supply intentions are influenced by factors other than the price of the product (which, if you think about it, is the most tangible expression of consumers' buying intentions). Other things are most certainly not always equal. Changes in these 'ceteris paribus' factors can be illustrated by shifts in the supply curve. A rightward shift indicates an increase in supply;

a leftward shift indicates a decrease in supply. Notice again how the language changes when we are talking about a shift in the whole curve rather than simply a movement along it – a change in supply rather than quantity supplied (see table 2.4 and figure 2.6).

Points to note:

♦ *Explanation of horizontal shift* – companies are now more willing and/or more able to supply PCs at each and every price. Whereas previously they had only been prepared to supply 3,000 units per week at £1,200, now they are prepared to supply 4,000.

♦ *Explanation of vertical shift* – companies previously wanted £1,200 per unit to persuade them to supply 3,000 units per week, now they are prepared to accept £1,000.

Price of a 'standard' PC (£)	Quantity supplied per week – supply curve S_2
800	2,000
1,000	3,000
1,200	4,000
1,400	5,000
1,600	6,000
1,800	7,000
2,000	8,000

Table 2.4 An increase in supply

Although this PC superstore is called Office World, many homes now have a computer

Self-assessment task

Use the information below to draw a new supply curve (S_1) and explain what has happened to that supply curve – remember you are showing a decrease in supply. Draw in supply curve S_0 as well so that you can use it as the basis for your comparison.

Price of a 'standard' PC (£)	Quantity supplied per week – supply curve S_1
1,000	1,000
1,200	2,000
1,400	3,000
1,600	4,000
1,800	5,000
2,000	6,000

Causes of shifts in the supply curve

Companies clearly differ in their willingness and ability to supply products and, as with demand, we could spend a long time building a list of possible factors other than price that will affect supply. If we were required (and paid!) to conduct a detailed analysis of supply conditions in a particular industry, that might be justified. For our purposes we need to simplify and generalise about the factors that can influence supply in most industries. As with demand, we can focus on three main influences:

◆ the costs associated with supplying the product;
◆ the size, structure and nature of the industry;
◆ government policy.

Let us discuss each in turn.

Costs

Since in a market-based economy, no firm (in the absence of government support) can exist indefinitely if it makes losses, companies will make supply decisions on the basis of the price they can get for selling the product in relation to the cost of supplying it. You will see in the next section how costs may rise as a firm increases production with a given capacity – this will influence the shape of the supply curve. What we are interested in here, however, is what factors can influence the position of the supply curve – in other words, what factors can cause an increase or a decrease in the costs of supplying each and every unit, since it is likely that this will impact on the price that companies charge for each and every unit. Below are listed some potentially

influential factors – if the factor pushes up costs, there is likely to be a leftward shift in the supply curve or decrease in supply; if the factor lowers costs, there is likely to be an increase in supply:

◆ wage rates;
◆ worker productivity (output per worker);
◆ raw material and component prices;
◆ energy costs;
◆ equipment maintenance costs;
◆ transport costs;
◆ the state of technology.

Self-assessment task

Go through each of the above factors in turn and work out what sort of change in that factor will cause:

◆ an increase in supply,
◆ a decrease in supply.

The size and nature of the industry

If it is clear that there is substantial profit to be made by selling a product, firms inside and outside the industry are likely to react. Firms currently in the industry may invest in capital equipment in an attempt to grow bigger and take advantage of the situation. Firms outside the industry may try to enter this market and of course new firms may set up in business. The ease with which they can do so will depend on whether there are any barriers to entry into the industry and, if there are, how easy it is to overcome them (see section 3). Nonetheless if the size of the industry increases, because there are more firms or bigger firms, then it is likely that the supply of the industry will increase. Equally, if firms in the industry start to compete more intensively on price, it is likely that the supply curve will shift to the right as the effects of this price competition start to affect the price that all companies are willing to accept for their products. Of course if a fierce price war does break out, then consumers, at least temporarily, may enjoy very much lower prices for any given level of supply.

Self-assessment tasks

1 Why might firms choose to leave an industry?
2 What is likely to happen to the industry supply if the size of the industry shrinks?
3 What might happen to supply if all firms decide to try and increase the amount of profit they make on each unit they sell?

Government policy

Governments influence company decisions in many ways. Legislation designed to protect consumers or workers may impose additional costs on companies and this may affect the supply curve. Governments may also impose indirect taxes (excise duties or value added tax) on companies. These taxes can act like a cost increase as companies may seek to pass the tax on to the consumer in the form of higher prices. As such, indirect taxes often result in a decrease in supply. On the other hand, a relaxation of certain types of legislation or government subsidies can increase supply by encouraging firms to lower prices for any given level of output.

Price of a standard PC (£)	Quantity supplied per week	Quantity demanded per week
800	1,000	7,000
1,000	2,000	6,000
1,200	3,000	5,000
1,400	4,000	4,000
1,600	5,000	3,000
1,800	6,000	2,000
2,000	7,000	1,000

Table 2.5 Market supply and demand schedules for PCs

Self-assessment task

Refer to the supply curve S_0 in figure 2.6. What would happen to this curve if the government introduced a tax of:

- ◆ £100 per computer?
- ◆ 10% on the pre-tax selling price?
- ◆ legislation that raised companies' costs by about 20 per cent on average?

Other supply-influencing factors

As with our treatment of demand, this is not intended to be a complete list of the factors that influence supply. Each industry will have some features that are relevant to it. For example, the supply of agricultural produce is particularly influenced by weather conditions. Some industries may be able to switch production from one product to another fairly easily and so the relative profitability of alternative product areas may be important. In financial markets, like the stock market or the foreign exchange market, supply may be significantly influenced by expectations of future prices. Once again the skill of the economist is to use theory, insight and observation to identify the key influences on supply in any situation to explain the past or to try to predict the future.

Putting supply and demand all together – markets in equilibrium and disequilibrium

We have now analysed each side of the market separately and it is time to put it all together. At any

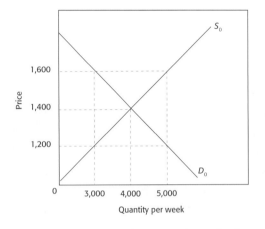

Figure 2.7 Equilibrium price and output in the market for PCs

point in time, there will be a given set of conditions influencing demand and a given set of conditions influencing supply (see table 2.5). Let us say that those conditions are reflected in demand curve D_0 and supply curve S_0 from earlier on – these relationships have been drawn for you in figure 2.7.

The term **equilibrium** refers to a situation of balance where at least under present circumstances there is no tendency for change to occur. In this particular situation, equilibrium will exist when the plans of consumers (as represented by the demand curve) match the plans of suppliers (as represented by the supply curve).

The market equilibrium in this case will, therefore, be at a price of £1,400 with 4,000 units bought and sold. Total consumer expenditure (and therefore industry revenue) will be £560,000 per week. Just think about what would happen if for some reason companies thought that consumers were prepared to pay £1,600 and supplied 5,000 units to the market. In this case the market would be in a disequilibrium (an imbalance where change will happen). At a price of £1,600, under present circumstances, consumers are only planning to buy 3,000 units. As such companies will build up excess stocks at the rate of 2,000 PCs per week. There is a **disequilibrium** of excess supply. Companies would be irrational to carry on with this unplanned stockbuilding. How might they react? Well for a start they could cut price; they would also probably start to reduce the quantity they supply to the market. Of course, as they cut price, some consumers who would not have been prepared to pay the higher price are now attracted back into the market – the disequilibrium starts to narrow. Provided there is no change to any of the conditions of supply or demand, and nothing prevented companies adjusting in this way, then eventually, perhaps through expert decision making or simply trial and error, the market price and quantity should move back to equilibrium.

Think now what would happen if the price was set at £1,000. Again we have a disequilibrium – this time of excess demand. Consumers are now keen to snap up what they consider to be a pretty good deal. However, given the low prices, supplies are fairly low and there are not enough PCs to meet demand – they run out of stocks far quicker than they had expected, so there are unmet orders. Profit-oriented companies, if they are reasonably sharp, will recognise this and will start to raise price and increase the number of PCs available for sale. However, as prices rise, some consumers will decide that PCs are a bit too expensive at the moment and the quantity demanded will fall. Once again, as a result of trial and error and good management on the part of businesses, the market will adjust back to the equilibrium.

Of course, this process of market adjustment may not happen instantly, there will be time lags, perhaps quite lengthy ones if companies are managed badly. The point, however, is that there will always be a tendency for the market to move back to its equilibrium because that is where the underlying motives and plans of consumers and suppliers are driving it.

Self-assessment task

In the figure 2.8 below symbols, instead of numbers, are used to represent the same situation.

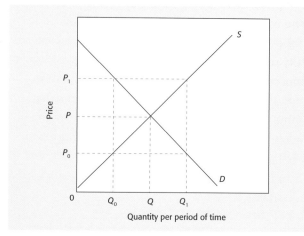

Figure 2.8 Typical supply and demand diagram

1 What is the market equilibrium price and quantity?
2 What area will show the total expenditure by consumers? This will be the same as the total revenue earned by companies.
3 What is the state of the market if the price is at P_1?
4 What is the state of the market if the price is at P_0?
5 Explain what will happen if the market is in a disequilibrium of:
   ◆ excess demand;
   ◆ excess supply.
6 What advantages/disadvantages are there in using symbols, such as P_s and Q_s, to analyse markets rather than actual numbers?

Changes in the equilibrium

The equilibrium will change if there is a disturbance to the present market conditions – this could come about through a change in the conditions of supply (the supply curve shifts) or a change in the conditions of demand (the demand curve shifts).

Self-assessment tasks

1 Review the factors that can cause the demand curve to shift.
2 Review the factors that can cause the supply curve to shift.
3 Review how disequilibrium positions are eliminated in a market.

A change in demand

Look at figure 2.9 – notice we are using P and Q symbols again instead of actual numbers – if there is an increase in demand (D_0 to D_2), then, at the original price, there is now a disequilibrium of excess demand equal to $Q_1 - Q_0$. As suppliers begin to recognise this they will start to raise price and increase quantity supplied. The rise in price will lead some consumers to decide they do not want to buy the product at the higher price. Although the process may take some time, the market will move back towards the new equilibrium at $P^*\,Q^*$, where the market is once more in balance. Note that the new equilibrium is at a higher price with a larger quantity traded than in the original situation.

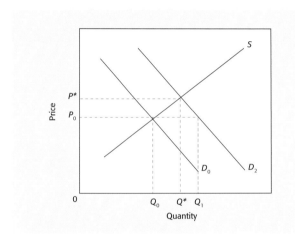

Figure 2.9 The effect of a shift of the demand curve on the equilibrium price and quantity

Self-assessment task

What will happen if there is a decrease in demand? Use a properly labelled diagram to explain clearly how both the market equilibrium price and quantity traded will fall.

A change in supply

Look at figure 2.10 – if there is an increase in supply (from S_0 to S_2) then, at the original price (P_0), there is now a disequilibrium of excess supply ($Q_1 - Q_0$). This would of course eventually be eliminated as price falls towards its new equilibrium level and the quantity traded in equilibrium rises from Q_0 to Q^* where the plans of consumers and companies once more coincide.

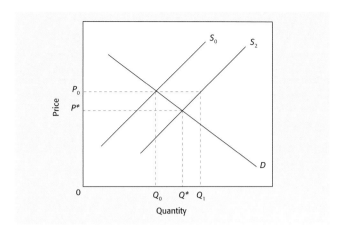

Figure 2.10 The effect of a shift in the supply curve on equilibrium price and quantity

Self-assessment task

What would happen if there was a decrease in supply? Use a properly labelled diagram to explain clearly how the market equilibrium price would rise but the equilibrium amount traded would fall.

A change in supply and demand

The above analysis is useful to deal with simple situations. However, in many situations the conditions of both supply and demand may change simultaneously. Look at figure 2.11. The initial equilibrium is at P and Q with the demand curve D_0 and the supply curve S_0. The increase in demand for the product (caused by, say, the increase in the price of a substitute) puts upward pressure on price. However, the simultaneous increase

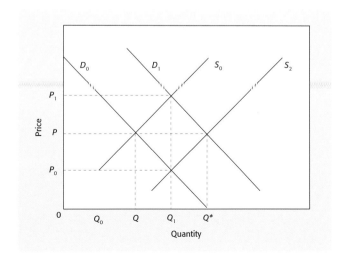

Figure 2.11 An unchanged equilibrium price and a changed equilibrium quantity

in supply (caused by, say, a fall in raw material and energy costs) puts downward pressure on price. The resulting effect is that the equilibrium price remains unchanged, although of course there is a fairly significant increase in the quantity traded (from Q to Q^*).

Self-assessment tasks

1 See if you can explain the following situations. Use a diagram to help you in each case – remember both curves are shifting now:
   (a) an increase in demand, but the equilibrium price falls;
   (b) a decrease in demand, but the equilibrium price goes up;
   (c) a decrease in supply, but the equilibrium quantity remains unchanged;
   (d) an increase in supply, but the equilibrium price increases.

2 (a) Explain the factors which might determine the demand for foreign holidays by households in the UK.
   (b) Discuss the impact of a reduction in air fares on the demand for holidays abroad and in the UK.

3 The opening of the Channel Tunnel increased the supply in the market for cross-Channel trips. With the aid of a diagram explain how this will affect travellers on cross-Channel trips.

4 Do some research, perhaps using the World-Wide Web (WWW), to find out what has happened:
   (a) to the numbers of people attending the cinema in the last ten years;
   (b) to house prices, nationally and in your area, in the last year.
   Use supply and demand analysis to explain why the changes may have occurred.

5 Analyse with the aid of diagrams:
   (a) the likely effect of a reduction in the price of pre-recorded compact discs (CDs) on the demand for visits to live music concerts;
   (b) the likely effect of a reduction in the entrance price to live music concerts on the demand for pre-recorded compact discs.

The Channel tunnel shuttle train emerges from the tunnel opening on the French side at Sangatte on 28 April as tests continued prior to the official opening ceremony on 6 May 1993.
Source: Popperfoto Reuters.

The importance of elasticity

So far our analysis of markets and sub-markets has concentrated on understanding the direction of any change in supply, demand, prices or output and sales. For example, we have looked at what can cause an increase or decrease in demand and whether this change will raise or lower prices or output. We now want to add more depth to our understanding by looking at the extent of demand changes and whether there is likely to be a large or a small impact on the equilibrium. In some cases a small increase in income, for example, may have a really big impact on demand and this in turn may have a really significant impact on the equilibrium price. In other cases, the same increase in income may have little impact on demand and the market equilibrium. We need some tools or concepts to help us understand these changes more precisely. The concept that allows us to move forward in this way is elasticity.

Elasticity is simply a way of quantifying cause and effect relationships. It is defined generally as a numerical measure of *the responsiveness of one economic variable (the dependent variable) following a change in another influencing variable (the independent variable), ceteris paribus*! Where relationships are elastic (responsive), a small change in the cause or the independent variable has a big effect on the other dependent variable. Where relationships are inelastic, a large change in the cause has limited effects on the dependent variable. This might seem a bit confusing, so let us look at specific examples of elasticity – this general definition will then start to become clearer.

Price elasticity of demand (PED)

Price elasticity of demand is a numerical measure of the responsiveness of demand for one product following a change in the price of that product alone. If demand is elastic, then a small change in price will result in a relatively large change in quantity demanded. On the other hand, if price goes up by a lot and quantity demanded only falls slightly, then demand would be price inelastic. A numerical example will help clarify this. First, however, we need a way of expressing PED in a numerical form – the formula we will use at this stage is:

$$PED = \frac{\%\text{ change in quantity demanded of a product}}{\%\text{ change in price of that product}}$$

Let us take two specific examples of price changes for two general products that we will call product A and product B (see figure 2.12). Assume that both of these unrelated products currently are priced at £100 and demand for them is 1,000 units per month. Consider what is expected to happen to the demand for A and B if the price rises to £105. The quantity demanded of product B only falls from 1,000 to 990, whereas the quantity demanded of product A falls from 1,000 to 900. Now let us put these values into the PED equation to calculate the elasticity.

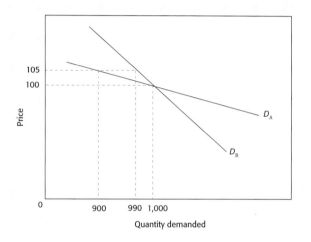

Figure 2.12 Elastic and inelastic demand curves

$$\text{Product A} \quad \frac{\%\text{ change in quantity demanded of A}}{\%\text{ change in price of A}} =$$
$$\frac{1\%\text{ fall}}{5\%\text{ increase}} = (-)0.2$$

$$\text{Product B} \quad \frac{\%\text{ change in quantity demanded of B}}{\%\text{ change in price of B}} =$$
$$\frac{10\%\text{ fall}}{5\%\text{ increase}} = (-)2.0$$

Notice that in both cases a negative figure is given, this is because of the negative (or inverse) relationship between price and quantity demanded, that is, as the price goes up, the quantity demanded goes down. Conventionally economists refer to PED in absolute terms either by ignoring the negative sign or by multiplying the PED value by –1.

Product A – because the numerical value (0.2) is less than one we say that the demand for this product is relatively inelastic or unresponsive to price changes. Over this particular range of prices, the 5 per cent increase has resulted in a much smaller change in quantity demanded.

Product B – because the numerical value (2.0) is greater than one, we say that the demand for this product is relatively elastic or responsive to price changes. Over this particular range of prices, the same 5 per cent price change has caused a much bigger change in quantity demanded.

Self-assessment tasks

1 Calculate the PEDs in each of the following cases and explain whether demand would be considered price elastic or price inelastic.

Original price	New price	Original quantity demanded	New quantity demanded
(a) £100	£102	2,000 units per week	1,950 units per week
(b) £55.50	£54.95	5,000 units per week	6,000 units per week

2 With the aid of a numerical example of your choice explain the meaning of these PED values:
   (a) PED = (–)1.5,   (b) PED = (–)0.6.

Some special PED values

It is important to realise that mathematically PED values can range from 0 to infinity. These values need explanation. Consider, for example, the demand curve shown below in figure 2.13. Irrespective of the price charged, consumers are willing and able to buy the same amount – in this case demand would be said to be **perfectly inelastic**. Let us just look at the PED calculation for an increase in price from £10 to £11

$$PED = \frac{\% \text{ change in quantity demanded}}{\% \text{ change in price}} = \frac{0\%}{+10\%} = 0$$

Hence, when the PED = 0, demand is perfectly inelastic, perfectly unresponsive to price changes.

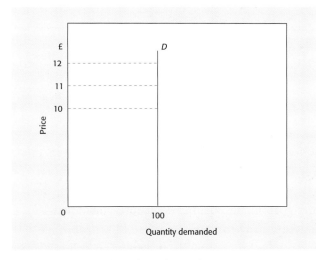

Figure 2.13 A perfectly inelastic demand curve

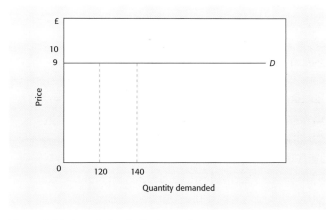

Figure 2.14 A perfectly elastic demand curve

Consider the demand curve above in figure 2.14. At a price of £10 per unit consumers are not prepared to buy any of this product; however, if price falls to £9, they will buy all that is available. The relative change in quantity demanded here, of course, is infinite, since the original demand was zero

$$PED = \frac{\% \text{ change in quantity demanded}}{\% \text{ change in price}} = \frac{\infty}{-10\%} = (-)\infty$$

Unitary elasticity

If the relative increase in price is exactly matched by the relative fall in quantity demanded, then the PED value will equal (–)1 and demand will be said to have **unitary elasticity** over that particular price range. So, for example, if the price of the product goes from £1,000 to £1,050 and quantity demanded decreases from 10,000 to 9,500, then the PED will equal (–)1 over this particular range of prices.

Factors that influence price elasticity of demand

There are three key factors that influence whether, over a particular price range, demand for a product is likely to be price elastic or inelastic.

◆ *The range and attractiveness of substitutes* – the greater the number of substitute (alternative) products and the more closely substitutable those products are, the more we would expect consumers to switch away from a particular product when its price goes up (or towards that product if its price falls).

It is important, however, to distinguish between the substitutability of products within the same group of products and substitutability with goods from other product groupings. For example, different types of wine are a group of products in their own right; they are also part of a larger group of alcoholic drinks and part of the even bigger category of products that we could label as 'drinks'. If we are concerned with the price elasticity of demand for a particular type of wine produced by a specific wine maker, then it will have a fairly high PED (probably) because of the range of substitutes. As we aggregate products into groupings, such as 'white wine', or 'all wines' or 'all alcoholic drinks', demand will start to become more price inelastic.

Other substitutability issues to consider include:
– the quality and accessibility of information that consumers have about products that are available to satisfy particular wants and needs;
– the degree to which people consider the product to be a necessity;
– the addictive properties of the product, that is, whether the product is habit forming;
– the brand image of the product.

◆ *The relative expense of the product* – a rise in price will reduce the purchasing power of a person's income (real income). The larger the proportion of income that the price represents, the larger will be the impact on the consumer's real income level of a change in the product's price. For example, a 10 per cent increase in the price of a flight to Malaysia will have a bigger impact than a 10 per cent rise in the price of a bus trip into town. The greater the relative proportion of income accounted for by the product, the higher the PED, ceteris paribus!

◆ *Time* – in the short term, perhaps weeks or months, people may find it hard to change their spending patterns. However, if the price of a product goes up and stays up, then over time people will find ways of adapting and adjusting, so the PED is likely to increase over time.

Self-assessment tasks

1 Classify the following products into whether, in your opinion, the PED is likely to be relatively high (elastic) or relatively low (inelastic):

◆ Coca cola
◆ Pepsi cola
◆ soft drinks in general

◆ Nike trainers
◆ Marlboro cigarettes
◆ all tobacco products

◆ Shell unleaded petrol
◆ all forms of car fuel

Justify your classification.

2 A tie manufacturer has received a market research estimate of PED values for their ties that are currently sold in three markets: to independent retailers, to prestige fashion stores and via mail order, mainly to sports clubs

Market	Current price	Current sales	PED value
Independent retailers	£8	40,000 p.a.	–1.0
Fashion stores	£15	10,000 p.a.	–0.2
Mail order	£10	3,000 p.a.	–3.0

Explain and comment upon the PED values shown above.

Source: UCLES, Paper 4381, March 1995 (adapted).

PED and a downward-sloping linear demand curve

So far the impression may have been created that PED and the slope of a demand curve are the same – this, however, is incorrect. Table 2.6 and the associated Self-assessment task will help you see the difference.

Self-assessment task

Use the information in table 2.6 to calculate the PED values as price falls from £10 to £9, from £9 to £8, from £8 to £7 and so on. You should see that the PED value falls as you move down the demand curve in figure 2.15. In the top half of the demand curve, PED > 1; in the bottom half of the demand curve, PED < 1. We could show that for very small changes in price PED = 1 at the mid point of the demand curve. That is why, in theory, a demand curve with unitary price elasticity throughout can be drawn – it is called a rectangular hyperbola. Total expenditure (the area beneath this curve) for any price quantity combination is constant.

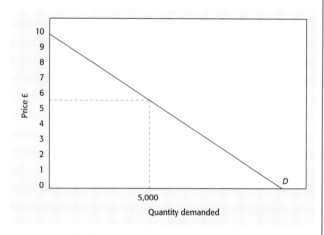

Figure 2.15 The demand curve for product R

Price of product R (£/unit)	Quantity demanded of product R (units per week)
10	0
9	1,000
8	2,000
7	3,000
6	4,000
5	5,000
4	6,000
3	7,000
2	8,000
1	9,000
0	10,000

Table 2.6 Demand schedule for product R

It is important to recognise that the relationship between income and demand changes may not always be positive. If an increase in income leads to an increase in demand (or a decrease in income leads to a decrease in demand), then there is a positive relationship and the product is classified as normal, and the YED has a positive value. However, there are some products (inferior goods) that exhibit a negative relationship between income and demand. Here an increase in income would cause a decrease in demand (a decrease in income would cause an increase in demand) and the YED has a negative value. So the sign that precedes the YED tells you the nature of the relationship between income and demand; the numerical value tells you the strength of that relationship.

There has been a 2 per cent increase in consumer income and that has led to the following changes in demand.

Income elasticity of demand

Income elasticity of demand (YED) is defined as a numerical measure of the responsiveness of demand following a change in income alone. Once again if demand is responsive, then it is classified as elastic; if unresponsive, it is inelastic.

The formula used in this case is

$$YED = \frac{\% \text{ change in quantity demanded}}{\% \text{ change in income}}$$

	Original demand (per period of time)	New demand
Product A	100 units at the current price (£10)	103 units at the same price (£10)
Product B	100 units at the current price (£10)	99 units at the same price (£10)
Product C	100 units at the current price (£10)	101 units at the same price (£10)

The YED of A = $\dfrac{\text{3% increase in demand}}{\text{2% increase in income}}$

= +1.5 (normal good – elastic response)

The YED of B = $\dfrac{\text{1% decrease in demand}}{\text{2% increase in income}}$

= –0.5 (inferior good – inelastic response)

The YED of C = $\dfrac{\text{1% increase in demand}}{\text{2% increase in income}}$

= +0.5 (normal good – inelastic response)

One of many laptop computers on the market – a normal good but with a positive cross elasticity of demand.

Self-assessment task

Use figure 2.16 to explain the YED calculations for each of these three products. Note: the sign indicates the direction in which the demand curve shifts, the numerical value indicates how far the curve shifts at the original price.

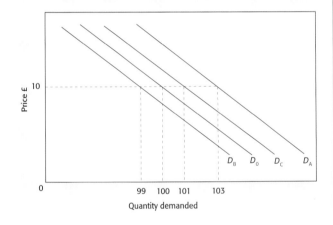

Figure 2.16 The effect of alternative income changes on the demand curve

Cross elasticity of demand

Cross elasticity of demand (XED) is a numerical measure of the responsiveness of demand for one product following a change in the price of a related product alone. Note the causal relationship that is being measured, and, since this has altered the conditions of demand, we would illustrate the impact of this change in the price of a related product by a shift in the demand curve (similar to YED above).

The formula used is

$$\text{XED} = \dfrac{\text{\% change in quantity demanded of product A}}{\text{\% change in the price of product B}}$$

Products that are substitutes for each other (e.g. different types of laptop computer) will have positive values for the XED. If the price of B goes up, then people will begin to turn to product A because of its more favourable relative price. If the price of B falls, then consumers will start to buy B instead of A. Products that are complements (e.g., computers and printers or software) will have negative values of XED. If the price of B goes up, the quantity demanded of B will drop and so will the complementary demand for A.

A numerical and diagrammatic illustration

Assume the current average market price of a standard type of personal computer is £1,000 and current sales are 100 units per day (figure 2.17). Consider what might happen if, following a 2 per cent decrease in the price of laptop computers (a substitute product), demand for PCs falls from 100 units to 98 units per day at the original price (D_0 to D_1). Our calculation becomes

$$\text{XED} = \dfrac{\text{2\% fall in demand for PCs}}{\text{2\% decrease in price of laptops}}$$

= +1

The positive sign indicates that the products are substitutes.

Self-assessment task

What would have happened to the demand for PCs if, following the same change in the price of laptops, the XED had been +2. Redraw figure 2.17 to illustrate this.

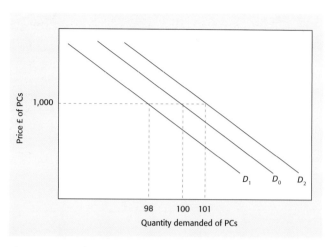

Figure 2.17 A change in the demand for PCs

$$PES = \frac{\% \text{ change in quantity supplied}}{\% \text{ change in price}}$$

Since the relationship between the price and quantity supplied is normally a direct one, the PES will tend to take on a positive value. If the numerical value of PES > 1, then we say that supply is relatively price elastic, that is supply is responsive. If the numerical value of PES < 1, then supply is relatively price inelastic, that is supply is unresponsive.

Figure 2.18 shows five supply curves each with different PES values.

Now consider that the average price of software (a complement) falls by 5% – this encourages extra sales of PCs so that demand for PCs rises to 101 per day at the original price and the demand curve shifts from D_0 to D_2.

The elasticity calculation is

$$XED = \frac{1\% \text{ increase in sales of PCs}}{5\% \text{ fall in price of software}} = -0.2$$

Note again the sign indicates the nature of the relationship (a negative one between complements), the numerical value indicates the strength of that relationship.

Self-assessment tasks

1 What would happen if demand for PCs had risen to 110 units per day? Calculate the XED and redraw the diagram to illustrate what has happened.

2 The owner of a local golf course loans out equipment to non-members who want to play occasional rounds. She estimates that in June and July, if she lowers the hire price of clubs by 10 per cent, the number of non-members playing will increase by 25 per cent. Calculate and comment on the XED. What other factors should the owner consider?

Price elasticity of supply

Price elasticity of supply (PES) is a numerical measure of the responsiveness of supply to a change in the price of the product alone. The supply could be that of an individual firm or group of firms; it could of course refer to the supply of the overall industry. It is expressed as

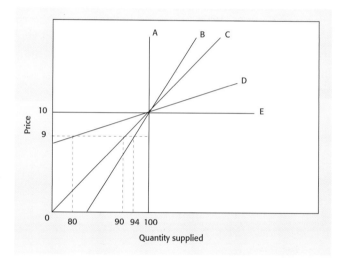

Supply curve	% change in quantity supplied	/ % change in price	= PES	Description
A	0%	/ 10% decrease	= 0	Perfectly inelastic
B	6% decrease	/ 10% decrease	= +0.6	Relatively inelastic
C	10% decrease	/ 10% decrease	= +1.0	Unitary elasticity
D	20% increase	/ 10% increase	= +2.0	Relatively elastic
E	Firms are not prepared to supply any at a price below £10 but will supply as much as they can at £10 (or above!)		= +∞	Perfectly elastic

Figure 2.18 Five different supply curves

Factors influencing PES

The key words in understanding PES are supply flexibility – if firms and industries are more flexible in the way they behave, then supply tends to be more elastic. The main influences on PES are:

◆ *The ease with which firms can accumulate or reduce stocks of goods.* Stocks allow companies to meet variations in demand through output changes rather than price changes – so the more easily manufacturing firms can do this, the higher the PES. Companies that provide services are, of course, unable to build up stocks.

◆ *The ease with which they can increase production.* In the short run firms and industries with spare productive capacity will tend to have a higher PES. However, shortages of critical factor inputs (skilled workers, components, fuel) or transport difficulties will often lead to inelastic PES. In recent years use of better management techniques and improved relations between firms and their suppliers has probably increased the PES in many industries.

◆ Over time, of course, companies can increase their productive capacity by investing in more capital equipment, often taking advantage of technological advances. Equally, over time, more firms can enter or leave an industry and this will increase the flexibility of supply.

Business relevance of elasticity
Price elasticity of demand

An understanding of PED is useful to help understand price variations in a market, the impact of changing prices on consumer expenditure, corporate revenues and government indirect tax receipts.

In figure 2.19 you can see how variations in PED can lead to price volatility following a change in the conditions of supply. D_e represents a demand curve with PED > 1 over the relevant price range. D_i represents a demand curve with PED < 1 over the relevant price range. In both cases, however, the current market equilibrium is at $P_e Q_e$. Now a decrease in supply resulting from an increase in, say, production costs would result in a leftward shift in the supply curve, from S_0 to S_1. Whilst we can see in both cases that the change in equilibrium leads to higher prices and a reduction in the quantity traded, the extent of the changes varies according to the PED. For D_e, as producers try to raise prices (to pass on

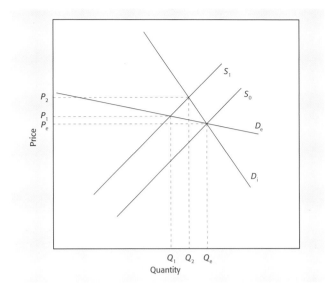

Figure 2.19 Price volatility following a change in supply

the higher costs to their customers), consumers reaction is to stop buying this product in their droves. This reaction constrains the extent to which prices rise only from P_e to P_1 – quantity, therefore, takes the strain here and falls considerably from Q_e to Q_1. On the other hand, when demand is relatively price inelastic, producers have the scope to raise prices considerably (P_e to P_2) without suffering from a significant drop in sales (Q_e to Q_2).

PED and total expenditure/total revenue

PED can help us understand how total spending by consumers will change as price rises or falls assuming the price change is caused by a shift in the supply curve.

$$\text{Total expenditure} = P \times Q = \text{Total revenue of a firm or industry}$$

In figure 2.20, assume there are two products each with the same equilibrium price (£10) and quantity traded (100 units per day). Total expenditure by consumers per day = £10 × 100 = £1,000 – this is of course equal to the revenue received by companies. Now, if the price rises to £11, the differences in PED indicate that consumers respond in different ways, and the total expenditure will change:

◆ D_e is relatively price elastic over the relevant price range, and quantity falls considerably to 80 units (PED = –2). Total expenditure is now down to £880 per day – the reason, of course, is that the relative fall in sales is greater than the relative increase in price.

◆ D_i is relatively price inelastic over the relevant price range and the quantity traded only falls slightly to

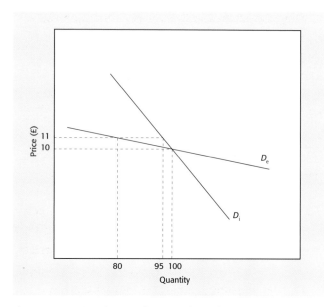

Figure 2.20 Price elastic and price inelastic demand curves

95 units (PED = –0.5). Total expenditure actually rises even though less is traded! The reason is that the increase in price exerts a more powerful influence in this case.

Income elasticity of demand

Since YED provides information about how demand varies as income changes, the concept is potentially of great importance to planners both in business organisations and government.

If the YED for a normal good exceeds unity, then demand for that product will grow more rapidly than consumer incomes during normal periods of economic growth – hence considerably greater productive capacity may be required. However, during a recession, when incomes fall, firms producing this sort of product will be extremely vulnerable, given the large reduction in demand that might be expected.

Self-assessment tasks

1 You used this demand schedule when we looked at PED on a linear demand curve at the beginning of this section. Figure 2.21 shows the resulting demand curve.

Refer back to how PED varies along a linear demand curve – note, in the top half of the demand curve PED > 1 whereas in the lower half PED < 1.

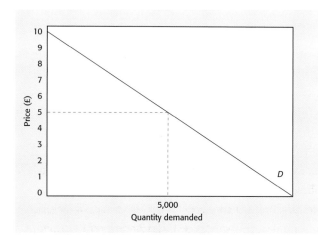

Figure 2.21 The demand curve for product R

Calculate the total expenditure (TE)/total revenue (TR) figures and graph the resulting values underneath the demand curve in figure 2.21 (put TE on the vertical axis and quantity on the horizontal axis – it will help if you use the same scale on the horizontal axis).

Price of product R (£/unit)	Quantity demanded of product R (units per week)	Total expenditure £ per week
10	0	
9	1,000	
8	2,000	
7	3,000	
6	4,000	
5	5,000	
4	6,000	
3	7,000	
2	8,000	
1	9,000	
0	10,000	

- What do you notice about TE/TR figures as price is cut from £10 towards £5 per unit?
- Why does this happen?
- What do you notice about the TE/TR figures as price is raised from £0 to £5?
- Why does this happen?
- Where is TE/TR maximised?

2 If a government is interested in raising more revenue from indirect taxes, such as VAT or excise duties, should it tax products that are price elastic or price inelastic? Explain and illustrate your answer with diagrams and examples.

If the YED is negative then firms producing such inferior goods will see their sales decline steadily over time as the economy grows – however, they may be the sort of business to benefit from the hard times of recession.

Self-assessment tasks

1 What will happen to sales of a product whose YED = + 0.6?

2 How could you use YED values to advise a company on how to produce a mix of goods and services that would reduce the risk often associated with only producing a very narrow range of products?

3 Why might government planners be interested in the YED values of different products?

Cross elasticity of demand

Many companies are concerned with the impact that rival pricing strategies will have, ceteris paribus, on the demand for their own product. Remember that substitutes are characterised by a positive XED: the higher the numerical value, the greater the degree of substitutability between these alternatives in the eyes of the consumer. In such cases there is a high degree of interdependence between suppliers, and the dangers of a rival cutting price are likely to be very significant indeed.

Companies are increasingly concerned with trying to tie consumers to buy not just one of their products but a whole range of complementary ones, for example computer printers and print cartridges. XED will identify those products that are most complementary and help a company introduce a pricing structure that generates more revenue. For instance, market research may indicate that families spend most money at the cinema when special deals are offered on ticket prices, even though the PED for ticket prices is low. In this case, for example, the high negative cross elasticity between ticket prices and the demand for food, such as ice cream and popcorn, means that, although the revenue from ticket sales may fall, this may be compensated for by increased sales of food. This points to the need for a more sophisticated pricing structure within the cinema looking at the relationships between the demand for all products and services offered, including other merchandise such as T-shirts and posters.

Price elasticity of supply

You have already seen how variations in PED will influence the nature of a change in the equilibrium following a given shift in the supply curve. Figure 2.22 also confirms that the PES will influence the nature of a change in the equilibrium following a given shift in the demand curve. The diagram illustrates two alternative supply curves with different elasticities over the relevant price range. S_e is relatively price elastic, S_i is relatively price inelastic.

If the initial equilibrium is at PQ and then demand for a normal good increases, perhaps because of an increase in income, in both cases the new equilibrium price and quantity are higher. However, in the case of S_e, the greater flexibility in supply allows companies to respond to this increased demand without raising prices so much. In the case of S_i, the inflexible nature of supply means that companies raise prices more sharply in response to the surge in demand.

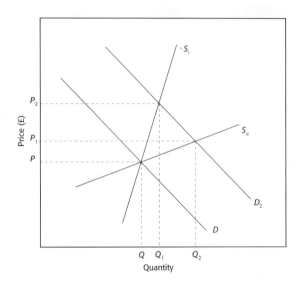

Figure 2.22 Supply curves with different elasticities

Self-assessment task

Redraw figure 2.22 to consider what will happen if there is a decrease in demand, perhaps because of a change in tastes and preferences away from this product. Remember you are analysing the impact of variations in PES on the new equilibrium.

◆ Under what conditions will prices fall most? Why is this?

◆ Under what conditions will there be the greatest decrease in sales? Why is this?

You will note that as with PED, prices tend to be more volatile when supply is inelastic, and quantity is more changeable when supply is price elastic.

Self-assessment tasks

1 (a) Explain the difference between price elasticity of demand, cross elasticity of demand and income elasticity of demand.

   (b) Discuss how an understanding of these concepts might be useful to a professional football club in deciding the price of tickets for its matches.

2 A market research company has recently published estimates about UK consumers' demand for holidays in certain countries. A summary of the main findings is given below:

Holiday destination	Price elasticity of demand	Income elasticity of demand
Spain	−1.8	−0.1
USA	−1.2	+1.3
South Africa	−0.5	+2.0

Price refers to the average combined price of a direct flight (economy class) and seven days accommodation, half board in a standard hotel.

With reference to the above data:

(a) Explain the difference between normal and inferior goods.

(b) Explain how an increase in consumers' income might affect the demand for each of the holiday destinations shown.

(c) Use the figures to discuss the possible effects that a 10 per cent increase in the 'average price' of each of the holiday destinations shown might have on demand.

(d) The directors of a small travel agency in the east of England have got hold of this research. Why would you advise them to treat the findings cautiously – what extra research might they need to undertake themselves before using elasticity figures as the basis for company policy?

Source: UCLES, Paper 4381, November 1996 (adapted).

Cautionary note

We have assumed that calculating elasticity values is straightforward. In fact there are enormous statistical problems. As an example consider the difficulties of calculating PED values from historical data. Have the price changes only been caused by supply variations? Have there been any non-price demand influences at work? Remember, if we are to calculate the PED value accurately, we need to separate out all the other influences and just measure the impact of the price change alone on quantity demanded – the difficulty encountered here is referred to as the identification problem. Collecting data from other sources, such as market testing, or surveys (using questionnaires and/or interviews), is costly in terms of time and money and may not be particularly valid or reliable. As such, many companies may prefer to make rough 'guestimates' of elasticity values or to work with incomplete data, particularly if they are operating in markets where rapid change means past data cease to be a good indicator of the future.

Factor markets and how they work

The previous section provided an introduction to the nature of factors of production. Like the product market, there is also a market in operation for land, labour, capital and enterprise. In particular, the case of the **labour market** will be described here, not least because its operation is something which affects all of us at some stage in our lives. The general principles which operate are the same as those described earlier in this section.

Labour earns an income in the form of hourly paid wages, monthly salaries or, in some cases, bonuses on top of such regular payments. It is a well-known fact, though, that in the labour market some people earn more than others. For example, if you have a part-time job, then you are likely to be paid £3 per hour or possibly £4. At the other extreme, a top Premier League footballer earns say £20,000 per week – he probably earns as much for a few minutes warm up before a game as you might earn for a whole day's work filling shelves in a supermarket. Why is this? In simple terms it is due to market conditions of demand and supply, which operate in the labour market.

The economic principles which apply are no different to those analysed earlier but with one important difference. This is that in factor markets it is firms that demand labour and it is households that supply them with labour. In other words, the positions are the reverse of those which have applied throughout the rest of this section. To provide a service or to produce goods firms need to employ factors of production, such as labour. For this reason the demand for labour is referred to by economists as a **derived demand**. Take the case of a sixth former working at the local supermarket. The reason for this is that the supermarket needs goods to be stacked onto shelves so that customers can buy them. If there were no goods on the shelves, then the supermarket's tills would be standing idle! Similarly, for someone employed in a car assembly plant or making CD players, that worker is employed as a consequence of the demand from consumers for new cars and CD equipment. The demand for labour is, therefore, derived from the demand for the final product.

In general the demand and supply curves for labour are the same as those illustrated earlier for goods and services. Figure 2.23 shows a typical example of the market supply and demand curves for hotel workers in London. Take the supply curve first:

◆ the higher the wages paid, the more people will want to work in hotels;
◆ consequently, the supply curve for hotel workers is upwards sloping.

For the demand curve:

◆ the higher the wages that hotel companies have to pay, the fewer workers they will want to employ;
◆ consequently, the demand curve for hotel workers is downward sloping.

Equilibrium in the market is determined by the intersection of the demand and supply curves for labour. The wage paid, W_1, is the price at which the particular market clears.

The above is a very simplified representation of the way labour markets actually operate. In practice they are much more complex than this and influenced by many things. The market supply curve for labour is very dependent on the elasticity of supply of labour. If wages change, only a few (or possibly a lot more workers) may join the labour market. A whole host of factors relating to labour immobility could explain this (see unit 2, section 5). Equally, the elasticity of demand for labour with respect to changes in wages depends on the ease of substitution of labour by other factors of production, the proportion of wage costs in total costs and the response time involved.

In conclusion, figure 2.23 assumes we are dealing unrealistically with a labour market which operates as a perfect market. In practice very few labour markets are perfect, although some do generally operate in this way, particularly where there are many buyers and sellers and the labour concerned has no particular skills and qualities.

Self-assessment task

Refer back to figure 2.23

1 Explain, with the aid of a diagram, how the equilibrium wage rate would change if:
   ◆ a major sporting event such as the European Football Championships or the Olympic Games were being held in London;
   ◆ hotels in London did not recruit migrant workers from the rest of the EU.

2 From your own experience what determines how much you might be paid for a part-time job? How does this relate to the simple theory of wages described above?

The money market

Section 1 of this unit introduced the idea of exchange and the benefits of specialisation. In practice, in all except for the most primitive economies, these fundamental processes are facilitated by means of money. Just think about how tedious our daily lives would be if we had to physically exchange one good we might have for others we might require. This is where money comes in, for it is money which facilitates the free flow of goods in an economy. But what is money?

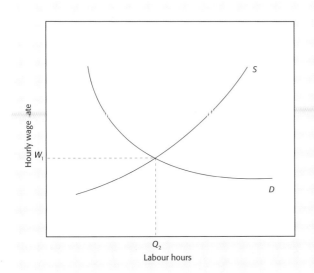

Figure 2.23 The market for hotel workers in London

This may seem an obvious question, with Bank of England notes and coins being an obvious answer. To the economist, though, money is rather more than this. For the time being money can be regarded as anything which is readily acceptable as a means of settling debt. Money need not be coins and notes – it could be something more tangible like precious stones, goats or salt (a very valuable resource a few hundred years ago). The item classed as money, though, must be acceptable to all concerned as a means of exchange. This overriding definition therefore covers the supply of money. At this stage, it is necessary to see the demand for money as the desire to hold money; in other words, to keep one's wealth or assets in the form of money.

The operation of the **money market** in practice is dealt with in detail in unit 7 of OCR's specification. At a simple level this market operates in the same way as all other markets analysed so far in this section. This is shown in figure 2.24. The supply curve of money is inelastic, whilst the demand curve is downward sloping

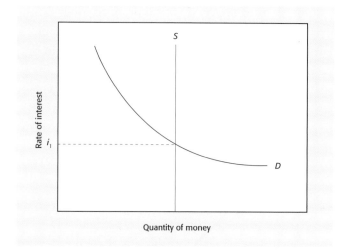

Figure 2.24 The market for money

like other demand curves. Where they intersect, is the **rate of interest**. To the borrower, this is the payment that has to be paid in order to obtain money; to the lender it is the reward received for parting with the money. In simple terms, it acts as a price in the money market.

Summary

In this section we have recognised that:

- A market exists whenever people come together for the trade or exchange of goods and services; it is also possible to identify sub-markets.

- The buying side of the market is referred to by economists as the demand side. It is possible to derive a demand curve for any market – this shows how the quantity which is demanded varies with the price of a product or service.

- Consumer surplus arises because some consumers are willing to pay more than the given price for what they buy.

- The demand curve shifts to the left or right when, 'other things being equal', the assumption is changed. Three important causes of this are a change in income, a change in consumer tastes or attitudes and a change in the price of related products.

- The selling side of the market is known as the supply side. It is possible to derive a supply curve for any market – this shows how the quantity which is supplied varies with the price of the product or service.

- Producer surplus can arise when firms produce below the market price.

- The supply curve shifts to the left or right when, 'other things being equal', the assumption is changed. Three important causes of this are a change in the costs of supply, a change in the characteristics of the industry and changes in government policy.

- Equilibrium occurs in the market where there is no tendency for change, when the plans of consumers match the plans of suppliers. A change to the equilibrium position will produce a new equilibrium price and quantity.

- Elasticity is a very important concept in markets; it is the responsiveness of one economic variable following a change in another variable.

- Price, income and cross elasticity of demand are relevant numerical measures which have considerable value and use in enhancing our understanding of how markets operate. The price elasticity of supply is relevant in understanding how producers can react in markets.

- The labour and money markets operate in the same way as any other market. Wages are the price of labour and the rate of interest is the price for obtaining or lending money.

Key words

Definitions of Key words can be found in the Glossary on page 240.

ceteris paribus
complements
consumer surplus
costs
cross elasticity of demand
demand
demand curve
demand schedule
derived demand
disequilibrium
effective demand
elasticity
equilibrium
income elasticity of
   demand
inferior goods
labour market

market
market demand
money market
normal goods
notional demand
perfectly elastic
perfectly inelastic
price elasticity of demand
price elasticity of supply
producer surplus
rate of interest
sub-market
substitutes
supply
supply curve
supply schedule
unitary elasticity

3 Firms and how they operate

On completion of this section you should be able to:

➤ understand what economists mean by costs

➤ distinguish between the short and the long run

➤ explain what is meant by economies of scale and how firms might benefit from them

➤ understand what economists mean by revenue

➤ describe what is meant by the profit maximisation objective

➤ understand other alternative objectives of firms

➤ describe the characteristics of the main forms of market structure in which firms operate

➤ explain why barriers to entry can be used to explain differences between market structures

The firm's costs of production

An entrepreneur must consider all the costs of the factors of production involved in the final output. These are the **private costs** directly incurred by the owners. Production may create costs for other people but these are not necessarily taken into account by the **firm**. In order to understand cost structures in business economists split costs into different categories and use specific cost concepts.

Fixed costs or overheads

These are the costs which are completely independent of output. Total **fixed cost** data when drawn on a graph would appear as a horizontal straight line. At zero output, any costs that a firm has must be fixed. Some firms operate in a situation where the fixed cost represents a large proportion of the total. In this case it would be wise to produce a large output in order to reduce unit costs.

Variable or direct costs

Variable costs include all the costs which are directly related to the level of output, the usual ones being labour and raw material or component costs. Sometimes a cost has elements of both; for example a firm's electricity bill may consist of the heating and lighting cost of the premises and the power to operate production machinery. Electricity, therefore, could be considered to be a **semi-fixed** and semi-variable cost.

Total cost (TC) equals fixed cost (FC) plus variable cost (VC).

From this information all the relevant cost concepts can be derived.

Average fixed cost (AFC)

$$\text{equals} \quad \frac{\text{total fixed cost}}{\text{output}}$$

Average variable cost (AVC)

$$\text{equals} \quad \frac{\text{total variable cost}}{\text{output}}$$

Average total cost (ATC)

$$\text{equals} \quad \frac{\text{total cost}}{\text{output}}$$

Marginal cost (MC) is the addition to the total cost when making one extra unit and is, therefore, a variable cost.

The most important cost curve for the firm will be the ATC. If it is U shaped, the most efficient output for the firm will be where the unit cost is lowest. If the firm chose to produce in the downward-sloping part of the average cost curve it would be experiencing **increasing returns** to the variable factors. The unit cost is falling because the fixed cost is being spread over an increasing output. The firm will be most efficient if it produces at the minimum point of the average cost curve. This is known as the **optimum output** and the marginal cost always cuts the ATC at this point. The most efficient output is not necessarily the most profitable. For a firm wishing to maximise its profits, its chosen output will depend on the relationship between its revenue and its costs.

Costs in the short run and the long run

The **short run** for the firm is a period of time when it cannot alter its fixed inputs. The level of production can only be changed by altering its variable inputs such as labour. The time taken to alter fixed factors differs , depending on how easy it is to get new capital installed.

In the **long run**, the firm can alter *all* of its inputs, so that they become variable in nature.

In the very long run, technological change can alter the way the whole production process is organised, even the nature of the products themselves. In a society with rapid technological progress this will be shrinking the time period. There are now examples in consumer electronics where whole processes and products have become obsolete in a matter of months.

Short-run costs

When a firm working with fixed factors increases the variable ones, there will come a point where the returns to the variable units begin to fall. This is the principle of **diminishing returns**. It will be reflected in an increase in the firm's marginal and, eventually, its average costs. The firm will be at its most efficient in the short run if it can operate at the optimum or the lowest point on the average total cost curve (see figure 3.1(a)).

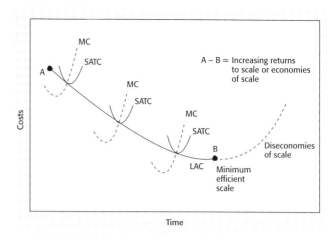

Figure 3.1(b) Costs in the long run

Costs in the long run

It is possible that a firm can find a way of lowering its cost structure over time. One way might be by increasing the amount of capital used relative to labour in the production process, with a consequent increase in factor productivity.

The long-run average cost curve shows the least cost combination of producing any particular quantity. Figure 3.1(b) shows a firm experiencing falling ATC over time. This would enable it to lower the price without sacrificing profit. Products such as Walkmans, personal organisers and games consoles are examples where prices have fallen through competition and changing technology.

Economies of scale

Where an expansion of output leads to a reduction in the unit costs, the benefits are referred to as **economies of scale**. They occur because the firm's output is rising proportionally faster than the inputs; hence the firm is getting increasing returns to scale.

What kind of economies of scale can be identified?

Internal economies are those benefits which only affect an individual firm, whereas external economies will benefit all the firms in a locality or in the market.

Technical economies refer to the advantages gained directly in the production process. Some production techniques only become economic beyond a certain level of output. The economy of increased dimensions occurs in a number of business applications.

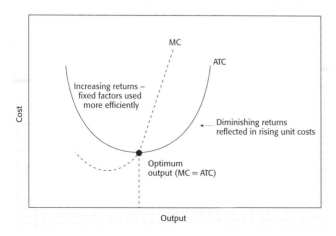

Figure 3.1(a) Costs in the short run

If one takes the production of a box structure, and doubles the scale, its production costs will double. If it is being used to carry something, then the operating costs may not increase in proportion. The capacity of the box will have increased eightfold, generating a much larger potential revenue. The trick is to make sure that the extra capacity is fully used. Making full use of capacity is also important on a production line. Car production is the result of various assembly lines. The number of finished vehicles per hour is limited by the pace of the slowest sub-process. Firms producing on a big scale can increase the number of slow-moving lines to keep pace with the fastest, so that no resources are standing idle and the flow of finished products is higher. One of the problems of the British motor industry was its small-scale output limited by low sales. Some firms produced at higher unit cost than competitors and this is one of the motives behind takeovers and mergers over the years, to get a bigger market share and benefit from economies of scale.

In addition to technical economies, economists have identified:

◆ *Marketing economies.* This is where large firms can achieve savings in unit cost from advertising or packaging. The usual one is the benefit of lower prices by buying in bulk from suppliers.
◆ *Financial economies.* Large firms will find both the access to borrowed funds easier, and the cost lower, than smaller firms will. This is because the perceived risk of lending to large-scale operators is lower.
◆ *Managerial economies.* Firms producing on a large scale may be able to re-organise the structure in order to get a more efficient management of resources. They may also attract the best management talent through higher salaries.
◆ *Risk-bearing economies.* These might explain why, as firms get larger, they become more diversified. It is a way of spreading business risks. A diversified conglomerate can cover any losses on one activity with the profits from another, an option not open to smaller firms. Risks can be further reduced by co-operating with rivals on large capital projects.

The last example above may be an illustration of an *external* economy since all firms will benefit from savings in research and development costs. Large firms may also benefit from locating close to others in the same market. The advantages may include a pool of skilled labour or a convenient supply of components. This may explain the trend for firms to cluster in business and science parks in certain parts of the country. The better transport infrastructure will be another advantage to all the firms.

It must be recognised that there are limits to economies of scale. A firm can expand its output too much with the result that unit costs start to rise. This may be the beginning of **diseconomies of scale**. The most likely source of these lies in the problems of co-ordinating large organisations and the effect size has on morale and motivation. A firm that is producing at its optimum output in the short run and at the lowest unit cost in the long run (sometimes called the minimum efficient scale [MES]) has maximised its efficiency (see section 4). Industries where the MES is low will have a big population of firms. Where it is high, competition will tend to be between a few large players.

The firm's revenue

In looking at the revenue of a firm, economists are dealing with the receipts the firm receives from the sale of the various products it produces. In general terms the total sales revenue will be influenced by the selling price of the product and the number of units bought by consumers at that price. The following general definitions apply:

Total revenue (TR) equals price (P) multiplied by quantity (Q);
Average revenue (AR) equals total revenue divided by quantity and is the same thing as the price;
Marginal revenue (MR) is the addition to the total revenue resulting from the sale of one extra unit of output.

A firm that accepts the ruling market price will get the same price whenever it increases its output. Therefore the marginal revenue will be constant and equal to average revenue. If, however, the market price falls as output increases, the firm will be facing a downward-sloping demand curve and its marginal revenue will be less than the average revenue. Any firm must look carefully at potential revenue together with its cost structure when determining its output. It is only possible to predict what this output will be if one has this data and the objectives of the firm are clearly understood.

The objectives of firms

The standard assumption made by economists is that firm's will seek to maximise their profits. Profit, in economic terms, is simply the difference between the firm's total revenue and its total costs. There will be a minimum level of profit necessary for the entrepreneur to stay in business. This is the concept of normal profit. It reflects the opportunity cost of the business capital used by the firm in the production process, that is what it could earn in its next most desired economic activity. This element of total profit can be considered as an essential cost of production and as such it is included in the firm's average costs. A firm making the minimum level of profit is said to be producing the break-even output. In most situations the firm could be expected to increase its profit by raising output. Any extra profit is termed abnormal or supernormal and it is assumed that this is the motive for firms to supply to the market. It is the reward for risk taking and managing resources.

If the firm produces up to the point where the cost of making the last unit is just covered by the revenue from selling it, then the profit margin will have fallen to zero and total profits will be greatest.

The rule for profit maximisation is therefore that the firm should produce where

MC equals MR

and the distance between TR and TC is greatest.

At any output below this, the firm is sacrificing potential profit, whilst any output above it is being sold at a loss, reducing the firm's total profit. Profit maximisation therefore is an ideal for firms to work to.

From a business standpoint, there may be several reasons why firms do not operate at the profit maximisation output:

◆ In practice it may be difficult to identify this output. It is also likely to be very difficult for firms to be able to calculate their marginal cost and their marginal revenue. Instead the firms may simply work out the cost per unit and add on a profit margin in order to determine the selling price. This cost plus pricing technique is unlikely to result in maximum profit, although it could produce a high level of profit.

◆ Short-term profit maximising may not be in the long-term interest of the company. Firms with large market shares may wish to avoid the attention of the Competition Commission.

◆ Large abnormal profit may attract new entrants into the industry and make existing firms vulnerable.

◆ High profits may damage the relationship between the firm and its stakeholders, such as the consumers and the company workforce. Profit maximisation may not appeal to the management, who may have different objectives.

◆ High profits might trigger action by the firm's rivals and it could become a target for a takeover.

Alternative objectives

Because of the problems of applying the profit maximisation objective, economists have recognised other objectives of firms. These are of particular significance from a practical standpoint. Some of the most important ones are described below.

Sales revenue maximisation

This is where a firm may be willing to accept lower short-run profit in order to increase its share of the market. A firm choosing this option would raise output beyond MC = MR until MR had fallen to zero. Extra sales after this would contribute nothing to total revenue; therefore it is the sales revenue maximisation output. There may still be abnormal profit if total revenue is higher than total cost.

Sales maximisation

This option maximises the volume of sales rather than the sales revenue. In this option the firm would increase output up to the break-even output where the total revenue just covered the total cost. A higher output implies loss-making behaviour. The only situation where this would be possible is where the firm could use the profit from some other activities to cover these losses, using the principle of cross subsidisation. The most likely motive for loss-making behaviour is to gain a toehold in a new market or to deter new entrants into an existing one. Short-term profit is therefore the opportunity cost of raising the level of sales.

Satisficing

This behaviour would occur when a firm is determined to make a reasonable level of profits to satisfy the shareholders but also to keep the other stakeholding groups happy. It may choose to sacrifice profit in order to improve the workforce's pay and conditions or to keep prices down for the benefit of consumers. Firms may have charitable or environmental objectives, which must be financed at the cost of profit. **Satisficing** can also be a feature of firms that have enjoyed a high market share over a long period of time. Complacency can lead to firms losing their focus on the cost structure or failing to devote resources to either product or process innovation. Either situation can lead to a loss of profits.

Where the ownership is divorced from the control in a company, the **managerial motives** may differ from those of the shareholders. If management salaries are linked to output, the management will prefer rapid growth and sales revenue maximisation. If the firm has close rivals and the growth strategy entails taking big

risks, it can lead to a more cautious managerial approach because job security and career advancement prospects will influence their decisions. Also, time and money may be used in improving the non-monetary rewards, such as company cars, private health insurance and company pension rights. In some firms a desire for greater prestige leads to the construction of expensive head offices and greater emphasis on corporate entertaining.

One must be careful of sweeping statements concerning firms' short-run behaviour. Extra long-run profits may follow from short-term sacrifices. As a working assumption, it is still valid to see profit maximisation as the major long-term objective influencing firms' competitive behaviour.

Self-assessment tasks

1 The following items are a selection of business costs. Indicate whether each one is fixed, variable or a mixture of both:

the rent of a factory	business rates
workers' pay	electricity costs
raw materials	advertising expenditure
interest on loans	management salaries
transport costs	depreciation on fixed capital

2 Calculate the firm's costs and revenue from the following information. The firm is operating at a fixed price of £60 per unit sold.

Output	FC	VC	TC	AFC	AVC	ATC	MC	TR	AR	MR
0	60									
1		50							60	
2		80								
3		105								
4		152								
5		225								
6		330								

(a) What is the profit-maximising output?
(b) What is the TR at this output?
(c) What is the TC at this output?
(d) How much abnormal profit is made?
(e) What output would maximise sales revenue?

3 Wok Stock and Barrel is a small family run engineering company with a production capacity of 9,000 units per year. Market research suggests that the market will take up all of this output at a price of £8 per unit. The firm's cost structure is as follows:

direct labour	£1.50 per unit
raw materials	£0.50 per unit
other variable costs	£1.00 per unit
total fixed costs	£27,000 a year

Calculate

- ◆ AFC
- ◆ AVC
- ◆ ATC
- ◆ AR

(a) If the factory produced its capacity output, what would the firm's abnormal profit be?

(b) Suppose that consumer tastes change away from the product and the firm has to reduce the price to £6 in order to get rid of unsold stock. What situation is the firm now in?

4 Study the information provided on the operating costs of a large goods vehicle and then answer the questions below:

(a) In this presentation of data, how has the annual total vehicle cost been calculated?

(b) Give examples of the business overheads.

(c) What is the economic term for the costs which depend directly on mileage?

(d) If the vehicle is operating at average mileage, what proportion of the annual total cost do the fixed costs account for?

(e) What is the average total cost (ATC) at average, higher and lower mileage?

(f) Using these data, what advice would you give haulage firms wanting to operate as efficiently as possible?

(g) Why might a profit-maximising firm not take this advice?

VEHICLE OPERATING COSTS
38 tonne gvw articulated vehicle
(2 axle tractor 3 axle curtain sided semi-trailer)

	Costs as at 1 April 1998		
	Average mileage	Higher mileage	Lower mileage
General information			
Annual mileage	70,000	85,000	60,000
Life (years) – tractor	6.0	5.0	7.0
– trailer	12.0	12.0	12.0
Life (miles) – tractor	420,000	425,000	420,000
Replacement cost (£) – tractor	51,580	55,533	48,615
– trailer	21,006	21,006	21,006
Fuel consumption – mpg	7.8	8.5	7.0
Fuel price – pence per litre	53.5	53.5	53.5
Tyre life (miles) – tractor	70,000	90,000	60,000
– trailer	65,000	75,000	55,000

	Costs £ p.a.			Costs pence per mile		
	Average mileage	**Higher mileage**	**Lower mileage**	**Average mileage**	**Higher mileage**	**Lower mileage**
Standing costs						
VED	3,210	3,210	3,210	4.59	3.78	5.35
Insurance	1,756	1,931	1,596	2.51	2.27	2.66
Depreciation – tractor	7,049	8,552	6,042	10.07	10.06	10.07
– trailer	1,751	1,751	1,751	2.50	2.06	2.92
	13,766	15,444	12,599	19.67	18.17	21.00
Running costs						
Fuel	21,818	24,311	20,838	31.17	28.60	34.73
Tyres – tractor	1,044	929	1,074	1.49	1.09	1.79
– trailer	1,044	989	1,032	1.49	1.16	1.72
Maintenance – tractor	4,823	5,409	4,429	6.89	6.36	7.38
– trailer	2,889	3,285	2,624	4.13	3.87	4.37
	31,617	34,923	29,996	45.17	41.09	49.99
Total vehicle cost	45,383	50,368	42,595	64.83	59.26	70.99
Employment cost of driver	22,502	24,676	19,466	32.15	29.03	32.44
Cost of vehicle and driver	67,885	75,044	62,061	96.98	88.29	103.43
Overheads						
Transport	5,694	5,694	5,694	8.13	6.70	9.49
Business	5,694	5,694	5,694	8.13	6.70	9.49
TOTAL COST	**79,273**	**86,432**	**73,449**	**113.25**	**101.68**	**122.42**

Source: FTA Cost Information Service

5 The following case study looks at some of the objectives of the firm. Read it and answer the questions which follow:

Chefaid plc

A row has broken out in the boardroom of Chefaid plc, the kitchenware company, over the firm's prospects and future direction. The marketing director announced a record level of sales for the last quarter and suggested that there should be a 10 per cent target for the growth of sales revenue over the coming year. It was suggested to him that this was unwise. The firm's latest product, an exclusive set of kitchen tools, has yet to break even. The sales record owes a lot to the current popularity of cookery programmes on TV; there is a danger that the sales boom is a flash in the pan.

The managing director was more interested in the firm's profitability. He was under pressure to declare higher future dividends and to get the funds to finance the planned new factory. He believed that a profit-maximisation strategy was the best way forward. The production director warned the meeting that cost pressures were building up and that industrial relations with the workforce were fragile because of the beginning of talks about wages and new working conditions. Management in general had been delighted with the new share option scheme and the bonus linked to sales performance.

It was suggested that the prospects for growth in general were good, because of the increase in consumer confidence, and the firm's market share had benefitted from the closure of two large rivals during the recession. It was argued that the market structure was becoming less competitive and this might give an opportunity for price rises. The company must not lose sight of its long-term drive to raise profitability by reducing unit costs. This sparked further disagreement over the firm's sponsorship commitments, its promotions budget and its charitable contributions.

(a) What do economists understand by the phrase 'the market structure is becoming less competitive'?

(b) What will be the best output for the firm if the profit-maximising strategy wins the day?

(c) What are the risks associated with this strategy?

(d) What output would maximise turnover?

(e) What does the phrase 'fail to break even' mean? What advice would you give to improve the performance of the new product?

(f) Explain why the management may not favour profit maximisation.

(g) To what extent does the case show that businesses have a range of objectives?

(h) Discuss the idea that each business decision to reach an objective has risks attached to it.

The market operations of firms

Firms operate in markets; in any particular market, though, there may be just one or many firms competing for business. The term *market structure* is used by economists to describe the context in which firms compete with each other and refers to the number of firms and their relative size in the market. Firms' behaviour from a business standpoint is influenced by the characteristics of particular market structures. The safest and potentially most profitable situation is that of a **monopoly**, a single seller without close rivals, whilst at the other end of the spectrum lies a theoretical structure economists have called **perfect competition**. The purpose of studying extreme models such as these is to provide benchmarks, against which real markets can be judged. **Monopolistic competition** has features of both the extreme cases, but is closest to perfect competition. **Oligopoly**, on the other hand, is closer to a monopoly situation. The important thing to understand is that the boundaries between these market structures can become blurred – this is particularly the case as an oligopoly moves towards a monopoly. One of the key economic concepts in explaining how firms come to be operating in a particular market structure is that of **barriers to entry**. The more difficult it is for new firms to compete, the closer the industry will be to a monopoly.

Barriers to entry

These consist of a mixture of obstacles, which either deter or prevent new firms from competing with the established players in a market. The construction and maintenance of these barriers can become part of a firm's competitive behaviour. Below are some of the main barriers that can be identified:

◆ Some industries such as car manufacturing and aircraft production have huge set up costs. The barrier to new firms is really the access to capital. Fixed capital represents a high proportion of total cost in these activities. In addition, the research and development cost necessary to compete

Concorde is the only operational supersonic transport aircraft. It was developed as a joint Anglo-French venture when it was realised that neither country alone could fund the project. The Concorde project would probably have never been started had it not been for hopelessly optimistic initial estimates of development cost. As the true costs escalated, and the British economy faltered, the British Government attempted to pull out, but this was implacably resisted by France. The Government was forced to scrap its advanced military aircraft the TSR2 instead. Initial entry of Concorde into service was hampered by American resistance on the pretext of the high noise levels. As a consequence it was some time before flights to New York were permitted. The aircraft now returns an operating profit, but the development costs will never be recovered. Subsequent studies for a replacement have so far always foundered on the inability of manufacturers to demonstrate a positive return on investment.
Source: This photo appears with kind permission of Dick Barnard.

effectively will put a strain on the resources of all but the largest firms. Where the new entrants would have to spend a huge amount on fixed capital and it would simply duplicate existing capital, for example railway infrastructure and electricity networks, this is sometimes referred to as a natural monopoly. It might therefore not make economic sense to have more than one producer

◆ The risk attached to entering such industries is increased if the capital cannot be recovered in the event of business failure. It will happen whenever the firm uses specialist capital that is not easily transferable to other economic uses. This is the concept of sunk cost and it acts as a barrier to exit from as well as entry into an industry.

◆ Advertising and brand names with a high degree of customer loyalty may prove to be a difficult obstacle to overcome. This explains why firms regard their marketing expenditure as an act of investment. Existing firms can make entry more difficult through brand proliferation, giving the customers an apparent abundance of choice and closing any market niches that new entrants could exploit.

◆ In a market dominated by firms with a large output, economies of scale can create an effective barrier. New entrants will naturally be at a cost disadvantage because the large ones can produce at lower average cost. This also gives them an opportunity to consider price cutting as a way of eliminating any high-cost producers. This is the concept of predatory or destroyer pricing.

◆ Some existing firms may have a monopoly access to either raw materials, components or retail outlets, which will make it difficult for new firms to break into the market. Vertically integrated manufacturing businesses are protected by the fact that rivals' costs will be higher. The firms may have also acquired specific technical knowledge through experience of production, which newcomers find difficult to match.

◆ The production process or the products themselves may be protected by patents. This is an example of a legal barrier to entry. In the past, when industries have been nationalised this has created state-owned legal monopolies. Some activities, such as the sale of alcohol and medicines, are still controlled by licensing, which limits access to approved suppliers. In the case of retail development, the refusal of planning permission for new outlets can create a legal protection for existing suppliers.

◆ In activities such as computer manufacturing and consumer electronics, the pace of product innovation is so rapid that the existing firms will be working on the next generation products whilst launching the current range. Unless the new entrants have new ideas or can exploit a new market segment, they are destined to fail.

◆ It may be possible for existing firms to hide the existence of abnormal profit by what is called entry limit pricing. This involves deliberately setting low prices to deter potential rivals. It may be in the interest of all the firms to do this, in which case a kind of restrictive practice might be the barrier to entry.

◆ Collaboration or co-operation between big firms to develop new products, though not a restrictive practice, may mean that the resources necessary to compete in such markets are beyond the means of any single firm, so deterring new entrants.

◆ Market conditions such as a fall in demand resulting from economic recession can leave firms with excess production capacity and this will deter entry.

Some of the barriers to entry are easier to overcome than others. New firms will only enter a market when they think that the economic returns will be greater than the cost of breaking the barriers. Where the barriers to entry and exit are low, the market is sometimes described as being **contestable**. In these market situations there are potential competitors, even if few actually appear.

Strong barriers to entry are associated with oligopoly and monopoly, but there are very good particular examples of monopoly power being eroded by new competitors. The Virgin Group for example has achieved this in the airline industry and the soft drinks market. Even firms with a domestic monopoly are likely to be challenged by imported goods, especially if large profits are possible. In a world where the financial resources of international firms is large, they may be prepared to break into markets by using cross subsidisation to cover initial losses.

Richard Branson, chairman of Virgin Atlantic Airways, addresses a gathering of US airline executives in Washington. Branson called upon the US Congress to allow him to own and operate a US airline.
Source: Popperfoto Reuters.

Self-assessment task

For each of the following business activities, consider what barriers to entry there might be for a new firm wishing to enter this particular market:

◆ a local newsagent's shop
◆ a town centre travel agency
◆ beer production
◆ car manufacturing

Characteristics of market structures

This unit will now be completed with a brief description of the main types of market structures identified and used by economists. (Models of these structures will be developed in the A2 stage of OCR's syllabus.)

One of the quickest ways of determining what kind of market structure exists in a particular industry is to use **concentration ratios**. Data on the sales revenue of the biggest three or five firms, relative to the total sales

revenue of the industry, will show the market power of the big firms. A high sales concentration ratio is associated with oligopoly and monopoly whilst a low one would be a feature of monopolistic competition. This is a very useful starting point for the analysis of any market – unfortunately data are not always readily available to allow this calculation to be made.

Figure 3.2 shows the main characteristics of each of the recognised market structures. The significance of barriers to entry, discussed earlier, is clearly shown in the competition roadmap in figure 3.3.

Monopoly

Market dominated by single firm.
In theory the monopoly firm is the industry.
Barriers to entry.
Abnormal profit is possible in short and long run.
Monopolist is a profit maximiser.
Monopolist is a price maker.

Oligopoly

Market dominated by handful of big firms.
Barriers to entry and exit.
Firms may or may not be profit maximisers.
Firms are price makers.
There is product differentiation.

Monopolistic competition

Market consists of large number of firms.
Products are differentiated.
There are no or few barriers to entry and exit.
Firms are profit maximisers.
Abnormal profit is only a feature of short run.

Perfect competition

Very large number of buyers and sellers with perfect knowledge.
Each firm is a price taker.
Firms are profit maximisers.
The products are homogeneous.
There is complete freedom of entry.

Figure 3.2 Economic models of competition

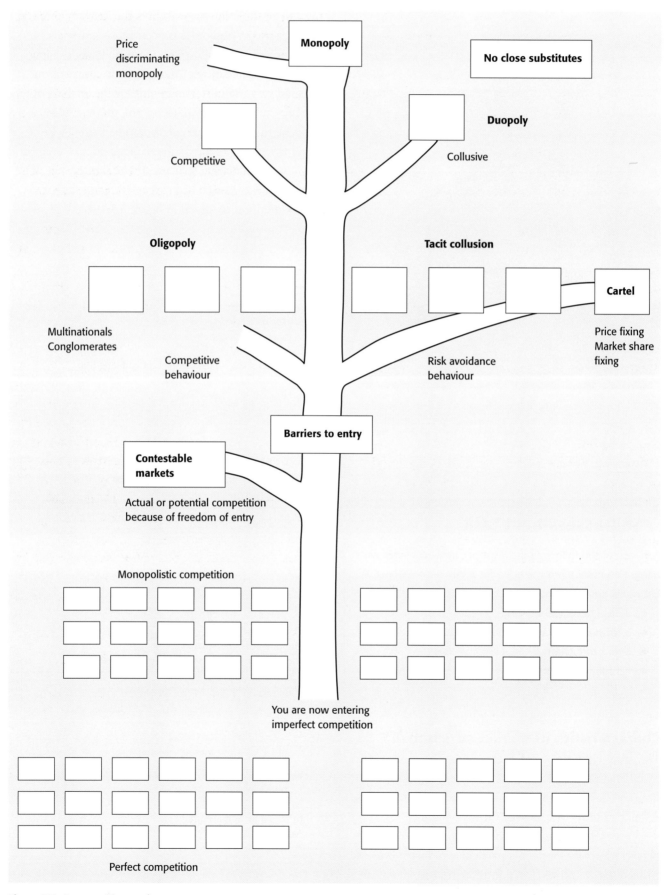

Price discriminating monopoly

Monopoly

No close substitutes

Duopoly

Competitive

Collusive

Oligopoly

Tacit collusion

Cartel

Multinationals
Conglomerates

Competitive behaviour

Risk avoidance behaviour

Price fixing
Market share fixing

Barriers to entry

Contestable markets

Actual or potential competition because of freedom of entry

Monopolistic competition

You are now entering imperfect competition

Perfect competition

Figure 3.3 A competition road map

Perfect competition

In this market structure, although there would be a large number of competing firms, the individual firm has little scope for competitive behaviour. This is because the products are all of the same quality, the firm has no power to alter the price it could charge and there are no barriers to entry. The firm is a **price taker** and its revenue depends on the output it chooses. The only way that firms will end up with different profits is if some of them have lower production costs than others. If any firms do make abnormal profit, it will only be temporary because in the long run new firms will be attracted into the industry and the abnormal profit will be competed away. From this description it is unlikely that there will be any markets that match this description. The nearest economic activity might be parts of the agricultural industry where large numbers of small producers supply a homogeneous product, such as milk or grain.

Monopolistic competition

The main feature which distinguishes this market structure from a perfect market is product differentiation. Each of the suppliers also has a degree of control over the price that is charged. Firms can therefore indulge in both price and **non-price competition**. The large number of substitute products makes this a very competitive market structure. Firms will only be successful in making abnormal profit in the short run because there are no or few barriers to entry. However a successful advertising policy to promote the brand, combined with product innovation, could shift the firm's demand curve to the right and at the same time reduce its price elasticity of demand if consumers no longer see rivals' products as close substitutes. The market power of firms is constrained by the ease of entry and the behaviour of rival firms. This is a very relevant type of market structure and includes hairdressers' shops, video rental outlets and driving schools.

Oligopoly

When an industry is dominated by a handful of big firms, action taken by one will have a big impact on the others. It becomes risky for a firm to alter its price because the reaction of the others is uncertain. Firms in this market structure may prefer to use non-price competition, such as product innovation, advertising and brand proliferation. The risks associated with competitive behaviour may become so great that firms are tempted to collude or settle for a quiet life; hence the relevance of the satisficing objective. There may be takeover and merger activity, which can take the market towards duopoly or monopoly. The difficulty of getting extra sales may lead to firms diversifying in order to grow in a different direction. In the real world, firms' behaviour in oligopoly is difficult to predict. Some oligopolies are highly competitive even though there are not many rivals. The example often quoted is the intense rivalry between Pepsi and Coca Cola. On the other hand, the giant petrol companies and breweries have in the past been accused of **collusion** and following the price leadership of a main player.

Monopoly

There are few situations where one firm has nearly all of the industry sales. The definition of monopoly used by the Competition Commission is where the dominant firm has more than 25 per cent of the market. This figure is deliberately set low to allow any potential monopoly situation to be investigated in the public interest. Sales concentration ratios show that a large number of firms operate in industries close to a monopoly structure. The reason for this is mainly to be found in barriers to entry. Monopolists have the power to raise prices and make abnormal profits at the expense of the consumer in both the short run and the long run, but monopoly does have some positive benefits. Some monopolies such as passenger train operating companies are a consequence of government action; others are not. Other monopolies have been created through a patent, for example cats' eyes and the Dyson vacuum cleaner.

Finally, table 3.1 summarises the characteristics of competitive markets in terms of their relevant economic characteristics.

	Perfect competition	Monopolistic competition	Oligopoly	Monopoly
Number of firms	Many	Many	Few	One or two
Entry into the industry	Easy, perfectly contestable	Easy	Barriers	High barriers
Products	Homogeneous	Differentiated	Varied	Lack of close substitutes
Pricing policy	Price taker	Price maker	Price maker	Price maker
Profit maximisers	Yes	Yes	Not necessarily	Yes
Profits	Abnormal profit only in short run	Abnormal profit competed away in the long run	Yes	Both short and long run
Non price competition	No	Yes	Yes	Yes
Choice for consumers	Yes	Yes	Yes	No

Table 3.1 Features of competitive market structures: a snapshot

Self-assessment tasks

Study the information below and then answer the questions which follow.

1 In December 1997, the former Monopolies and Mergers Commission presented a report to Parliament on the foreign package holiday market and the role of travel agents. It estimated that there were over 1000 tour operators and 2100 travel agents with a total of 6935 retail outlets involved in a business worth £5 billion in 1996. The structural characteristics of the market are illustrated in the following data.

Airline company used	Tour operator	Market share %	Travel agent	Market share %
Britannia	Thomson	24.6	Lunn Poly	23
Airways	Airtours	15.9	Going Places	16
Air 2000	First Choice	10.1		
Airworld	Thomas Cook	4.2	Thomas Cook	12
Caledonian	Inspirations	2.3	A T Mays	6
	Cosmos	1.9	Co op	8
	Flying Colours	1.8	Others	35
	Others	39.2		

(a) Calculate the 3 and 5 firm sales concentration ratios for tour operation and for the retail travel agent business.

(b) What other measures of concentration might you use in this case if you were able to obtain data?

(c) Why might the Monopolies and Mergers Commission have been interested in investigating the relationships between tour operators and travel agents?

2 Read the following short case study opposite and then answer the questions below.

(a) Explain using examples relevant to this case, what is meant by the term low overheads.

(b) Using economic theory, explain why price rises will not make a fish and chip shop owner better off.

(c) How would behaviour differ, if the owner was in a local monopoly situation?

(d) Discuss the non-price methods of boosting revenue. What will determine their success in this case?

(e) Suggest three reasons why the barriers to entry are low in this example.

(f) Explain why a fish and chip shop owner may not be a profit maximiser.

Fish and chip sales take a battering

Over the past few years, fish and chip shops have been doing a roaring trade especially in the North. The typical shop is family run, has low overheads, and the owners have a pride in supplying traditional food to local people. Many of them look at their costs, add on a profit margin and hope that sales will be high enough to give them a reasonable income. Prices range from as low as £1.60 to £2.80, but there are significant regional variations and local prices are influenced by the number of direct competitors. Sales are sensitive to price changes, but the suppliers think that the quality of the product is most important. Reputation is everything in maintaining sales in an increasingly competitive market.

The short-term problems that have hit the suppliers are a rise in fish prices reflecting the growing scarcity of high-quality white fish and the weather conditions that have increased potato prices. A spokesman for the Fish Fryers Association was recently reported as saying:

Things are getting so bad that some of our members are barely covering their wages and the cost of materials. Normally, businesses would react to this by raising prices. Our members are reluctant to do this because of the economic circumstances of their customers. Price rises and cutting the size of portions will not make us better off. The take-away food business is easy to start and is getting more diverse all the time. Our members are trying to increase the range of food served and must have an eye on long-term business rather than short-run difficulties.

Trends and fashions in food consumption may be starting to affect the most loyal of fish and chip consumers. The demand for low fat foods is increasing and survey data show that, as they get better off, consumers are widening the range of take-away food they eat. Even in the world of fish and chips the market is changing. Although there are a huge number of shops, a growing proportion are franchise outlets of large businesses, such as Harry Ramsden's. This business grew rapidly from a single shop near Leeds to a multinational operation in only a few years. All in all, the traditional chippy may be a disappearing feature of urban life. Will only grandparents remember fish and chips with salt, vinegar and bits wrapped in newspaper? Is the future trend towards up-market fish restaurants serving fish in sauces rather than batter and chips that are low fat and from organically grown potatoes?

Harry Ramsden's in Bournemouth. Harry Ramsden's has broken the world record on four occasions for selling the most portions of fish and chips in a day. The current record being 12,105 in Melbourne.
Source: Harry Ramsden's.

3 Read the following on recent merger issues in the brewing industry and then answer the questions that follow.

Brewing comes to a head

Brewing is a manufacturing activity characterised by a large number of producers. In 1996 there were 70 large regional brewers, 200 smaller ones and another 200 micro breweries with a very small output. The national market is somewhat different. The major firms are part of larger conglomerate groupings. The Bass group for example has diversified into hotels, pubs, bingo clubs, betting shops and soft drinks. Brewing only accounts for 36% of its turnover each year.

Brewery group	Share of total beer sales	Number of tied houses, i.e. pubs owned by the brewery group
BASS GROUP	23%	4400
CARLSBERG TETLEY	14%	None
SCOTTISH COURAGE	28%	2700
WHITBREAD	13%	4400

The former Monopolies and Mergers Commission (MMC) first investigated the brewing industry in 1989, when it found evidence of a complex monopoly situation operating against the public interest in the following ways:

♦ the retail price of beer had risen too fast;
♦ the price of lager was not justified by production costs;
♦ regional price variations were excessive;
♦ consumer choice was restricted by control of the brands sold in tied houses.

It investigated the industry again in 1997 when Bass proposed to merge with Carlsberg Tetley. It found that the beer market had seen considerable changes on the demand side as illustrated in table 2. Partly as a consequence, the market had become much more concentrated. All the major brewers gave evidence that the competition in the market was intense. Only 33% of pubs are now owned by the brewery compared with 50% in 1985. The vertical ties have been loosened following a massive selling off of tied houses at the suggestion of the Monopolies Commission in

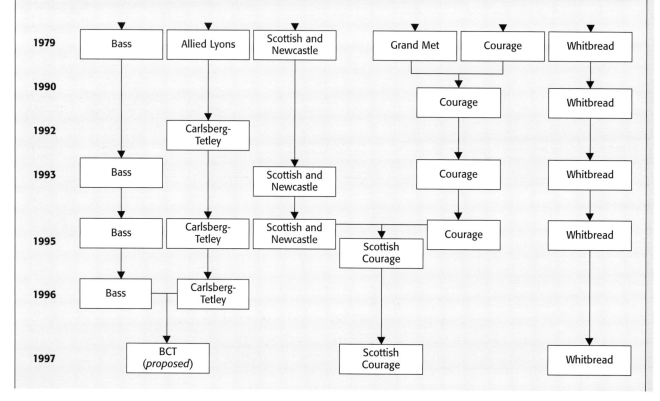

Year	Consumption '000 hl	Consumption '000 barrels	By type of beer Ale and stout %	By type of beer Lager %	By container Draught %	By container packaged %
1960	45,118	27,561	99.0	1.0	64.0	36.0
1970	57,300	35,003	93.0	7.0	73.0	27.0
1980	66,658	40,720	69.3	30.7	78.9	21.1
1990	65,184	39,819	48.6	51.4	71.6	28.4
1991	63,038	38,508	48.9	51.1	70.3	29.7
1992	60,937	37,247	48.6	51.4	69.3	30.7
1993	59,177	36,150	48.1	51.9	68.2	31.8
1994	60,575	37,004	47.0	53.0	67.0	33.0
1995	59,129	36,120	45.2	54.8	65.3	34.7

Table 3.2 UK beer consumption, 1960 to 1995
Source: HM Customs and Excise, BLRA.

1989. Even the tied houses can now sell guest beers from other producers. All of this has increased real choice for consumers who are becoming more brand conscious. Sales of beer are now highly dependent on advertising. More beer is now sold through off licences and supermarkets, which have 28% of beer sales compared with 17% in 1985.

The argument for the merger was that Carlsberg Tetley would benefit from the export reputation built up by Bass. Bass needed more production capacity and suggested that there would be efficiency savings resulting from economies of scale. It also wanted major names in the lager market to widen its product range. In 1996, Bass had a total of 68 beer brands and Carlsberg Tetley had 64.

Bass contended that there were no barriers to entry into the brewing industry and that the regional brewers had increased their share of the total market. In addition Bass argued that there was strong competition from imports, stating that 37% of all brands sold were foreign owned. Both companies suggested that the competition would continue to be fierce after the merger.

The rival brewers' contention was that the merger would give significant economies of scale. This would allow the new group to cut the prices to a level at which they could not compete. They feared that they would be driven out of the market and that the new group could then raise prices at will.

The MMC was concerned that no new major brewers had entered the industry in recent years because of the level of sales necessary to keep production costs low, and the difficulty in setting up a new distribution network. It was concerned that the new group would have too much market power and that it might lower or raise the prices of its products according to whether it wanted to increase market share or increase its profits. The MMC concluded that the benefits of the merger would not outweigh the adverse effects and therefore could be expected to operate against the public interest.

Source: MMC Report July 1997.

(a) What evidence is there to suggest:
   ◆ that brewing is an oligopoly?
   ◆ that the retail market is also highly concentrated?

(b) What has happened to the volume and pattern of beer consumption between 1960 and 1995? Explain the possible connection between these changes and the increasing horizontal integration that has happened.

(c) What barriers to entry may explain the lack of new entrants into brewing?

Summary

In this section we have recognised that:

- A firm's costs of production can be broken down into fixed and variable costs.

- The marginal cost is the addition to total cost when producing one extra unit of output.

- Diminishing returns take place in the short run when the returns to variable units begin to fall.

- The benefits associated with a reduction in unit costs due to an expansion of output are known as economies of scale. Various sources of internal and external economies of scale can be recognised.

- A firm's revenue is the value of the output which is sold.

- Profit maximisation is the usual assumption made in economic theory as to how firms behave. It occurs at the output where the revenue from an extra unit of sales equals the cost of making this last unit, i.e. $MR = MC$.

- Firms do not always seek to maximise their profits and may pursue alternative objectives.

- Economists recognise various types of market structure in order to explain the behaviour of firms.

- The degree of competition in these markets is largely determined by the extent of barriers to entry.

- Perfect competition acts as a very important benchmark against which all markets can be measured.

- A monopoly is in theory a single firm controlling the entire output of an industry. Extensive barriers to entry are the source of monopoly power.

- Monopolistic competition and oligopoly are particularly relevant real-world market structures.

Key words

Definitions of Key words can be found in the Glossary on page 240.

abnormal or supernormal profit
average fixed costs
average revenue
average total costs
average variable costs
barriers to entry
collusion
concentration ratio
contestable market
diminishing returns
diseconomies of scale
economies of scale
firm
fixed costs
increasing returns
long run
managerial objectives
marginal cost
marginal revenue

monopolistic competition
monopoly
non-price competition
normal profit
oligopoly
optimum output
perfect competition
price taker
private costs
profit
profit maximisation
sales maximisation
sales revenue maximisation
satisficing
semi-fixed costs
short run
total revenue
variable costs

Unit 2

Market failure and government intervention

4 Economic efficiency within competitive markets

On completion of this section you should be able to:

➤ describe what is meant by efficiency in Economics
➤ explain what is meant by productive efficiency
➤ explain what is meant by allocative efficiency
➤ explain what is meant by Pareto efficiency
➤ illustrate how the concepts of efficiency can be applied to the production possibility curve
➤ understand how competition can lead to an efficient allocation of resources

Efficiency in economics

How might we judge whether any type of economic system (be it a market system or any other type of system) is 'doing a good job'? This is clearly a very important question. The answer to it might affect the whole way that we would want to try to organise the running of an economy. The answer that economists give to this question is to say that an economic system is doing well to the extent that it is delivering economic efficiency.

Efficiency is a word often used in our society. It is usually seen as 'a good thing'. However, it is important to think what it actually means. It probably has a range of different meanings when it is used by different people in different contexts.

The best way of understanding the term 'efficiency' is to return to the key issues of Economics, as discussed in section 1, unit 1. If Economics is a study of the use of scarce resources in order to meet our infinite wants, then efficiency is to do with using those scarce resources in the most effective way possible to meet the highest possible level of wants.

If resources are being used in this 'best' possible way, then economists are clear that this must imply that two different types of efficiency are being achieved, namely **productive efficiency** and **allocative efficiency**.

Productive efficiency

This type of efficiency is all to do with using the least possible amount of scarce resources to produce any particular product. To put it another way, it involves producing things at the lowest possible cost.

Productive efficiency can be understood through figure 4.1, which shows a firm's or an industry's average total cost curves.

In this diagram, the point marked 'x' indicates the point of productive efficiency. It is worth noting that productive efficiency can thus be seen as implying two things about the point of production by a firm or an

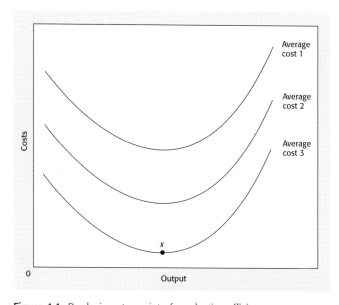

Figure 4.1 Producing at a point of productive efficiency

industry. First, it implies that production takes place on the lowest possible cost curve. This means that the lowest possible cost techniques of production are being used. Secondly, it implies that production occurs at the lowest point on the lowest cost curve. Production at this point on an average cost curve is referred to as a point of 'technical efficiency' by economists.

Allocative efficiency

To achieve full economic efficiency, it is not enough simply to produce goods and services at the lowest possible cost. Even had the former command economies of Eastern Europe produced everything with full productive efficiency (which seems unlikely), it would be hard to argue that this represented efficiency in its full sense. Economies must not only produce things using the least possible resources, they must also make the products that consumers most want. There would be little of merit in an economy that produced many products at very low cost that nobody particularly wanted and yielded little satisfaction (see also section 5).

Allocative efficiency is all to do with producing those products that are most wanted by consumers, given their cost of production. This can be seen from the following:

1 Two products, x and y, cost exactly the same amount to produce. However, product x gives consumers twice as much satisfaction as product y. If allocative efficiency is to exist, product x should be produced in preference to product y.

2 Two products, a and b, yield the same amount of consumer satisfaction. However, product a costs half as much to produce as product b. It would be allocatively efficient to produce product a in preference to product b in this situation.

Allocative efficiency can be thought of more precisely than this. It will exist when the selling price of a product is the same as the marginal cost of producing that product. In this situation, the price paid by the consumer will represent the true economic cost of producing the last unit of the product. This should ensure that precisely the right amount of the product is produced.

The idea that when price is equal to marginal cost there will be allocative efficiency (the right amount of the product made) is best understood through a simple example:

Quantity	1 2 3 4 5 6 7
Price (£)	5 5 5 5 5 5 5
Marginal cost (£)	2 3 4 5 6 7 8

For this product, an output of one unit would not be allocatively efficient. Here, the cost of producing the product is less than the value put on it by the consumer (as represented by the price that the consumer is prepared to pay for that product). The product should clearly be produced, but there is scope for further worthwhile production from this point. This is also true when two or three units of the product are made. On the other hand, an output of seven units of the product should not be produced. Here, the seventh unit costs £8 to produce, but is only valued at £5 by the consumer. The same problem exists with output levels of 5 and 6. Thus, there is only one ideal output level (that is, one output level that will yield allocative efficiency) and that is an output of four units where price is equal to marginal cost.

Pareto efficiency

A related way of defining economic efficiency is in terms of what economists call 'Pareto efficiency' (named after an Italian economist, Wilfredo Pareto, who suggested the idea at the beginning of the twentieth century). This is said to exist when it is not possible to make any one person in society better off without making someone else worse off. If this situation exists, then there will be productive efficiency as nothing more could be produced with the resources available (and thus there is no possibility of any overall extra production). It also implies that allocative efficiency exists because, if it does not, then it may be possible to swap production in such a way that consumers can be made better off (without necessarily having to make any others worse off).

Efficiency and the production possibility frontier

One way to illustrate the concept of economic efficiency is to think in terms of the production possibility frontier. This is illustrated in figure 4.2.

Point a on the diagram can be considered to be productively efficient. At this point, nothing more can be produced in total than is currently being produced.

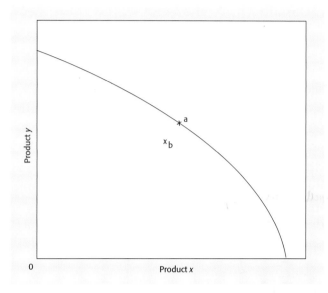

Figure 4.2 Efficient points on the production possibility frontier

This is as opposed to point b where it is possible to increase production with the scarce resources that are available in the economy. Equally, point a can be considered to be a possible point of Pareto efficiency as it is only possible to increase the production of one product by reducing the production of another (and hence potentially making someone worse off). This is not true about point b from where it is possible to increase the production of either product without sacrificing any other production. It is only possible to establish whether point a (or any other point on the frontier itself) is allocatively efficient by knowing consumer preferences. This information about consumer demand is not given by the production possibility frontier alone, and thus we cannot say for sure whether this point represents the point at which the combination of products x and y that are being produced is that which satisfies the maximum amount of wants (or gives the highest possible level of consumer satisfaction).

Competition and efficiency

It is often suggested by economists that efficiency, as defined above, will exist in a fully competitive market (specifically, a perfectly competitive market). This is seen as the crucial argument in favour of competition. It is why competition is seen as 'a good thing'.

Productive efficiency

A competitive market could lead to productive efficiency as it provides firms with the incentive to produce things at the lowest possible cost as represented by the lowest point of their average cost curve (see section 3). It does this by providing both a 'carrot' and a 'stick'. The 'carrot' of a competitive market is that, if a firm can produce at a lower cost than its competitors, then its profits will be higher. The 'stick' of a competitive market is failure to keep costs low will lead to the firm going out of business either because it cannot maintain competitive prices or, if it does, it is selling at a loss.

Allocative efficiency

Competitive markets could also force allocative efficiency upon an economy. The 'carrot and stick' of competition once more come into play. If firms wish to make maximum profit (the carrot), then they will only succeed in doing so by producing those products that are most demanded by consumers. Equally, the threat of bankruptcy (the stick) will force firms to produce only products that are clearly in demand, as a failure to do so will result in losses being made.

In perfect competition, it can be noted that the specific requirement of allocative efficiency, that the selling price is equal to the marginal cost of production, is always true. In other words, the price paid in the market is exactly equal to the cost of producing that unit of output.

Pareto efficiency

A free and competitive market can also be seen as leading to Pareto efficiency. The key to understanding this is to recognise that people will only trade with each other if they believe that trading is mutually beneficial. No one will trade with someone else unless they believe that they will benefit from that trade. If this is true, then it can be concluded that, in a totally free market, all trades that are advantageous to both traders involved will occur, but no trades in excess of this will take place. In other words, Pareto efficiency will exist. It will not be possible to improve on the situation described by making someone better off without making someone else worse off. The free market automatically leads to Pareto efficiency.

Self-assessment tasks

1 Discuss what type of efficiency each of the following might lead towards:

   (a) A firm uses a new machine that costs less than its old one but produces more.

   (b) A company swaps production to a different product that sells at the same price but is in greater demand.

   (c) A car plant makes 1,000 workers redundant because their jobs can now be done by robots that cost less over a period of time than paying workers' wages.

   (d) Following privatisation, firms in Eastern Europe have to change what they produce in order to make a profit.

Automatic robots weld parts of a Mercedes-Benz A class car in the new Mercedes-Benz plant at Juiz de Fora, 110 miles northeast of Rio de Janeiro. The new Mercedes-Benz plant is expected to produce 30,000 A class compact cars a year
Source: Popperfoto.

2 Read the following newspaper article and then answer the questions that follow.

Consumers in a power struggle

Sparks will fly as the electricity revolution unfolds. Regional energy companies are now allowed to go looking for business on rival turf: but who will really benefit – the householder or the corporation?

The dream is that competition will drive prices down. The Office of Electricity Regulation (Offer) says: 'For typical domestic consumers, their electricity supplier will be charging among the highest prices in the area. They can save by switching supplier.'

But Offer's figures suggest the biggest saving possible for an average user is just £21.00 a year or 40p a week. Benet Middleton, who heads policy research at the Consumers Association, says: 'Until there is more competition in electricity generation, as opposed to sales, it is unlikely we will see anything like the savings in other utilities.'

John Over, Yorkshire Electricity's marketing director, believes domestic electricity prices are about as low as they are likely to get for some time and thinks that competition will centre on service instead. He says: 'Clearly, we've got competitive electricity prices. I think competition will impact not only on price, but also on the range of services you expect to get.'

Source: Paul Slade, *The Independent*, 19 September 1998 (adapted).

   (a) Explain why it might be expected that the price of a product, such as electricity, will fall when competition is introduced into a market.

   (b) Why might it be reasonable to anticipate that service to electricity consumers will improve now that consumers can choose their electricity supplier?

   (c) In what ways does the article suggest that consumers of electricity may not enjoy the benefits of the introduction of competition into electricity supply?

Summary

In this section we have recognised that:

- Efficiency is an important concept in Economics relating to how well scarce resources are used.

- Three types of efficiency are recognised: productive efficiency is achieved when firms produce at the lowest possible average cost; allocative efficiency is when the price paid is equal to the marginal cost; and Pareto efficiency occurs when it is not possible to make one person better off without making someone else worse off.

- The concept of efficiency can be applied to the production possibility frontier and to market structures.

Key words

Definitions of Key words can be found in the Glossary on page 240.

allocative efficiency
economic efficiency

Pareto efficiency
productive efficiency

5 Why markets may not work efficiently

On completion of this section you should be able to:

➤ describe what is meant by market failure

➤ understand why market failures arise

➤ describe what is meant by positive and negative externalities and explain these in terms of a divergence between private and social benefits and costs

➤ analyse why market dominance can lead to inefficiency

➤ differentiate between public, quasi-public and private goods with an understanding of the terms 'non-excludability' and 'non-rivalry'

➤ explain why public goods may not be provided by the market

➤ explain the problems created by information failures, including the concepts of merit and de-merit goods and why these create market failures

➤ explain the possible inefficiencies caused by factor immobility, such as structural and regional unemployment

➤ understand that markets can lead to an 'unacceptable' distribution of resources such as 'unfair' access to health care and education

➤ apply these concepts of market failure to a range of possible economic issues

➤ comment upon their likely impact

Defining market failure

It is stating the obvious to say that **market failures** exist when markets fail. However, the question needs to be asked: 'Fail at what?' The answer is: 'Fail at delivering economic efficiency.' Market failure exists any and every time that a free market, left to its own devices and totally free from any form of government intervention, fails to lead to the best, or optimum, use of scarce resources. In terms of the previous section, it is when the interaction of supply and demand in a market does not lead to productive and/or allocative efficiency.

The first section of this unit suggested that there are reasons to expect that freely functioning markets could lead to economic efficiency. There are reasons why this may not be the case. The purpose this section is to explain the different reasons for this failure of markets to work as well as might be hoped. Specifically, it will look at the following different reasons why markets fail:

1 The existence of externalities.
2 Merit and de-merit goods.
3 Public and quasi-public goods.
4 Occupational and geographical immobility of labour.
5 The concentration of power in markets.
6 Concerns about distribution and equity.

Externalities
Defining externality

If the market system is to work well and lead to economic efficiency, it is important that the people who make economic decisions are those who are affected by those decisions. A transaction between a supplier and a consumer for a product needs only to affect the supplier and consumer involved. As long as this is the case, then both sides will act only so long as both feel that they will benefit from any action – all is well in the market. However, a problem could clearly arise if someone else, not party to the economic decision, is affected by that decision. This is the economic concept known as **externality**.

An externality is said to arise if a third party (someone not directly involved) is affected by the decisions and actions of others. If you decide to shout loudly to your friend in public, then others (third parties) not involved in making that decision are affected by the assault on their ear drums.

Private and social costs

Another way of understanding the same concept is to define an externality as any divergence between private

79

and social costs or benefits. The social costs of any action are all of the related costs associated with that action. The private costs are those costs involved in an action that accrue to the decision maker.

Negative externalities

It is quite possible that these private and social costs are the same: all of the costs of an action accrue to the decision maker and there are no further costs. If this is the case, then there are no externalities. However, it is possible that there will be a difference: private and social costs may not be equal to each other. For example, if you make a decision to take a journey in my car, you consider the costs of the petrol and the time taken. However, you do not consider the further costs that you may be imposing on others in terms of your contribution to road congestion, to environmental damage and to possible car accidents. In this situation, a negative externality, or an external cost, is said to exist. The situation is illustrated in figure 5.1. Here, private costs are part of the social costs involved in a decision. However, they do not represent all of the social costs. The difference between the two is the negative externality.

Private and social benefits

A similar situation can also exist with benefits rather than costs. The social benefits of a decision are all of

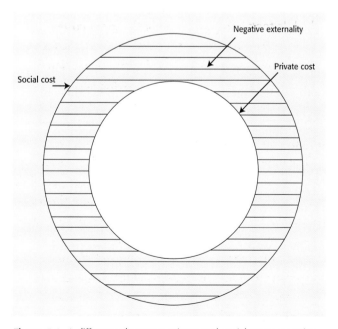

Figure 5.1 A difference between private and social costs: negative externalities

the benefits that accrue from that decision. The private benefits are those that accrue solely to the decision maker. Again, these may or may not be the same.

Positive externalities

It is possible that the social benefits of a decision may exceed the private benefits. If this is the case, then a positive externality, or external benefit, is said to exist. For example, if you make a decision to go to the doctor to be inoculated against a particular disease, then clearly you receive the private benefit of not catching that particular disease against which you have been inoculated. However, you may not be the only one to benefit. The fact that you do not get the disease has some possible benefit to all others with whom you come into contact, who will now not catch the disease from you.

The problem created by externalities

The essence of the problem created by externalities is that they will lead to an inappropriate amount of the product involved being produced: the free market will lead either to too much or too little production.

Consider a firm that produces a chemical. There are costs that the firm will have to meet in producing a certain quantity of this chemical. These would include such things as:

◆ raw material costs;

◆ labour costs;

◆ energy costs.

All such costs would be termed 'private': they have to be paid for by the decision maker (the firm) (see section 3). These costs form part of social costs. However, there are further social costs likely to be involved as well. These might include any dumping of chemical waste, perhaps in a local river, which creates clean-up costs, any atmospheric pollution that creates clean-up costs and ill health, and possible road congestion that results from the transportation of the chemicals. These are negative externalities. The problem is that only the private costs of producing the chemical will be taken into account by the firm when making the pricing decision about its chemical. The further external costs, which are real costs to society, will not be taken into account. This will mean that the price will be lower than if all social costs were taken into account. In turn, demand and production will be higher than if the full

A coal-fired power station belching CO_2 emissions into the atmosphere: a typical case of negative externality
Source: Electricity Association.

social costs had been considered. Thus, a negative externality will lead to too much of a product being produced. The situation can be seen in figure 5.2.

The price that will occur in the market will be P_1 where the supply schedule that takes account of the private costs, S_1, is equal to demand. This price is associated with production of Q_1. However, if the supply schedule took into account all of the social costs, S_2, which are greater than just the private costs, then this would result in a price of P_2. This price is associated with a lower production of Q_2. Thus, the negative externality has led to $Q_1 - Q_2$ too much production. Too many scarce resources are being devoted to the production of this product. The market has failed.

The opposite problem is true of a positive externality. Here, the problem is that too little of the product will be produced. If only the private benefits, and not the full social benefits, are considered, then there will be under-production. This is illustrated in figure 5.3.

This time, the problem is with demand. If only the private benefits are registered, then demand is represented by the demand schedule D_1. This leads to a price of P_1 and an associated production of Q_1. However, if the further extra benefits to society were registered (which they will not be by the private

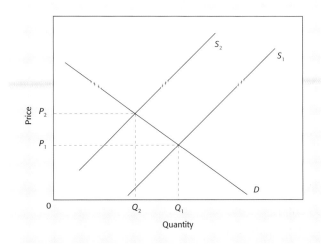

Figure 5.2 Over-production caused by a negative externality

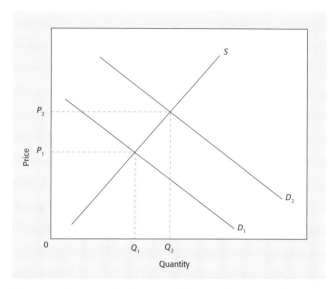

Figure 5.3 Under-production caused by a positive externality

decision maker involved), then demand would be greater at D_2. This would lead to a price of P_2 and a production of Q_2. Thus there is an under-production of $Q_1 - Q_2$ associated with the positive externality. Insufficient scarce resources are being devoted to the production of this good or service. The market has failed.

We must, therefore, suggest that externalities are likely to be a source of market failure as they will mean that resources are not allocated in the ideal way: too few or too many resources are likely to be directed to the production of certain products.

Self-assessment tasks

1 Identify and explain whether each of the following involves a positive or a negative externality:
   - a next-door neighbour playing his/her music loudly;
   - a person being educated beyond the compulsory school leaving age;
   - the dropping of litter;
   - smoking in a public place;
   - a new, well-designed and pleasant public building;
   - the use of pesticides.

2 Read the adaptation of a newspaper article on the page opposite and then answer the questions below:
   (a) Explain what is meant by Professor Gershunt's phrase, 'The retail industry in effect externalises a large part of its costs.'
   (b) Identify and explain the different negative externalities arising from the development of out-of town supermarkets that are mentioned in this article.

Merit goods, de-merit goods and information failures

Defining merit and de-merit goods

Another way in which markets may fail is due to the existence of what are termed **merit** and **de-merit goods**.

Sometimes, merit and de-merit goods are simply seen as an extension of the idea of externalities in Economics, as discussed above. A merit good may be described as a good that has positive externalities associated with it. Thus, an inoculation might be seen as a merit good as others who may not catch the disease from the innoculated person also benefit. A de-merit good is seen as any product that has negative externalities associated with it. Thus, cigarettes can be seen as a de-merit good insofar as secondary smoking can be viewed as a possible cause of ill health (a clear negative externality). If this is all there is to merit and de-merit goods, then they cannot be seen as a separate category of market failure from externalities.

However, merit and de-merit goods can (and indeed should) be defined in a different way, which does make them clearly different from externalities. The essence of merit and de-merit goods in this definition is to do with a **failure of information** to the consumer. Consumers do not perceive, it is suggested, quite how good or bad a particular product is for them: either they do not have the right information or they simply lack some relevant information.

Cheap food – at a huge price

Why do the British shop in supermarkets? Easy. Price, convenience, quality and choice: the mantra of the market economy. But is perception matched by reality?

Supermarkets are very cheap for some goods, but what you save on the loss-leading swings, you lose on the marked-up roundabouts. Take fruit and vegetables. Last summer we compared prices between supermarkets and street markets of the old-fashioned endangered variety. Like for like, the markets won on almost every count.

If they're not such paragons on price, at least supermarkets are safe, convenient and accessible by car. Or are they? If, like a third of the population, you don't have the use of a car, they are not. But even getting to the store by car may be far from convenient. Over the past 20 years, the number of shopping trips has increased by a third, and driver shopping mileage has more than doubled. Given Britain's congestion, more journeys of increasing length doesn't sound very convenient. Nor is it: in the Sixties, according to Professor Jonathan Gershuny of Essex University, consumers spent on average 41 minutes per day shopping and in related travel. In the Eighties this has risen to 70 minutes, with studies showing that food shopping accounts for more than three-quarters of total shopping time. According to Professor Gershuny, 'the increase in shopping time reflects the growth of "self servicing" and the growth in the size of supermarkets ... the larger the supermarket the more walking for the shopper and the greater the average distance from the shopper's home ... The retail industry in effect externalises a large part of its costs.'

On quality and choice, supermarket products may be varied and consistent – but is what you see what you really get, and are you paying the real costs? Supermarkets' huge buying power and demand for absolute consistency means that fruit and vegetable production are now industrialised processes. Multiples have 60 per cent of the market and suppliers who cannot supply 52 weeks a year need not supply. Your Brussels sprouts may be perfectly formed, but at what costs to the countryside? Biodiversity on the shelf is increasingly at the cost of biodiversity in the field.

While it has long been recognised that the perceived benefits of the supermarkets are not evenly spread between social groups (the chief executive of the supermarkets' own research organisation acknowledges that old and poor people will have serious problems over where to buy food because of the growth of superstores and the lack of town centre stores), our research leads us to believe that, even for the better-off and mobile, the advantages of supermarkets are beginning to be outweighed by the drawbacks.

The decline of the town centre is well documented and attributable, at least in part, to the development of out-of-town shopping centres. The big retailers' claims to efficiency in transport are bogus. Much freight transport is unnecessary – produce could be sold locally. More than a third of the increase in freight transport since the late Seventies has been food, drink and tobacco – which together account for less than one tenth of the economy. Next time you use a motorway, count the supermarket trucks. No wonder the big retailers are such lavish supporters of the British Road Federation.

It's the same story with packaging. According to the government, 'the stocking policies of supermarkets ... largely contributed to non-returnable [packaging] attaining [its] present share of the market', while MEPs reported that an EU directive to reduce packaging was 'the most lobbied issue in the (EU) Parliament's history'. The supermarkets are used to getting their way; the directive was duly changed.

Britain's retailing policies need a radical shake-up. We need more smaller shops, buying locally, and revitalised street and covered markets. We still need tougher rules on out-of-town development, and freight companies could pay the real cost of their operations.

Source: Hugh Raven and Tim Lang, *The Independent*, 10 January 1995 (adapted).

Merit goods

With this idea of a failure of information, a merit good is defined as a good that is better for a person than the person who may consume the good realises. Under this definition, education is often defined as a merit good. The individuals who make decisions about how much education to receive (or how much to allow their children to receive) do not fully appreciate quite how much benefit will be received through being educated. We do not appreciate how good education is for us. We do not perceive its full benefits at the time of making the decision about how much education to receive.

De-merit goods

De-merit goods, on the other hand, are those products that are worse for the individual consumer than the individual realises. Cigarettes are taken to be a good example here. It is suggested that, when a person makes a decision to smoke a cigarette, he or she is not fully in possession of the information concerning the harmful effects of smoking. If he or she were in possession of such information, then there would be a greater reluctance to smoke.

It is interesting to note that the example of a de-merit good given here, namely smoking, is the same as the example of a product that can be seen as having negative externalities associated with it. However, the reason for identifying the product is different. Here, it is not due to the damage done to others that the issue arises, but rather due to the unperceived damage done to the person through consuming the product.

Merit goods, de-merit goods and value judgements

It may have been noticed in the above definitions that a significant question poses itself with regard to merit and de-merit goods. Who is to say what is 'good' or 'bad' for a person? If an individual consumer makes a presumably rational decision to consume a product, what right has the rest of society to say that he or she is making a 'wrong' decision. It seems clear that if this is what is going on, we have entered the area of **value judgements** and thus normative economics. If society is able to say to consumers that they do not fully realise what is good or bad for them, then we are accepting that 'society knows best' and has some right to make such a

judgement. In effect we are allowing **paternalism** to be a legitimate part of Economics. It is acceptable for us to say that society can judge what is, or is not, good for a person, regardless of what that person believes. In this area, then, we may have gone beyond our allegedly 'value-free' positive economics (see section 1).

The problems caused by merit and de-merit goods

Why, then, might merit and de-merit goods be identified as a failure of the market? The problem is that their existence will cause an inappropriate amount of the products concerned to be produced.

Merit goods will be under-produced in a free market situation. Insufficient scarce resources will be devoted to their production. The problem is that the lack of information about how good the product is for individuals will result in insufficient demand being registered for the product in the market. This is illustrated in figure 5.4. Here, the 'correct' level of demand, if consumers appreciated the true value of the product to themselves, would be D_1. This would lead to a market price of P_1, where D_1 is equal to the supply of product, S. This price would be associated with a level of production and consumption of Q_1, the ideal quantity of the good. However, because consumers undervalue the product, demand is only registered as D_2. This leads to a market price of P_2 (where D_2 is equal to supply S),

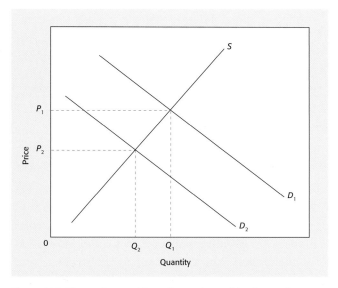

Figure 5.4 The under-provision of a merit good by the market

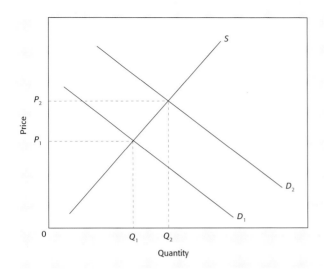

Figure 5.5 The over-provision of a de-merit good by the market

which is associated with production and consumption of Q_2. This is below the optimum level: the market has failed.

Figure 5.5 illustrates the problem of a de-merit good. Here, the 'correct' demand should be at D_1, which will lead to a price of P_1 and a production and consumption of Q_1. As consumers over-value the product, demand is registered at the higher level of D_2. This leads to a market price of P_2 and a production and consumption of Q_2. Too many scarce resources are devoted to the production of this de-merit good: the market has failed.

Further market problems caused by information failures

It is worth noting that there are other significant examples of market failure, as we have defined it, that can arise due to failures of information. Two specific examples are noted below:

The health care market Why does anyone go to the doctor? The most usual answer to that question is presumably because we are not sure what ailment we may have and/or are unsure what can be done about our ailment. To put it another way, we lack appropriate information. Thus we go the doctor to try to gain the necessary information. On the basis of the advice that we are given, we then make a decision about what to do. This system may be satisfactory as long as the doctor does not inadvertently or deliberately give us the wrong information. Our problem is that we have no way of knowing the veracity of the information that we are given. If it happens to be wrong, we may well make an undesirable choice about possible treatment. In economic terms, there will be a misallocation of resources. There is a market failure.

The insurance market It is suggested that markets for insurance may not work well because of information problems. The health care market could be an example again. This time it is the insurer who does not possess all the necessary information about the person who is to be insured. The insurer wishes to know how great a risk the person seeking insurance may be in order to set an appropriate premium. They must rely on the person accurately disclosing information. If insurers are not made aware of relevant information about a person's state of health, then too low a premium is offered. In order to pay for the forthcoming health treatment, the premium that has to be paid by those who are healthy may rise. In the worst case, healthy people will no longer seek insurance as they consider the price to be too great and the insurance company is left with just the 'bad risks'. This could mean that the whole operation becomes unprofitable and the market for health insurance in an entirely free market could collapse.

Public goods
Defining public goods

A different type of good from a merit or de-merit that may cause the market to fail is referred to as a **public good**. Here, it is not a matter of too much or little provision of the good in question, but rather whether the product will be provided at all.

There are two specific characteristics that a good must possess if it is to be classified as a public good:

1 It must be **non-excludable**. This means that once the good has been provided for one consumer, it is impossible to stop other consumers from benefiting from the good.

Self-assessment tasks

1 Discuss whether each of the following may be considered to be either a merit or a de-merit good:

- ◆ wearing a seatbelt;
- ◆ visiting a museum;
- ◆ children eating sweets;
- ◆ listening to very loud music;
- ◆ the provision of health care.

2 Read the short newspaper extract below and then answer the questions which follow.

Museum charges will always be too high a price to pay

If you wish to continue to look at this painting, please insert another compulsory donation token.' Can the day be far off when our museums and art galleries are cordoned off from the rest of public space and charges introduced across the board? That will be a shame. Either this country continues to glory in a series of great national art and cultural collections into which citizens can walk on a whim, in their lunch breaks or in between shopping. Or it slips and slides into a state of affairs in which 'culture' is seen as a segmented economic activity, marked

Natural History Museum, London

off, labelled as elite, and paid for.

Yes, of course this is an elitist issue. Many cultural institutions already charge. The Science and Natural History Museums in London are not cheap. You have to pay to go to a theatre or listen to a concert. Why are the fine arts and provincial museums different? Well, they are different because as communities we recognise that we all gained from them, even if we personally never understood why a photograph would not be a better likeness, or why we could not read about the Rosetta stone in a book.

Source: Leader article, *The Independent*, 1 December 1997 (adapted).

(a) In what way does this article suggest that fine art and certain museums might be viewed as merit goods?

(b) Discuss whether it can be justified to provide admissions to certain museums free while consumers have to pay for virtually all other services.

2 It must be **non-rival**. As more and more people consume the product, the benefit to those already consuming the product is not diminished.

Once one begins to think about these characteristics, there are a number of goods that can be seen as public goods. Take the example of a lighthouse. Once a

lighthouse is built to warn one ship at sea away from a dangerous area of rocks, then, by its very nature, this service will automatically be provided to all ships that sail within a certain distance of the lighthouse. It is non-excludable. Equally, the fact that other ships see the light given by the lighthouse and are warned away from the dangerous rocks does not reduce the benefit that any one particular ship receives from that warning. It is non-rival.

Quasi-public goods

While there may be some goods that can clearly be defined as 'public' in nature, there are others that have some of the nature of such goods without possessing fully the two required attributes mentioned above. Such goods are referred to as **quasi-public goods**. They are like public goods without truly being public goods.

In practice, it is not possible to classify all products as being either 'public' or 'private' (private goods being goods that are excludable and rival: others can be excluded from their consumption and once more people start to consume the good, those already consuming it have their satisfaction reduced). Many products lie somewhere in between these two extremes. A good that is closer to a public good than to a private good, but is not fully a public good, is a quasi-public good.

A good example might be a sandy sea-side beach. Such a beach is available to all those who wish to use it. It appears non-excludable. However, it is possible to conceive of ways of excluding consumers. Privately owned beaches have techniques of doing this. Equally, the beach is non-rival up to a point. If you are the first person on this pleasant beach on a warm sunny day, it does very little to diminish your enjoyment of that beach if a few more people arrive to enjoy the benefits. However, there may well come a point at which this is no longer the case. As the beach becomes crowded, space limited, and other people's conversations and music become ever more audible, enjoyment may be perceptibly reduce. Thus the beach has something of the characteristic of non-rivalry, but not the full characteristic. It is a quasi-public good.

The problem caused by public goods

The problem that may be caused in a free market by the existence of public goods is a serious one: the market may fail to produce them at all. There may be a consumer demand for such products (consumers are willing and able, in principle, to pay for the product's services), but the free market may not have a mechanism for guaranteeing their production.

Pendeen Lighthouse, Cornwall – a classic example of a public good.
Source: Turid Nyhamar and Roy Valentine photographers.

The essence of the problem is summed up in the phrase **free riding**. Consumers attempt to gain a 'free ride' on the back of other consumers' purchases of the public good. It is entirely reasonable that they may attempt to do this. One of the key characteristics of public goods as stated above is that they are non-excludable. This implies that once one consumer has purchased the product, all other consumers cannot be prevented from benefiting from that product. Take the example of the lighthouse. Once one particular fisherman has provided a lighthouse close to some dangerous rocks for his benefit, then all other fishermen in the area will benefit equally from the lighthouse. Their advantage, however, is that they do not have to pay for this lighthouse: they have received a free ride on the back of someone else's purchase. The logical thing to do, then, would seem to be for all fishermen to sit back and to wait for one fisherman to be foolish enough to provide a lighthouse so that those not purchasing can benefit without paying. Unfortunately, the implication of this is that the lighthouse is never provided: everyone waits for everyone else to provide it, and nothing happens.

It could be argued that a more likely scenario to the one described above is that all fishermen in an area might agree to club together in order to make the purchase and thus the lighthouse would be provided. However, there is still a problem here as it is in the interest of any one fisherman to conceal his desire for the lighthouse, refuse to pay but still to gain the final benefit once it is provided. Again, if all fishermen behave thus, the lighthouse is not provided.

The existence of public goods may thus mean that scarce resources are not used in a way that would be desirable. People may wish for the provision of such goods (they yield utility), but the demand may never be registered in the market.

A further difficulty arises due to the existence of quasi-public goods. This is a specific issue with regard to concern over the environment. In many ways, the problems that appear to exist with the environment are due to the fact that it is a quasi-public good rather than a pure public good. If one thinks of the earth's atmosphere, it is non-excludable in terms of its use (for example, in terms of the production of greenhouse gases that are released into the atmosphere). Up to a point, it might be argued that the atmosphere is also non-reducable; there are no costs to anyone due to its use by others. However, there clearly comes a point where this is no longer true and all may suffer due to the ever-increasing use of the atmosphere (for releasing greenhouse gases). A problem is created because the environment possesses some, but not all, of the attributes of a public good.

Failures in the labour market
The mobility of labour
If markets are to work with full efficiency, then labour markets must function well. There are a number of particular factors that will have to exist for this to be true. One important one is that labour must be fully mobile. Only if labour is fully mobile will labour markets function efficiently.

Self-assessment tasks

1 Explain whether each of the following may be described as a private, a public or a quasi-public good:
   ◆ a nuclear defence system;
   ◆ a chocolate bar;
   ◆ a public park;
   ◆ a firework display;
   ◆ a motorway;
   ◆ street lighting.

2 Read the following short case study and answer the questions which follow.

The prisoners and their dilemma

The two prisoners lay in their cells as night descended. Tomorrow morning they would both have to give their respective pleas: 'Guilty' or 'Not Guilty'. Both had been arrested for the same crime. The judge and jury knew that at least one of these prisoners was guilty, but were unsure whether both were. If both prisoners were to plead guilty, then both would be assumed to be guilty and would receive five years each in prison for their crime. If one were to plead guilty and the other not guilty, then the one pleading guilty would receive eight years in prison and the other would be assumed to be innocent and would be set free. However, if both prisoners pleaded not guilty, then both would be assumed to have committed the crime and would receive seven years each in prison. The dilemma of each prisoner is thus whether to plead 'Guilty' or 'Not guilty' in the morning.

(a) Assuming that the prisoners make their decisions separately and that all they are interested in is minimising the length of time they spend in prison, explain why they are both likely to plead 'Not Guilty'.

(b) Explain how the prisoners could do better if they managed to agree to make the same plea of 'Guilty'.

(c) Discuss how this illustration can help to explain the principle of attempted 'free-riding' that can lead to the free market failing to provide public goods, even though many people might in principle want them and be prepared to pay for them.

There are two types of labour mobility:

1 **Occupational mobility** of labour. This means that workers are able to move quickly and easily from one occupation to another. A redundant coal miner can rapidly move into a new form of employment.

2 **Geographical mobility** of labour. This means that workers are quickly and easily able to move from one part of a country to another in order to find employment. The loss of a job in one region means that the worker concerned rapidly moves to a different region in order to gain new employment.

The problem is that these two types of labour mobility often do not fully exist, or sometimes do not exist at all. This results in further examples of market failures.

Occupational immobility of labour

In practice, workers may not easily be able to move from one form of employment to another. It might make economic sense for a coal miner to leave the coal mining industry as it contracts and move into a job in computer programming as that industry expands, but it may not be that simple. The redundant coal miner may possess few, if any, of the relevant employment skills to become a computer programmer. Considerable re-training would be needed.

This can create a serious problem for a country. As some industries decline (such as coal mining) and others grow (such as computer programming) due to changes in consumer demand and technological developments, workers need to move occupations. The problem is that they may not be able to do so. The redundant workers do not have the necessary skills to move. They can thus get 'stuck' and cannot get a new job: they are unemployed. This type of unemployment in Economics is referred to as 'structural unemployment'. If this occurs, it represents a very clear failure of the market. The scarce resource of labour is simply not being used. It is not a case of a scarce resource not being used as well as might be possible. The resource is not being used at all in order to meet infinite wants. It is the clearest possible case of a market failure (see section 7).

Geographical immobility of labour

Workers may also not easily and quickly be able to move from employment in one region of a country to employment in a different region. There are various possible reasons for this. Family and social ties may be very strong for people in a particular region and this may prevent geographical movement. House prices can differ greatly between different regions. This can make it very difficult for a worker to move from a low-cost to a high-cost housing region.

The effect of geographical immobility of labour may be that when employment contracts in one part of the country and expands in another, as may happen with changes in tastes and costs in a market economy, workers are unable to move from the region where employment is contracting to the region where it is expanding. Thus unemployment may once more be created. This type of unemployment is referred to as 'regional unemployment' in Economics. As with structural unemployment, it represents a clear market failure.

The concentration of power in markets
Competition and markets

For markets to work well, it is generally accepted in Economics that there must be a high level of competition. To work as well as is possible, the competition needs to be as great as is possible. Economists refer to this very high level of competition as 'perfect competition' (see section 3).

There are good reasons for believing that a high level of competition will mean that markets work well. Some of the following are important:

1 If there is a high level of competition between firms, then it is likely that these firms will produce exactly what consumers most want. There will be consumer sovereignty. Any firm that does not produce what consumers want will find itself out of business very quickly as there will always be plenty of other firms managing to produce what is most wanted.

Self-assessment tasks

1 Explain whether each of the following is likely to experience occupational immobility or geographical immobility (or both):

- ◆ a redundant steelworker;
- ◆ a schoolteacher who loses his/her job;
- ◆ an unemployed doctor;
- ◆ a footballer forced to end his career early due to injury.

2 Read the following newspaper article and answer the questions which follow.

More artists than artisans in Britain by year 2006

Well-meaning parents should advise their children to head for the stage – or the screen, the music business, design, journalism or professional sport. The creative professions will be the fastest-growing source of new jobs between now and 2006, says a report published today.

The report's moral is that young people should be aiming high. Modern Britain offers better prospects in acting or football than in hairdressing or secretarial work.

The increase in demand for people with literary, artistic and sporting skills will even outpace the need for more computer programmers and lawyers, two other high-growth categories of employment. By the year 2006, there are likely to be nearly as many luvvies as construction workers in Britain and they will also outnumber engineers or security guards.

Within a decade there will be twice as many 'creative professionals' as car workers or doctors. The number is predicted to rise by 5 per cent a year, outstripping growth in all other job categories.

Traditional craft and manual jobs will shrink in number. Within three years there will be only just over three million in the traditional manufacturing craft-related occupations, and even demand for secretaries and hairdressers is falling.

Source: Diane Coyle, *The Independent*, 16 April 1998 (adapted).

(a) Why might a successfully functioning market economy expect to see the sort of changes in employment mentioned in the passage?

(b) Discuss the implications for geographical and occupational immobility of labour, given the projections for jobs stated in the passage.

2 A high level of competition will mean that firms will produce products at the lowest possible cost. The least possible scarce resources will be used to produce the products that consumers most want. Any firm that fails to do this will be in great difficulty as other competitors will have lower costs and be able to charge lower prices for the same product.

3 A competitive market will mean that firms have to charge a price to the consumer that is not much, if at all, above the cost of production. Any firm charging too high a price will soon lose out to others charging a price closer to the true production cost. Thus, when consumers buy a product, they pay a price that represents how much that product truly costs to produce in terms of scarce resources.

The problem is that in very many markets, nothing close to a high level of competition exists. This causes markets to fail.

Lack of competition and markets

There are two very valid reasons to expect many markets in developed economies to not be highly competitive:

1 The existence of economies of scale. Economies of scale imply that the larger a firm becomes, the lower the cost of producing any particular product is likely to become. In many industries, there are considerable economies of scale available and thus firms have to become very large to benefit fully from them. In some cases, this could mean that there is room for very few

or even just one firm (a monopoly) to exist in any particular industry (see section 3).

2 The profit motive. As also stated in section 3 the dominant motivation of firms is seen as being to make maximum profits. Perhaps the most effective way that profit can be made by a firm is either to get rid of all competitors or to enter into agreements with those competitors. In either case, competition ceases to exist.

The implication of these two important forces in markets is that there is often a concentration of power in many markets, which means that the benefits of competition mentioned earlier are reversed:

1 Firms may not produce what consumers most want. Given the control that firms have in a market, firms may not have to produce those things that are most desired by consumers. Consumers cannot easily turn to an alternative. Thus, infinite wants may not be as

fully satisfied as in a competitive situation. The market has failed.

2 Firms do not have to produce goods and services at the lowest possible cost. There is no constraint from competitors forcing firms to minimise their costs of production. Thus, firms may 'take it easy' and use more scarce resources for production than is necessary (economists refer to this as 'x'-inefficiency). The market fails.

3 Firms are able to charge a price that is higher than the cost of production. With no competitors, a firm does not have to worry that consumers will turn elsewhere if price rises above costs. In this case, the price paid by the consumer is higher than the cost of production in terms of scarce resources and the demand for the product will be lower than it should be. There will be an under-production of the product. The market has failed.

Self-assessment tasks

1 Explain why each of the following situations may well arise in a market that is dominated by one or just a few firms:
  ◆ a poor quality product;
  ◆ unnecessarily large expenditure on management perks;
  ◆ a selling price well in excess of the cost of producing a product.

2 Read the following article and answer the question that follows.

Important competition issues

One of our competitors, *The Times*, is next month planning to cut the cover price of its Saturday edition to 10p a copy. There is also some talk of it doing the same to its Thursday edition. *The Times* already charges just 10p for its Monday edition and sells at a significant discount to its main rivals throughout the rest of the week.

On a number of occasions Rupert Murdoch, proprietor of *The Times*, has expressed the view that there are too many national newspapers in Britain. An aim must therefore be to bring about the closure of a competitor. Why does this matter? It is because

diversity of choice is the best and only reliable way of safe-guarding consumer and other public interests. It is in diversity and the innovation that flows from it that we find the greatest chance of economic success for all.

This is particularly important in newspapers and broadcasting, because diversity of opinion, information and reporting is such a fundamental part of the democratic process. But the same arguments also apply to other industries from supermarkets to banks, and from software providers to metal bashers where big companies use their greater clout and spending power to undermine and crush smaller competitors.

Source: Business Leader Article, *The Independent*, 30 December 1997 (adapted).

Discuss the ways in which consumers of daily newspapers in Britain might suffer if Rupert Murdoch were to succeed in reducing the number of competitors to *The Times* (as this article suggests he is attempting to do).

Distributive and equity issues
An economic democracy

One argument in favour of markets is that they can be seen as allowing the economic equivalent of a political democracy.

In the place of voters in our economic democracy, we have consumers. In the place of votes, we have money (claims on scarce resources). Our consumers (or voters) 'elect' those products that are to be produced by use of their money (or votes). The products that have most money votes are the 'winners'. These are the products that will be produced most and be most successful as these are the products that are most desired by consumers and thus those products that consumers will be most willing to purchase. Firms that wish to make a profit will produce exactly what consumers elect.

There is one important flaw in this analogy. One of the key tenets of a political democracy is 'One person, one vote'. This cannot be said to be true of the so-called 'economic democracy' that has just been described. Here, there are very greatly varying numbers of votes between different voters. In terms of £s or $s, some voters are able to cast millions of votes in order to elect those products that should be produced. Other voters have very few, if any, votes to cast. This is often seen as a major problem (or failure) of markets: a lack of fairness or equity. Both income and wealth may be very unevenly distributed.

'Fairness' and Economics

The concept of fairness or equity is one with which Economics as a subject has considerable difficulty. So-called 'positive' economics claims not to deal at all with value judgements (as mentioned in the discussion about merit goods). However, ideas of equity go straight to the heart of serious and important value judgements in society. We must therefore state here that the notion of 'market failure' with regard to concerns over the equity of the market system is a different idea of market failure from the others discussed in this section. While the others are to do with observations about how scarce resources are not being used as effectively as possible to meet the infinite wants of consumers, this 'failure' is to do with value judgements that the scarce resources are not being fairly distributed in a free market economy.

Income and wealth

There are two separate aspects of resources that could be unevenly distributed in a market system: income and wealth. They are not the same. Income is a flow of earnings over a period of time (perhaps a year) usually in return for services rendered. Wealth is a stock of owned assets or properties. The most important wealth owned by most people in the UK is their house. There may be considerable inequalities in both income and wealth arising from the operation of markets.

In a free market, income, in the form of wages for labour, will be determined by the forces of supply and demand. If a person is blessed with a particular talent that is in very high demand (perhaps the ability to score goals for a top soccer club), then the income commanded by that person will be very high. Others may not be so fortunate and may thus receive far lower incomes. This may be judged as 'unfair' (or inequitable).

The principle means of gaining significant wealth is through inheritance. This is sometimes seen as even more inequitable than significant inequalities in income. A person born into one family has a far greater ownership of scarce resources than one born into another family. The strength afforded by such wealth could allow inequalities to persist or even widen as better education and other opportunities may be available through the greater level of wealth. This might all be judged as an unacceptable aspect of the operation of markets.

Self-help in redressing the problem of equity

Self-assessment tasks

1 (a) Explain the difference between income and wealth in Economics.

(b) Explain why equity concerns over the distribution of income and wealth are different from other examples of market failures.

2 The following figures state the average annual rates of change in real earnings at the 90th (top), 50th and 10th (bottom) percentiles, per cent for the time period, 1979–90.

FRANCE		GERMANY	
90th percentile	1.1	90th percentile	3.7
50th percentile	0.6	50th percentile	3.5
10th percentile	0.6	10th percentile	4.2
ITALY		UNITED KINGDOM	
90th percentile	2.2	90th percentile	3.4
50th percentile	0.5	50th percentile	2.2
10th percentile	2.0	10th percentile	1.2
UNITED STATES			
90th percentile	0.4		
50th percentile	–0.6		
10th percentile	–1.4		

(a) Discuss the extent to which these figures support the view that there has been an increase in the inequality of income in the western world during the time period 1979–90.

(b) What comments might an economist make about any such perceived rise in the inequality of earned income?

3 Local hospital closure threatened

Read the case study opposite and then answer the questions below. (This is indicative of what you can expect in OCR's examination paper for this unit.)

(a) ◆ Define the term 'merit good' in economics.
   ◆ Explain why the provision of preventative health care can be considered to be a 'merit good'.

(b) ◆ Explain what economists mean by the term 'economic efficiency'.
   ◆ Explain what type of efficiency the government is referring to in the last paragraph.

(c) ◆ Why might the income distribution of a society be considered as a possible market failure?
   ◆ How might an economist comment on the suggestion made by the local residents that they 'have a right to easy access to a hospital'?

(d) ◆ Why would monopoly power be expected to lead to market failure?
   ◆ Explain, referring to the passage, why there might be a tendency for the provision of health care to be dominated by large hospitals.
   ◆ Explain what other possible market failures might exist in the market for health care.

(e) ◆ Explain the term 'externality' in Economics.
   ◆ Discuss the possible externalities that could arise from the closure of the hospital in Nilton.

Local hospital closure threatened

A recent government re-organisation of hospital provision has raised the possibility of the closure of the hospital in the town of Nilton. As with many such small local hospitals, the government believes that their services can be more cheaply provided by the nearest large town's hospital. It is not surprising that local residents are very unhappy about the suggestion of the closure.

A government enquiry has been ordered to consider whether the closure should go ahead. An organisation of local residents has been invited to present the case for allowing the local hospital to remain open while government officials will be presenting evidence as to why they believe that the hospital should be closed.

The main points raised against the closure by the local residents are as follows:

(a) The hospital is a major local employer. Unemployment will result from its closure.

(b) Local people, especially those without a car, have a right to easy access to a hospital.

(c) The town may not prove so popular with future house buyers if there is no hospital. This will affect house prices and local trade.

(d) Local people will not make the effort to receive preventative medical care if they have to travel a considerable distance to do so.

The principal point made by the government is that keeping open the local hospital does not represent 'efficiency'. The hospital is seen as not sufficiently large to benefit from the economies of scale that are available in the provision of health care and is thus not a good use of taxpayers' money. The costs of treating all patients at the larger hospital in the large town will be considerably less than keeping the local hospital open.

Summary

In this section we have recognised that:

- Markets do not always operate as suggested by economic theory. There are various reasons why markets fail.

- Where negative and positive externalities exist in a market, the outcome is an inappropriate level of production.

- Merit and de-merit goods will not be provided in the right quantities by the market.

- Public goods will not necessarily be provided by the market.

- The occupational and geographical immobility of labour creates particular unemployment problems.

- Where there is a concentration of power in particular markets, there is an undesirable effect upon consumers.

- Equity concerns over the distribution of income and wealth may arise from the operation of markets.

Key words

Definitions of Key words can be found in the Glossary on page 240.

de-merit goods
equity
external benefit
external cost
externality
fairness
free rider
geographical mobility
information failure
market failure
merit goods
negative externality
non-excludable

non-rival
occupational mobility
paternalism
positive externality
private benefits
public good
quasi-public goods
social benefits
social costs
value judgement
wealth
x-inefficiency

6 Making choices and the impact of government intervention on market outcomes and efficiency

On completion of this section you should be able to:

➤ understand what is meant by a cost–benefit approach

➤ understand and interpret information collected in a cost–benefit study

➤ understand the limitations of a cost–benefit approach

➤ describe the various methods by which governments intervene in markets

➤ analyse how the imposition of taxes and subsidies affects equilibrium in markets

➤ analyse the effects of price control and minimum wage control in product and factor markets respectively

➤ explain how state provision, regulation and standards can be applied in markets

➤ discuss the possible role of information provision in a range of possible market failures

➤ examine the role and analyse the impact of competition policy in tackling problems of market power

➤ discuss how governments may create inefficiencies when they intervene in markets due to such factors as political objectives distorting incentives and lack of information

The cost–benefit approach

The previous section of this unit identified various causes and consequences of market failure, in particular situations:

- where there is a divergence between private and social benefits and costs;
- where market dominance can lead to an inefficient allocation of resources;
- where public goods may not be provided by the market;
- where merit goods may be under-provided by the market;
- where there is factor immobility.

It is in such circumstances that a cost–benefit approach has been used by economists as a means of decision making, not least to ensure that the right choice of action is being made. Here we will be concerned with situations where major projects produce important and often controversial side effects, in particular where there are substantial costs and benefits which fall upon people and communities who have no direct connection with the particular project, either as consumers or suppliers.

A particularly relevant and widespread case of this occurring is where a new retail development is planned

(see Self-assessment task). The so-called **spillover effects** upon third parties (those not involved in the particular project) can be far-reaching and substantial. **Cost–benefit analysis** genuinely attempts to quantify the opportunity cost to society of the various possible outcomes or sources of action. It is therefore a procedure for making long-run decisions where present actions have implications far into the future.

The cost–benefit approach differs from private sector methods of appraisal in two main respects. These are:

- It seeks to include all of the costs and benefits, not just private ones.

A new housing development on former agricultural land

95

◆ It often has to impute **shadow prices** on costs and benefits where no market price is available. Very relevant examples here would be how to value the degradation of scenic beauty or the loss of agricultural land in the case (say) of building new houses on an attractive area of green belt. Other examples might be how to value the benefit of cleaner air or being able to live in a less noisy environment.

The framework of cost–benefit analysis

Whatever the problem under investigation, there are four main stages in the development of a cost–benefit analysis. These are shown in figure 6.1.

The first stage is to identify all of the relevant costs and benefits arising out of any particular project. Systematically, this involves establishing what are the private costs, the private benefits, the external costs and the external benefits (see unit 1, section 3 and unit 2, section 5 for details and definitions). On the surface this may seem a relatively simple task. In reality, and with a

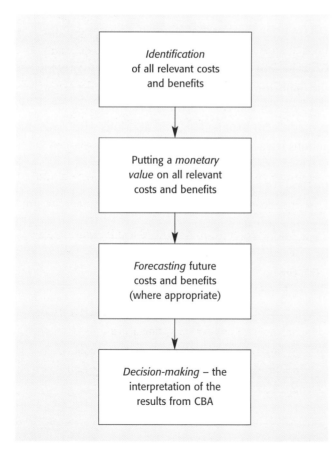

Figure 6.1 Stages in a cost–benefit analysis

little more thought, it is not so. There are particular problems when it comes to establishing external costs and benefits. These are often controversial, not easy to define in a discrete way and have the added difficulty that it is not always possible to draw the line in terms of a physical or geographical cut-off. The spillover effects of a new retail development, for example, are wide-reaching and often affect people and communities way beyond the immediate vicinity of the proposed development (see self-assessment task, question 1).

The second stage involves putting a monetary value on the various costs and benefits. This is relatively straightforward where market prices are available. For example, in the case of a new retail development, a monetary value can be put on the jobs created or the increased profits arising from the development. For other variables, though, a monetary value must be inputed for costs and benefits where no market prices are available. This particular measurement difficulty has occupied economists for thousands of hours over the years. It has also been a very controversial matter in situations where cost–benefit analysis has come under close public scrutiny. A particularly good example of this is the issue of valuation of time, especially travel time and savings in travel time. Another relevant example is how to put a monetary value on the cost of accidents, particularly where serious injuries or a loss of life is involved. (OCR's Transport Economics module looks at these in more detail in the context of the appraisal of new road schemes.)

The third stage of the cost–benefit analysis applies in situations where projects have longer-term implications which stretch well into the future. Here, economists have to employ statistical forecasting techniques, sometimes of a very crude nature, to estimate costs and benefits over many years. This particularly applies to proposed projects where massive capital expenditure is involved (see self-assessment task, question 3 for example). In other cases, this stage may actually not be needed, particularly if two alternatives are being considered (see self-assessment task, question 2).

The final stage is where the results of the earlier stages are drawn together so that the outcome can be presented in a clear manner in order to aid decision making. The important principle to recognise is that if the value of benefits exceeds the value of the costs, then the particular project is worthwhile since it provides an overall net benefit to the community (see self-assessment task, question 2 for a simple example of such a situation).

The four stages in a cost–benefit analysis provide a coherent framework by which decisions can be made in situations of market failure. Students should therefore see any cost–benefit study or application in these terms. Of the respective stages, though the identification stage is in many respects not only the most interesting, it is also the one most relevant for OCR's examination of this unit, as the self-assessment tasks indicate. Students should also consider how the information which is required for a CBA might be collected (see the Introduction for information on how to plan an investigation).

Finally, to conclude, it is relevant to recognise that in practice cost–benefit analysis is fraught with many difficulties. Some have already been stated such as:

♦ which costs and benefits should be included;
♦ how to put monetary values on them.

Additionally, there are others, particularly when it comes to the acceptance of the outcome by the community as a whole. For example:

♦ CBA does not always satisfactorily reflect the distributional consequences of certain decisions, particularly where public sector investment is involved. In the case of a new retail development, external costs are likely to be highly localised whilst external benefits, in terms of employment creation for instance, are likely to be more widely spread.
♦ Many public sector projects (for example that analysed in self-assessment task, question 3) are very controversial and subject to much local aggravation from pressure groups. It may be the case that the outcome of the CBA is rejected for local political reasons, with the consequence that the most expedient decision may not be the one recommended by economists. Where this happens, it is easy to dismiss the technique of CBA as irrelevant. This is not a fair conclusion, not least as CBA has at least brought out the issues involved so that a decision can be taken on the basis of all of the information available. CBA is an aid and not a replacement for decision making.

Self-assessment tasks

1 Read the short case study below on Shopping in Bamfield, which is an adaptation of an A-Level question set by UCLES in March 1997, and then answer the questions which follow.

Shopping in Bamfield

Bamfield, a market town in the Cotswolds, is a thriving shopping centre, which attracts customers from many surrounding villages. It has various food and non-food shops, including a small privately owned supermarket trading as 'Cheap Away'. Virtually all of the shoppers travelling into Bamfield come by car as there are very few local bus services. Cheap Away does not have a car park of its own and consequently it is often difficult for shoppers to park on Bamfield's narrow streets.

Recently, Bamfield Town Council has received a planning application from a national supermarket chain, Fineways, to construct a new large store on agricultural land on the outskirts of the town. This proposed store would have a large car park and provide an extensive range of products. Many of the shoppers who currently use local shops and Cheap Away welcome the proposal. Others are against it, claiming that it will lead to the closure of existing shops, an argument which is endorsed by the local shopkeepers and the owner of Cheap Away.

Suppose you have been asked by Bamfield Town Council to produce a cost–benefit analysis of the Fineways supermarket proposal.

(a) What costs and benefits would you include in your analysis?
(b) How would you set about collecting this information?
(c) On what basis would you make a recommendation to the Town Council? Why might this recommendation not be entirely acceptable to all parties who have an interest in the proposed development?

2 This case study is an adaptation of an A-Level question set by UCLES in June 1997. Read it and then answer the questions that follow.

Cavalier Pet Products

Cavalier Pet Products is a large privately owned manufacturer of canned pet foods based in Bolton, Lancashire. The company, which employs 300 people, is long-established and has been on its present site since it was founded by its owners, the Fazackerley family, in 1906. It is a market leader, producing own-branded products, which are widely advertised and well known.

Through the nature of its manufacturing processes, the company is a polluter of the local environment. The nauseating smells from the factory, particularly in hot weather, are the main source of complaint; the firm also creates noise disturbance and quite recently was successfully prosecuted for discharging effluent into a local stream running alongside the factory. There is increasing local pressure from residents for something to be done about the whole question of the firm and its operations.

The obvious answer is for the firm to move to another location. The Managing Director of Cavalier Pet Products, Basil Fazackerley, favours such a move but is quite adamant that, 'We shall not pay the full cost. If the local council want us to move, then they will have to help us to do so.'

The decision to relocate the factory has long-term implications both for its owners and for the community. In particular, new jobs will be created as the firm increases output and the local environment within the vicinity of the present site will experience environmental gain.

The local authority have agreed to contribute to the relocation, as they can see a benefit to the community. Cavalier Pet Products remain concerned that they should pay a realistic contribution to the cost of relocation.

In order to sort out these difficulties, a local university was asked to carry out a cost–benefit analysis of the proposed relocation. A summary of their findings is given in the table below

Costs		Benefits	
Private costs of the relocation	1,300	Private benefits	1,500
Contribution from local authority	300	External benefits	1,200
External costs	400		
Total costs	**2,000**	**Total benefits**	**2,700**

Estimated discounted[1] costs and benefits of the relocation of Cavalier Pet Products (£000)

Note: [1] Discounting is a procedure whereby a present value is given to costs and benefits that will occur some time in the future.

(a) What is the specific purpose of the cost–benefit analysis in this case?

(b) With reference to the proposed relocation, give an example of:
   ◆ a private benefit,
   ◆ an external benefit,
   arising from the proposed relocation. Explain your choice.

(c) Use the information in the table to state what conclusions you could draw from the cost–benefit analysis.

(d) You are asked to plan an investigation to estimate the various external costs and benefits of the proposed relocation. Explain how you might do this and comment upon some of the problems you might face.

3 Read the two local newspaper articles on the following page on the problems of waste disposal in Huddersfield and then answer the questions that follow:

(a) Why has the decision been made to close the Vine Street incinerator?

(b) Use the evidence in the articles to identify:
   ◆ the private costs,
   ◆ the external costs,
   ◆ the private benefits,
   ◆ the external benefits,
   of the incinerator's operations. What additional information do you need in order to complete this task?

(c) You are required to produce a cost–benefit analysis on two alternative ways of disposing of Huddersfield's waste, namely:
   ◆ continuing to transport waste to landfill sites in the vicinity of Huddersfield;
   ◆ building a new 'state of the art' incinerator on the Vine Street site.
   What information would you require in order to carry out this study and on what basis would you reach a decision?

Vine Street waste site to close

Huddersfield's 330ft-high incinerator chimney is doomed to be a thing of the past, it was revealed today.

Waste officials confirmed the Vine Street rubbish plant would close in the next year.

And it could be replaced by extending a tip at Blackley on the Kirklees-Calderdale border.

Proposals went on show from today for public comment.

The move to shut the incinerator follows the failure to get backing for an ambitious plan to generate electricity from waste.

Cash was needed to update ageing furnace equipment because it did not reach Euro pollution standards.

Environmental group Greenpeace claimed last year that dioxin levels were 187 times higher than the safety limit.

Now West Yorkshire Waste Management says the site will be scrapped within a year.

An exact date has yet to be given for the shutdown.

Campaigners have long called for the incinerator to be closed because it is too close to the town centre – and only 500 yards from homes.

It opened in 1975 at a cost of £2m.

Two waste tips – at Cromwell Bottom, Elland, and Lower Spen Valley, Ravensthorpe – will also close around the same time.

Initial plans have been drawn up to replace them with a bigger tip at Hollins Hey, Blackley.

This would allow an extra 300,000 cubic metres of rubbish to be dumped over three years.

The exhibition of the proposals opened at Elland library today and runs until August 6.

But a West Yorkshire Waste Management spokesman said: "No decision has yet been taken on whether or not to submit a planning application."

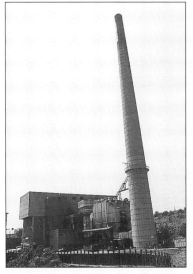

The 330ft-high incinerator chimney which dominated the Vine Street plant has now closed. It opened in 1975 at a cost of £2m and stood just 500 yards from nearby homes. Anti-pollution campaigners succeeded in having it closed down in July 1996.
Picture by Julian Hughes

Source: Andrew Baldwin; this article and photograph appear with the kind permission of the *Huddersfield Examiner*, 19 July 1996.

Lorry plan as incinerator shuts down

A vast fleet of lorries is to be brought in to transport Huddersfield's waste when the Vine Street incinerator shuts this week.

The plant closes on Saturday and thousands of tons of rubbish will have to be transported by road to landfill sites across the county.

But speculation is growing that new talks could lead to a new incinerator being built on the site.

After 18 months of failed negotiations and scrapped plans, the incinerator at Vine Street is to shut.

In a move which has been branded "environmental nonsense", rubbish will be transported by road to two different landfill sites.

Euro laws are forcing the closure of the incinerator, which does not reach pollution standards.

And negotiations to get financial backing from a private company for an ambitious plan to generate electricity from waste at the site failed.

Environmental group Greenpeace claimed last year that levels of allegedly cancer-causing dioxins were 187 times higher than the recognised safety limit.

Campaigners have been calling for the incinerator – which deals with 55,000 tons of waste a week – to shut for many years. They claim it is too close to both the town centre and houses.

Strategy to take the area into 21st century

Kirklees Council's environmental waste services manager Steve Noble said from next week, waste will still be taken to the site but there it will be compacted before being transported by road to landfill sites at Honley and just over the Kirklees/Calderdale border.

Mr Noble is drawing up a waste strategy to take Kirklees into the 21st century.

"We want our waste management to have the minimum environmental impact," he said. "And that could involve a new incinerator."

West Yorkshire Waste Management's engineering manager Dr David Baines explained two different groups were linked to the site.

While the collection of refuse is dealt with by Kirklees Council, whose binmen bring the waste to Vine Street, the incinerator itself and what happens next to the rubbish is the responsibility of West Yorkshire Waste Management.

"It all stems from the abolition of West Yorkshire County Council," he explained. "But ultimately I think Kirklees will have this land handed back.

"And the council will redevelop the site and build a new incinerator using private cash.

"Using landfill is environmental nonsense – especially if it is being sent to someone else's patch – and Kirklees knows that."

The incinerator plant was built by the former Huddersfield borough council and was brought into use in 1975. Since then it has handled the bulk of the town's household refuse.

Source: Claire Horton, *Huddersfield Examiner*, 26 November 1996.

Government intervention

You have only to glance at a newspaper, listen to the news or a political debate for a few minutes to realise that one of the more controversial areas of Economics is concerned with the extent and reasons for government intervention in markets. All governments in the world intervene to a greater or lesser extent and the reasons for intervention vary enormously between them. However, the justification for intervention is usually given under two broad headings:

> *market failure* and the desire to achieve a *fair or equitable distribution of resources* in economy.

These have been analysed in section 5. The first intervention occurs when markets do not allocate resources efficiently and the second is concerned with ensuring that all members of society have fair access to goods and services. The role of the government is to intervene in markets that are not seen to be allocating resources in the most efficient or the most equitable manner. In attempting to achieve this aim it must also be recognised that there is also the possibility that governments will fail and create rather than remove distortions.

Methods of government intervention

Government policy and methods of intervention can be summarised under four broad headings: regulation, financial intervention, production and transfer payments. The method chosen will depend to a large extent on whether the reason for intervention is concerned with market failure or with the desire to achieve equity.

Regulation

The government uses a large number of methods of **regulation** as a means of controlling a market. Legal and other methods are used to control the quality and quantity of goods and services that are produced and consumed. For example, the government may regulate the sale of certain drugs by making them only available on prescription from a qualified doctor. Hygiene laws set standards for the production of foods. There may be **controls** on shop opening hours or the setting of a minimum age at which a person can buy certain products, such as alcohol, cigarettes and lottery tickets. Other forms of regulation may include the requirement

for an individual to purchase an insurance policy before being legally permitted to drive a car, the age at which people are required to attend school and the payment of social insurance contributions.

Regulation may not only apply to the quantity and quality of goods and services sold but may also refer to prices. Examples of price controls include minimum wage legislation and rent controls.

Finally, the government has powers to control abuse of monopoly power through regulatory organisations such as the Competition Commission (CC) or bodies set up to investigate and regulate production and pricing policies by public utilities such as Oftel (telecommunications), Ofwat (water), Offer (electricity) and Ofgas (gas).

Financial intervention

Financial tools, such as taxes or subsidies, are also frequently used by governments to influence production, prices of commodities, incomes or the distribution of wealth in an economy. Price subsidies may vary. They might be in the form of a partial subsidy, as in the case of public transport, or total, as in the case of free eye tests for children in full-time education.

Tax instruments may also vary. For example consider two different forms of taxation that are currently applied to the use of vehicles in the UK. Vehicle Excise Duty is paid once every six months or year, unless the vehicle is more than 25 years old. The same amount is paid whether the car is used daily or only once a month. In addition vehicle users pay a tax on petrol. In this case the amount of tax paid rises with the number of miles driven. The first type of tax may deter ownership of a vehicle whilst the second deters use of the vehicle.

Governments also provide the finance that is needed to produce a good or service. It is very important to note at this early stage that, just because the government provides the finance for a product, it does not necessarily mean it has to produce the product too. For example, the government could finance education but all schools, colleges and universities could be privately owned and run. Health care may be provided free (**financial intervention**) but the drugs used in prevention and cure of illness could be privately produced.

State production

In addition to providing the finance it is also possible for a government to take over the production of a good or service, either in whole or in part. State-owned industries are often referred to as **nationalised industries**. Industries such as the electricity, coal mining and railway industries are entirely owned and managed by the state in many countries. This is no longer the case in the UK following the major shift towards privatisation that took place in the 1980s and 1990s. It is also very common to find some goods and services being produced by both the state and the private sectors. Education and health care are particularly good examples of these types of service industries. NHS hospitals function alongside private hospitals and independent schools operate alongside state schools.

Income and other transfers

Income transfers are used by governments as a means of redistributing income or transferring income from one group in society to another group, for example from people in work to those who are retired or from relatively rich people to those who are in poverty. The justification for these transfers is to achieve fairness or equity in an economy. These transfers of income may be in the form of a cash benefit paid by the government to someone with a low income. Income transfers may also be used to cover the unexpected loss of income when a person is not working due to illness or unemployment. These cash transfers include social security benefits, such as income support, a job seeker's allowance or a state pension. The recipients of these benefits are free to spend this money as they see fit.

Other cash benefits are tied to specific areas of spending. An example of this would be housing benefits, which are given to low-income families to help with their housing costs. In this case the cash must be spent on housing.

It would be wrong to think that all transfers are in the form of a cash payment. **In-kind transfers** occur when a particular person is given a service or good free whilst other groups have to pay. An example of this type of transfer would be free dental check-ups, which are available to recipients of income support and to all children. In the first case free dental care is directed to those on low incomes whilst in the second it is directed to a specific age group.

The impact of government intervention on markets

The impact of these different methods of government intervention will vary according to both the reasons for market failure and the conditions facing the markets.

Public goods

Public goods, such as defence, need to be financed by the government but they do not necessarily need to be produced by the government. The government will decide upon the optimal amount of defence expenditure and raise revenue through taxation to fund it. The problem facing the government is deciding on the best or fairest method of raising the tax revenue required. One approach is to tax individuals according their ability to pay tax. Thus those who have the highest incomes (or wealth) will pay most in taxation. Many governments use the 'ability to pay' principle as a basis for the tax system and it has a wide acceptance amongst the electorate as being the fairest means of raising tax revenue. In most countries the government takes a larger percentage of income in tax from the rich than the poor. This is called a **progressive tax** system.

An alternative approach is to tax individuals according to the benefits they receive from the public good. The main problem is valuing the benefits that an individual receives from a public good, defence being a particularly good example. Mrs Thatcher's government in the 1980s argued that all households received the same amount of benefit from local authority spending in the form of sewerage disposal, refuse collection, local road building, leisure centre and library facilities, parks and other such goods and services. All households were therefore required to pay the same amount of money to the local authority. This was called the Community Charge and it was in fact a 'poll' tax. Its introduction caused a lot of resentment and it was abandoned in favour of the Council Tax in 1991.

Externalities

Setting standards and regulation Governments frequently use regulation to overcome market failures caused by externalities. Let us consider the case of an electricity company that pollutes the surrounding countryside. The government might intervene by setting standards which restrict the amount of pollution that can be legally dumped. The government would then need to regulate and inspect the company to make sure that these restrictions are enforced. It can do this in several ways, for example by imposing large fines on any company that contravenes the law.

Exhaust fumes from cars pollute the atmosphere and to reduce this problem the government can set legal limits on the amount of carbon particles that is emitted from a car's exhaust pipe. This can be tested in the annual MOT test, although it also possible to conduct random on-the-spot tests. Regulations of this type are particularly effective when there are a large number of potential sources of the external cost. There are 17 million vehicles using Britain's roads and it is not possible to individually test every vehicle every day.

Financial intervention – taxes Financial intervention will take the form of taxes or subsidies and they can also be used in the case of externalities. A tax would normally be imposed on the individual or firm that causes the externality. If this happens then economists say that external costs are internalised.

In figure 6.2, in the case where there is no government intervention, the equilibrium occurs at point E, where supply, S_1, which is given by MPC or marginal private cost, equals demand, D, which is given by MPB or marginal private benefit. However, if external costs are included in this diagram, then the supply curve becomes

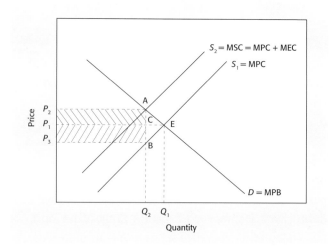

Figure 6.2 External cost and use of taxation

S_2 or MSC, marginal social cost. The vertical distance between these two supply curves is marginal external cost, MEC. The socially optimal level of output is therefore equal to Q_2, where S_2 cuts the demand curve. At this socially optimal level of output, the marginal external cost is equal to the vertical distance AB.

The government intervenes in this market and imposes a tax which is equal to the marginal external cost. This tax is added to the cost of producing the product and thus the supply curve S_2 is also equal to the MPC plus tax. Looking at the diagram, you can see that the price at which the product is sold has increased from P_1 to P_2. This is less than the tax applied by the government. At first sight this may appear a little strange, but the producer has accepted a cut in the price received from P_1 to P_3. The producer has borne the burden of part of the tax. The total tax paid is equal to the area P_2ABP_3, of which the consumer's share of the burden is P_2ACP_1 and the producer's share is P_1CBP_3.

Financial intervention – subsidies Financial intervention to overcome market failure caused by external benefits or positive externalities will take the form of a subsidy. This is shown in figure 6.3. The equilibrium without government intervention is at point F where MPC = MPB or $D = S_1$. In this case marginal external benefit is added to the MPB curve to give the MSB or marginal social benefit curve. The MSB represents society's demand curve for the product.

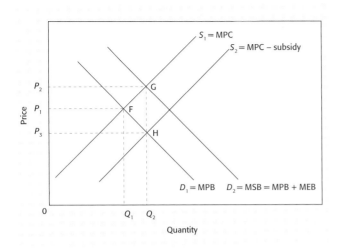

Figure 6.3 External benefits and use of a subsidy

If the government subsidises production of this product then the supply curve moves to the right from S_1, which equals MPC, to S_2, which equals MPC minus the subsidy. The marginal cost of supplying the good is reduced by the amount of subsidy and the vertical distance GH is equal to the value of the subsidy. Thus the equilibrium after the subsidy is given by point H, which is where D_1 crosses S_2 and the optimal amount of goods Q_2 is sold by the market.

As you might expect, there is considerable debate over which is the best method of government intervention when externalities are present in a market. If we accept the argument that education provides external benefits, then one solution would be to provide a subsidy to education. This can be seen in the UK where the government subsidises university education. Students still have to pay towards their education in the form of a fee, which can be represented by P_3 in figure 6.3. The government provides the difference between P_2 and P_3 in subsidy.

Information failures

Methods of intervention for market failure caused by information failures are varied. Consumers do not have perfect information about every good and service that is available on the market. The obvious question is why doesn't the government insist that correct and relevant information is made available to consumers and then they can correctly formulate their demand curve for the product. The short answer is that for many goods and services it does.

Providing information and government intervention

It is a legal requirement for shops and other suppliers to provide the consumer with information about the price of the product being offered for sale. Information about the product is also provided to the consumer. For example, food products are clearly labelled with details of weight, ingredients and the nutritional content of the product. Consumers are also protected against the possibility of buying products that have been sold using misleading information and against buying a faulty product. For example, it is not possible to tell by looking at the outside of a washing machine whether it has been manufactured to acceptable standards. The government therefore requires that products have a guarantee period, which protects the consumer against faulty manufacture. If a product needs repair during the guarantee period then consumers can claim their money back or have the good replaced.

Consumers may also be able to claim compensation if they are given misleading information, which led them to purchase the good or service. For example, a rail company may provide a timetable that gives the times a train is expected to deliver you at your destination. If you purchase a rail ticket for a train that is subsequently late, you are entitled to claim compensation if the delay is more than one hour.

In many cases, however, the information is either not available or it is so complicated that it cannot be interpreted by the consumer. In this case you could pay someone to provide and interpret this information for you. The consumer might buy a publication such as a car price guide or a computer magazine to obtain information about a product. These magazines usually give 'star' ratings for products, stating which is the best value for money in the eyes of the magazine. Alternatively you might pay an independent garage or the Automobile Association to send an expert to examine a second-hand car and provide you with a report before you purchase it.

When it comes to health care or the purchase of insurance, it is likely that the information is so complex that you need to obtain advice and information from an expert such as a doctor or an insurance broker. The government has to intervene in this market to make sure that the advice you receive is both good and appropriate to your needs. The consequences of poor or incorrect advice from a doctor could result in permanent injury or even death. Thus the medical profession is very strictly controlled and doctors are required to undertake regulated training before they can prescribe medicine and offer treatment to patients.

Over-consumption of a product and regulation It can be argued that a drug, such as heroine or tobacco, is over-consumed because individuals do not realise the true extent of the harm that the product causes. The government has several policy options that it can employ to try and limit the amount of the drug that is consumed.

For example, it can impose legal regulations on the market, such as an outright ban (as in the case of heroine), or limit the market, as in the case of alcoholic drinks and cigarettes, by restricting purchase to certain age groups. Such types of policy can cause anger amongst some consumers, who argue that these are infringements of civil liberties. The government could respond to this criticism by engaging in an advertising campaign to inform the consumer of the dangers of taking drugs and then allow individuals to decide how much they should consume. Warnings of the possible effects of smoking are printed on the side of cigarette packets. The success of this policy will be determined by the extent to which cigarette smokers take notice of these warnings. Thus the government attempts to control the behaviour of consumers by providing information.

Over-consumption and financial intervention Another option is to impose a tax on the good, which shifts the supply curve to the left. The government imposes a high tax (called a customs and excise duty) on both cigarettes and alcoholic drinks in order to reduce the consumption of these products. Figure 6.4 illustrates the case where a consumer over-values the product. The demand is incorrectly placed at D_1. The correct demand curve (with perfect information) would have been at D_2. Therefore an amount, Q_1, is consumed that is above the correct equilibrium quantity, Q_2. The tax shifts the supply curve of the product from S_1 to S_2 and so as the prices rise the consumer moves along the incorrect demand curve to point A. The consumer now consumes Q_2, which is the optimal amount of the product.

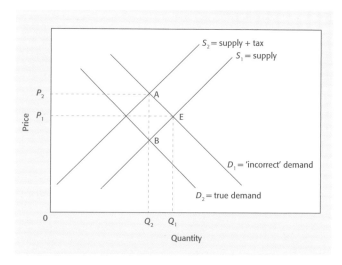

Figure 6.4 Over-consumption and the use of a tax

Under-consumption and regulation If a consumer underestimates the demand for a good then the policies are reversed. The government can make purchases of a good compulsory. Many of the compulsory purchase requirements are in insurance markets. All workers might be required by law to contribute to a state pension scheme or to a National Health Service via their national insurance contributions because the government estimates that they would under-consume these goods if purchase was not compulsory.

It is a legal requirement in the UK for all children to receive education between the ages of five and 16. In addition, state schools are required to follow a 'national curriculum' to ensure that all children receive a minimum standard of education. Thus the government considers that, without the legal requirement, some children would not attend school and thus education would be under-consumed.

Under-consumption and financial intervention
Financial intervention, in this case, will take the form of a subsidy or alternatively a financial incentive in the form of a tax reduction to encourage consumers to buy the product. Let us assume that the government believes that without government intervention individuals will not purchase sufficient pensions. The government could offer a subsidy to the pension providers. This subsidy may be offered to the customer in the form of a tax reduction.

A government may state that a consumer does not have to pay any income tax on the interest payments paid into a pension fund. (Income tax is normally payable on interest payments made on savings held in a financial institution such as a bank or building society.) This means that interest payments added to pension funds would be larger than those added to other forms of saving. For example if the interest paid on savings was 5 per cent per annum and the income tax rate was 25 per cent, the pension fund saver would receive the full 5 per cent whereas those saving money in a building society account receive 3.75 per cent (5 per cent interest payment less tax at 25 per cent).

Alternatively the government could say that any payments into a pension fund that are made from a worker's income will not count towards that person's taxable income. An example illustrates how this works. An individual earns £20,000 and is in the basic income tax band. For simplicity assume that the income tax rate for this consumer equals 25 per cent. Now this individual decides to pay £1,000 into a pension fund. The Pension Company refunds the income tax that would have been paid on this sum and thus the individual has a refund of tax which equals £250. In this simplified example, the net cost (or price) of the pension therefore becomes £750. The individual pays the Pension Company £750 and the Pension Company claims back £250 from the tax authorities. The government has given a subsidy to the Pension Company which is equal to the tax rebate. The effect of this is illustrated in figure 6.5.

Without government intervention the equilibrium quantity of goods bought and sold will be Q_1; this is given by point M where S_1 crosses D_1 (the 'incorrect'

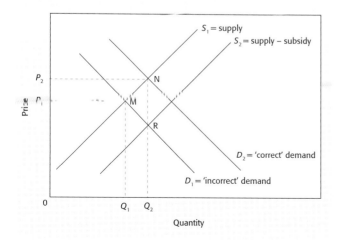

Figure 6.5 Under-consumption and subsidy

demand). However if information had been both made available and understood, the consumer would have purchased amount Q_2, given by the point where the 'correct' demand curve, D_2, cuts the supply curve.

The government intervenes by giving a subsidy to the pension company and this reduces the supply price by an amount equal to the amount of the subsidy. The supply curve shifts from S_1 to S_2 and equilibrium moves from point M to point R (note point R lies vertically below point N) and thus the equilibrium quantity bought and sold rises from Q_1 to Q_2. The supply shift means that the consumer has moved down the 'incorrect' demand curve from point M to point R.

Mixed goods and intervention

It is highly likely that many, if not all, of the product markets in which governments intervene have both externalities and imperfect information problems. These products can be referred to as **mixed goods**. The method of government intervention, therefore, has to allow for both potential causes of market failure. As an example, consider the case of a drink driving.

Drivers may underestimate the effects of drinking alcohol on their ability to drive. If they do drink and drive they are more likely to be involved in an accident. It is often the case that drivers will underestimate the probability or likelihood of having an accident and thus over-consume alcohol. If as a result of excessive drinking they are actually involved in an accident they will incur both private and social costs. Private costs include both loss of earnings incurred by the driver whilst in hospital and also repairs to the driver's car. External costs will include injuries to others who were hurt in the accident or damage to another individual's property or vehicle. The government imposes legal limits on the amount of alcohol that can be consumed before driving a car.

Smoking not only affects the smoker, who may not fully appreciate the harm that cigarette smoking causes, but it also affects other individuals who inhale the smoke. Thus smoking has both elements of imperfect information and externality.

Concentration of power in markets

Governments intervene in situations in which market power is concentrated in a small number of firms. In these situations markets are not operating efficiently because firms abuse their market power. There are several methods that a government can use to prevent abuse of this market power. The government can use standards and regulation or financial intervention in the form of price controls. In some cases governments may also decide that market efficiency is best achieved if the product is produced by state-owned firms. Barriers to entry will protect the power of a monopolist. Some of these barriers may be artificial and the government can remove these barriers and thus make the market more 'contestable' (see unit 1, section 3).

Regulation and control of monopoly power

Governments have three key methods of controlling monopoly power. They can prevent the formation of monopolies by blocking the merger of companies that would potentially lead to one large company that is likely to dominate the market. Alternatively they can regulate firms that dominate the industry. Finally, the government can remove any artificial barriers that have allowed the monopolist to dominate the market.

All mergers that are likely to lead to a company gaining dominance in a market can be referred to the Competition Commission (CC). This government body is charged with ensuring that the merger is not against the public interest, in other words, that the result of the merger will not lead to a situation in which the consumer will be exploited through high prices and reduced output.

If a company already has a dominant position within the market, then this company can also be referred to the CC if it is considered to be acting against the public interest. A dominant position is usually seen to occur when a company controls more than 25% of a market. There are a wide range of methods by which these dominant firms can act against the public interest and against which the CC will act.

The dominant firm may charge prices that are considerably higher than the marginal cost of production, safe in the knowledge that there are no competitors to which the consumer can turn for a lower-priced product. As we have shown in Section 4, this leads to an allocatively inefficient use of resources. Price is also unlikely to equal minimum average cost, which leads to productive inefficiency. The government

may place price controls on a firm to ensure that prices are not set above a certain limit. Thus the maximum price that a firm in this situation can charge is set by the government. This type of price control is typical in the case of public utilities, such as privately owned gas, electricity and water companies.

The dominant firm may also exploit the consumer by offering a poor quality product or service. An example of this might by a train-operating company that frequently gives poor service in terms of the late running or cancellation of trains. Other companies may produce products with shoddy workmanship and lack the willingness to honour guarantees. The government can intervene and fine these companies or, in the case of rail companies, withdraw their franchises so that they are no longer able to operate train services.

As a final example, the firm may exploit consumers by using a practice that has become known as 'bundling'. In this case the company insists that if you buy their product then you *must* also buy other products that are associated with it. Thus a consumer has to buy a 'bundle' of products from the company. Until recently a tour operator could insist that if you bought their holiday product you also had to purchase their holiday insurance. Thus the holiday and insurance were bundled together. This practice has now been made illegal. Similarly a building society (or other mortgage provider) would insist that you could only have their mortgage if you also bought their life insurance policy and their house and contents insurance policy. A final example is given by the Microsoft company which insists that if you buy their 'Office' product you must also buy their Internet browser as the two are bundled together.

State ownership and monopoly power

In many countries, natural monopolies are placed into the hands of state ownership to avoid the problems of exploitation by dominant firms. The state-run, or nationalised, industry then charges prices that are equal to the marginal cost of production. Large economies of scale are present in special markets referred to as natural monopolies. These include public utilities and railways. In the UK many of these industries have been **privatised** because it was believed that privately run companies would be more efficient as a result of the discipline placed upon them by the profit motive. However, without control these privatised companies may abuse their dominant position and charge high prices or provide a shoddy product or service.

The government has a clear choice: state ownership or private ownership plus rigid regulation and control. Products such as water, gas and electricity are seen by some governments as being so important to the welfare of their population that their production cannot be entrusted to large privately owned companies. This appears to be a political rather than an economic decision.

Removal of barriers to entry and contestable markets

One possible barrier to entry that leads to monopoly power is the legal barrier that only allows a single company to supply the product. Until July 1996 the Royal Mail had an exclusive right to deliver letters charged at less than £1. This was removed in order to make the market 'contestable' and new firms entered, giving more competition to the Royal Mail. It was argued that this was 'cream-skimming' with the new competitors taking the most profitable areas for delivery and that these companies would not be prepared to deliver anywhere in the UK for a single unit price. The Royal Mail's own profits would be severely reduced, meaning that it too would no longer be able to offer a complete service to every inhabitant in the UK at the same price.

Royal Mail van stops to collect post from a village post box

Self-assessment task

Explain how different methods of government intervention can be used to correct market failures caused in the following:

- the purchase of a technically complex good such as a computer;
- a national airline, which is given sole rights to fly certain routes;
- a chemical plant that discharges its waste products into the local river;
- street lighting;
- the potential health risk caused by BSE-infected cattle;
- noisy neighbours;
- inoculation against a disease;
- university education.

Equity, redistribution and government intervention

The methods of intervention used by governments to ensure a fair or equitable distribution of resources are different to those described earlier. First, if markets fail then the government needs to raise taxes in order to provide the finance to correct the market failures. For example, finance is needed to pay for public goods, such as defence, and it is also necessary to pay for goods and services, such as roads, education and health. These taxes should be raised in a fair and equitable manner.

Second, the government may want to redistribute income, wealth or other resources for social or political reasons. These involve value judgements but nonetheless require government intervention in markets. Society, through its elected members of government, decides that it is socially unjust to have a very unequal distribution of income or wealth. Thus these types of argument to justify redistribution are referred to as **social justice** reasons.

There are several possible strands to such equity objectives. The government may intervene to achieve any one or any combination of the following:

- the elimination of poverty (all individuals are entitled to a minimum standard of living regardless of personal circumstances);
- a reduction in unacceptable inequalities in the distribution of income and wealth;

Unit 2 Market failure and government intervention

◆ equal access, regardless of a person's income, to certain goods and services such as education, health and housing – for example, all children should have equal access to high-quality education regardless of their family background;
◆ the protection against a sudden and unexpected loss of income – for example, protection against loss of income due to an unexpected illness that prevents a person from being able to work.

If the government decides to intervene for social justice reasons it then has to decide how to redistribute these resources. It may do this in the form of cash payments or social security benefits. These benefit payments may be 'means-tested' (that is, only paid to people on low incomes) or 'universal' (that is, paid to everyone with a particular need regardless of their income).

Alternatively these benefits may be paid 'in-kind'. This means that government provides a good or service free of charge rather than give cash to individuals to arrange their own consumption. An example of this would be entitlement to free prescriptions or dental

treatment that is given to people on low incomes or to people in certain age groups, such as children or pensioners.

Redistributive taxes and paying for welfare The government needs to raise a considerable sum of money each year to pay for its expenditure. A tax that raises this money by taking a larger percentage of income from the rich than the poor was referred to earlier and is known as a **progressive** tax. Alternatively, if a larger percentage of income is taken from the poor than the rich, it is called a **regressive** tax.

Table 6.1 gives a simple example of both types of system. First note that the total amount raised in tax from both systems is £5,000 and, equally importantly, that the poor person has paid less in tax than the rich person in both cases. In the regressive tax system, Person A (the person on the lower income) has paid 20 per cent of their income in tax whilst Person B has paid only 5 per cent. By redistributing the tax burden it is possible to shift to a progressive tax system. Person B now pays a higher percentage in tax than Person A.

The last gathering of all peers in the House of Lords prior to its reconstitution. Although the distribution of wealth has become more equal, those, such as the hereditary peers, who inherit wealth still account for many of the country's rich. New wealth, however, has been created through privatisation sales, through increased housing values and through share prices. Nevertheless, statistics on the distribution of wealth still indicate much inequality, with the top 50 per cent of the population having 82 per cent of the wealth, the top 10 per cent have 33 per cent and the top 1 per cent have 10 per cent.
Source: Eddie Mulholland.

Type of tax system		Regressive tax system			Progressive tax system	
	Income	Tax Paid	Percentage of Income paid in tax	Tax Paid	Percentage of Income paid in tax	
Person A	£10,000	£2,000	20%	£500	5%	
Person B	£50,000	£3,000	6%	£4,500	9%	
Tax Paid		£5,000		£5,000		

Table 6.1 Regressive and progressive tax systems

Redistributive taxes and social justice Redistribution for social justice reasons is achieved through a combination of taxation, benefit payments and in-kind transfers. Let us assume that the government wants to redistribute wealth because it believes that the current distribution is too uneven. It might do this by taxing inheritances. An example will illustrate how this might work.

Assume that the first £100,000 of an inheritance is free of tax but any additional receipt of an inheritance is taxed at 40 per cent. If a someone dies and leaves £200,000 to say, Person A, then £40,000 is paid in tax and the person receiving the inheritance actually receives £160,000. However, if the person leaves the money to two people who receive £100,000 each then no tax is paid. This system of tax may encourage people to leave their money in smaller amounts to a larger number of people and thereby redistribute or spread the wealth over a wider number of people.

Although the British system of taxation of wealth is called an Inheritance Tax, it is confusingly named because it does NOT in fact tax the amount of money that a person inherits. In the British system the amount of tax paid is determined by the total amount of money in a person's estate (that is, left by a person after death). It does not matter whether the deceased leaves this money to one

person or to several people as the amount paid in tax is exactly the same. This is more properly called an Estate Duty. Thus in table 6.2, the deceased's estate would be required to pay £40,000 in tax in both cases and £160,000 would either be paid to one individual or, in the second case, shared between the two individuals. There is no tax incentive to redistribute the wealth.

The income tax system in the UK is a progressive tax system and thus redistributes resources from the higher-income earners to those on low or no income. In our tax system expenditure taxes are either regressive or progressive. VAT is generally regarded as being mildly progressive in its current form, which is mainly because the UK government does not impose VAT on food. The rich spend a higher proportion of their income on goods and services that have VAT imposed on them than the poor and so pay a higher proportion of their income in VAT. If VAT was imposed on food then, because the poor spend a much higher proportion of their income on food than the rich, they would pay a higher proportion of their incomes in VAT and the tax would become regressive. The tax on beer and cigarettes (that is, excise duties + VAT) is regressive because the poor spend a higher proportion of their income on these items than the rich.

	Inheritance tax system				Estate duty system			
	All to Person A		Equal shares		All to Person A		Equal shares	
	Amount of inheritance	Tax paid	Amount of inheritance	Tax paid	Amount of inheritance	Tax paid	Amount of inheritance	Tax paid
Person A	£200,000	£40,000	£100,000	0	£200,000	£40,000	£100,000	£20,000
Person B	0	0	£100,000	0	0	0	£100,000	£20,000
Totals	£200,000	£40,000	£200,000	0	£200,000	£40,000	£200,000	£40,000

Table 6.2 Different wealth tax systems

Redistributive social security benefit payments The government uses a range of social security benefits or payments to redistribute resources, usually in the form of income, from one group in society to another. Different criteria are used to judge who is entitled to claim these benefits. Some benefits are targeted towards those on low incomes, some towards those with children and others towards those who are over a certain age.

Social security benefits that are used to transfer income from high-income earners to low-income earners are referred to as 'income-targeted' or 'means-tested' benefits. This is because the type of benefit, such as income support, is targeted towards low-income earners. There are two major problems with this type of redistributive benefit system. A considerable amount of information is required about an individual's financial position and thus long and detailed claims forms need to be completed by the claimant.

There are two problems associated with this type of benefit. First, it is administratively expensive to collect information about a person's income and, secondly, claimants are put off making a claim for several reasons. For example, the form is complex, they feel uneasy about releasing sensitive personal information and a certain amount of 'stigma' is attached to admitting publicly that you are poor. For this reason, many 'means-tested' benefits have very low 'take-up rates', that is, the number of people who claim the benefits as a proportion of those who are entitled to claim them is low. In the case of a benefit such as income support only around 50 per cent of those entitled to make a claim will do so.

To overcome the problem of stigmatisation and low take-up rates the government frequently uses other methods of targeting benefits to those who are poor. For example, it is known that a very large percentage of people who are living in poverty in the UK are either over 65 (that is, pensioners) or have children. Benefits are therefore targeted to these groups. Old age and having children can be used as an 'indicator' of poverty. These benefits are known as 'indicator-targeted' benefits.

These benefits are not 'means-tested' but are given to everyone regardless of their income. The general name for a benefit that is given to everyone regardless of income is 'universal benefit'.

Child benefit, an example of a universal and indicator-targeted benefit, is paid to all families who have children regardless of income. Child benefit is very easy to claim – you make one claim soon after the baby is born and the benefit is paid until the child reaches a certain age or leaves full-time education. This is obviously very cheap to administer and has no stigma attached to it as everyone receives the payment. In consequence the take-up rate for child benefit is close to 100 per cent. However, many people argue that child benefit is poorly targeted because it is paid to many people who are not in poverty.

The government is willing to accept payment to all because the rich in effect pay more into the tax system than they claim in benefits, whilst the poor pay little or

Two decades of rising poverty mean today's children face the same problems as earlier generations
Source: Family Service Units.

	Progressive tax system			Universal benefit	
	Income	Tax paid	Percentage of income paid in tax	Annual payment	Income after tax and benefit
Person A	£10,000	£500	5%	£2,500	£12,000
Person B	£50,000	£4,500	9%	£2,500	£48,000
Tax raised		£5,000		£5,000	

Table 6.3 Redistribution under a universal benefit system

nothing in tax and still receive the benefit. Thus a combination of a progressive tax system and a 'universal' benefit payment system means that income is redistributed from high-income earners to the poor. Table 6.3 gives a simplified example to illustrate how this works.

A total of £5,000 is paid in tax using the progressive tax system discussed earlier in table 6.1. This is used to pay a universal benefit of £2,500 to each of the taxpayers (half the tax raised). We can see clearly that Person A pays £500 in tax and receives £2,500 in benefits. Person A's disposable income after subtracting tax and adding benefits is equal to £12,000 – a rise of £2,000. However, Person B has a disposable income of £48,000, which is a fall of £2,000. Therefore, £2,000 has been transferred from Person B to Person A under this system. In the real world the tax and benefit system is much more complicated, but this simple example shows how universal indicator-targeted benefits can transfer income from one group to another.

Redistributive benefits paid 'in-kind' Not all redistributive benefits are paid in the form of cash. 'In-kind' benefits are usually provided in the form of entitlement to a good or service without the need for payment. Thus goods and services such as medical prescriptions, eye tests and dental care are given free of charge to children and pensioners. In this case the benefit is targeted towards certain age groups.

Benefits paid 'in-kind' are also targeted at those with low incomes and/or in receipt of certain means-tested benefits, such as a job seeker's allowance or income support. Receipt of one benefit therefore automatically acts as the ticket or passport to other benefits. A person on low income is therefore spared the indignity of filling in a multitude of forms.

Some 'in-kind' benefits are paid to every person in the country. All residents are entitled to free access to the National Health Service and to free education in a state school for their children. These universal 'in-kind' benefits are provided to allow everyone to have equal access to services that the government believes to be important. However, in this case they should not be seen as redistributing resources from the rich to the poor. In fact the opposite is probably the case as the rich tend to make greater use of both the health service and the education system. The economic justification for providing health care and education free of charge to all is based on market failure rather than equity arguments.

Self-assessment tasks

1 Explain which of the following are regressive and which are progressive taxes:
   ◆ a Poll Tax which takes the same amount of tax from everyone regardless of income;
   ◆ VAT on children's clothing;
   ◆ income tax.
2 Explain which of the following redistribute resources and how this redistribution occurs:
   ◆ free long-term care in residential homes for pensioners;
   ◆ reduced bus fares for individuals receiving job seeker's allowance;
   ◆ a state pension paid to everyone;
   ◆ a tax on the purchase of houses costing more than £100,000;
   ◆ tax on beer.

Government failures

It is not only markets that fail. It is important to recognise that government intervention can also fail. To illustrate this point we begin by considering an economy in which *all* of the decisions are taken by the state, the extreme opposite to an economy in which *all* decisions are taken by the market with no government intervention. Both extremes are unlikely to occur in reality as most economies can be considered mixed economies and thus we consider the case of **government failure** in a mixed economy too.

Government failure in a non-market economy In the state-controlled economy, all prices, all production levels and the allocation of all resources are decided by some central authority. This requires central planning, which is an extremely complex business. If planners make errors in determining production levels and demand exceeds supply at the government-set prices, then a shortage and queues will form. There will be unsold surpluses for goods where supply exceeds demand.

Although used extensively by many Socialist and Communist countries during the twentieth century, most of these countries, such as the Soviet Union, Poland, Bulgaria and China, have now abandoned central planning of this type. Four government failures were significant in this decision. First, a centrally planned process finds difficulty in coping with rapid change, such as technological advance or sudden harvest failure. Secondly, it proved difficult to control the quality of products produced. Thirdly, there was no incentive for workers to undertake training or move jobs as they were guaranteed employment at a fixed wage. Similarly, companies had little incentive to innovate and introduce new products or technology into their production processes. Finally, environmental degradation occurred on a massive scale as production plants were concerned only with meeting production targets and were not concerned at all with pollution (section 13 covers these issues in more depth and detail).

Government failure in a market economy
Governments intervene in mixed and market economies to correct market failures. Through intervention a government introduces a distortion or rigidity into a market. If the government makes a mistake with the type, size or extent of intervention, then rather than correct a market failure the government will itself create a more inefficient distribution of resources.

It takes time to change government policies and, if there is a sudden and unexpected change in the market, then governments may be slow to react as policy changes have to pass through correct parliamentary procedures. For example, tax rates are usually only adjusted in an annual budget.

The government may use the best information available at the time the policy decision was made but the introduction of the policy will itself undoubtedly cause behaviour to alter. In a highly uncertain world, the government may not always be able to fully judge the effect of its policy change. The government may impose a tax on petrol to correct for the external cost that arises from the pollution that is emitted by car exhaust fumes, but, if car producers invent a new form of car engine that radically reduces the amount of pollution, then a lower tax rate will be required to correct for the market failure.

Many members of the public will always attempt to find legal (and sometimes illegal) ways of avoiding paying tax. Thus, if the government increases the tax rate on high incomes, the tax payers will attempt to find loopholes in the tax laws which allow them to reduce their tax liability or attempt to find alternative ways of receiving this income payment which avoids the tax payment. The government then has to play catch-up and close these loopholes or extend the tax to cover all other sources of income. For example, a company director may not take all of his earnings in the form of income but may accept perks, such as a company car. The government (as it does in the UK) will tax the company car as though it was an addition to the company director's income. The company director may then take payment in the form of free private health care. The government will need to close this loophole too. It could be argued that if the government has to keep altering the tax laws to close these loopholes then it has failed, *but* it has to be remembered that the government cannot work out how the public will respond to many of these policies and many of the loopholes will only be discovered once the policy is put into practice.

The government has political objectives as well as economic objectives. Governments have to face elections and the implication of some policies, such as those which involve increasing taxes or regulating the behaviour of individuals when an election is close, may have an influence on when and if to introduce the policy. It can be argued that a government is more likely to introduce unpopular changes at the start of its term of office rather than at the end.

Self-assessment tasks

1 (a) Explain why governments might fail to allocate resources efficiently in a command economy.

  (b) Explain how a government can fail in its attempt to achieve a more equitable distribution of income.

  (c) Explain how a government might fail in setting a tax to reduce the external costs caused by pollution.

2 Local residents claim that a planned pop festival will causes several problems for their community. They claim that roads will become congested, excessive noise will be created throughout the day and night, litter and waste products will be thrown into the local countryside and drugs introduced to the local community. The organisers argue that if the residents had good information they would realise that these claims were exaggerated and in any case the pop festival will bring benefits to the community in the form of increased expenditure in local shops and campsites.

  (a) Explain the potential causes of market failure in this case.

  (b) Comment upon the different policies that could be used to overcome the problems caused by market failure.

3 The government gives both child benefit and income-targeted benefits to families with children who are considered to be poor.

  (a) Explain why a government might want to redistribute resources from one sector of the population to another.

  (b) Comment upon the use of child benefits and income-targeted benefits as a means of achieving the aim of redistributing resources to families who are considered poor.

4 The market for education might fail if the provision of education was left entirely to the private sector.

  (a) Explain why the market for education might fail.

  (b) Comment upon the alternative policies that a government might use to correct for these market failures.

The following tasks bring together various concepts – they are typical of those that will be set by OCR in the examination for this unit.

5 Government intervention

The annual budget speech is a chance for the Chancellor of the Exchequer to explain why and how the government intervenes in the economy. It also enables the government to alter taxes and government expenditure in order to overcome problems generated from a freely operating market economy. This case study takes selected parts from the 1999 budget speech. As you read these highlights from the speech, it will become obvious that it is a political speech but it is also obvious that there are many reasons for government intervention in an economy.

Chancellor's Budget Speech, 10 March 1999

With this the last Budget of the 20th century – we leave behind the century-long sterile conflicts between governments of the left that have too often undervalued enterprise and wealth creation, and governments of the right, too often indifferent to public services and fairness.

The sharpest spur to enterprise, the ingredient too often missing in our country today, is competition… And it is time for more competition and lower prices in basic essentials like the utilities, financial services, indeed the whole range of consumer goods, where too often British people are paying more than they should for what they need to buy. It is wholly unacceptable that consumer goods can still cost up to twice as much in Britain as in America.

Tomorrow so that competition will be encouraged for the long-term needs of the economy and consumers, the Secretary of State for Trade and Industry plans to set out a new competition policy for Britain. The Office of Fair Trading will now be charged with a pro-active remit to root out cartels and restrictive behaviour. Wherever there is monopoly power we will open the way to competition… Britain will have the most open competition policy the country has seen.

As Britain works to lead in the new economy we must resolve to lead in respecting the environment. Our target is to reduce greenhouse emissions by 12.5 per cent by 2010. And today I will announce a programme of measures that will cut carbon pollution by 3 million tonnes.

My first proposal alone will reduce carbon pollution by 1.5 million tonnes… We will now… introduce a levy on business use of energy from April 2001.

We also intend to set significantly lower rates of tax for energy intensive sectors that improve their energy efficiency … We will also allocate an extra £50m to encourage business to invest in the new environmental technologies and in renewable fuels.

In line with the fuel escalator first introduced by the previous government at 5 per cent above inflation and now 6 per cent, petrol duty will rise from 6pm today.

Vehicle excise duty for smaller cars will, from 1 June this year, be cut by £55 – the first cut in the licence fee in 50 years. Other cars' rates are only increased in line with inflation.

Children are 20 per cent of the British people but 100 per cent of Britain's future. To build that future, this Budget provides a better deal for families and children …

In the Budget last year I set down the two principles that govern my approach: that we must substantially increase support to families with children and we must do so in the fairest way.

Every year a quarter of a million children, even at the moment they are born, are born into poverty. This too is wrong. … When we came into power, one child in every three in our country was in poverty. With our measures today 700,000 children are being lifted out of poverty. Families with children are better off…

On top of the £40bn extra we are already investing in education and health, we will today allocate increased resources for our key public services…

We are allocating an additional £170m for crime prevention in areas where crime is highest. The Home Secretary will make a detailed statement to the House. For public transport, in addition to the rural transport fund, we will make a further allocation to be announced by the Deputy Prime Minister.

The £190 bn extra we are already providing for education will finance smaller class sizes, more nursery education, better pay for better teachers, our drive to improve literacy and numeracy – and we will help 700,000 more young people to go on to further and higher education.

I turn to the NHS: £21bn extra money is making possible the largest hospital building programme since the war: a £1bn investment in modern technology in the health service, the recruitment of 7,000 new doctors; 15,0000 more nurses; and a fair pay award for nurses.

To enhance in every part of the United kingdom the health care that people most urgently require we today make an additional and immediate cash allocation, to be spent in the next 12 months, for the upgrading of every single accident and emergency unit which needs it

Today's Budget is a better deal for work, a better deal for the family, a better deal for business – for a Britain now united around values of fairness and enterprise, and I commend this Budget not just to the House but to the country.

(a) ◆ Why does the government want to intervene in markets whenever there is market power?

   ◆ How can the government open the way to competition?

   ◆ How can the government root out cartels and restrictive behaviour?

(b) ◆ Explain why the government is keen to reduce pollution tax.

   ◆ Using a diagram, show how you can determine the rate of tax that would need to be charged to reach the optimal level of production.

   ◆ How will the proposed changes in vehicle excise duties help?

   ◆ What other policies could the Chancellor choose to cut carbon pollution by 3 million tonnes?

(c) ◆ Explain two different methods by which the government could help families with children.

   ◆ Is increasing 'Child Benefits' the best way of helping children who are 'born into poverty'?

   ◆ What 'in-kind' transfers does the government use to help children? How would increasing expenditure on these help children 'born into poverty'?

   ◆ Discuss the advantages and disadvantages of the Chancellor using means-tested benefits to help children 'born into poverty'.

(d) ◆ Why does the government spend money on crime prevention, education and health care?

   ◆ Could the private market provide all or part of crime prevention, education or health care?

6 Read the following article and then answer the questions below:

Pensioners face to face with ghost of policy past

The state earnings-related pension scheme is a state pension scheme which allows people who are not members of an occupational pension scheme (i.e., one run by their firm) to make contributions to an additional state pension scheme. As the name suggests, this pension scheme pays a pension which is related to earnings. The state pension scheme to which all workers contribute pays the same amount to everyone regardless of their earnings.

Back in 1986, Sir Norman Fowler, the then Conservative social security secretary, decided that one of the most generous provisions of the state earnings related pensions scheme – or SERPS – needed to be axed. SERPS then paid out – and still does – the full pension to widows and widowers after the death of their spouse. This is an arrangement that is far more generous than most occupational schemes, which generally pay out only a half pension to surviving spouses. But it made SERPS expensive, and the then government decided the cost of SERPS in the 21st Century would be unsustainable.

Sir Norman decided to bring SERPS in line with occupational schemes, halving survivor benefits. But it was decided that the change would only take effect way into the future – from April 6 2000, some 14 years after the decision was announced. At the time the government knew people had been contributing to SERPS on the understanding that a full widow's pension would be paid when the time came. It would have been grossly unfair to axe it overnight.

Department for Social Security, DSS, leaflets were not altered and staff were not briefed on the changes as they seemed a long way off. The DSS claim that few people ask about survivors' benefits. But from the few cases that have come to light, it appears that when pensioners did, they were told their surviving spouse would be entitled to full benefits – strictly true, but only if their partner died before April 6 2000.

The issue resurfaced in 1995 when Peter Lilley, the then Social Security Secretary, halved the value of SERPS again. At this point, there may have been a chilling realisation that the change was now a mere five years off. Staff started giving the right advice and the leaflets were altered. But an unknown number of people will have taken decisions about a new mortgage, for example, or a higher private pension now in return for reduced survivors' benefits later – on the assumption SERPS would pay out a full pension to their survivor.

According to parliamentary answers, next year's change will cut the average widow's benefit in SERPS from £33 a week to £12. But Age concern says it has cases where survivors will lose £25–£100 a week if their partner dies after April 6 2000. The saving to the government is £60m in the first year and £2,300m by 2020.

Age Concern is urging the government to cancel the change 'given that many of those potentially affected were unaware of it'. To have a case for compensation, individuals are likely to have to demonstrate they took financial decisions based on misinformation.

The DSS said yesterday no such cases would even be considered until a pensioner affected died after April 2000 and the survivor could demonstrate he or she had lost out as a result. Even then, the department said, it did not believe it had misled people, because the advice it gave between 1986 and 1988 was 'correct at the time'.

Age Concern and others will not accept that, and the department seems certain to face at least some compensation claims. 'No occupational scheme would make such changes without notifying all members of the plan', Age Concern said. The government had castigated the personal pensions industry for mis-selling and was insisting on compensation for victims. 'Many people will see this as an example of the same thing.'

One thing is certain. At some point there will be a report from the Ombudsman condemning the department for exactly what is so plainly guilty of – maladministration.

Source: *Financial Times*, 18 February 1999.

(a) Why does this case study represent an example of government failure?

(b) Age Concern argued that pensioners will lose £25–£100 a week because of bad advice given by the DSS. Explain why this is a case of information failure.

(c) Using a demand and supply diagram explain how this 'information failure' could lead to a fall in demand for private pensions.

(d) Explain how the government, in retrospect, could have made these changes without causing information failure.

Summary

In this section we have recognised that:

- The cost–benefit approach through cost–benefit analysis is an important aid to decision making in situations where markets fail.

- The limitations and weaknesses of the cost–benefit approach should also be recognised.

- Government intervention can take various forms including regulation, financial intervention and the provision of public goods.

- Different methods of intervention can be used to achieve specific market outcomes.

- Financial intervention in the form of taxes and subsidies has been widely advocated for use in markets where there are negative and positive externalities.

- Where there is a concentration of power in a market, the government can use standards and regulation or financial intervention in the form of price controls to prevent the abuse of this power.

- Governments too may fail in market and non-market economies.

Key words

Definitions of Key words can be found in the Glossary on page 240.

controls
cost–benefit analysis
financial intervention
government failure
income transfer
in-kind transfer
mixed goods
nationalised industry
privatisation

progressive tax
regressive tax
regulation
shadow prices
social justice
social security benefit
spillover effect
subsidy

Unit 3

The national and international economy

7 Government macroeconomic policy objectives and indicators of national economic performance

On completion of this section you should be able to:

➤ define, in broad terms, employment and unemployment, inflation, the balance of payments account and economic growth

➤ understand the objectives of government economic policy in terms of the above and why it is necessary for governments
➤ to establish such objectives

➤ define GDP

➤ outline its measurement through the output, income and expenditure approaches

➤ explain the difference between real and nominal values of GDP

➤ define unemployment and explain how it is measured in the UK economy

➤ explain the difficulties of measuring unemployment

➤ define inflation and explain the main methods by which it is measured in the UK economy

➤ outline the broad structure of the balance of payments account of the UK economy

➤ define economic growth and explain how it is measured in the UK economy

➤ show an awareness of trends in these key policy indicators

➤ discuss the consequences of unemployment, inflation and balance of payments problems

➤ discuss the benefits and costs of economic growth

➤ explain the reasons for, and consequences of, possible conflicts in macroeconomic policies

Introduction

'Barclaycard cuts 1,100 jobs over three years.'
The Times, 3 September 1998

'The G7 must make some painful choices now if it is to halt the crisis in the world economy.'
The Financial Times, 16 September 1998

'No interest rate rise but respite may be short-lived.' *The Independent*, 10 July 1998

'Thousands face dole as the Chancellor admits: "It's grim."' *The Sun*, 7 October 1998

These are all recent newspaper headlines. Every day stories appear in the newspapers and on the television news about how the UK economy and other economies are performing. As the fourth headline shows even the tabloid press cover certain economic issues!

These stories appear in the media because people are interested in events which affect their lives. For example, when a company such as Barclaycard makes staff redundant it not only has an impact on the lives of the

redundant workers but also reduces demand in the area where they were previously employed. People working in other financial institutions may become concerned about their own job security. The redundancies may also be taken as an indicator that the economy is running into difficulties. **Unemployment** as an indicator of economic performance is starkly referred to in the fourth headline.

The global crisis mentioned in the second headline led to falling incomes throughout the Far East, Russia and Latin America. To minimise the impact of this crisis on the UK, the Bank of England initially held interest rates constant and then cut them. A fall in interest rates may benefit borrowers but reduces the return which savers receive.

So how the economy is performing can have a major impact on people's lives. It influences the types of jobs we have, indeed whether we have jobs at all, and the quantity and quality of goods and services we are able to buy.

Government policy objectives

The main government macroeconomic policy objectives are:

◆ low unemployment;
◆ low and stable **inflation**;
◆ a satisfactory **balance of payments** position;
◆ avoidance of excessive **exchange rate** fluctuations;
◆ steady **economic growth**.

Key indicators

To assess how successful a government is being in achieving its objectives and to judge the performance of an economy, economists examine a number of key indicators. These include:

◆ the level of **output**;
◆ economic growth;
◆ the inflation rate;
◆ the level and rate of unemployment;
◆ the balance of payments position.

In broad terms an economy can be judged to be performing well if it has a high and growing output, a low and stable inflation rate, low unemployment and a healthy international trade position.

There are a number of stages involved in analysing any of the key indicators. First, economists define what they mean by, for example, unemployment; then they measure it and then they interpret their findings (see Introduction). As discussed below these tasks are neither as easy nor as straightforward as they may first appear.

The level of output and economic growth

One of the main indicators of a nation's economic performance is its level of output. Tables are produced by a number of organisations, which rank countries according to their level of output or more commonly level of output per head.

Output can be measured in terms of **Gross Domestic Product** (GDP) and **Gross National Product** (GNP). Gross means total, domestic refers to the home economy and product means output. So UK GDP is a measure of the total output produced by factors of production based in the UK.

There are three ways of calculating GDP. These are the output, income and expenditure methods. They should give the same total as they all measure the flow of income produced in an economy. Figure 7.1

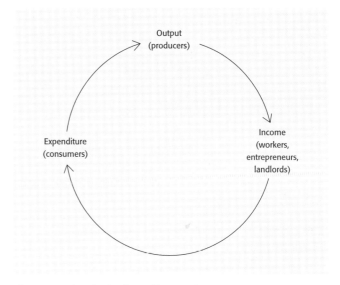

Figure 7.1 The circular flow of income in an economy

illustrates this **circular flow of income** in a simplified model of the economy.

The value of output is equal to the incomes which it generates, that is wages, rent, profit and interest. If it is assumed that all income is spent, expenditure will equal income and in turn, by definition, equal output.

The output method

This measures the value of output produced by industries including, for example, the output of the manufacturing, construction, distributive, hotel and catering and agricultural industries.

In using this measure it is important to avoid counting the same output twice. For example, if the value of cars sold by car manufacturers is added to the value of the output of tyre firms, double counting will occur. So economists count only the value added by each firm. **Value added** is the difference between the sales revenue received and the cost of raw materials used. It is equal to the payments made to the factors of production in return for producing the good or service. So that if a TV manufacturing firm buys components costing £60,000 and uses them to make TVs which it sells for £130,000, it has added £70,000 to output. It is this £70,000 which will be included in the measure of output.

The income method

The value of output produced is based on the costs involved in producing that output. These costs include wages, rent, interest and profits. All of these payments represent income paid to factors of production. For instance, workers receive wages and entrepreneurs receive profits. In using this measure it is important to include only payments received in return for providing a good or service. So **transfer payments**, which are transfers of income from taxpayers to groups of individuals for welfare purposes, are not included.

Self-assessment task

Decide which of the following should be included in measuring GDP by the income method:
- government subsidies to farmers;
- the pay of civil servants;
- the pay of nurses;
- supernormal profits;
- state pensions.

The expenditure method

As discussed above, the total amount spent in a year should also equal total output and total income:

Output = Income = Expenditure

What is produced in a year will either be sold or added to stocks. So, if additions to stocks are added to expenditure on goods and services, a measure is obtained which will equal output and income. In using this method it is necessary to add expenditure on exports and deduct expenditure on imports. This is because the sale of exports represents UK output and creates incomes in the UK, whereas expenditure on imports is spending on goods and services made abroad and creates incomes for people overseas. It is also necessary to deduct indirect taxes and add subsidies in order to get a value which corresponds to the incomes generated in the production of the output.

Nominal and real GDP

Nominal (or money) **GDP** is GDP measured in terms of the prices operating in the year in which the output is produced. It is sometimes referred to as GDP at current prices and is a measure which has not been adjusted for inflation.

Nominal GDP may give a misleading impression of how a country is performing. This is because the value of nominal GDP may rise not because more goods and services are being produced but merely because prices have risen. For example if 100 million goods are produced at an average price of £5, GDP will be £500 million. If in the next year the same output of 100 million goods is produced but the average price rises to £6, nominal GDP will rise to £600 million. So to get a truer picture of what is happening to output, economists convert nominal into **real GDP**. They do this by measuring GDP at constant prices, that is, at the prices operating in a selected base year. By doing this they remove the distorting effects of inflation. For example, in 2000 a country's GDP is £800 billion and the price index is 100. Then in 2001 nominal GDP rises to £864 billion and the price index is 105.

Real GDP is nominal GDP × price index in base year

Price index in current year

$$£864bn \times \frac{100}{105} = £822.86bn$$

To conclude, Figure 7.2 shows the way in which the UK's real GDP has changed since 1980. As this shows, the overall trend has been upwards despite the economic downturn between 1990 and 1992.

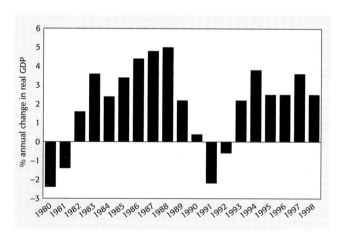

Figure 7.2 UK real GDP growth 1980–1998
Source: OECD, figure for 1998 is a November 1997 forecast.

Self-assessment task

In 2002 a country's nominal GDP is £1,000bn. In 2003 nominal GDP rises to £1,092bn and the price index increases by 4%. Calculate:
- real GDP;
- the percentage increase in real GDP.

Economic growth

If a country's output is increasing, this suggests that its citizens will be able to enjoy more goods and services and so a higher living standard. Most countries now measure changes in output by examining changes in GDP. Indeed the most common definition of economic growth is that it is an increase in real GDP. So that a growth rate of 3 per cent means that GDP this year is 3 per cent greater than it was the year before.

Actual and potential growth

Increases in output can be referred to as actual growth whereas increases in the productive capacity of a country can be called potential growth. Figure 7.3 illustrates this distinction. A shift outwards in the production possibility curve from AB to CD means that the country is capable of producing more goods and services – potential growth (see section 1).

A movement outwards of the production point, for example from point D to point E or from point D to point F, means that the economy is actually producing more output. So actual growth, increases in GDP, can occur in the short run by utilising previously unemployed resources. Once all resources are being fully utilised output can only be increased as a result of more resources (factors of production) or better quality resources. So in the longer run, for output to continue to grow, there has to be an increase in potential output.

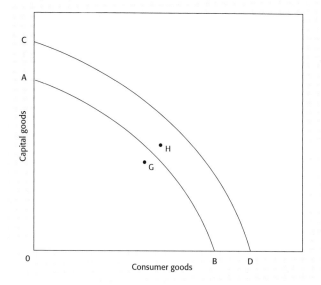

Figure 7.4 The output gap in an economy

Output gap

If potential output grows at a faster rate than actual output there will be an increase in spare capacity. Figure 7.4 shows that, as potential output increases from AB to CD but actual output only increases from G to H, the shortfall between actual and potential output widens.

Production and productivity

A country's output can increase either because more resources are employed or because productivity rises. Whereas production is output, productivity is output per factor of production. For example, labour productivity is output per worker. If productivity rises but fewer resources are employed production may actually fall. An increase in production means that actual growth occurs. An increase in productivity means that potential growth occurs but whether this is matched by an increase in actual output will depend on what happens to the level of employment of resources.

Measurement problems

The output, expenditure and income methods are all used in an attempt to gain an accurate measure of national output and changes in national output. However, in practice, a number of difficulties arise in achieving a completely accurate figure. The key difficulties are:

1 The existence of a black economy. The output of some goods and services are deliberately not declared.

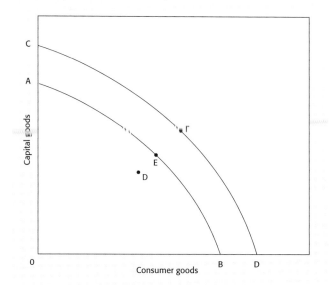

Figure 7.3 Potential growth in an economy

There are two reasons for this. One is that people are seeking to avoid paying tax. For example, a plumber may receive payment for undertaking jobs in his spare time and not declare the income he receives to the Inland Revenue. So some of the services he produces will not be included in GDP. Another reason for not declaring economic activity is that the activity is in itself illegal, for example prostitution and the trading in hard drugs.

Some idea of the size of the black economy can be gained by measuring any gap between GDP as measured by the expenditure and income methods. This is because people will be spending income they have not declared!

The existence of the black economy means that the official GDP figures will understate the quantity of goods and services actually produced. However, if its size is relatively constant, the rate of economic growth can be calculated reasonably accurately.

The size of the black economy does vary between countries. It is influenced by the marginal rates of taxation, the penalties imposed for illegal activity and tax evasion, the risk of being caught and social attitudes towards, for example, drug taking, prostitution and tax evasion. Of course this can and does vary over time. A recent estimate has put the size of the black economy in the UK at 15–20 per cent of GDP and increasing.

2 **Non-marketed goods and services.** The GDP figures only include marketed goods and services, that is goods and services which are bought and sold and so have a price attached to them. Services which are produced and which are either not traded or which are exchanged without money changing hands go unrecorded. For example DIY activities, domestic services provided by homeowners and voluntary work are not included in the official figures. The proportion of goods and services which people produce for themselves and the proportion of voluntary work varies from country to country.

3 **Government spending.** In the expenditure method government spending on final goods and services is included. However, some government spending goes on producing public goods, for example defence and the fire service, which are not sold. In the past in the UK the output was valued at cost, normally in terms of the value of inputs. This gave a somewhat

Charity shops – staff are usually unpaid volunteers and second-hand goods do not always command a true market price

distorted view of what was happening to output. For instance, if productivity increased in the fire service, fewer firemen and women might have been needed. This reduced the cost of providing the fire service. Output as officially recorded fell, although the level of service provided might have been unchanged or may even have increased. To overcome this problem, in 1998 the Office for National Statistics developed a system for measuring government outputs of services other than through the value inputs. This method covers education, health and social security, around 50 per cent of the public sector, and uses a variety of key performance indicators (such as student numbers for education and claimant numbers for social security) in order to estimate output.

Inflation

A low and steady rate of inflation provides a number of benefits for a country, in particular that of enabling businesses to forward plan with confidence. A country with a rapidly rising inflation rate in excess of that of its main trading partners will be likely to experience a number of problems, including difficulty in selling its goods and services at home and abroad.

One of the main measures of inflation used in the UK is the Retail Prices Index (RPI), which is a measure of changes in the prices of consumer goods bought in the UK. Much attention is paid to this index by the media, economists, business people, politicians and wage bargainers. As a result it is often known as the headline rate of inflation.

Calculating the RPI

The RPI is a weighted price index. Employees of the Office for National Statistics (ONS) calculate it in three main stages:

1 They carry out a 'Family Expenditure Survey' to find out what items people buy and how much they spend on them. Approximately 7,000 households are asked to keep a record of what they spend over a two week period and to give details of other major items, for example telephone bills, over a longer period. These households are drawn from across the country and from different socio-economic groups. Two groups are excluded because their patterns of spending are noticeably different from most households – these are households in the top 4 per cent of income earners and low-income pensioners who are mainly reliant on state pensions. (Separate one-pensioner and two-pensioner price indices are calculated.)

   The weights for the RPI are drawn from the information gathered in the Family Expenditure Survey. Price changes of items on which people spend a significant amount obviously have a greater impact. So the statisticians attach a greater 'weight' to them. This is expressed as the amount spent on the item as a fraction of total expenditure. For example a person, spending £500 in total, spends £100 on food and £5 on postage stamps. In this case food would be given a weighting of 1/5 and stamps a weighting of 1/100. The weights are revised every year to reflect changes in spending patterns.

2 They record how much the prices of some 600 selected items have changed. Around the middle of each month prices are collected from a range of retail outlets in 180 areas throughout the country. These outlets include supermarkets, department stores and small retailers. Some prices are collected by visiting the same shops on a monthly basis. Other prices, for example electricity and rail fares, are gathered from central sources and from large retailers which charge the same price throughout the country – these businesses send in information direct to the ONS. In total approximately 150,000 price quotations are collected each month. When they have all been collected, an average price is calculated for each item in the index.

3 The data are checked and fed into a computer. Then the percentage change in price for each item is multiplied by its weight. There are currently 14 main categories of items in the RPI. These are:

food	household services
catering	clothing and footwear
alcoholic drink	motoring expenditure
tobacco	fares and other travel costs
fuel and light	leisure goods
household goods	leisure services
housing	personal goods and services

The total of the weighted price changes for each of the items gives the RPI which represents the average change in the prices of millions of consumer purchases.

Other measures of inflation

RPIX is sometimes known as the underlying or target rate of inflation. It is the RPI minus mortgage interest payments. There are two main arguments for not including mortgage payments in a measure of consumer prices:

1 A number of other countries do not include it.
2 Mortgage interest payments are affected not only by changes in the prices of houses but also by changes in the rate of interest. So a rise in interest rates, perhaps designed to reduce inflation, will have the effect of raising RPI. This may have a longer-term impact if it stimulates workers to press for wage rises to compensate for the rise in the RPI.

The UK government has set a target for the RPIX measure of inflation of 2.5 per cent with a 1 per cent point margin either side.

The RPIY is the RPI minus not only mortgage interest payments but also local authority taxes and indirect taxes. The advantage of this measure is that it shows the underlying inflation rate undistorted by changes in interest rates and taxation. For example, raw material costs and wage costs may not be changing and there may be no excess demand in the economy. In this case an increase in the rate of VAT will be reflected in a rise in the general price level as measured by the RPI and the RPIX but not as measured by the RPIY.

Measurement problems

Among the problems involved in gaining an accurate measure of changes in the general price level are:

◆ Changes in quality. Measures of price changes do not take into account changes in quality. This can be significant as over time the quality of many goods and services improve. For example, a video recorder purchased now may be less expensive than one purchased ten years ago. However it is debatable whether they are really the same products. If today's video recorder has more features and is of better quality consumers may be gaining better value for money. So, in effect, its 'real' price has fallen even more than its nominal price.

- Special offers. Inflation indexes do not take into account special price offers or prices charged in charity shops and car boot sales. So people may be purchasing some goods and services more cheaply than the indexes suggest.

- Changes in the pattern of expenditure. The weights in the indexes are reviewed every year to reflect changes in consumer spending. However even this may not be frequent enough. Consumer tastes change quickly and new products are always coming on to the market.

- Sampling. To gain information about weights a sample of households is selected and to gain information about price changes a sample of goods is monitored. To obtain an accurate measure these samples have to be representative of the whole population and this is not easy to achieve.

Finally to conclude this introduction to inflation and its measurement, figure 7.5 shows recent trends in inflation for the UK economy. The overall trend has been very encouraging despite the marginal increasing annual percentage change since 1996.

Employment and unemployment

Countries measure both the numbers in employment and the numbers of those unemployed. If there is unemployment, output will be below its potential level, tax revenue will be lower and more state benefits will have to paid out. The unemployed, in addition to having lower incomes, may experience higher rates of divorce and mental and physical illnesses and will miss out on training and work experience. There is also increasing evidence of a link between levels of unemployment and crime.

The level of unemployment should be distinguished from the rate of unemployment. The level refers to the number of people who are unemployed whereas the rate of unemployment is the number of people unemployed as a percentage of the number of people in the labour force (that is, the employed and the unemployed).

Measures of employment

The Office for National Statistics collects data on employment. It carries out a 'Labour Force Survey', which asks people about their employment status and the nature of their main job. In addition it draws on information from employers and from administrative sources, for example those on government training schemes.

Measures of unemployment

One of the measures of unemployment in the UK is based on those in receipt of unemployment-related benefits, principally the job seeker's allowance. It is called the claimant count.

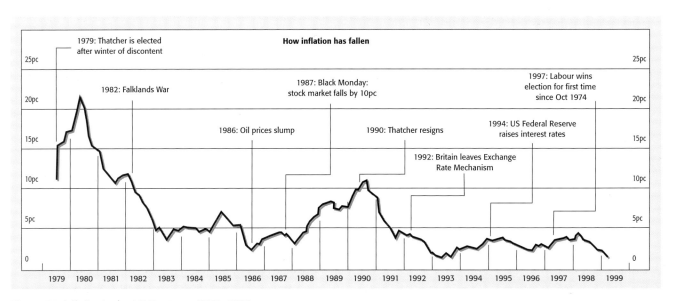

Figure 7.5 Inflation in the UK Economy, 1979–1999

As a measure it has the advantage that it is relatively cheap and quick to construct since it is based on information which the government collects as it pays out benefits. However it has come in for criticism on the grounds of accuracy. Some of those who are receiving the job seeker's allowance may not be very actively seeking employment (although this is carefully checked) or they may be working and so claiming the benefit illegally.

On the other hand, a number of groups who would like to work but who are unable to find employment do not appear in the official figures. These groups include those who are over 60, those under 18, those on government training schemes, married women looking to return to work and those who choose not to claim benefits. As unemployment is a measure which is based on those receiving benefits, it changes every time there is a change in the criteria for qualifying for benefit.

An alternative measure is based on the 'Labour Force Survey'. This uses the International Labour Organisation definition of unemployment, which includes all people of working age who, in a specified period, are without work, but who are available for work in the next two weeks and who are seeking paid employment. Since April 1998 this measure has been given greater prominence whilst the claimant count has been downgraded.

As its name suggests the measure is based on a survey which is carried out four times a year. Sixty thousand people are asked whether they have a job and if not whether they are seeking employment and what steps they have taken to find employment. It picks up some of the groups not included in the claimant count and so measures unemployment rather than those eligible for unemployment-related benefits. It collects more information, for example on ethnic origin, qualifications and those seeking part-time as opposed to full-time employment. It also has the advantage that as it is based on internationally agreed concepts and definitions it makes international comparisons easier. However it is a more expensive and time-consuming method than the claimant count. Also as it is based on a sample survey it is subject to sampling error.

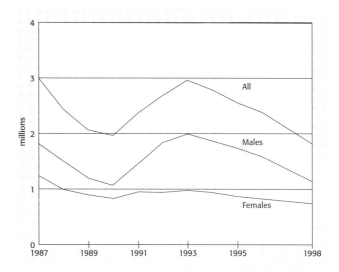

Figure 7.6 Unemployment by gender in the UK
Source: Office for National Statistics, 1999.

Measurement problems

Among the problems involved in gaining an accurate measure of unemployment are:

- If the claimant count method is used, any government changes in the eligibility criteria for job seekers' allowance will affect the figure. For example, if it becomes more difficult to qualify, the official unemployment figure will fall even though there may have been no change in actual unemployment. Changes in the criteria will also make it more difficult to compare figures over time.
- If the 'Labour Force Survey' measure is used there is a risk that the sample may not be truly representative.
- Whichever measure is used it can be difficult to assess whether people claiming to be unemployed are genuinely seeking employment.
- It may also be hard to decide whether some people should be included in the unemployment figures or counted as sick or disabled. Some without a job may actually be physically or mentally incapable of keeping a job, whilst others receiving disability benefit may actually be capable of working.

Figure 7.6 shows the trend in UK unemployment since 1987. Although some cyclical tendency is clearly evident, the underlying trend is downwards.

The balance of payments

The balance of payments is a record of the UK's economic activities with other countries. Economists, politicians, the media and the business world study this

Self-assessment task

Using any appropriate source, compare the UK unemployment rate with that of other EU countries at the present time and over the last five years.

account to gain information on the UK's current and future international competitiveness and net movements of income and assets. The first part of the balance of payments is in three main sections – the **current account**, the **capital account** and the **financial account**. These are a record of all money entering and leaving the country over the period of a year. There is also now a second part, the International Investment Position, which shows the level of external assets and liabilities at the end of the calendar year.

The current account

This in turn has four main headings:

1 Trade in goods. This covers the **exports** and **imports** of goods. For example, the export of toys to the USA brings money into the country and so is a credit item, whereas the import of video recorders from South Korea will result in money leaving the country and so is a debit item.

2 Trade in services. This covers exports and imports of services, for example financial services, insurance, transport, tourism and information services.

3 Income. The main item in this category is investment income. This covers profits, dividends and interest receipts from abroad minus profits, dividends and interest paid abroad. These receipts and payments arise from lending and borrowing money and from the sales and purchase of assets between countries.

4 Current transfers. These include central government and other sector transfers. The former includes the UK's net contribution to the EU and aid which is provided to developing economies. The latter covers items such as money sent back to relatives by UK citizens working abroad and taxes on income paid to the Inland Revenue by foreign workers in the UK. Debit items include money sent home by foreign workers in the UK and taxes paid by UK citizens to foreign governments.

The capital account

A new capital account came into being in 1998. This shows capital transfers, including government investment grants, and the acquisition/disposal of non-produced, non-financial assets, including the purchase and sale of patents, trademarks and land for foreign embassies. This is a very minor part of the balance of payments.

	£m	£m
Current account		
Trade in goods and services	−7,920	
Income	15,782	
Current transfers	−6,388	
Current account balance		1,474
Capital balance		438
Net financial transactions		−9,094
Net errors and omissions		7,182

Table 7.1 Summary of the UK balance of payments in 1998
Source: ONS, *Monthly Digest of Statistics*, April 1999.

The financial account

Known previously as the capital account, this is concerned with investment leaving or entering the country. This can take many forms including the purchase and sale of companies, portfolio investment and reserve assets of foreign exchange. Outward investment will later generate income and will be shown as such in the current account, whilst inward investment is likely to result in certain income streams leaving the UK as debit items in the current account. This is an important part of the balance of payments and can involve huge flows of money.

Net errors and omissions

In theory the balance of payments should balance. In other words the net of the current account plus the capital account plus the financial account when added together should equal zero. This last part, formerly known as the balancing item, is included to reflect any discrepancies in what is a highly complex accounting system. Table 7.1 shows a highly simplified summary of the UK balance of payments in 1998.

The international investment position

Whereas the financial account shows the purchase and sale of external financial assets and liabilities in one year, this account shows the total of external assets held by the UK government, companies and individuals and the total UK assets held by overseas governments, companies and individuals.

Self-assessment tasks

Allocate each of the transactions (a)–(f)

(a) interest paid by a UK company to a French bank,

(b) the hiring of a UK tanker by an Arab oil company,

(c) UK citizens travelling on an Australian aircraft,

(d) the sale of UK cars to America,

(e) the payment of dividends on Italian shares held by UK citizens,

(f) the purchase by a UK company of raw materials from Germany

to one of the following parts of the UK balance of payments:

1 trade in goods section;

2 trade in services section;

3 investment income section.

International competitiveness

In terms of the balance of payments most attention is focused on the trade in goods and services. A deficit on the trade in goods and services means that more has been spent on imports than has been earned from exports and may be a symptom of poor economic performance. The country's goods and services may be uncompetitive in terms of price and/or quality or the country may be concentrating on producing goods and services which are in low demand.

Other measures of international competitiveness

A number of international organisations now seek to measure comparative international performance. For example the OECD annually publishes a 'league table' based on countries' real GDP per head. In its 1997 report, which uses 1996 figures, the UK was placed twenty-second.

Whereas real GDP per head gives an indication of current economic performance, indexes of international competitiveness seek to throw light on future economic performance. The World Economic Forum and the International Institute of Management Development (IMD) compile lists of world competitiveness. Whilst they use different methods to measure competitiveness, they both base their indexes on a range of indicators including progress on growth, trade, investment, employment, education and technology. In 1997 both organisations reported an improvement in the UK's performance. According to the IMD the UK rose from nineteenth to twelfth place and according to the World Economic Forum it rose from fifteenth to seventh place.

Self-assessment tasks

1 Study the table below and then answer the questions which follow.

| | Gross domestic product | | | | | | | | Gross product per person employed | | | | | | |
	US	Canada	Japan	France	Germany	Italy	UK	OECD	US	Canada	Japan	France	Germany	Italy	UK
	Constant prices														
1994[a]	37.1	3.4	14.1	6.3	9.2	5.9	5.9	100.0							
1989	91.7	94.0	89.8	94.3	80.6	95.3	94.4	90.8	96.2	95.5	94.5	93.6	106.1	91.5	90.3
1990	92.8	94.3	94.4	96.7	85.3	97.4	95.0	93.2	96.2	95.2	97.5	95.1	109.4	91.8	90.2
1991	92.0	92.5	98.0	97.4	96.7	98.5	93.6	94.5	96.1	95.2	99.3	95.8	94.0	92.0	91.1
1992	94.5	93.3	99.0	98.6	98.5	99.0	93.6	96.2	98.1	96.6	99.3	97.5	97.0	93.5	93.7
1993	96.7	95.5	99.3	97.3	97.3	97.9	95.8	97.3	98.9	97.5	99.4	97.4	97.0	95.9	96.7
1994	100.0	100.0	100.0	100.0	100.0	100.0	100.0	100.0	100.0	100.0	100.0	100.0	100.0	100.0	100.0
1995	102.3	102.6	101.4	102.1	101.3	102.9	102.8	102.0	100.8	100.9	101.3	101.2	101.4	103.3	101.5
1996	105.8	103.9	106.6	103.7	102.6	103.6	105.4	105.0	102.8	100.9	106.1	102.6	103.2	103.4	102.6
1997	110.0	107.8	108.1	106.1	105.0	105.2	109.1	108.3	104.5	102.8	106.4	104.5	106.1	105.0	104.4

Gross product and productivity in industrial countries and OECD (*Seasonally adjusted, Index numbers, 1994 = 100*)

Note: [a] % of OECD total.

Source: Table 13, page 124, *National Institute Economic Review*, 167, January 1999, National Institute of Economic and Social Research.

(a) Explain what is meant by GDP at constant prices.

(b) Estimate which country experienced the most rapid economic growth in the period shown.

(c) Estimate which country experienced the most rapid increase in productivity in the period shown.

(d) Comment on the other economic data it would be useful to examine in assessing the UK's comparative international competitiveness.

2 Study the tables below and then answer the questions which follow.

Governments in the modern world regard low inflation as an important target. The tables below give some relevant historical data.

1986	103.4	1991	141.8
1987	107.7	1992	146.4
1988	113.0	1993	148.7
1989	121.8	1994	152.4
1990	133.3	1995	157.1

Table 1 Index of retail prices, UK (1985 = 100)

	1975	1984	1993
Germany	5.9	2.4	4.1
Japan	11.8	2.2	1.3
UK	24.2	5.0	1.6
USA	9.1	4.3	3.0
Industrial Countries	11.2	4.7	2.7
World	12.2	10.6	13.0

Table 2 Inflation in selected countries
(percentage change in consumer prices from previous year)

(a) Inflation in the UK, during the period 1985–1995, was at its highest in 1990, and at its lowest in 1993. What evidence in table 1 supports this statement?

(b) An alternative way of measuring inflation is to consider how the pound loses real value over time. Thus, taking £1 in 1965 as the basis for comparison, this was worth 47.6p in 1975, 15.9p in 1985 and just 9.6p in 1995.
   ◆ Explain how inflation and the real domestic value of a currency are related.
   ◆ In which ten-year period between 1965 and 1995 did UK prices rise most rapidly? Explain your answer.

(c) Use the information in table 2 to compare the UKs inflation performance with that of other countries.

Adapted from OCR Modular A Level Economics, The National Economy, 4382, June 1998.

3 Read the case study below and answer the questions which follow.

	Treasury forecasts				Average latest independent forecast for 2000
	What happened in 1998	Nov. 1998 forecast for 1999	Yesterday's forecast for 1999	Yesterday's forecast for 2000	
Economic growth (GDP)	2.25	1 to 1.5	1 to 1.5	2.25 to 2.75	1.8
Balance of payments (current account £bn)	−2.25	−7.5	−10	−10.5	−6.8
RPI	2.5	2.5	2.5	2.5	2.1

Gordon Brown is braced for a rise in unemployment of around 250,000 this year as the recession in manufacturing is set to deepen.

But the Chancellor has stuck to his prediction of a soft landing for the economy as a whole despite the global downturn according to the Treasury's new economic forecast.

In recognition of the bleak outlook for exports, the current account forecast has been revised to show a deficit of £10bn this year and £10.25bn in 2000 against £7bn and £8.75bn in the pre-budget report.

Although the economy is expected to avoid a recession, Mr Brown is basing his public spending plans on a rise in unemployment to 1.55 million by the end of this year from 1.305 million at the moment.

The figure for the end of 1999 is one cited by independent forecasters as the most likely outcome given the slowdown in growth predicted for this year and it is endorsed by the National Audit Office as a realistic basis for planning social security expenditure.

Source: 'Mark Atkinson on the great unmentionable at the heart of the Chancellor's speech', 'The Guardian', 10 March 1999.

(a) How did the Treasury's March 1999 current account forecast compare with its November forecast for 1999?

(b) Was the state of the UK economy predicted to improve or worsen in 2000? Explain your answer.

(c) Did independent forecasters view the prospects for the UK economy more or less favourably than the Treasury? Explain your answer.

(d) Discuss the effects on economic growth, inflation and the balance of payments on current account of a greater than anticipated rise in unemployment.

4 Study the article below and then answer the questions which follow:

Quality of life gets a higher profile

A radical move to extend the yardstick of progress from economic output alone to quality-of-life measures, such as education, pollution, and even the number of birds in the countryside, was yesterday unveiled by the government.

A series of 13 new headline indicators [see below] intended to reflect everyday concerns will for the first time allow the government's performance to be judged not only by growth rates but by the effect of policies on the environment and social welfare.

Launching the indicators yesterday, the Deputy Prime Minister, John Prescott, said, 'Sustainable development links the standard of living and the quality of life, not just in Britain, but right across the world.'

Charles Secrett, executive director of Friends of the Earth, said, 'Often policy has been driven by the idea that more is always better...'

The 13 quality of life indicators:

Economic growth: Total output of the economy. Standard measure is gross domestic product (GDP). Since 1970 output has increased by 80 per cent in real terms.

Social investment: Measures investment in 'public assets' such as railways, buses, roads, hospitals, schools, water and sewerage. Accounts for 10 per cent of all capital spending and about 2 per cent of GDP.

Employment: Income enables individuals to improve living standards. Since 1994, the employment rate has increased slowly to 73 per cent of the population of working age.

Health: Average life expectancy is now around 74 years for men and 79 for women, but the time people can expect to live in good health is some years less.

Education and training: Based on qualifications at age 19.

Housing quality: Measures numbers of homes unfit to live in. In 1996, the private rented sector had the highest proportion of unfit stock – 15.1 per cent.

Climate change: Based on greenhouse gas emissions. UK emissions of the 'basket' of greenhouse gas fell by 5 per cent between 1990 and 1996.

Air pollution: In urban areas, the average number of days when pollution was recorded as moderate or worse fell from 62 days in 1993 to 40 in 1997.

Transport: Motor vehicle traffic in 1997 was more than eight times the level in 1950, and car traffic was over 14 times higher.

Water quality: According to number of rivers of good or fair quality – currently 95 per cent of UK river network.

Wildlife: Based on population of wild birds – regarded as a good indicator of wildlife and the health of the wider environment. Populations of farmland and woodland birds have been in decline since the mid 1970s.

Land use: New homes built on previously developed land. In England, about 55 per cent of homes are built on brownfield sites, against a government target of 60 per cent by 2008.

Waste: An estimated 145 million tonnes of waste are produced in the UK each year, of which over 60 per cent are disposed of in landfill sites.

Typical 1960s high-rise flats – now often unpopular with those who live in them

Source: Lucy Ward, *The Guardian*, 24 November 1998 (adapted).

(a) What do you think is meant by 'sustainable development'?

(b) Does more growth always mean that 'things get better'?

(c) What evidence is there in the comments on the 13 quality of life indices that social welfare may have improved in recent years?

(d) Discuss two additional quality of life indicators you would like to see added.

Macroeconomic problems

In managing the economy, governments are acutely aware of the problems that can arise when (say):

◆ the rate of inflation is higher than they would like;

◆ there is a recession and the rate of unemployment is excessive;

◆ there is a surge of imported goods into the country.

Such problems as these have consequences for the economy as a whole. In managing these problems, though, the dilemma governments face is that not all of their stated policy objectives can be achieved simultaneously. Choices and priorities must therefore be established.

For many years, economists and governments took it for granted that a high rate of economic growth was a very appropriate objective to follow. Growth does of course bring many benefits; it should also be recognised that when not managed effectively, a high rate of growth is not without its costs. Issues such as these will be discussed in the remainder of this section.

Consequences of inflation

The effects of inflation depend on:

◆ the rate at which it is rising;

◆ whether the rate is accelerating or stable;

◆ whether the rate is the one which had been expected;

◆ how the rate compares with that in other countries.

The inflation rate

An inflation rate of 20 per cent is likely to cause more problems than an inflation rate of, say, 2 per cent because money will be losing its purchasing power at a rapid rate. A very high rate of inflation is known as **hyperinflation**. When this occurs people will lose confidence in money and may even go back to barter.

In Germany between 1913 and 1923 the price level rose 755,700 million times and people switched from using cash to using cigarettes to buy goods. More recently in Georgia in 1994 when inflation reached 15,000 per cent, a wheelbarrow was needed to carry enough money to purchase a loaf of bread.

Hyperinflation can also cause political instability. People become dissatisfied with the government's failure to control the high rise in prices and may look to parties offering radical solutions to the problem. Even less dramatic inflation rates of, say, 10 per cent can cause problems. People who are on a fixed income or on an income which does not rise as fast as inflation will experience a fall in their purchasing power.

High rates of inflation also mean that people and companies may lose considerable purchasing power if they keep money lying idle and not earning interest. Economists refer to **shoe leather costs**. These are the costs involved in moving money from one financial asset to another in search of the highest rate of interest. The term can also be applied to firms and consumers spending more time searching out the lowest prices.

Inflation makes it more difficult to assess what is happening to the price of goods and services. A rise in the price of a good may now not mean that it has become more expensive relative to other goods – indeed it may have risen by less than inflation and so have become relatively cheaper. This tendency for inflation to confuse price signals is referred to as inflationary noise. It can result in consumers and producers making the wrong decisions. For example, producers seeing the price of their good rising may increase output when this higher price is the result of inflation rather than increased demand. This will result in the misallocation of resources.

Firms will also suffer from menu costs. These are the costs involved in changing prices. For example, catalogues, price tags, bar codes and advertisements have to be changed. This involves staff time and is unpopular with customers.

Whilst there are clear disadvantages of a high rate of inflation there can be advantages of a low, stable rate of inflation of, say, 2 per cent. If the rise in the general price level is caused by increasing aggregate demand firms can feel optimistic about the future. They will also benefit if prices rise by more than costs since this will mean that profits will increase.

Inflation may also stimulate consumption. This is because real interest rates may be low or even negative as the nominal rate of interest does not tend to rise in line with inflation. So debt burdens may fall and people may be able and encouraged to spend more. For example, those who have borrowed money to buy a house may experience a fall in their mortgage interest payments in real terms. At the same time the price of their house is likely to rise by more than inflation, which may make them feel better off, and so they may spend more.

The existence of inflation may also help firms which need to reduce costs to survive. For most firms the major cost is wages. With zero inflation firms may have to cut their labour force. However, inflation would enable them to reduce the real costs of labour by either keeping nominal (money) wages constant or not raising them in line with inflation. During inflation workers with strong bargaining power are more likely to be able to resist cuts in their real wages than workers who lack bargaining power.

Accelerating versus stable inflation

An accelerating inflation rate is likely to have more serious consequences than a stable rate. If, for example, inflation three years ago was 5 per cent, two years ago was 8 per cent and last year was 15 per cent, people and firms will be likely to expect a further rise in inflation. The way they react is likely to bring about what they fear. For example, workers may press for higher wages, firms may raise prices to cover expected higher costs and consumers may seek to purchase goods now before their prices rise further. Accelerating, or indeed fluctuating, inflation will also cause uncertainty and may discourage firms from undertaking investment. The

need to devote more staff and effort to estimating future inflation will also increase administration costs. Whereas if inflation is stable it will be easier to predict future inflation and hence easier to plan and protect people from the harmful effects.

Self-assessment task

The rate of inflation in France was reported to have been 8 per cent in 1996. Explain what this figure means and how it might have been calculated.

UCLES, Modular A Level Economics, The National Economy, 4382, June 1997.

Anticipated versus unanticipated inflation

Anticipated inflation is when the rise in the general price level is the one, or close to the one, expected. If firms, workers, consumers and the government have correctly predicted the inflation rate then, as mentioned above, they can take measures to avoid the harmful effects. For example, firms can adjust their prices, nominal interest rates can be changed to maintain real interest rates if considered desirable, consumers may be able to distinguish between changes in the general price level and relative prices, and the government can adjust tax thresholds and index-linked pensions, benefits and civil servants' pay (that is adjust them upwards in line with inflation).

In contrast unanticipated inflation occurs when inflation was either not expected or is higher than had been expected.

Unanticipated inflation can bring with it a number of problems. As people and firms have been caught unawares they are likely to be uncertain about future inflation. This can result in a fall in consumption and investment.

Fiscal drag may also occur. With no adjustment of tax thresholds, higher nominal pay will drag incomes into higher tax bands and workers' disposable real income will fall.

There can also be an arbitrary redistribution of income. Borrowers tend to gain and lenders to lose. This is because nominal interest rates usually rise more slowly than the inflation rate. So real interest rates often fall with inflation. Indeed in some years they have been negative.

Income may also be transferred from the old to the young as the former tend to be net savers whilst the latter tend to be net borrowers. It is also because, whilst state pensions are raised in line with inflation, they fall behind wages, which usually rise at a faster rate than inflation.

International price competitiveness

Inflation may make a country's goods less price competitive. This may result in balance of payments problems. Consumers at home and abroad may switch away from buying the country's goods and services, which may cause a deficit to arise or get larger in the trade in goods and the trade in services sections. The uncertainty that arises from inflation may also discourage financial and capital investment in the country.

In a **floating exchange rate** system, a fall in demand for a country's goods and services and a reduction in the inflow of investment from abroad will reduce the exchange rate. This in turn will lower export prices and, at least initially, restore price competitiveness. However, there is danger that a vicious cycle will develop with inflation causing a lower exchange rate which in turn results in higher import prices, cost–push inflation and then a fall in the exchange rate. Also, if the root cause of the inflation is not tackled, it will continue.

However, inflation will not necessarily have adverse effects on the country's international trade position. If the country's inflation rate is below that of its main competitors, its goods and services will become more price competitive. In addition, if a country's goods and services were originally cheaper than their rivals, even with a higher inflation rate they may still be at a lower price.

It also has to be remembered that, whilst price is an important influence on demand, it is not the only one. A country may be able to sustain its output and sales at home and abroad even with inflation if the quality of its goods and services is rising or if, for example, its marketing is improving.

Consequences of unemployment

The consequences of unemployment will depend on its rate and duration. A high rate of unemployment will tend to have more significant effects than a low one. However, the length of time which people are unemployed also has to be considered. An unemployment rate of say 12 per cent with an average duration of two months will have less serious consequences than a 6 per cent unemployment rate which lasts on average for a year. Unemployment will have consequences not only for the unemployed themselves but also for firms and the economy.

Consequences for the unemployed

There may be some benefits of being unemployed. It may encourage those who are unemployed to reassess their career objectives and provide them with the time to search for a job which may be better paid and/or which they may enjoy more. It may also provide them with more time to pursue their leisure activities. However, whilst they may have the time, they will lack the income. Indeed, for most, any advantages of being unemployed are likely to be outweighed by the disadvantages.

Most of the unemployed will experience a fall in income. The amount they receive from benefits is likely to be lower than the amount they were earning when in work. This fall in income will lower their living standards and can make people more prone to certain forms of physical illness. In addition the loss of status and the stress involved can lead to mental illnesses and the break-up of relationships.

The longer someone is unemployed, the more they will miss out on training, changes in technology and changes in work practices. The chances of regaining employment diminish as the duration of unemployment increases.

Consequences for firms

If unemployment is high the demand for a firm's goods and services will be relatively low. High unemployment may also reduce workers' morale, which in turn may reduce labour productivity.

However, some firms may gain some benefits from unemployment. They may find it easier to recruit staff and the people applying for jobs may possess higher

One of the many 'drop-in' centres where the unemployed can get help in obtaining work

Self-assessment task

Discuss why a government might allow significant levels of unemployment to exist.

Adapted from UCLES, Modular A Level Economics, The National Economy, 4382, June 1996.

skills. The existence of unemployment may make workers fearful of losing their jobs. As a result they may reduce their wage claims, be more willing to agree to adopt flexible working practices and be more reluctant to take industrial action.

Consequences for the economy

The most significant disadvantage of unemployment is the opportunity cost involved. Having people out of work means that output and hence living standards are lower than they could be. The output is lost for all time. Even if unemployment falls next year, the output can never be regained.

Higher unemployment increases government expenditure on unemployment-related benefits, health and possibly the police force whilst it reduces revenue from direct and indirect taxes. Crime levels may increase with some of the unemployed feeling disaffected from society. A positive correlation has been found between unemployment rates in young men and crime levels.

The distribution of income will become more uneven and, if the rise in unemployment is not evenly spread, regional differences will increase.

There are few benefits of unemployment for the economy, which is why governments usually seek to keep unemployment at a low level. However unemployment provides some slack which can permit the economy to expand. Some economists also claim that the existence of unemployment can put downward pressure on inflation by reducing wage claims and limiting increases in aggregate demand (see section 8).

Consequences of instability of exchange rates

Countries, or groups of countries, may operate fixed, managed or floating exchange rate systems. A **fixed exchange rate** system is one determined by the government or international body. The rate is maintained by the purchase and sale of the currency and by changes in interest rates. A **managed exchange rate** system is usually one in which the exchange rate is permitted to move within bands. A floating exchange rate is one which is determined by market forces and which varies with changes in the demand and supply of the currency. In a floating exchange rate system there is a risk of frequent and large changes in the value of the currency. Speculation on changes in the value of currencies and interest rates can result in large changes in demand and supply of the currency and hence the exchange rate (see section 10 also).

Planning problems

Frequent changes in the exchange rate may create a number of problems. Firms will find it difficult to plan if there are frequent changes in the price of exports and imports, particularly if these fluctuations are unpredictable. They will be uncertain about how much they will earn from export sales and how much they will have to spend on imported raw materials and components. To overcome this uncertainty they may seek to agree in advance the price at which they will buy or sell the currency.

Effect on international trade

Frequent changes may even discourage firms from engaging in international trade. If they are worried about how much they will earn from exporting they may decide to concentrate on the home market. This will reduce their potential market and hence their opportunity to take advantage of economies of scale. Uncertainty about the amount that will have to be paid for imports may mean that the highest quality raw materials and components may not be purchased.

Effect on productive potential

The uncertainty created may also reduce investment. This will have consequences for current output and for future economic growth. The productive potential of the economy may also be reduced as a result of firms going out of business when the exchange rate is high.

The ratchet effect

Changes in the exchange rate can push up costs of production and cause inflation. When the exchange rate goes down import prices rise and this increases the cost of living. As a result workers may press for wage rises. If these are awarded the price level will rise further. In contrast, when the exchange rate goes up and import prices fall workers do not ask for a wage cut. This tendency for exchange rate movements to move the price level in only one direction is known as the **ratchet effect**.

Self-assessment task

Plot the movements in the value of the £ sterling against another major currency such as the $US or DM over the last year and discuss the likely consequences of fluctuations in its value.

Consequences of a balance of payments deficit

The effects of a balance of payments deficit will depend on

◆ its size;
◆ its duration;
◆ its cause.

The size and duration

A deficit will mean that more money is leaving the country than entering it. This will reduce the country's money supply and may also reduce inflationary pressure as there will be less money to spend on more goods and services. The country's citizens will enjoy more goods and services than the country is producing. However it will mean that the country is adding more to the demand and hence output and employment of other

countries than to its own demand, output and employment. It also means that the country will be getting into debt with other countries.

However these may not be serious problems if the deficit is small and/or is of short duration. If a deficit is relatively quickly followed by a surplus, some of this can be used to repay any debt and it may indicate that there are no fundamental problems in the economy.

Cause

A deficit which arises as a result of an increase in imports of raw materials may be self correcting. When the raw materials are converted into finished goods at least some are likely to be exported.

A deficit may also arise because of cyclical factors. When income levels are rising demand for goods and services will increase. More imports are likely to be purchased and goods and services, originally intended for the export market, may be diverted to the buoyant home market.

More significant is a deficit caused by structural problems. There may be fundamental weaknesses in the economy, which means that foreign goods and services are more attractive than domestic ones. For instance, the quality of the domestic goods and services may be low, they may not be price competitive, after sales service and marketing may be poor and the country may be making goods and services which are not in high domestic nor world demand.

With a floating exchange rate, a deficit would result in a fall in the value of the currency. However, without measures being taken to make the domestic goods and services more attractive, the deficit will reappear again and the country's output and employment are likely to be below their potential levels.

Benefits and costs of economic growth
Benefits

The main benefit of economic growth is the increase in goods and services which become available for the country's citizens to enjoy. This raises their material living standards. If you have difficulty in believing this, ask your parents what life was like when they were your age!

Economic growth also makes it easier to help the poor. Without any increase in output and income, the only way in which the living standards of the poor can be raised is by taking income and hence goods and services from higher income groups. Whereas if economic growth occurs at least some of the extra income can be given to the poor in the form of higher benefits, thereby enabling them to enjoy more goods and services.

A stable level of economic growth increases firms' and consumers' confidence. This makes planning easier and encourages investment. Economic growth may also increase a country's international prestige and power. For example, China's rapid growth in the early 1990s increased its status in world politics.

Costs

Economic growth may bring with it a number of costs. If the economy is operating at the full employment level there will be an opportunity cost involved in achieving economic growth. To produce more capital goods, in order to increase the country's productive capacity, some resources will have to be moved from producing consumer goods to producing capital goods. So current consumption of goods and services will have to be reduced. However, this will only be a short-run cost since in the long run the increased investment will increase the output of consumer goods and services.

Economic growth may also bring increased stress and anxiety. A growing economy is a dynamic economy with changes in the structure of the economy. Workers may have to learn new skills and may have to change their occupation and/or where they live. Some workers may find this difficult to cope with. Economic growth may also be accompanied by increased working hours and pressure to come up with new ideas and improvements. When Japan was growing rapidly in the 1980s some workers put in very long hours and students felt under considerable pressure to pass examinations.

Economic growth may also be accompanied by the depletion of natural resources and damage to the environment. Higher output may, for example, involve firms using more oil, building on green field sites and creating more pollution. However, this does not have to be the case. Output can be increased in ways which do not damage the environment.

Sustainable economic growth

Very rapid growth may be achieved but this may be at the expense of the living standards of future generations if it results from the reckless use of resources. Countries are now becoming more concerned to achieve **sustainable economic growth**. This occurs when output increases in a way which means that increases in output can continue into the future. Materials such as aluminium, paper and glass can be recycled. More use could be made of renewable energy resources in preference to non-renewable resources and improvements in technology may increase both output and reduce pollution.

Conflicts in macroeconomic policy objectives

Government policy objectives may not be compatible. A government wishing to raise employment may seek to increase aggregate (total) demand. Higher demand is likely to encourage firms to expand output. As well as reducing unemployment this will also accelerate the rate of economic growth. However the higher demand may lead to demand–pull inflation. The increase in spending may also result in more imports being purchased, and goods and services being diverted from the export market to the home market. To reduce inflationary pressure and correct a deficit on the current account a government may seek to restrain or reduce aggregate demand. This tendency for governments to seek to expand economic activity and then, when their other objectives are threatened, to limit it is sometimes referred to as a **stop–go policy** – although a more appropriate term might be a 'go–stop policy'.

As policy aims can conflict, a government may have to decide, at any particular time, what is its priority. To achieve its key aim or aims it may be prepared to sacrifice other objectives. For example if unemployment is very high a government may be prepared to raise aggregate demand even if it means a rise in the inflation rate. It is prepared to trade off higher inflation for lower unemployment.

Due to the difficulty of achieving a number of objectives a government may follow Tinbergen's rule, which states that a different policy instrument should be employed to achieve each objective.

Self-assessment tasks

1 Discuss which government macro-economic objective is currently receiving the highest priority.

2 The following question is adapted from UCLES, National Economy, 4382, June 1996.

Country	Trade in goods 1993 $bn	Balance of payments on current account 1993 $bn	1995 forecasts		
			Balance of payments on current account (% of GDP)	% change in retail prices	% change in real GDP
UK	−19	−12	−2.1	3.7	3.2
France	+16	+13	0.6	1.8	2.9
Germany	+43	−22	−0.6	2.2	2.1
Italy	+19	+8	1.5	3.5	2.5
Japan	+143	+132	2.2	0.7	2.1
USA	−147	−116	−1.9	3.5	3.0

(a) How is the trade in goods balance calculated?

(b) Compare the current account of payments of the UK in 1993 with those of Japan and Germany.

(c) Compare the forecast performance of the UK economy in 1995 with those of the other five countries shown in the table.

3 Read the following and answer the questions that follow.

Economic activity in France has continued to strengthen, with GDP rising by 0.5 per cent in the third quarter of last year to a level of 2.8 per cent higher than a year earlier. Domestic demand has been strong, although there are some signs that growth may be about to slow, with new orders having begun to weaken, particularly from abroad.

There are few signs of any inflationary pressure. Consumer prices in the fourth quarter were unchanged from those in the third, with the annual inflation rate declining to 0.3 per cent by the year end, the lowest since 1954. The annual rate of growth in the consumer price index dropped to 0.2 per cent in November.

Over the year to the third quarter of 1998 total exports increased by 5.4 per cent, whilst total imports rose by 6.6 per cent supported by robust domestic demand. Over the first three quarters of 1998, it is estimated that exports to the Asian economies were some 32.2 per cent lower than a year earlier.

Total employment rose by 0.5 per cent in the third quarter of last year, to a level 2.3 per cent higher than a year earlier. Nearly all the new jobs created have been in the services sector. The unemployment rate fell by 1 percentage point to 11.5 per cent over the year to November, reaching the lowest level since 1995.

Source: Extracts from 'Prospects for the Euro Area', by R. Barrell, N. Pain, F. Hubert, D. te Velde, D. Holland and V. Genre, *National Institute Economic Review*, 167, January 1999, pp. 61–3.

(a) Define the following terms:
- GDP;
- consumer price index;
- inflationary pressure.

(b) Explain what is meant by a slowdown in economic growth.

(c) Discuss the advantages and disadvantages of an inflation rate of 0.3 per cent.

(d) Explain how the rise in the unemployment rate could have been greater than the fall in the unemployment rate.

4 The following question is adapted from UCLES, National Economy, 4382, June 1995.

Jobless total falls as Britain 'bucks European trend'

Unemployment in the UK fell by 13,600 in September 1993 to 2.91m, 10.3 per cent of the working population. This was the sixth time in 1993 that a monthly fall has been recorded, and the seasonally adjusted trend suggests that it may well continue to fall throughout the winter, which is relatively unusual. The

Employment Secretary, David Hunt, said 'Britain is bucking the trend. While unemployment continues to rise generally across Europe, unemployment in the UK is falling and is now below the EC average.' The latest unemployment figures were welcomed by the government after recent disappointing news about a rise in inflation to 1.8 per cent.

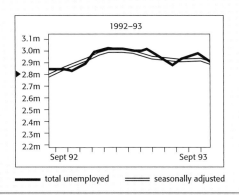

(a) How is unemployment officially measured in the UK?

(b) Give one reason why the official figure may understate the actual level of unemployment and one reason why it might overstate it.

(c) What might have been the opportunity cost to society of rising unemployment between 1990 and 1993?

(d) Comment upon the apparent relationship between changes in the level of unemployment and changes in the rate of inflation between September 1992 and September 1993.

5 Read the following and answer the questions that follow.

The current crisis can be traced back to the adoption of the anti-inflationary Real Plan in July 1994, although Brazilian policymakers have been struggling to achieve macroeconomic stabilisation through a series of anti-inflationary programmes since the mid 1980s. The Real Plan which linked the real to the US dollar in a gently crawling peg exchange rate regime, was extremely successful in achieving a

sustained reduction in inflation, which was rising at an annual average rate of 2,500 per cent before the Plan was introduced. Inflation fell sharply, reaching single digits after two years, and maintained this downward trend until the recent devaluation. Moreover, also unlike its predecessors, the Plan's rapid reduction in inflation was achieved in the context of relatively strong positive GDP growth.

Source: 'The Brazilian Debacle', *Lloyds Bank Economic Bulletin*, No. 25, February 1999.

	Consumer prices % increase on a year earlier	Balance of payments on current account $bn	GDP % change on a year earlier
1993	2,489	−2	4.8
1998	17	−36	0.4

(a) Explain what is meant by macroeconomic stabilisation.

(b) Discuss the benefits which Brazilians may have experienced as a result of the fall in the inflation rate from 1993 to 1998.

(c) A 'crawling peg exchange rate regime' is a form of fixed exchange rate system which allows some movement. What are the benefits of exchange rate stability?

(d) Compare the state of the Brazilian economy in 1998 with that in 1993 and discuss what other information would be useful in making such an assessment.

Summary

In this section we have recognised that:

- The four main government policy objectives are low unemployment, low and stable inflation, a satisfactory balance of payments position and steady economic growth.

- Among the indicators of a country's economic performance are its growth rate, its inflation rate, its unemployment rate and its balance of payments position.

- Production is output whereas productivity is output per factor of production.

- Economic growth is measured in terms of percentage annual increases in GDP.

- GDP is measured by the output, income and expenditure methods.

- Real GDP is nominal (money) GDP adjusted for inflation.

- Countries with high inflation may experience problems in competing on price with other countries.

- Various measures of inflation are used by economists.

- The main cost of unemployment is foregone output.

- The three main sections of the balance of payments are the current account, the capital account and the financial account. The section which receives the most attention is the current account.

- A deficit on the current account may indicate a lack of price or quality competitiveness.

- A whole range of indicators can be used to assess the international competitiveness of an economy relative to those of others.

- The effects of inflation on an economy depend on the rate, whether it is fluctuating or stable, whether the rate has been anticipated or not and its rate relative to that of other countries.

- High, unstable, accelerating and unanticipated inflation will involve more costs than low, stable, declining and anticipated inflation.

- Low and stable inflation may bring advantages including encouraging producers to increase output and permitting real wages to be adjusted downwards.

- The effects of unemployment will depend on its rate and duration.

- The costs of unemployment for the economy include lost output, lost government revenue and increased expenditure on benefits.

- Instability of exchange rates creates uncertainty, makes planning more difficult, may discourage international trade, may cause inflation and may lead to upward or downward spirals.

- The effects of a balance of payments deficit depend on its size, its duration and its cause. A deficit is particularly serious where this is caused by structural weakness in the economy.

- Economic growth increases material living standards and makes it easier to help the poor but may involve some costs.

- Policy conflicts may occur with unemployment and economic growth benefiting from increases in aggregate demand whilst higher aggregate demand may cause inflation and a balance of payments deficit.

Key words

Definitions of Key words can be found in the Glossary on page 240.

aggregate demand	fiscal drag	living standard	real GDP
anticipated inflation	fixed exchange rate	managed exchange rate	shoe leather costs of
balance of payments	floating exchange rate	net errors and omissions	inflation
black economy	government spending	nominal GDP	stop–go policy
capital account	Gross Domestic Product	non-marketed goods and	sustainable economic
circular flow of income	Gross National Product	services	growth
current account	hyperinflation	output	transfer payments
economic growth	imports	output gap	unanticipated inflation
exchange rate	income method	output method	unemployment
expenditure method	inflation	potential growth	value added
exports	international	productivity	
financial account	competitiveness	ratchet effect	

8 Aggregate demand and aggregate supply

By the end of this section you should be able to:

➤ define aggregate demand

➤ explain why the AD curve slopes down from left to right

➤ describe the main components of AD and explain what determines each of them

➤ account for why the AD curve in an economy shifts outwards or inwards

➤ define aggregate supply

➤ distinguish between the short-run and long-run aggregate supply curve

➤ explain why AS curves may shift

➤ explain what is meant by equilibrium in the macroeconomy and how the equilibrium output and price level is determined

➤ analyse how the equilibrium is affected by changes in aggregate demand and aggregate supply

➤ show a broad awareness of the multiplier effect and the concept of leakages and injections

➤ use AD and AS analysis to illustrate the macroeconomic problems in an economy

Introduction

Economists often disagree, particularly when it involves macroeconomic policy issues. This section provides an introduction to the basic workings of the economy and, in so doing, provides a perspective on one of the most controversial areas of economic policy, namely whether the economy is best managed through the application of demand-side or supply-side policies. Central to this debate is the role of government in managing the economy.

The traditional view, advocated by J. M. Keynes over 60 years ago and applied for many years in the UK, is that governments must intervene in the affairs of the economy if the objectives stated in section 7 are to be met. The management of aggregate demand through both **fiscal** and **monetary policies** (see section 9) is crucial to achieving full employment, low inflation, balance of payments stability and economic growth. Other economists, especially since the election of Mrs Thatcher's Conservative government in 1979, have taken a different view. Their belief is that macroeconomic objectives can be best met when the economy is allowed to function naturally, with little interference from government. In other words, the forces of aggregate demand and **aggregate supply** combined will allow the

John Maynard Keynes, the creator of modern macroeconomics

139

market economy to operate in the most effective way to allow governments to meet their objectives for the macroeconomy. **Supply-side policies**, which focus explicitly on managing the total amount of output in the economy, are combined with policies which manage aggregate demand, in order to provide the most appropriate ways of allowing governments to meet their macroeconomic objectives. This particular approach is the one which will be applied in this section and in section 9. In order to understand its operation and relevance, it is first necessary to establish and define its basic parameters.

Aggregate demand

Aggregate demand is the term used by economists to denote the total spending on goods and services produced in an economy. It consists of four elements:

◆ consumer spending (*C*),
◆ investment expenditure (*I*),
◆ government spending (*G*),
◆ net expenditure on exports and imports (*X–M*),

and is usually represented by means of the following expression:

$$AD = C + I + G + (X - M)$$

Figure 8.1 shows a typical aggregate demand curve. In certain respects this is very similar to the demand curves introduced in section 2. It is for example downward sloping. The axes of this graph are of course different –

real GDP is shown on the horizontal axis and the average price level is on the vertical axis. Any point on the AD curve therefore shows total real GDP required in an economy at a specific overall price level. Because the curve relates to *real* GDP, it takes into account the effects of inflation. Unlike the demand curves seen in section 2, though, the downward-sloping nature of the curve cannot be explained by inflationary changes.

There are three main reasons why the AD curve is downward sloping. These are:

1 Exports of goods and services are likely to be greater if the domestic price level is lower, as long as there is no compensating adjustment in the exchange rate to offset the lower price level. In addition, imports are likely to appear more expensive in these circumstances. Consequently, domestic demand may switch from imported commodities to home-produced ones, so increasing aggregate demand. The international economy is highly competitive and those economies with a low and stable rate of inflation may find it easier to sell their products in their own domestic markets. For example, in such circumstances, a Rover car made in the UK is likely to appear cheaper than a Volkswagen made in Germany, so demand for UK-produced cars may remain strong. Exchange rate fluctuations though may often have a more important bearing on this particular factor, often wiping out the benefits of low domestic inflation.

2 It is fair to assume that a reasonable proportion of domestic consumers possess a stock of wealth, in the form of savings in banks and building societies and holdings of stocks and shares. If the overall price level were to fall it would mean that this wealth would be capable of being used to buy an increased quantity of goods and services. People would feel better off. When this occurs there will be a tendency for them to go out and buy more, so the aggregate demand increases. Essentially this argument supposes that peoples' savings are for a 'rainy' day in the future – such as wanting to buy a new car or a house, or keeping a stock of money in case they need to go into a nursing home when they become elderly. When the price level is lower their savings or wealth has a greater real value. It seems less essential either to keep so much money in the bank, or to save quite as much of their income as they have been doing. So consumers' expenditure and aggregate demand will be greater.

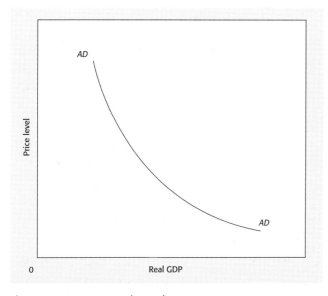

Figure 8.1 An aggregate demand curve

3 The third rationale for a downward-sloping demand curve again relates to consumers, but this time concerns their expectations of movements of prices. If the present price level is low it seems reasonable to expect that in the future prices will increase. If it is possible, it makes sense to buy goods and services now, while they are cheap, rather than wait until they become more expensive. As long as commodities are desired, and people can store them if necessary, demand will be higher when the price level is low but expected to rise in the future. Similarly, if the price level is high but expected to fall, demand will be low because people will hold off their purchases as long as possible until prices have fallen.

These three ideas, based on exports, wealth and price expectations, provide a sufficient reason to expect the aggregate demand curve to slope downwards from left to right.

Using aggregate demand curves

The use of AD curves follows a similar approach to the discussion of microeconomic curves in section 2. There are some circumstances that lead to movements along the AD curve, and some that cause shifts in the AD curve. Movements along the AD curve were discussed earlier above when considering the rationale for its downward slope. Three basic reasons were given for the curve sloping down from left to right. If the basic circumstances underlying those causal factors alter then there will be shifts of the AD curve. For example, if the world economy moves into a boom there will be a boost to UK exports at any given price level, and the AD curve may be said to shift to the right. On the other hand, if a tax on wealth holdings is imposed so that stocks of monetary assets fall dramatically, then the AD curve may be said to shift to the left. If, at any given price level, consumers' price expectations alter then the AD curve will shift (figure 8.2).

On the other hand, more dramatic changes in aggregate demand may arise from changes in the underlying constituents of aggregate demand – that is, consumer spending, investment, government spending, exports and imports. To see the factors that may cause changes in these categories it is necessary to briefly consider their underlying determinants. Let us look at each in turn.

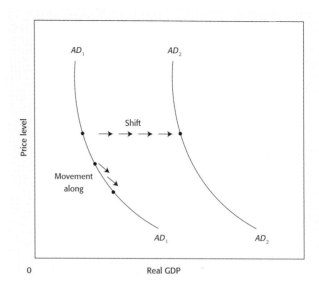

Figure 8.2 Shifts of and movements along the aggregate demand curve

Determinants of consumer spending

Consumer spending (or consumers' expenditure as it is more technically known) is the most important component of aggregate demand. It is the amount of money spent by individuals on goods such as food, clothing, drink, cars, personal computers, housing, travel, entertainment and so on. A key determinant of consumer spending is the level of income or, more correctly, the level of disposable income (income after the payment of compulsory direct taxes and social security contributions). It is very obvious that as one's income level increases so too does spending on the above items. For the economy as a whole, therefore, an increase in the level of income will lead to an increase in consumer spending.

This is though a great simplification. What is often important is the marginal propensity to consume (mpc) – that is, the proportion of any increase in income that is spent on consumption. The general belief is that at low levels of living any increase in incomes is taken up entirely on increased consumption – the mpc is 100 per cent. That is, if you are very poor additional funds are likely to be spent on food, clothing, shelter and other essential items. Even at living standards beyond this it is still likely that the mpc may be high – 90 per cent or so – although it will decline a little because some provision is now made for saving. However, when income levels are so high that there is general affluence people become less concerned about spending any additional income, and the mpc falls to 60–70 per cent or so. The rest of the increase in incomes is saved and adds to wealth.

But the key thing is that when incomes increase, so does consumer expenditure. In that case, the effect on the AD curve is that it shifts to the right. At any given price level, consumers have more income and demand more. Note that a key way in which consumers may receive more (or less) disposable income is through the effects of direct taxation and social security contributions. If the government raises income tax, incomes decline, consumer spending declines, and the AD curve shifts to the left.

Two further important factors affecting consumer spending are:

1 Government policies which affect the distribution of income. For example, if the government increases old age pensions and increases tax thresholds for low-income earners whilst increasing income taxes for the high-income earners, total disposable income may remain the same. Consumer spending, though, will increase, as will aggregate demand. The effect will be a shift outwards of the AD curve.

2 Interest rate changes. Some forms of consumer spending are sensitive to variations in interest rates, particularly expenditure on consumer durables and housing. Higher interest rates will deter consumer spending and require mortgage borrowers to make higher monthly repayments. Consumer spending overall falls, as does aggregate demand. Consequently, the AD curve shifts inwards.

Self-assessment task

Read the article below and then answer the questions which follow.

High points of Japan's recession

It feels like a Golden Recession. The official Japanese statistics may be dismal: the economy contracted by 1.4 per cent in the six months to September last year, new vehicle sales last month fell 24 per cent while supermarket sales figures for 1997 fell 2.8 per cent. But the streets are not filled with the homeless, high street shops are not boarded up and there is evidence of pockets of spending.

Yumino Tanaka, a 24-year office worker, recently spent Y3.5m (£16,600) on a four-wheel-drive Mitsubishi and has also taken a holiday to Hong Kong on a shopping tour. 'I didn't like the car I bought a year ago so I decided to change it for a new one', she says blithely.

Ms Tanaka is not the only one with the propensity to spend. In Shibuya, one of Tokyo's main shopping areas popular with the young, the streets are packed and there is a five-minute queue to pay for a compact disc at Tower Records.

'The young are among the few groups supporting consumption in Japan at the moment', says Ken Egusa, retail analyst at UBS in Tokyo. Those in their twenties with jobs but no dependants and teenagers who work part-time are buying personal items, including clothing, footwear and accessories, and taking trips abroad.

European luxury goods manufacturers are still experiencing steady demand. Bulgari, the up-market jewellers, for example, expects turnover for the past year to increase 26 per cent and plans to open more stores.

Although not spending as lavishly as during the economic 'bubble' of the late 1980s consumers in the top income brackets have not turned the tap off completely either, say analysts. Toshiko Binder, retail analyst at HSBC in Tokyo, says that over the past couple of years, low income households have cut their spending, while those with higher incomes seem to have been less affected by the downturn.

But spending by the rich and young has not offset the fall in consumption by the country's core spenders – people in their thirties and forties. Comprising a third of the population, they have been the main buyers of household goods, electronic equipment and cars. Faced with declining incomes and increasing uncertainty over jobs, many households have deferred spending on high priced items.

Office workers, who bought property and have mortgages – often lasting more than 30 years – have become especially cautious.

Economists warn that things could get worse, especially unemployment, now at a record high of 3.5 per cent and expected to rise. Although the government has announced cuts in income tax of Y26,000 per worker over the next month, scepticism is rising over its effectiveness in fuelling consumer demand.

Source: Emiko Terazono, *Financial Times*, 5 February 1998.

1 List all the factors mentioned in the passage that have an effect on the level of consumer spending.
2 Obtain data on the age distribution of the population in the United Kingdom and the spending patterns of different types of UK households. (Population figures are given in the Annual Abstract of Statistics and spending patterns in the Family Expenditure Survey, both published by the Office of National Statistics (ONS). Also check the ONS website.) What value are these data to an economist?
3 Do you think that consumer spending in the United Kingdom would be as difficult to boost as it seems to be in Japan?

Determinants of investment expenditure

This is a very complex area of Economics. Let us therefore look very briefly at some of the issues involved. Investment expenditure can be split into three main categories – private investment, public investment and household investment in houses, flats and other types of accommodation.

Investment by the private sector, in say a new factory or distribution centre, varies inversely with the rate of interest, the cost of borrowing money. If interest rates rise, businessmen will find that fewer projects will earn a sufficient rate of return for the investment to be profitable. In this instance, the AD curve will shift inwards. On the other hand, if interest rates fall, projects become more profitable, investment expenditure increases and the AD curve shifts outwards to the right.

Another relevant factor to consider is the role of expectations of the future. Firms often base investment plans on all sorts of external factors which might affect business well-being, such as the outcome of an impending election or England succeeding in its bid to host the World Cup in 2006. These expectations are very volatile and investment expenditure may fluctuate quite markedly, leading to shifts outwards and inwards of the AD curve.

Public investment is rather less volatile, given that on-going investment is necessary to ensure the future viability of the armed forces, the road network, hospitals, schools and other important areas of capital investment. Such investment is very much dependent on the state of the economy. For household investment in dwellings, the rate of interest has a substantial effect on mortgage payments and, in turn, on disposable income and aggregate demand.

Determinants of government spending

This element of aggregate demand mainly includes current expenditure on goods and services and spending on employment in central and local government services. It is particularly sensitive to a change in economic policy on the part of government in order to achieve their macroeconomic objectives (as stated in section 7). On a wider basis, the pattern of taxation and expenditure may be manipulated in line with political beliefs and aspirations. Changes in government spending act directly to cause a shift in the AD curve. However, as we have seen, in recent years, when government spending has been restricted in real terms, there has been little change in the AD curve as a consequence of changes in this particular component. A sudden boost in government spending would alternatively lead to an outward shift in the AD curve.

Determinants of net expenditure on exports and imports

It is quite difficult to summarise these determinants in a simple way but one key aspect is the nature of a country's resources and the structure of its industries. If a country possesses oil or cheap labour supplies, or has strength in industries, such as car manufacture or pharmaceuticals, then it will have a greater chance of being a successful exporter than if it does not. However, possession of desirable characteristics is not sufficient in itself. The industries must also be efficient and competitive in many different dimensions: good quality products, swift delivery, a steady stream of product innovations based on research and development, well-thought-out marketing campaigns, salesmen with an ability to converse in several languages and so on. All these characteristics are needed to make a success out of exports. In addition, exporting will be easier at times of a world boom than when there is a global recession.

The other key element in export success is the level of the exchange rate. If US importers are purchasing Scottish knitwear they will be offering US dollars for the goods, whereas the Scottish producers will seek to be paid in pounds sterling. There therefore needs to be some way of exchanging dollars for pounds. This is achieved through banks and other financial intermediaries, who use the foreign exchange market.

Through this market system there will arise an exchange rate of dollars for pounds. The level of the exchange rate is crucial for the exporter. The Scottish producer may be selling sweaters at £30. If the exchange rate is $1.50 for £1 the US importer will pay $45 for each sweater. If the exchange rate is $2 for £1 they will have to pay $60. Clearly, export sales will be much more difficult to achieve in the latter case. (See section 9 for details of exchange rate determination.)

Many of the factors which determine exchange rates in the modern world are beyond the power of a government to influence. International capital flows or hot money have a significant effect, as witnessed in the SE Asian currency crisis of 1997/98, when certain currencies experienced substantial depreciation in value over a very short period of time. Such unplanned and unexpected variation in the exchange rate had a major impact on trade and on most of the world's economies.

Imports of goods and services do not contribute to aggregate demand directly, but they do indirectly by diminishing its size. If imports make substantial inroads into the home market then there is less scope for domestic industry to respond to home demand. The extent to which this is possible will clearly depend upon the relative success of exports, and the factors that contribute to that success. Of these the key one will be the level of the exchange rate.

Beyond this the key element that determines imports is the overall level of demand in the economy. When GDP rises there is an automatic increase in imports. This is particularly the case for those imports that are needed for the production process. If the manufacture of cars needs steel, copper and rubber, all of which are imported, then an increase in the production of cars will require additional imports. In addition, growth in standards of living tends to increase demand for imported products, often more than proportionally so, as consumers seek greater variety and quality of commodities from other countries. It is difficult for government to resist this trend other than by manipulating the exchange rate.

Self-assessment task

Study the table below, which brings together each of the main components of aggregate demand, and then answer the questions which follow:

	£ billion			Growth rates per cent per annum	
	1980	1990	1997	1980–1990	1990–1997
Household final consumption expenditure[2]	303.7	427.4	490.6	3.5	2.0
Government expenditure on goods and services	121.9	133.0	142.9	0.9	1.0
Investment	73.9	117.8	132.4	4.7	1.7
Exports of goods and services	111.1	156.6	236.0	3.5	6.0
Imports of goods and services[4]	−104.9	−176.4	−245.2	5.3	4.8
GDP at 1995 market prices[1]	504.8	658.5	756.1	2.7	2.0

	Per cent of GDP		
	1980	1990	1997
Household final consumption expenditure[2]	60.2	64.9	64.9
Government expenditure on goods and services[3]	24.1	20.2	18.9
Investment	14.6	17.8	17.5
Exports of goods an services	22.0	23.8	31.2
Imports of goods and services[4]	−20.8	−26.8	−32.4
GDP at 1995 market prices[1]	100.0	100.0	100.0

UK gross domestic product at constant (1995) prices[1]

Notes: 1 The term 'at constant 1995 prices' means that the statisticians have tried to eliminate, as far as possible, the effects of inflation. Other ways of expressing this are to say that the data are in *real* or *volume* terms.   2 Including the expenditure of non-profit institutions serving households.   3 Individual and collective government final consumption expenditure.   4 Including the statistical discrepancy.
Source: United Kingdom National Accounts, 1998, Office for National Statistics.

1 Briefly describe how the composition of the UK's Gross Domestic Product changed between 1980 and 1997.
2 Discuss the likely reasons for the changes in composition which you have identified.
3 Suppose in 1997 the government wished to reduce aggregate demand in the UK economy. What possibilities were available to it and what problems would it have experienced in carrying out such a policy.

Aggregate supply

So far in this section we have been concerned with aggregate demand or the demand side of the economy. Let us now turn our attention to aggregate supply or the supply side of the economy.

Aggregate supply is the total output of the economy. In our modern economy this would be anything that is produced by the factors of production (as described in section 1). Aggregate supply is simply the total output of the economy at a given price level and at a given point in time.

The key factors needed to produce aggregate supply are those needed to produce any good or service. Usually there is a need for land, some input of labour and capital equipment. We must also consider the level of technology as this is a very specific input into the production of goods and services. The role of enterprise and entrepreneurship must also be included. It is, though, beyond the scope of this book to look at these key factors other than in this very cursory way. To help you grasp the idea of aggregate supply, and what factors underpin it, look at the self-assessment task below.

Self-assessment task

Consider any particular production or service activity known to you. This could be where one of your relatives or friends works, where you work or possibly somewhere you have visited from school or college. Try listing the production inputs in terms of land, labour, capital and specific forms of technological input. Also, think about some of the problems you experience in classifying inputs in this way.

The aggregate supply curve

The aggregate supply curve shows the relationship between the total quantity supplied in an economy and the price level. Given this we would expect it to resemble the supply curve introduced in the microeconomic context of section 2 and slope upwards from left to right.

We can also rationalise this picture of the supply curve quite easily, in the same way as we do for the microeconomic curve. At low price levels businessmen collectively do not feel that it is worth producing commodities, because they do not expect to be able to sell them and make a profit, or break even. As the overall price level increases, more and more businessmen feel that it is worthwhile to start producing, or produce more, and so supply expands. However, again as in the case of the individual businessman, we must expect that, in the short run at least, as supply expands it starts to meet bottlenecks and this carries on until, eventually, the economy is running at full capacity. Given the stock of land, labour, capital and entrepreneurship, it is not possible to produce any more. At this point the AS curve will become vertical. Whatever the price, only a fixed amount can be produced. On this basis, the aggregate supply curve is shown in figure 8.3. Note that the axes are the same as for an aggregate demand curve (figure 8.1) and, like all supply curves, it is upward sloping.

It is now necessary to distinguish between the short-run and long-run aggregate supply curves. Thinking

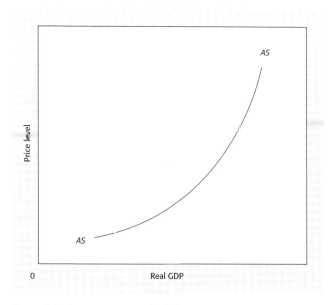

Figure 8.3 An aggregate supply (AS) curve

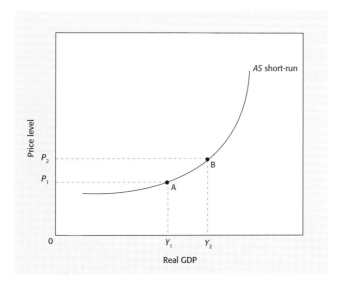

Figure 8.4 The short-run aggregate supply curve

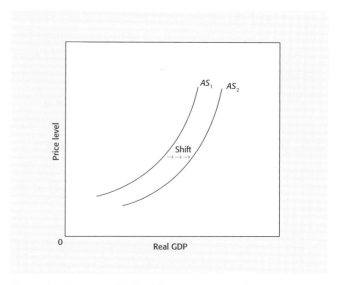

Figure 8.5 An outward shift of the aggregate supply curve

back to the factors which might affect aggregate supply, it becomes clear that almost all of them are relatively long term in nature. Any change in these factors will lead to shifts of the aggregate supply curve. In the short term, though, we are looking at a movement along the curve – this would be as a consequence of a change in the overall price level in the economy. If there is spare capacity in the economy, any increase in demand will have a much bigger effect on output than it will have on prices. Looking at figure 8.4, this is shown by the movement along the AS curve from A to B. Beyond B, though, as firms are reaching their full capacity and costs are rising, the AS curve becomes steeper. Further increases in demand will have a bigger effect on prices than output.

From a long-run standpoint there are many factors which may shift the whole of the aggregate supply curve. Some examples are:

◆ an increase in the capital stock due to a reduction in interest rates;
◆ an improvement in the expectations of businessmen;
◆ continuing technological change;
◆ increased investment in education and training;
◆ a reduction in direct taxation or unemployment benefits which may increase the incentive to work;
◆ schemes to increase the geographical mobility of workers.

In all cases the effects of such actions will be to shift the aggregate supply curve outwards, as shown in figure 8.5. The last twenty years or so have seen a strong commitment on the part of the government to create economic conditions which favour such a shift (see also section 9).

The problem is that all these actions are relatively uncertain in impact and will take a long time to have any marked effect. In addition, their use is likely to impinge on other government policies because they may involve greater government expenditure, interfere with other social objectives, involve foregoing tax revenue or reduce interest rates when other government objectives require that interest rates be raised. Consequently, government supply-side policies are intrinsically difficult to introduce, uncertain in their impact and may take a long time to have an effect. The only policies that may have a short- to medium-term impact will be changes in income tax levels and unemployment benefits and eligibility for them. However, some of these may have a 'once-and-for-all' impact. Once instituted, they will be hard to repeat.

Self-assessment task

Read the article below and then answer the questions that follow.

Investing in the school system will not pay off for decades

What's so great about education? The Government has driven home the lesson that this is its top priority, but the lecture has the ring of motherhood and apple pie. It is fair to ask, in a spirit of intelligent enquiry, how exactly education boosts the economy and how it enhances fairness and opportunity…

Like all economics, this is a tale of demand and supply; the demand for and supply of the skills needed in the workforce. Demand for skill depends upon the kind of capital equipment businesses need their employees to work with and how they work with it, so changes in demand are determined by technical developments and investment. Supply of skill depends upon the education system…

The technical changes introduced during the Industrial Revolution tended to deskill the workforce requiring factory fodder rather than artisans and craftsmen. By contrast, during the 1910s and 1920s, the spread of electricity led to a profusion of processes that required new skills, such as knowledge of chemistry and machine drawing. In addition, goods ranging from cars and radios to refrigerators and office calculators boosted the need for a wider spread of skills. The productivity gains permitted by the new technologies could not have been realised without improved education…

Goldin and Katz have recalculated the increase in the US stock of educational capital between 1910 and 1950 based on new data. They find that the increase in years of schooling of the workforce was greater than earlier work indicated. 'The increase in the US educational stock was a major contributor to American growth across much of the twentieth century. Education's role in economic

Comprehensive school that tries to meet the increasing demand of the modern educational system

growth may have been larger than previously thought,' they concluded…

The clear conclusion is that boosting the national investment in education will have the desired results. Past experience suggests a more skilled workforce does boost economic growth when technology changes in such a way that extra skills are required to make best use of it…

Unfortunately confirming the diagnosis does not make the cure easy. For instance, there is the issue of how to improve the education system and the quality of its output. The other important point is that these kinds of shift in levels of skill in the workforce take decades to achieve. If our school system improved substantially tomorrow the full effect would not show until today's infants joined the workforce in 2020.

Source: Adapted from the article by Diana Coyle in *The Independent*, 12 June 1997.

1 Summarise the arguments put forward in the article.

2 Why might improved education and training be regarded by economists as investment?

3 Use aggregate supply curves to illustrate the historical arguments being put forward in the article.

Equilibrium in the macroeconomy and the determination of output and prices

The AD/AS diagram

We are now in a position where the aggregate demand curve of figure 8.1 can be combined with the aggregate supply curve of figure 8.3. The outcome is shown in figure 8.6.

Inevitably, the AS and AD curves cross at a point, marked as P_1 and Y_1. These indicate the *equilibrium* price level and real output, in exactly the same way that microeconomic supply and demand curves cross to give

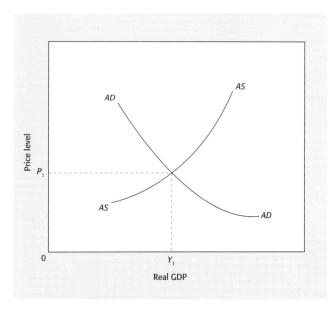

Figure 8.6 Equilibrium between AD and AS

an equilibrium price and output. The price level P_1 is the only price level which will lead suppliers to produce exactly the right output to satisfy the aggregate demand from consumers, government, overseas customers and investors in fixed capital, at that price level. At any other price level there will be an imbalance between aggregate supply and aggregate demand. If some other price level is somehow set up, then there will either be excess demand or excess supply. If price is below equilibrium there will be excess demand, but those demanding goods and services will become more willing to pay higher prices, and the price level will be bid back up towards the equilibrium. If price is above equilibrium there will be excess supply, stocks will start to build up, and suppliers will be forced to cut prices in order to sell stocks. So the price level will be forced down towards equilibrium.

Changes in aggregate demand and supply

The accepted relationship between output and employment is that, as output increases, employment also increases and unemployment falls. Particularly in the short run, this is valid although in practice by no means as simple as might be assumed. In the long run, if aggregate supply increases, the situation is complicated by the factors that cause this shift. Take for example an improvement in technology or a better-educated workforce; these may enable output to increase

without there being an increase in employment. Indeed, a firm that installs some new high-tech machinery may be likely to make some workers redundant and add to unemployment. Overall, a 10 per cent increase in output capacity caused by increased capital investment might imply only a 3 per cent increase in labour requirements and a lesser impact on unemployment. This is the reality of how the economy works although, for the time being, the accepted relationship is the one that will be assumed.

Figure 8.7 shows that a shift in aggregate demand from AD_1 to AD_2 will raise output (real GDP) but at the same time increase the price level from P_1 to P_2. This shift can be due to an increase in any one of the components of aggregate demand. For example:

♦ Consumer spending would increase if the government reduced the rate of income tax.
♦ A reduction in interest rates is likely to stimulate investment expenditure by business.
♦ The government could increase its own spending by giving more money for new teachers and textbooks.
♦ Exports could increase if our labour costs were competitive relative to some of our EU trading partners.

There are many other possibilities. The effect though is a shift of the AD curve to the right in an AD/AS diagram. If the economy is running below capacity with some unemployment, there is likely to be an increase in output and probably an increase in prices.

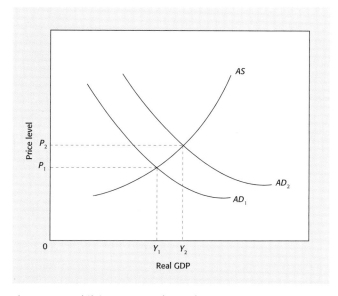

Figure 8.7 A shift in aggregate demand

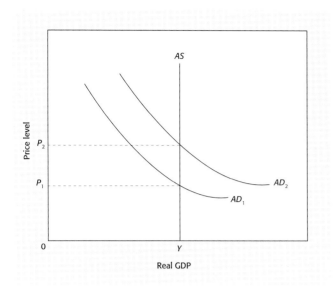

Figure 8.8 Equilibrium with a vertical AS curve

Some economists would argue that the AS curve should be vertical, indicating that any increase in aggregate demand can only increase prices. The reasoning behind this is the time it takes to move additional resources into supply following an increase in demand. They would further argue that the only way to increase output in the long run is by increasing aggregate supply, not by boosting aggregate demand (figure 8.8).

Figure 8.9 shows that an increase in aggregate supply, shown by the AS curve shifting to the right, is likely to have the general effect of leading to an increase in output and a lower price level. As mentioned earlier, the short-run impact will be very small. The longer-run effects may be more substantial but take a considerable time before they are anything other than modest in size. Factors which might be responsible for the shift in the AS curve have already been stated.

Injections and leakages and the multiplier effect

We have so far looked at aggregate demand and aggregate supply or aspects of total spending and total output in the economy. In producing this output, factors of production receive payments for their services (see section 1). In turn these payments are used to purchase the output produced by firms. This simple relationship was referred to earlier in section 7 as the circular flow of income. Figure 8.10 is a development of figure 7.1 for a simple economy.

This economy consists of households who are consumers and firms who are producers. The two flows between them are physical flows (goods and services and factor services) and monetary flows. It is assumed that all output is sold and all income is spent and that in this simple representation, there are no **injections** or **leakages**. This is unrealistic as in the modern economy there are various injections and leakages, which have to be recognised since they add or remove income from the circular flow. All have been considered at some point in this section.

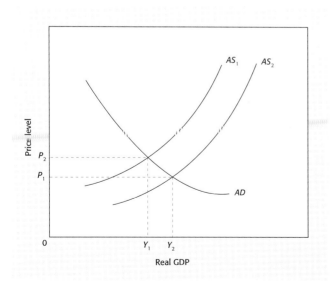

Figure 8.9 A shift in aggregate supply

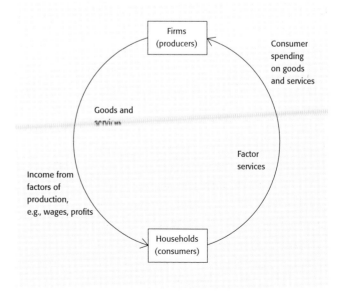

Figure 8.10 The circular flow of income and expenditure

The three injections into the circular flow of income are:

◆ *i*nvestment expenditure (I);
◆ government spending (G);
◆ exports (X).

Each represents an autonomous addition to the circular flow. Leakages, on the other hand, represent a withdrawal of income and expenditure from the circular flow and are:

◆ **savings** (S);
◆ taxation (T);
◆ imports (M).

At any one time, all of these are likely to be operating in the economy, making for a much more complex situation than might at first be obtained from the earlier analysis in this section.

It should also be recognised that changes in AD and AS may have a larger total effect on GDP than the particular tax reduction or increase in government expenditure that set it off. This is known as the **multiplier effect** and can be used to explain why say a reduction in income tax of £500m may produce an expenditure boost of £800m to the economy.

The rationalisation for this result is as follows. Suppose that government increases expenditure on health and education. This means not only that the salaries of teachers and nurses increase but also that there is new expenditure on school buildings and hospital wards, new computer facilities, new brain scanners and so on. Consequently there is a big boost to consumer spending and to investment expenditure, equal to the value of the additional government expenditure. This is known as the **first-round effect**.

However, the pattern of increased expenditure does not end there. Teachers and nurses, with increased salaries, go off to cinemas and nightclubs drink beer and whisky, and buy new curtains for the home. As a result, the cinemas, nightclubs, breweries and distilleries, curtain manufacturers and others are soon faced with increased demand. This is also true of the building industry, manufacturers of computers and brain

scanners. All these manufacturers have to increase output, which may mean employing more labour (who receive incomes) and buying in more raw materials, such as hops, cotton fabrics, computer cases and digital imagery software. This sets up a second round of purchases. In their turn, the second round of purchases leads to a third round, as the workers making curtains get more overtime, have an increased income and spend more.

These successive rounds of expenditure carry on, and would seem to have all the potential of carrying on for ever, with an infinite addition to consumers' expenditure and the GDP. This happy result does not occur, because there are leakages out of the system at every turn. As referred to earlier, every time a person gets additional income some of it will be taken as income tax before they even receive it; in any case they will not spend all of the income they receive because they will save some of it; when they spend it, some of the expenditure may return to the government as VAT or excise duty; and they may purchase imports, which do not add to the domestic GDP. Consequently the first-round impact of expenditure is less than the full value of the increased income, the second round expenditure is only a fraction of the first, and so on. Eventually successive rounds are so small as to add nothing to the multiplier effect, and it peters out.

In principle multiplier effects result from any additional expenditure, whether it be through changes in government taxes or expenditures, the result of a spontaneous increase in investment expenditure, or the result of a boom in exports. They may also operate on a small scale in an area, for example when a large new factory employing a lot of previously unemployed workers is set up, and they can also operate in reverse, so that a rise in income taxes may lead to a *reduction* in consumer expenditure greater than the original amount. Regardless of how they might have occurred, multiplier effects have to be taken into account by policymakers when investigating the impact on the economy of a change in aggregate demand.

Summary

In this section we have recognised that:

- Aggregate demand refers to the total spending on goods and services produced in an economy. It consists of consumer spending, investment expenditure, government spending and net expenditure on exports and imports.

- The aggregate demand curve is downward-sloping.

- Each of the components of aggregate demand is in turn determined by various economic variables.

- Aggregate supply is the total output in the economy. It is determined by factors of production and the level of technology.

- The aggregate supply curve is upward-sloping.

- Equilibrium output and prices are determined where the AD and AS curves intersect.

- Any change in AD or AS will lead to a shift in these functions and will have an effect upon the equilibrium level of output and prices.

- Any economy has various injections into the circular flow of income and leakages from it.

- Any change to injections and leakages will have a multiplier effect on expenditure in the economy.

Key words

Definitions of Key words can be found in the Glossary on page 240.

aggregate supply
consumer spending
disposable income
expectations
first-round effect
fiscal policies
hot money
injections
investment expenditure

leakages
marginal propensity to consume
monetary policies
multiplier effect
net expenditure on imports and exports
savings
supply-side policies

9 The application of macroeconomic policy instruments

On completion of this section you should be able to:

➤ describe what is meant by fiscal policy

➤ define monetary policy and understand the basic relationship between money supply and interest rates

➤ outline how exchange rates are determined by the supply and demand for currencies

➤ explain how interest rates are determined by supply and demand for money

➤ explain how the AD/AS model may be used to analyse the way fiscal, monetary and supply-side policies and exchange rate changes can affect the levels of employment, rate of inflation, economic growth and the balance of payments

Fiscal policy

Previous sections have, rather casually, referred to instruments of fiscal policy, such as variations in income taxes and social security benefits, without discussing them in any depth. This section remedies this deficiency by considering fiscal policy in more detail. In doing so it will stress the ways in which variations in fiscal policy instruments may affect aggregate demand and supply.

Fiscal policy refers to the use of taxation and government spending in pursuit of particular policy objectives. It is used by governments to influence the level of aggregate demand in the economy and it can also affect aggregate supply through changing incentives facing firms and individuals. In simple terms it is best seen as referring to changes in the income or expenditure sides of the government accounts.

Table 9.1 shows the UK government's sources of income for the period 1989–97, and table 9.2 shows the pattern of its expenditures over the same period. In each case the data are at current prices, so it must be assumed that some of the variations in the relative importance of some of the tax and expenditure items in the tables will reflect differences in the rate of inflation. For example, it is possible that the pay of the armed forces could increase more rapidly than that of nurses, so defence expenditure might rise more rapidly than expenditure on health. Or it could be that prices for electronic goods, on which VAT is levied, rise more rapidly than incomes, on which income tax is paid, so VAT receipts rise more rapidly than income tax.

However, many of the trends shown in the tables stem from changes in government policy, together with

changes in the economy and society. For example, as was discussed in section 5, government has a responsibility to the public for arranging for the provision of public goods and merit goods, or for limiting the effects of negative externalities. As a

	£ billion		
	1989	**1993**	**1997**
Primary incomes			
Operating surplus, gross	2.7	2.9	4.1
Value added tax (VAT)	28.6	38.3	52.3
Other taxes on products	23.2	28.4	40.7
Other taxes on production	1.5	15.0	16.7
Property income	12.0	9.7	9.6
Balance of primary incomes (gross)[1]	*68.0*	*94.3*	*123.4*
Secondary incomes			
Taxes on income and wealth	75.5	80.7	110.5
Social contributions	36.2	42.9	54.4
Other	4.4	7.0	6.3
Total resources (gross)	*184.0*	*224.8*	*294.4*

	Percentage of total resources		
	1989	**1993**	**1997**
Value added tax (VAT)	15.5	17.0	17.8
Other taxes on products	12.6	12.6	13.8
Other taxes on production	0.8	6.7	5.7
Taxes on income and wealth	41.0	35.9	37.5
Social contributions	19.7	19.1	18.5

Table 9.1 UK Central government: sources of income
Note: 1 Before any primary income expenditures.
Source: United Kingdom National Accounts, 1998, Office for National Statistics

	£ billion		
	1989	**1993**	**1997**
General public services	9.0	12.0	15.1
Defence	21.7	24.4	23.4
Public order and safety	9.6	14.5	16.3
Economic affairs	15.6	20.7	21.7
Environmental protection	2.0	2.6	2.6
Housing and community services	5.8	9.5	6.3
Health	25.4	37.0	44.0
Recreation, culture and religion	3.3	4.6	4.1
Education	23.9	30.7	36.2
Social protection	68.2	115.3	113.2
Other	21.0	20.0	30.1
Total outlays	205.5	291.3	331.0

	Percentage of total outlays		
	1989	**1993**	**1997**
General public services	4.4	4.1	4.6
Defence	10.6	8.4	7.1
Public order and safety	4.7	5.0	4.9
Economic affairs	7.6	7.1	6.6
Environmental protection	1.0	0.9	0.8
Housing and community services	2.8	3.3	1.9
Health	12.4	12.7	13.3
Recreation, culture and religion	1.6	1.6	1.2
Education	11.6	10.5	10.9
Social protection	33.2	39.6	39.6
Other	10.2	6.9	9.1
Total outlays	100.0	100.0	100.0

Table 9.2 UK Central government: total outlays
Source: United Kingdom National Accounts, 1998, Office for National Statistics.

'Steady Eddie' – one of many transport operators using central government funded motorways

consequence it may alter its expenditures on health and education, or change excise duties on whisky, tobacco and petrol, for general political reasons that have nothing to do with using them as part of macroeconomic policy. Again, a change in government from a political party of one set of beliefs to another party with a different view of the responsibilities of government may produce a slow, but steady, turn-round of the government's expenditure pattern. In addition, a boom in the economy will raise employment and hours worked and reduce unemployment. Without lifting a finger, because of the increased incomes and expenditures, the government automatically receives more revenue from income tax, excise duties and VAT.

Because of the reduced unemployment the government automatically pays out less in social security benefits, such as unemployment benefits.

The instruments and their effects

In practice there are severe limitations on the ability of the government to use fiscal policy. On the income side, the key areas that may be manipulated are income tax rates and allowances; Value Added Tax (VAT); excise duties, such as those on tobacco, alcohol and petrol; social security payments, such as National Insurance contributions. On the expenditure side, there is no key area as such. An increase in almost all types of government expenditure will have an impact on aggregate demand, but increases in some areas may have a greater impact on aggregate supply than others. Expenditure on fighter aircraft will not add much to productive capacity; new motorways will.

To boost aggregate demand the government essentially has two options. It can either *cut* taxes, or it can *increase* expenditure. In either case the net effect is the same. The general public have greater real incomes than before, consumer expenditure rises and aggregate demand is boosted (shown by the AD curve shifting to the right). In more detail, a reduction in income tax will mean that large sections of the population will receive more money in their pay packets or as salary payments. Not unnaturally, a high proportion of this increased income will be spent, the exact proportion depending upon the marginal propensity to consume. Consequently, consumer expenditure will rise. Alternatively, a fall in excise duty on petrol means that people have to spend less on petrol. As petrol is a good inelastic in demand, expenditure on petrol will fall, implying that people have more money to spend on other things, whilst buying at least as much petrol as before. Consequently consumer expenditure rises. Finally, if the government increases its expenditure on health and education, it is possible that the salaries of nurses and teachers will increase and in turn, therefore, consumer expenditure will increase.

The discussion above has concentrated on the impact of fiscal policy instruments on aggregate demand. In addition, there may also be an impact on aggregate supply, and this should not be neglected. Such impacts may occur in two ways.

First, changes in income taxes and social security benefits may have *incentive* or *disincentive* effects on workers. This may cause aggregate supply to increase, or to decrease, in the short to medium term. Secondly, depending upon the nature of the change in government expenditure, there may be long-term effects on aggregate supply. This is most obviously the case for direct expenditures on roads, but it can also occur in a multitude of other ways. Changes in subsidies to capital, or for research and development, may lead to increases in the size and productivity of the capital stock. Improved education and training will improve the efficiency and productivity of the workforce.

The result of this is that some areas of fiscal policy have fairly direct, short-term impacts on aggregate demand whilst also affecting aggregate supply in the long run. Both effects need to be considered when analysing fiscal policy.

Self-assessment task

1 What will be the effects of the following on aggregate demand and aggregate supply in the short and long run?
   (a) a reduction in income tax allowances;
   (b) an increase in compulsory pensions contributions;
   (c) an increase in VAT;
   (d) an increase in expenditure in further education colleges;
   (e) an increase in unemployment benefits;
   (f) a reduction in expenditure on subsidising firm's expenditures on investment in capital goods.

Monetary policy

Monetary policy is normally interpreted as government induced changes in either the supply of money or interest rates. Over that last twenty years or so it has become the dominant means of macroeconomic policy, specifically enabling successive governments in the UK to maintain a low rate of inflation (see section 7).

A simple definition of money was introduced in section 2. Although this is a great simplification compared with the real world, it will suffice. Defining the **money supply**, though, is far more complex (see the A2 module, the UK Economy).

Clearly it must include notes and coins, but nowadays many purchases are not paid for with such currency. Instead people pay with Visa cards, Switch cards or personal cheques. What is happening is that they are paying using money balances that stand in their name in banks and building societies. The effect of the cards or cheques is to transfer some of their bank balance from their account to the payee's account. Obviously these bank balances are serving as money, and they are therefore counted as part of the money supply. Taken together currency in the form of notes and coin, plus balances that are available for use in normal transactions, is often called **narrow money**. Beyond this amount of money there is an additional vast amount of balances at banks and building societies that stand in the names of individuals, but which is not so immediately accessible and cannot be used for direct transactions. This is usually called **broad money**.

In a very simple and logical way economists view the growth of the money supply as a prime cause of inflation, particularly where this involves the cavalier printing of notes by the monetary authorities. Changes in the money supply will affect aggregate demand indirectly. So, if the supply of money increases, people will have more spending power and they will demand more goods and services. What we are saying here is that aggregate demand has increased and the AD curve has shifted to the right. This will put pressure on suppliers, bottlenecks will appear and prices will rise. It also follows that a means of keeping underlying inflation at a low level is to restrict the supply of money. Consumer spending in turn is restricted, so there is less danger of the economy over-heating and prices will be relatively easy.

A change in the money supply, though, can also affect aggregate demand in less direct ways:

1 Individuals may not necessarily spend their income on goods and services; instead they may decide to purchase a security in the form of a **government bond**, which is usually issued at a given face value and pays a fixed annual sum as a rate of interest. For example, it may be a £1,000 bond paying £80 per year – representing 8 per cent on the face value of the bond. However, such bonds may be traded in financial markets, in the City of London, New York, Frankfurt or Tokyo. If the markets move the price of the bond down, so that it now only has a value of £800, but it is still paying £80 per year, then the rate of interest is now effectively 10 per cent. If the market price of the bond rises to £1,600, but it is still paying £80 per year, the rate of interest is now effectively 5 per cent. Hence the market price of bonds and the rate of interest are inversely proportional. So, when the supply of money increases, the demand for such securities will rise and, in turn, their price will rise.

2 Individuals may spend some of their income on imported goods and services (see section 10). So when the money supply increases, so too will the demand for imports, necessitating an increase in (say) pounds on the foreign exchange market. With floating exchange rates, the price of pounds will fall, in turn making exports rather more competitive and imports rather more expensive. In turn, some consumers will switch their expenditure from imports to home-produced goods, so eventually increasing aggregate demand.

The basic theoretical relationship for the determination of interest rates was shown in figure 2.24 in section 2. Building on this a change in the money supply will in turn affect interest rates, as figure 9.1 shows. So, when the money supply is reduced from S to S_1, the rate of interest increases from r_0 to r_1. On the other hand, if the money supply were to increase from S_1 to S, the rate of interest would fall from r_1 to r_0. Any further increase, to say S_2, would lead to a very slight fall in the rate of interest to r_2.

This relationship between the money supply and the rate of interest has very substantial implications for macroeconomic policies, as we shall see at the end of this section.

Supply-side policies

As mentioned in section 8, there are various policies which can result in a shift of the aggregate supply curve. Collectively these measures are referred to as supply-side policies in so far as they seek to increase the aggregate supply available in the economy. When combined with policies to manage aggregate demand they provide an effective means for allowing governments to meet their stated macroeconomic objectives. A wide range of supply-side policies are potentially available. Unlike the relatively blunt instruments of fiscal and monetary policy, these policies are much more focused in their objectives, although they can be expensive to introduce and have limited and relatively uncertain long-run effects on the economy. In promoting these policies the role of government is to remove market imperfections and restrictive practices so that the economy can operate in a more efficient manner. A few examples are outlined below.

Providing incentives to work

The guiding principle here has been to encourage more people to join the labour force and so bring about an increase in output. Underlying this particular approach is the idea that direct taxation and the welfare payments system can actually act as a disincentive to work and through evading taxation, promote the growth of the 'black economy' (see also section 7). It should be emphasised though that this relationship is by no means clearly evidenced from an empirical standpoint, although, in theory, it is more obvious.

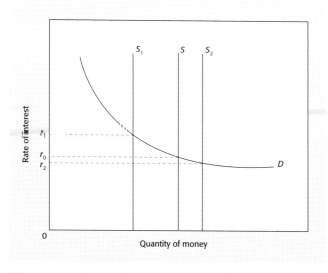

Figure 9.1 Relationship between money supply and interest rates

The last Conservative government in the UK firmly believed that high rates of direct taxation were very much a disincentive to work. When elected in 1979, the top rate of income tax was a massive 83 per cent – systematically and deliberately this has been reduced to a top rate of 40 per cent and the basic income tax rate has fallen from 33 per cent to just 24 per cent. Tax thresholds for low-income earners have also been revised with the objective of encouraging more people to join the labour force. Lowering income tax in this way will shift the AS curve to the right (see figure 8.9).

The Conservatives also reformed the unemployment benefit and social security system, a process which has been continued by the Labour government elected in 1997. The Conservatives' objective was to encourage low-income earners and the unemployed to seek work rather than rely on state handouts. Because of the system some individuals actually receive more in benefits than they would be paid if they were in a job. This so-called **unemployment trap** acts as a clear disincentive to work. The objective of supply-side policies here is one of widening the gap between the wages received through working and the welfare payments received whilst unemployed or economically inactive. Its effect on the AS curve is the same as indicated by figure 8.9.

Education and training

Many people who are unemployed lack the skills that are necessary to obtain a job. This particularly applies to many sixteen-year old school leavers and some people who have been unemployed for a long time. By providing opportunities for such people to train, wider skill shortages in the economy can be addressed and the workforce can become more effective, more mobile and more flexible, so enhancing the country's international competitiveness compared with our trading rivals.

In recent years there have been many schemes designed to promote this particular objective. Many of these are managed by local Training and Enterprise Councils (TECs), which provide vocational training and work placements for teenagers and unemployed adults. Job clubs, Restart schemes, Access courses and personal counselling, managed by the local offices of the Employment Services Agency, provide opportunities for the longer-term unemployed to rejoin the labour market. The theoretical impact of all such schemes is once again as shown in figure 8.9.

Interviewing and assessment are an important role of staffing agencies
Source: Select Appointments plc.

Trade union reform

This has been another area where the last Conservative government pursued a vigorous supply-side policy, in this case aimed at reducing the power of trade unions in the labour market. By restricting the supply of workers, trade unions seek to increase the wages of their members but at the cost of a decrease in the numbers employed. Such action, it is argued by supply-side economists, increases costs, impairs efficiency and reduces international competitiveness. During the 1980s, a mass of new legislation was introduced to reduce the power of the trade unions and consequently produce a more flexible, adaptable and responsive labour force. The number of working days lost through strike action, for example, has fallen remarkably and in many companies highly restrictive working practices have been removed. The outcome again has been to shift the AS curve to the right.

Privatisation and deregulation

Structurally the most important change in the economy over the past twenty years or so has been the transfer of ownership of former state-owned activities to the private sector. This is a supply-side policy in so far as it is argued that, under private ownership, companies are more efficient, more competitive and less of a drain on the public purse. As a consequence market conditions provide for a shift to the right of the AS curve.

Privatisation in the UK economy since 1979 has been extensive, particularly for the fuel and power and transport industries. **Deregulation**, the removal of barriers to entry into an industry, has also taken place on an extensive scale, as indeed has the contracting-out of activities normally undertaken by the public sector. Although we cannot ignore the political motive, the outcome has arguably been the creation of a much more competitive market in many areas of the economy where previously there had been a public sector monopoly.

It is beyond the scope of this text to look at the arguments for and against privatisation. The significance of privatisation and deregulation though cannot be ignored from a supply-side standpoint.

Self-assessment task

Study the short article below and then answer the questions that follow.

Benefit 'will not provide work incentives'

Only between 30,000 and 45,000 families are likely to be tempted back to work by the government's new flagship benefit for the low paid, the Working Families Tax Credit, (WFTC), the independent Institute for Fiscal Studies said yesterday.

As the government launched the bill to replace family credit with WFTC, the Institute said most of the gain from the new, more generous credit would go to people already in work.

Relatively few individuals are likely to be tempted into the labour market, despite the estimated £1.5bn extra cost of the credit, because for those on housing benefit the combined means-tests will still not leave them markedly better off, the Institute said.

While people who do not receive housing benefit will make significant gains, those who do will lose 89p of each extra £1 they earn as they start to pay tax and national insurance and begin to lose WFTC itself and housing and council tax benefit as their earnings rise. Under the present system they lose 92p in the £1.

Alan Duncan, a senior researcher at IFS, said some further reform to housing benefit and its interaction with the new credit would be needed to provide bigger work incentives.

The estimates have been made for the Bank of England's Monetary Policy Committee, which wanted to know the likely labour market effects of the new credit.

Source: N. Timmins, *Financial Times*, 27 January 1999 (adapted).

1 With the aid of a diagram, briefly explain the economic logic underpinning the Working Families Tax Credit (WFTC) scheme.

2 Comment upon the views made by the Institute for Fiscal Studies about this new scheme.

Exchange rate determination

As stated in the early part of section 8, net receipts from exports and imports are one of the four contributors to aggregate demand in an economy. Section 10 will look at the international economy in detail but, in order to complete our perspective of macroeconomic policy instruments, it is now necessary to understand how exchange rates are determined. The concluding part of this section will then explain how exchange rate changes can affect the performance of the macroeconomy.

The exchange rate of a currency, as its name suggests, is the rate at which one currency is exchanged for another. For example, £1 can be exchanged for (say) $1.6 US, FF 10 or DM3 at any one time on the foreign exchange market. It is therefore the price of one currency expressed in terms of any other tradable currency.

Foreign exchange is needed because of the nature of international trade. If a UK resident buys a good which has been produced abroad and imported into the UK, currency exchange must take place. This is because the producer of this in, say, France will require payment in their own currency, French francs. At some stage of the trading process currency exchange must take place. The buying and selling of foreign exchange takes place on the foreign exchange market. Importers of goods into the UK will use £s to buy the currency of the country from which they are purchasing the goods, so providing a supply of £s to the foreign exchange market. Similarly, those who have bought products from the UK will be using their own currencies to purchase £s on the foreign exchange market. This action creates a demand for £s.

The exchange rate of a currency is determined by the relative strength of the supply and demand for a currency. Figure 9.2 shows the supply and demand for £s on the foreign exchange market. For simplicity, the relationship between just two currencies, £s and $USs, is shown. In this diagram the demand for £s (D£) slopes down from left to right because when the price of the £ in terms of $USs is high, UK goods are relatively expensive to US consumers. As a result the demand for British goods and services will be low, with few £s being demanded on the foreign exchange market. As the value of the £ falls against the $US, American consumers can gain more £s for their $USs and so more £s are demanded on the foreign exchange market. The supply

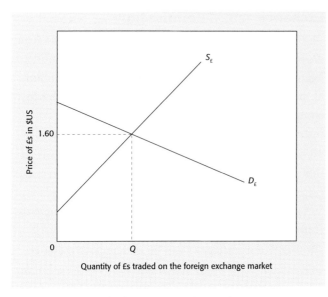

Figure 9.2 The simple determination of an exchange rate

curve for £s (S$_£$) in figure 9.2 is upward sloping from left to right, as when the value of the £ against the $US is low, American goods are relatively expensive in the UK. Fewer British consumers will buy such goods and, as a result, few £s will be supplied to the foreign exchange market. As the value of the £ rises against the $US, however, American goods become more affordable to British consumers and therefore more £s are supplied to the foreign exchange market.

Suppose the price of the £ on the foreign exchange market moves from the position shown in figure 9.2 to one where £1 = $2 US. The £ is now overvalued and British exporters find it difficult to sell their goods in the US market. The demand for £s is low but in contrast, because American goods are relatively cheap in the UK market, British consumers have increased their demand and more £s are being supplied. At this exchange rate therefore there is an excess of £s on the foreign exchange market. In such a situation the usual principles of market economics apply – the excess supply results in a fall in price until it reaches the equilibrium rate of £1 = S1.60 US, where once again supply equates to demand.

The above analysis is a great simplification of how the foreign exchange market really operates. It is necessary, though, to understand these basic principles to be able to analyse how exchange rate changes can affect the level of employment, rate of inflation and the balance of payments position in the economy.

Applications of the AD/AS model

Let us conclude this section with a brief overview as to how the policies described so far can be applied through the AD/AS model to allow governments to achieve the objectives given in section 7. First, though, a few words of warning!

1 The policies described so far in theory might seem relatively easy to comprehend. Unfortunately in practice their outcome is far from easy to predict and, on occasions, very uncertain.

2 The policies themselves do not operate independently. At any one time, a whole mass of fiscal, monetary and supply-side policies are being applied by governments in pursuit of their objectives. It is also the case that indirectly one policy may trigger off an unwanted reaction. For example, if the government tries to boost aggregate demand in the economy by lowering taxes, this increases the demand for money with the resulting effect that interest rates must rise. In turn, this reduces aggregate demand. So, fiscal policy designed to expand aggregate demand leads to interest rate rises that reduce investment expenditure and demand, cutting back the positive effects of fiscal policy. These interest rate changes may also lead to a higher exchange rate and lower exports. Overall, the effect of reduced investment and exports is referred to as crowding out, that is exports are crowded out by increased consumption.

3 The application of fiscal, monetary and supply-side policies involves a time lag. Some policies tend to be more immediate than others in their effects. Changes to indirect taxes on fuel, drink or VAT are relatively quick to apply and relatively immediate in their impact. Other fiscal changes, say to government

spending or direct taxes, take much longer both to be applied and to have an effect on the macroeconomy. Monetary policies are in general more longer term in their effects than fiscal policies.

4 Supply-side policies tend to be long term and uncertain in their measurable outcome since they require structural changes to be made to increase aggregate supply in the economy. They therefore have little relevance from the point of view of short-term economic management.

Table 9.3 provides a summary of the main applications of fiscal, monetary and supply-side policies that governments can use in pursuit of their macroeconomic objectives. In terms of the AD/AS model, you should refer back to figures 8.7 and 8.9, which show how the equilibrium position is affected with shifts in AD and AS respectively.

Policies to reduce unemployment

It might seem easy to reduce unemployment. All the government needs to do is to create more jobs and produce a greater output. In terms of the AD/AS model, it means shifting either the AD curve to the right or the AS curve to the right or both simultaneously.

In the short run, as table 9.3 indicates, fiscal and monetary policies can operate to increase aggregate demand and so reduce unemployment. The only adverse effect would seem to be the increase in prices that will follow such an expansion in the economy. If interest rates are lowered, this could lower the exchange rate, allowing export prices to fall but leading to higher import prices, in turn feeding domestic inflation. In the long run the main hope for reducing unemployment must lie with supply-side policies targeted at the labour force. Some examples of such policies are also shown in table 9.3. If effective these will shift the long-run AS curve to the right. As figure 8.9 showed, this has the added benefit of reducing the price level. As section 8 explained, by definition, fiscal and monetary policies are ineffective in dealing with the problem of long-term unemployment – only policies designed to enhance training and skills or improving home circumstances will make it easier for such people to obtain work.

Policies to control inflation

It follows from the above that appropriate short-term policies to bring down prices are the reverse of those to reduce unemployment. In the case of fiscal policy this

Problem	Short-run policies	Long-run policies	Difficulties
↓ Unemployment	Fiscal and monetary e.g. ↓indirect taxes ↑government spending ↓rate of interest shift AD to right	Supply-side e.g. retrain long-term unemployed, reduced welfare payments → shift AS to right	Higher prices in short run Not all unemployed can realistically re-join labour force
↓ Rate of inflation	Fiscal and monetary policies e.g. ↑indirect taxes ↓government spending ↑rate of interest → shift AD to left	Supply-side e.g. remove restrictive practices, privatisation → shift AS to right	Reduced output and increased unemployment in short run Appreciating exchange rate
↓ Balance of trade deficit	Fiscal and monetary policies e.g. ↑direct taxes ↑rate of interest Exchange rate policies e.g. depreciation → shift AD to left	Supply-side e.g. measures designed to promote increased international competitiveness → shift AS to right	Increased unemployment in short run

Table 9.3 A summary of macroeconomic problems and policy options

would mean raising income taxes, reducing social benefits or cutting government spending. These are by no means popular measures politically, but have often to be used to control inflation. On the monetary policy front, raising interest rates is an obvious measure to keep down the rate of price increases. The AD/AS model is the reverse of that shown in figures 8.7 and 8.9 (see self-assessment task below). Unfortunately all of these policies have the unpopular side effect of reducing output and increasing unemployment.

In recent years the UK government has had as its principal economic objective, that of stabilising the rate of inflation. This has been necessary for it to meet its macroeconomic objectives (as outlined in section 7) and the convergence criteria set for Economic and Monetary Union (EMU) (see section 12). Conservative and Labour governments have turned away from fiscal measures to control inflation; the consequence is that monetary policy in the form of regular changes in interest rates has been the means of controlling inflation. This task is now in the hands of the specially created Monetary Policy Committee of the Bank of England who were given a target rate of 2.5 per cent per annum. Their response was initially to raise interest rates in small cautious steps. Inevitably, as table 9.3 shows, this led to an upward movement of exchange rates against the US dollar and major European currencies. Good news for UK holiday-makers but not good news for exporters! It is only when the inflation rate is seen to be reaching its target that interest rates have been lowered.

The only effective long-run policy of reducing the price level, avoiding the above problems, is to use supply-side policies to expand aggregate supply. Such policies, as mentioned on numerous occasions, are designed to improve international competitiveness and economic efficiency. Like all supply-side policies, they are very slow to have any measurable impact.

Policies to promote economic growth

Economic growth is an objective in all modern economies as, through growth, living standards can improve as more goods and services become available to the population. To achieve this is difficult and the effects of policies to promote growth are by no means certain. One thing that economists do agree, though, is that an increase in the quality and quantity of factors of production is essential if a positive rate of growth is to be achieved through an outward shift of the PPC (see figure 1.4).

It follows from the analysis of actual growth and potential growth in section 7 that the two main factors contributing to the latter are:

- an increase in the quantity of resources available;
- an increase in the efficiency with which these resources are being used, for example through increased labour productivity and advances in technology.

One of the most important ways to foster economic growth is to increase labour productivity. In other words, the amount of goods and services produced per worker must increase. This can be achieved by making the capital stock more efficient, either by replacing old outdated machinery and buildings by improved new ones or expanding the stock with new efficient capital. Alternatively, it can be achieved by making the labour force more efficient through education and training as we discussed earlier.

In modern economies, it is essential that improved technology through better equipment, improved organisation and management is used to achieve this important objective. It can, though, be a difficult process not least because the introduction of new technology invariably seems to lead to job losses and unemployment. One can see this process quite clearly in activities such as banking and retailing as well as in manufacturing where robots and mechanised production have taken over from process workers.

How best governments can achieve growth is a complex matter and subject to certain disagreement amongst economists. On the one hand, policies can focus on the demand side, in particular to create conditions where demand is strong, firms wish to invest and potential output is achieved. On the other hand, supply-side policies can be used to increase potential output through measures such as those referred to in section 8. The disagreement really centres on how best to implement such policies. Some economists argue very strongly that this has to be done through the free market; others are not convinced, arguing that planning and control can best lead to the high levels of investment needed to sustain long-term growth.

Policies to affect the balance of payments

In recent years the balance of payments in the UK, including the balance of trade, has been rather low key and down-played as a policy objective. The reasons for this are quite complex and complicated by the UK's membership of the European Union (EU). The flow of capital in response to interest rate changes has had an important bearing on the exchange rate. As a result, if the exchange rate is 'too high', and the balance of trade in goods and services is out of balance, a massive deficit is caused by increasing volumes of imports from the rest of the EU and the rest of the world (see section 10). In such circumstances, firms in the UK will find it difficult to export goods, output will be affected and workers made unemployed. Under such circumstances, the government finds it necessary to consider policies that affect the exchange rate in order to move a deficit on the current balance of trade away towards a more balanced position.

In theory, the most effective way to redress this situation is to apply fiscal and monetary measures to depress the economy by cutting aggregate demand. So, if consumer spending and capital investment are cut back, imports will fall. In other words, UK consumers will buy less French wine and fewer German cars, less sports clothing from China and Taiwan and firms will cut back on purchases of machinery from the USA. Imports of raw materials should also fall as there will be less domestic output being produced. The shift of the AD curve to the left will be indicative of a rise in unemployment. Such policies are unpopular and do nothing to enhance the 'feel good' factor which politicians openly like to promote.

Otherwise the possible policies to address balance of payments problems are long-run supply-side ones, which seek to improve the efficiency and competitiveness of the UK economy. These imply making factories and services more efficient, cutting costs, improving the quality and design of products, putting more effort into marketing and after-sales service and so on. This is a long and slow process, carried out against the background of a global economy where all other countries are following the same set of procedures.

Self-assessment tasks

1 Look back at figure 8.7. Re-draw this to show how a shift to the left of AD affects the equilibrium position. Briefly say what this means, how it might apply and what are the consequences for the economy.

2 The level of capital investment in the UK is currently below that of many other EU countries. Briefly explain what fiscal, monetary and supply-side policies could be used to improve this position and how these might be represented on the AD/AS model.

Summary

In this section we have recognised that:

● Fiscal policy, which involves the use of taxation and government spending, has an important bearing on the level of aggregate demand in the economy. It can also affect aggregate supply.

● Monetary policy involves the manipulation of the supply of money or interest rates in the economy.

● Supply-side policies are longer term in their effects and their outcome is less certain than fiscal and monetary measures. They are designed to affect the total output in the economy.

● All three types of policy tend to be in operation at any one particular time.

● The exchange rate in simple terms is the price of one currency in terms of another currency.

● The AD/AS model can be used to show how fiscal, monetary and supply-side policies can affect the level of employment, the rate of inflation, economic growth and the balance of payments in the economy.

Key words

Definitions of Key words can be found in the Glossary on page 240.

broad money	money supply
crowding out	narrow money
deregulation	unemployment trap
government bond	

10 Structure and essential determinants of international transactions

On completion of this section you should be able to:

➤ recognise the similarities and differences between internal and external trade
➤ understand the main types of goods and services traded internationally, the main destinations of UK exports and the main sources of UK imports
➤ describe the broad impact of EU membership on the pattern of UK international trade
➤ explain the gains from international trade in general terms
➤ understand the meaning and advantages of free trade
➤ explain tariff and non-tariff methods of protection using relevant diagrams
➤ discuss the arguments for and against protection

The UK and the international economy

Many of the goods and services produced in the UK will not be consumed by domestic households. They will be exported to satisfy the wants of consumers in foreign economies. Similarly, many British consumers' wants will be satisfied by goods and services which are produced abroad and imported into the UK. In addition, many UK firms will import capital goods from abroad, just as some British firms will produce capital goods for export. Buying and selling goods and services across national frontiers is called **international trade**. It is based upon international specialisation and has led to a tremendous growth in world living standards over the years. Because goods and services are traded across national frontiers, different currencies are involved and it is necessary at some stage to exchange one currency for another. This takes place in the foreign exchange market. The flows of currencies to pay for imports and exports of goods and services are recorded in a country's balance of payments account. In addition to recording receipts and payments for exports and imports of goods and services, the balance of payments account also records international flows of currency for other reasons. These include, for example, flows of funds for investment in other economies and the receipt of income from these investments (see section 7).

Overseas trade and investment is particularly important to the UK economy. In 1997, the population was 58.6 million which represents only about 1 per cent of the world's population and yet the United Kingdom was the fifth largest trading nation, accounting for around 5% of world trade in goods and services. This is a considerable decline since the mid nineteenth century when Great Britain was responsible for over 25 per cent of the world's exports of goods and services, but this declining share has only occurred as a result of the tremendous expansion in world trade over the years as other countries have begun to import and export goods and services. The volume of goods and services exported by the UK economy continues on a steady upward trend.

Just as the UK remains an important nation in international trade, so trade has had a very great impact upon the UK economy. The significance of international trade can be assessed by the degree of 'openness' of an economy. Openness is measured by the proportion of total final expenditure in an economy which is taken up by sales abroad of goods and services.

In 1997, this proportion was about 22 per cent of GDP for the UK compared with 10 per cent for the United States and 9 per cent for Japan. This means that although the United States and Japan are responsible for more exports than the UK, they are relatively more 'closed' economies. This means that international trade is less significant for the average US or Japanese citizen than it is for a citizen of the UK. This is emphasised by the fact that the UK exports more per head of the population than both the United States and Japan.

The UK is also the world's second biggest foreign investor with a higher percentage of overseas investment relative to Gross Domestic Product than any other leading economy. It should also be noted that the United Kingdom, as a major economy within the European Union, is part of the world's largest established trading group with access to a market of over 390 million citizens. Through its membership of the European Union, the United Kingdom has significant influence on world international trade policy (see unit 4).

	Value (£ millions)			%	
	Exports	Imports	Balance	Exports	Imports
European Union	95,892	99,979	−4,087	55.8	54.5
Other Western Europe	7,845	10,748	−2,903	4.6	5.9
North America	23,858	27,170	−3,312	13.9	14.8
Other OECD countries	10,769	14,503	−3,734	6.3	7.9
Oil exporting countries	9,416	3,317	6,099	5.5	1.8
Rest of the World	24,019	27,871	−3,852	14.0	15.2

Table 10.1 Distribution of trade in goods, 1997
Source: Office for National Statistics.

The pattern of UK trade

The United Kingdom was the first industrial nation and the first economy to take off into self-sustained economic growth. The traditional pattern of UK trade was related to this early industrialisation and the fact that much trade was with former or existing colonies. Although the UK was deficient in certain raw materials, it was able to import these from the Empire, which also provided a market for British manufactured goods. Although the trade in goods section might be in deficit, the trade in services was often sufficient to provide a surplus on the Current Account. There was an inevitability about this pattern of trade given Britain's political dominance of her Empire and the fact that new entrants to world markets in the second half of the nineteenth century, such as the United States and Germany, imposed tariffs on British imports to protect their infant industries.

So the traditional pattern of UK trade was the import of raw materials and foodstuffs from the Colonies and the export of manufactured products. Trading links with Europe developed gradually during the twentieth century, but in 1955 Europe was the destination for only about 25 per cent of UK exports, and approximately 25 per cent of imports came from Europe. By contrast the less-developed economies, including the Colonies, accounted for just under 40 per cent of both imports and exports.

In more recent years (see table 10.1) there have been very significant changes in the United Kingdom's pattern of trade:
- The greatest proportion of trade is now with other developed economies. Other countries in the OECD took over 80 per cent of UK exports and supplied 83 per cent of imports into the UK in 1997.
- Imported manufactures have taken an increasing share of the domestic market in recent years. Import penetration ratios in some products have risen to over 90 per cent. (The United Kingdom has not had a surplus in manufacturing since 1982.)

At the same time:
- The surplus on trade in services continues to grow. In 1997 the surplus was £11,160 million, reflecting large surpluses in insurance, financial services and other business services.
- Manufactured goods continue to provide the biggest proportion of exports. Manufacturers represented 84 per cent of UK exports in 1970. Although this declined with the rise in North Sea oil exports, by 1997 it had again risen to 84 per cent. The United Kingdom has significant surpluses in chemicals, beverages and tobacco products.

Causes of the changing pattern of UK trade

The changing pattern of UK trade in recent years has been caused by two very closely related issues:
1 The entry of the UK into the European Economic Community (EEC) in 1973 and the development of this community into an Economic Union (EU).
2 The decline in the competitiveness of the UK manufacturing sector, leading to extensive deindustrialisation.

In assessing the significance of these changes, we need to consider how each has affected the pattern of UK trade. We then need to consider how this has affected resource allocation in the United Kingdom and to consider whether resources are put to their best use. This is known as optimal resource allocation. Another way of expressing this is that we need to consider whether the UK's pattern of trade reflects comparative advantage which is predicted to lead to maximum economic welfare. We then need to consider the costs and benefits of a movement to optimal resource allocation to assess whether, on balance, the changes have been beneficial to the United Kingdom

The gains from international trade

It is generally acknowledged today that international trade based upon specialisation and exchange will lead to an increase in world economic welfare. The guiding principle in trading relationships between nations is that trade should be based upon co-operation and any barriers to trade which exist should be removed. Several organisations such as the World Trade Organisation (WTO) exist to promote **free trade** between nations. Government support for free trade between nations has not always existed. In the seventeenth and eighteenth centuries, the dominant view was that nations should aim for **self-sufficiency** and an excess of exports over imports. This body of thought was known as **mercantilism** and was based upon the idea that a nation's wealth and power were directly related to the gold and silver circulating in the economy and in the state's reserves. The greater the gold and silver in circulation, the greater the prosperity of the citizens of the country.

Adam Smith and absolute advantage

In *The Wealth of Nations* (1776), Adam Smith attacked mercantilist ideas. This was part of his general attack on any state interference in industry and his support for **laissez-faire** policies, which suggested that in a free market with no state regulation economic welfare would be maximised. This Smith believed to be true in both the domestic and international economy. Smith put forward the principle of **absolute advantage**. For a

given set of resources, a country should specialise in the production of those goods in which it can actually produce more than another country. If specialisation then took place, total world production would increase and, through trade, each country would also be better off.

This is a very simple idea. It describes a situation where one country is superior in the production of one commodity and the other country is superior in the production of the other. We now need to examine a situation where one country has an absolute advantage in the production of both commodities.

David Ricardo and comparative advantage

An economy's ability to produce goods and services depends upon that economy's factor endowments. This means the quantity and quality of the factors of production in the economy. These change over time but at any point in time one economy, by the nature of its factor endowments, might have an absolute advantage in the production of all commodities compared to another. Is specialisation and trade still worthwhile? In the early part of the nineteenth century, David Ricardo developed the principle of **comparative advantage**, which states that trade between two countries will be mutually beneficial as long as their **domestic opportunity costs** of production differ. As a result, consumption increases through specialisation and trade compared to a situation of self-sufficiency. Although highly simplified, both principles help our understanding as to why international trade is important in leading to a better allocation of the world's scarce resources.

Free trade and protection

Since free trade leads to a rise in world economic welfare, why should any country adopt policies which prevent free trade? Sometimes policies are adopted which distort market forces in order to give a competitive advantage to the domestic industry of an economy. Such policies are called **protectionist** policies because they provide some degree of protection from foreign competition. There are various methods of protecting domestic industry.

A modern UK-registered container vessel
Source: Bibby Line Group.

Tariffs

A **tariff** is a tax on imports. It can be either specific, that is so much per unit or *ad valorem*, which is a percentage of the price. Like all indirect taxes, tariffs have the impact of reducing the supply and raising the equilibrium price of the import. This gives a competitive advantage to home-produced goods and services, which become more attractive to consumers, resulting in a fall in imports.

Consider the economy in figure 10.1. If it did not engage in world trade, consumers would pay price P and consume quantity Q. This would be determined by the domestic supply and demand for the commodity. If

the economy engaged in international trade, then consumers would benefit from international specialisation. World supply is shown as supply (world). Under these circumstances prices would fall to P_1. Consumption of the good would rise from Q to Q_4. At this price, however, only Q_1 would be supplied by the domestic producers. This means that domestic production has fallen from Q to Q_1. Lower-cost overseas producers have free access to the market, which has benefitted consumers, but domestic producers have suffered, leading to a fall in employment in the industry. The imposition of a tariff, like all indirect taxes, would shift the supply curve upwards. This would increase the price to domestic consumers from P_1 to P_2. Production by domestic producers would increase from Q_1 to Q_2. Some jobs in the domestic economy would be saved.

Clearly, tariffs distort market forces and prevent consumers from benefiting from all the advantages of international specialisation and trade.

Quotas

Quotas are restrictions on the maximum quantity of imports. Their effect will be to reduce the supply of imports on the domestic market. This will lead to a higher equilibrium price than would occur in a free market. Just as with tariffs the impact is to prevent the domestic consumer from benefiting from all the advantages of international trade. One difference is that, whereas the government gains revenue as a result of tariffs, with quotas the increased price paid by consumers results in the foreign firm which supplied the imports earning higher profits. One answer might be for the government to sell licences to foreign firms to allow them to sell some allocation of the quota on the domestic market. The prospect of raised profits would ensure a market for the import licences.

Exchange control

One way of preventing excessive spending on imports is to set legal limits on the dealings in foreign currency that a country's citizens can make. If importers are limited in their access to foreign currency, they cannot pay for imports to the full extent of the domestic demand that exists. Imports will fall to a level below that which will occur in a free market. Again the consumer would suffer. **Exchange controls** existed in the UK before 1979 and there have been periods when

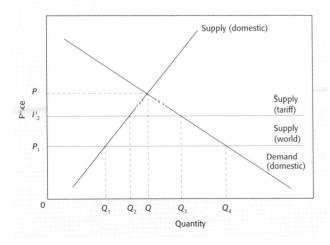

Figure 10.1 The effects of a tariff

there was a limit to the amount of foreign exchange that British citizens could take on overseas holidays. In 1979, all exchange controls were abandoned by the newly elected Conservative government. All member states of the European Union abandoned exchange controls in 1993.

Export subsidies

We have defined 'protectionism' in terms of any policy that distorts market forces to give competitive advantage to domestic industry. Sometimes, this is achieved through direct subsidies on exports. The impact of an export subsidy is to increase the supply of an industry's exports on the world market, which will have the impact of reducing price below that determined in free market equilibrium. Foreign consumers will enjoy an increase in their economic welfare as the price of the good falls. Those employed in the domestic market might also benefit as production increases to match demand for the lower-priced goods. They might enjoy higher wages and their jobs might be more secure but only as long as the subsidy lasts. Those who lose are the tax payers who have to pay for the subsidy. In addition, as firms divert output to the overseas market, the supply of goods may fall in the domestic market, leading to rising prices and reduced welfare for domestic consumers.

Other methods

The methods of protectionism described so far are all quite clear and obvious ways in which domestic industries can be given a competitive advantage over foreign industry in order to reduce imports and/or boost exports. Because these methods so obviously distort international market forces in pursuit of the more narrow national interest, they are all generally forbidden, except under very limiting circumstances, under the terms of international trading agreements such as the General Agreement on Tariffs and Trade (GATT).

Protectionist policies are sometimes called **expenditure switching** policies because their aim is clearly to switch expenditure, both domestic and foreign, to the output of goods and services of the domestic economy.

An assessment of the arguments in favour of protectionism

International specialisation and free trade are justified because they lead to an optimal allocation of resources on a world scale and leads to a rise in the economic welfare of consumers. Any arguments advanced in justification of protectionist policies can only be assessed if the impact on world resource allocation and consumer welfare is considered.

It is often argued that protectionism is justified:

◆ *To safeguard employment in the home economy.* An examination of the UK's trade accounts over the last few years will reveal the extent to which imports of manufactured goods have increased. The **import penetration ratio** is the proportion of the domestic sales of a product which is taken up by imports. For example, in 1968 the import penetration ratio in textiles was 16 per cent. This means that out of every £100 spent on textiles in Britain, £16 was spent on imported textiles. By 1997 the figure had risen to 53 per cent. In the category radio, television and communications equipment, the import penetration ratio was as high as 98% in 1997. As import penetration rises, domestic firms come under increasing pressure to maintain sales and the less successful will have to lay off workers and some may close down completely. This can result in considerable structural unemployment and can lead to calls for some degree of protection from imports. Very often interest groups, such as trade unions, will call for tariffs when faced with a flood of cheap imports from abroad. In 1966 full-time employment in manufacturing in the UK reached a peak of 11m. By 1998 this had fallen to just over 4m. Many of those made unemployed found jobs in the expanding service sector where full-time jobs increased from 6m jobs in 1966 to 11.7m by December 1998. However, at the same time there was a considerable increase in the number of long-term unemployed, especially in those regions which had formerly relied heavily upon manufacturing. This was because there was insufficient occupational and geographical mobility of labour to shift labour away from manufacturing jobs towards jobs in the service sector (see section 5). A long-term decline in the absolute levels of employment in manufacturing is termed **deindustrialisation**. If this process is a reflection of shifting comparative cost advantages in different economies, then we would predict that the process would lead to improved resource allocation and a rise in economic welfare. Clearly, import controls cannot be used to justify protection of jobs on economic grounds. Any argument in favour of import controls to protect jobs can only be justified on social grounds. To maximise economic welfare, labour should be considered as a resource that must be swiftly allocated and reallocated to its best use. This process can be aided by any measures to improve the occupational and geographical mobility of labour. Looked at in this way 'a flood of cheap imports' should be welcomed as a benefit to the consumer rather than seen as a threat to jobs.

◆ *To correct balance of payments disequilibria.*
During the 1950s and 1960s the UK's economic policy was often described as stop – go (see section 7). As governments implemented go policies to expand the economy, there was a rise in imports to satisfy increased demand and, as a result, the balance of payments went into deficit. At this time the UK was part of a managed exchange rate system and as a result the deficit led to downward pressure on the value of the £ and a fall in the UK reserves. This led to the government being forced to implement stop policies to slow the economy down and remove the deficit. These policies included raising income taxes and interest rates to prevent consumers purchasing imports. These policies were sometimes known as **expenditure dampening policies**. In addition to preventing imports, such policies also reduced consumer spending on the output of domestic industry, so the side effect was a rise in unemployment. This resulted in a call for expenditure switching policies as an alternative way of protecting the balance of payments and the exchange rate. The potential for such pressures will always exist when it is a government's policy to follow a managed exchange rate system rather than allowing the exchange rate to float. This argument for protectionism again cannot be justified on economic grounds because it leads to a less than optimal resource allocation.

Consumers will again suffer as they are prevented from purchasing the goods of their choice. The answer to the problem caused by balance of payments disequilibria is to consider how international trade is financed and to ensure that deficits do not create pressures which lead to the underutilisation of resources in an economy.

◆ *To prevent the exploitation of labour in developing economies.*
Very often as cheap goods are imported into a market, there are claims that the goods are cheap because labour in the exporting countries is paid a very low wage. It is claimed that the labour is exploited and as a result imports should be prevented. This results in a call for import controls on moral grounds but also often on the grounds that firms in the importing country cannot compete with the cheap imports because they have to pay higher wages. This argument in favour of import controls is often combined with the argument that they are required in order to protect jobs. Such arguments in favour of import controls have no economic justification whatsoever. If labour is cheap in an economy this is a reflection of that economy's factor endowment. A large supply of unskilled labour will lead to low wages and usually low priced products. The law of comparative advantage suggests that this will lead to increased economic welfare as those economies with cheap labour specialise in those products in which they have the lowest opportunity costs. This will be in those products which are highly labour intensive. It should be noted that there may well be moral arguments to justify protectionism in this case, but it should also be considered that any measures which reduce imports from such countries are likely to make the problem of low wages worse. This is because any fall in demand for imports from such economies will reduce the demand for labour further and make wage rates fall even lower.

◆ *To prevent dumping.*
Dumping is a term in economics which describes the process of selling goods in an overseas market at a price below the cost of production. This is a form of price discrimination because consumers in the home market will pay a higher price than those in the overseas market. The purpose of dumping

might be to destroy existing competition in the overseas market or to prevent newly established firms in the overseas market from becoming established. Dumping can be achieved through export subsidies provided by the home government or through ensuring that consumers in the home market pay a sufficiently high price to cover total costs. Alternatively, firms might be prepared to suffer losses in the short term if this allows them to destroy competition and create a monopoly, increasing excess profits in the long term. Clearly, if dumping leads to anti-competitive behaviours in the long run and prevents the emergence of comparative advantage, then import controls on products dumped in a market can be justified. It should be noted, however, that firms which face competition through cheap imports will often claim that goods are being dumped, when in reality the low prices of such goods are merely a reflection of the greater efficiency of the exporting firm. Whether a good is truly being dumped on a market needs careful investigation before import controls can be justified.

◆ *To safeguard infant industries.*
As shifts in comparative advantage occur, conditions for the location of industries in particular economies can become favourable. Establishing a fledgling industry can be quite difficult in the early years, however, especially if the new industry faces competition from a long-established company. The '**infant industry**' with only a small part of the market will not be able to benefit from all potential economies of scale and will be unable to compete in the market. It will be in the interests of the established firm to try to drive the new industry out of business and it might cut prices fiercely to retain its market. If the infant industry does have the potential to develop into an efficient producer in line with comparative advantage, then import controls may well be justified in this case. It should be noted, however, that many industries call for protection in their fledgling state but they then develop a vested interest in maintaining this protection once they have become established. Interest groups develop to lobby politicians to prevent import controls from being removed

Developments in World Trade Policy

During the 1930s, the world was gripped by a massive depression with millions unemployed. Governments resorted to protectionist policies to try to safeguard jobs. Tariff levels rose and often governments resorted to competitive devaluations of their currencies to reduce imports and boost exports. These policies were often called 'beggar-my-neighbour' policies because they tried to solve domestic problems with policies which could only have a detrimental impact upon other economies. Of course, if all countries engage in 'beggar-my-neighbour' policies, then none can win and the problems for all get worse. In fact, during the 1930s the volume of world trade reduced drastically under the impact of protectionist policies. After the Second World War, there was a resolve amongst the world's major trading nations that there should not be a return to the disastrous protectionist policies of the 1930s. As a result, three institutions were established to help to regulate the international economy. These institutions were:

1 The International Bank for Reconstruction and Development (later renamed the World Bank). This was established to assist in the reconstruction of the war-damaged economies of Europe and Asia. Once this had been achieved, its focus became the provision of funds to assist projects in the less-developed countries (LDCs).

2 The International Monetary Fund (IMF). This was established to promote international monetary stability and co-operation. It aims to avoid competitive devaluations through the provision of loans to those countries faced with balance of payments problems.

3 The General Agreement on Tariffs and Trade (GATT). This was founded in 1948 with the intention of promoting international trade. It established a series of multilateral trade negotiations between member countries designed to reduce the protectionist measures which remained in place from the 1930s. The negotiations were known as 'rounds' and they resulted in 45,000 tariff concessions covering about one fifth of world trade. These tariff reductions helped to contribute to high world growth rates averaging 8 per cent in the 1950s and 1960s. By the early 1980s deteriorating world trading conditions led to the Uruguay Round, which concluded in 1994. This updated and extended the

rules governing international trade. It has been estimated that world merchandise trade will be 755 billion US dollars higher in the year 2005 than it would have been without the package of measures agreed during the 4th Uruguay Round.

In 1995 the functions of GATT were taken over by the World Trade Organisation (WTO). This organisation, based in Geneva, has a potential membership larger than the 128 countries which signed up to GATT. It also has more extensive responsibilities. Whereas GATT supervised trade in goods, the WTO also has responsibility for services and ideas or 'intellectual property'. The WTO is also a permanent institution with an annual budget of 80 million US dollars.

Self-assessment task

Read the newspaper editorial below and then answer the questions that follow.

Free trade is fair

'Fair trade, not free trade' is the banner carried by protestors outside the World Trade Organisation conference. It is code for quotas, tariffs and prohibitions. So when Britain's man in Seattle blathers approvingly about 'fair trade', it matters. By adopting the language of the protectionists, Stephen Byers, the DTI Secretary, advertised before the hard bargaining had even started that this Government will not exert leadership to defeat obscurantism. Nor will President Clinton, who is backing away from America's commitment to free trade in order to appease the rioters and their friends in the media. If the two powers that built the world's open trading system – and are still seen as its custodians, even if Britain has surrendered trade policy to the EU – do not have the gumption to face down Dyke Action and the Raging Grannies, God help us.

Free trade does not happen of its own accord. The natural condition of the world is protectionist: the gains of increased commerce are spread widely, and to some degree invisibly, while the losses are concentrated heavily in sectors that mobilise quickly for political action – as French farmers and Detroit's motor industry have shown in their time. Trade barriers are rarely reduced without a Herculean effort by far-sighted leaders, acting in concert, at grand summits like this one in Seattle. So far, it looks as if the current generation of leaders is incapable of making such an effort.

The European Union is seeking to do little more than protect its ruinous system of farm subsidies, while suggesting otherwise with disingenuous demands for a comprehensive agenda. President Clinton – already electioneering for Al Gore – has abruptly changed US trade policy in a sop to the trade unions, calling for the WTO to extend its power into the area of labour rights. Mr Clinton is making emotive noises about 'child labour', but the real issue is cheap labour, which is the one competitive advantage left to poor countries. The gambit is rightly regarded as an invidious form of rich world protectionism by most of the WTO's 134 members. If pressed, it will wreck the meeting.

It is lamentable that the governments of the world's richest countries cannot find the political will – in the easiest of conditions, at the height of a long economic boom – to uphold the system that made them so rich. The best that can now be expected from this miserable summit is a fudge that does no damage.

Source: Daily Telegraph, 3 December 1999.

1 What is meant by 'fair trade'?
2 Discuss why the EU is reluctant to reduce its quotas, tariffs and prohibitions on trade with developing economies.

Summary

In this section we have recognised that:

- International trade is extremely important for the UK economy.

- The pattern of the UK's trade has changed much over the past 150 years; at the present time it is strongly focused on the EU and on other developed economies.

- Absolute advantage occurs when one country can produce a particular commodity with fewer resources than another country.

- Comparative advantage is a situation where trade is beneficial because the domestic opportunity costs of production vary between countries.

- Tariffs, quotas, exchange control and export subsidies distort the picture of free trade in the world economy.

- Under certain circumstances, the application of protectionist policies may be appropriate.

Key words

Definitions of Key words can be found in the Glossary on page 240.

absolute advantage
comparative advantage
deindustrialisation
domestic opportunity cost
dumping
exchange control
expenditure dampening
  policies
expenditure switching
  policies

free trade
import penetration ratio
infant industry
international trade
laissez-faire
mercantilism
protection
quota
self-sufficiency
tariff

Preparing for examinations

➤ Know how to plan your work and how to use your study time effectively before an examination
➤ Know what sort of examination questions to expect and how to apply a simple method to understand what they mean
➤ Know what OCR Economics examiners are looking for when marking your examination script
➤ Know the most common errors students make in Economics examinations

Introduction

In many respects this is the most important section in the book. To make a sporting comparison, the examination is your FA Cup Final, your Wimbledon tie break or your Superbowl decider. If you approach it in an appropriate way, it should be the means by which you realise the grade you were expecting, consistent with helping you achieve a result based on the effort you have put into your work. For some students, though, this is not the case. It can be like missing a penalty in the last minute or serving a double fault at match point. When this happens it is very unfortunate and examiners do not derive pleasure in witnessing it. For many students who are in this situation it is *not* that:

◆ they have failed to complete the work for the module;
◆ they have not understood the main concepts involved.

The principal cause of under performance or even failure can be bad examination technique. Experience has shown over and over again that some students make basic errors in their Economics examinations. The consequence of these errors is that they can make at least a grade difference in the final assessment or, in some cases, the difference between a pass grade and an unclassified result.

These common faults are explained at the end of this section. But before you get to this, it is important that you know what you need to do to succeed in OCR AS Economics. The seeds for success are sown well before you enter the examination room. The key to success is preparation! A well-used and highly relevant phrase for you to remember is:

'A FAILURE TO PREPARE IS A PREPARATION TO FAIL'

For many years, this was on the office wall of Howard Wilkinson, the former Leeds United Manager, and one of the longest serving football club managers in the UK. Why not put it on your wall? But, if you do, remember to practise what it says.

How to plan your work and study effectively

Get into the study habit and plan ahead

As a student, study is something you do from the first day of your AS course. The process of study involves the gradual accumulation of knowledge and should also include its regular review. Revision is not something you should do just before an examination. *Make study a habit. Make revision a habit.*

Each of us has our own preferences for when and where to study in an effective manner. Some people are most receptive to study in mornings; others prefer to work late and 'burn the midnight oil'. Think about what is best for yourself and do it.

At school or college, *use your time effectively*, particularly if you are in a situation where you have only to attend for time-tabled classes. Think about how much additional time there is at your disposal; by all means have a social life, but reserve regular periods for your own private study *and do it*. In other words, build breaks into your study time – not the other way around. So, get into a routine of regular study. Have a set time and place to work, and stick to it.

Adaptation from an original drawing by Emily Bamford

A second important aspect of time management is that of *planning*. As a student, this is something you should try to do. It is particularly important where you are taking AS subjects on a staged basis, as there is only about four and half months time between the start of teaching and you taking the first examination. So, here are a few simple things you should do:

◆ Read through your class notes on a *daily* basis; follow this by reading about the subject matter in this text. You will also find it useful to use some of the other texts on the recommended reading list, particularly to obtain other examples and applications of economic concepts.

◆ Make a *weekly* plan of what you have to do and what you have actually done. Tick off items as you complete them. Table 1 shows an example of a simple planner you might like to use.

◆ Above all, *think and plan ahead*. Find out when mock examinations are to be held; know precisely when your actual examinations will be taking place.

And remember what was said earlier: 'A failure to prepare is a preparation to fail.'

Week commencing 16 October	Lesson topic	Homework due	Study tasks
Monday			Homework for 19 October completed
Tuesday	Price elasticity of demand – definition, calculations, meaning		N R
Wednesday			
Thursday	Business relevance of price elasticity of demand. Other elasticities – income and cross elasticities	Essay on how prices are determined	N
Friday			
Saturday			
Sunday			OCR assessment task from Section 2 completed
Outstanding work for next week	Read up about topics from Thursday's lesson. Look at past papers for other questions on elasticities of demand.		

Table 1 A daily and weekly study planner pro-forma
Notes: N – notes checked through
R – topic read up in text books

A few hints on how to study effectively

Each of us has a preferred study environment where we can work in an effective and efficient way. For most of us it is likely to be a bedroom or a school library where the distractions going on around us can at least be shut off for an hour or two. The best time for study may also vary – much will depend upon your family circumstances and how you can arrange to study in relation to these and other commitments on your time. Whatever the best time, the following advice should help you.

◆ Put yourself in a position where you can *concentrate on your work*. This is most unlikely to happen if your CD player is turned on or there is your favourite television programme being broadcast in the same room.

◆ The *attention span* of most people is 40–60 minutes. After such a period, have a drink and a rest, maybe watch a short television programme before studying for a further period.

◆ When reading, *make notes* on what you have read and incorporate these into your class notes on a particular topic. You will also find it useful to do the self-assessment exercises in this book and work through sample examination questions on a topic. Writing and working in this way greatly enhances your understanding of a topic. *Do not just read material on its own* – the problem with this approach to study is that you will very quickly forget what you have read. The big advantage also of making notes is that they will be there for future revision when you need them.

◆ Once you have completed the study of a particular topic, condense your notes down onto a *revision card*, which you will find invaluable for use shortly before examinations. An example of such notes is shown in figure 1.

So, it is not so much how long you study but how effective you are in your studying. Make sure you use your time effectively so that you *feel in control of your own learning experience*.

And remember: 'A failure to prepare is a preparation to fail.'

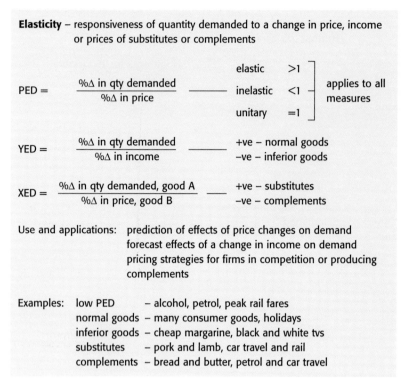

Elasticity – responsiveness of quantity demanded to a change in price, income or prices of substitutes or complements

$$PED = \frac{\%\Delta \text{ in qty demanded}}{\%\Delta \text{ in price}}$$

elastic   >1
inelastic   <1   applies to all measures
unitary   =1

$$YED = \frac{\%\Delta \text{ in qty demanded}}{\%\Delta \text{ in income}}$$

+ve – normal goods
–ve – inferior goods

$$XED = \frac{\%\Delta \text{ in qty demanded, good A}}{\%\Delta \text{ in price, good B}}$$

+ve – substitutes
–ve – complements

Use and applications: prediction of effects of price changes on demand
forecast effects of a change in income on demand
pricing strategies for firms in competition or producing complements

Examples: low PED   – alcohol, petrol, peak rail fares
normal goods – many consumer goods, holidays
inferior goods – cheap margarine, black and white tvs
substitutes   – pork and lamb, car travel and rail
complements – bread and butter, petrol and car travel

Figure 1 Example of revision card

The OCR case study

All AS Economics question papers consist of a case study from which a series of questions are drawn. The case study represents a concise, self-contained economic situation indicative of the subject content of the module. The Self-assessment tasks include many examples of the kinds of questions and case studies you can expect in OCR's examination papers. In addition the appendix to this section shows some typical examples of complete specimen examination papers.

There are two types of case study. These are:

1 Case studies which are 'synthetic' in so far as they have been produced specifically for examination purposes. The Molar Dental Practice case study in the Market System specimen paper is one such case. It has, though, been derived from an actual situation, involving real economic problems and issues.

2 Case studies which contain 'actual' or 'real world' information, which is reproduced in the same way as it appears in the original source or some adaptation of this. The case studies in the other specimen papers are of this form.

All case studies have an actual theme or themes, drawn from the subject content of the module. When you read through the case study, you should think carefully and deliberately about the following:

1 Look for the economic theory or concepts around which the case study has been compiled and from which questions have been derived. If the case contains data, think about how these concepts are embedded in the data.

2 Look at the title of the case study – this may well give you some clues.

3 Where the case study contains real data, look for any dates, labels or footnotes and if there is a stated source. Again, these may help you to understand its context. If the data are in the form of a table, look for any trends and important features. Questions are likely to be drawn from these. (Refer back to the Introduction for more advice.)

4 If the case study contains a chart or diagrams, look to see if you can identify any patterns or outstanding features. If there are, then there is likely to be a question on these. (Again, refer back to the Introduction.)

5 Once you have done these simple yet fundamental tasks, you will feel more confident to answer the questions that follow.

Self-assessment task

Spend ten minutes reading through each of the case studies in the appended question papers. When you have done this, ask yourself the following questions:

(a) What is the key economic concept or concepts in the case?

(b) Is this confirmed by the title? Or is the title of little relevance?

(c) Can you identify any important features in the data provided?

(d) Do you recognise how these features can support your knowledge of the key concept or concepts? Make a few notes on each.

Examination questions

Types of question

The appendix contains specimen question papers for each of the three OCR AS Economics units. These papers contain the following general types of question:

◆ short answer questions;
◆ questions where continuous prose is required;
◆ questions which require you to interpret the data provided in the case study.

In all instances the mark allocation is clearly shown in brackets. This indicates how many marks are allocated to each part out of the total marks available for the examination.

Short answer questions require short answers. It is important for you to remember this. In some cases, the answer required may be no more than a single word, a phrase or a number. In other cases, it may be a diagram with a sentence or two of explanation. What is required for a particular question should be clear from:

◆ the precise wording of the question;
◆ the marks allocated to it, relative to others on the question paper.

Questions where continuous prose is required will always be those at the end of the set of questions in a particular examination paper. For example, Qs (d) and (e) on the Market System specimen paper are this type of question. In the case of questions which have five marks available, a paragraph or so of writing is normally needed to answer the question effectively. Questions with higher marks usually require rather more writing than those with lower marks allocated to them.

Questions which require you to interpret the data provided in the case study. The use of data and their interpretation is a very important part of the economist's 'tool kit'. Some of the basic data handling skills you need were outlined in the Introduction. Each of OCR's AS case study questions will contain some data, either in the text of the case study or in a separate table, graph or diagram.

In all AS units, these data will be actual information, usually from a published source, or data which have been compiled specifically for the case study.

Whatever the type of question, all of the AS units are seeking to examine your knowledge and understanding of the case material. It is therefore very important for you to use this material as directed in your answers and draw upon it consistently throughout your examination script. This skill is a very important one for you to acquire.

The wording of questions

A lot of care, thought and attention goes into the final production of all OCR examination papers. So, when you sit an examination, it is important to appreciate that the questions which are on the examination paper have been set by an examiner who is requiring you *to answer these questions.* Put another way, examination papers never contain questions such as:

Write all you know about ...

or:

Write as much as you can remember about ...

Unfortunately, this point is not always appreciated by some students.

All examination questions contain two very important instructions. These are called:

◆ *Directive words* – these words indicate what form the answer should take. For example, it could be in the form of a description, a discussion, an explanation or merely a statement. These words are there for a purpose, namely that they have been used by the examiners to say what they are looking for (in skill terms when you answer a particular question).

◆ *Content words* – these are much more diverse in nature since they cover the whole of the subject area of the AS syllabus. Their aim is to make clear to you, the candidate, what is the focus of the question being set, and indeed, what examiners expect you to write about.

Table 2 shows a list of key directive words which will be used in OCR AS Economics examination questions. *You should study these carefully and understand what each means.* You will then appreciate that a question which asks:

Define price elasticity of demand

is not the same as

Explain what is meant by price elasticity of demand

is not the same as

Discuss the relevance of price elasticity of demand in business

Directive word	What it means	Where you can expect it to be used
Calculate	Work out using the information provided	All AS
Define	Give the exact meaning	units,
Describe	Give a description of	usually in
Give (an account of)	As 'describe'	the early parts
Give (an example of)	Give a particular example	of the questions
How	In what way or ways	
Illustrate	Give examples/diagram	
Outline	Describe without detail	
State	Make clear	
Summarise	Give main points, without detail	
Which	Give a clear example/state what	
Analyse	Set out the main points	All AS units
Apply	Use in a specific way	
Compare	Give similarities and differences	
Explain	Give clear reasons or make clear	
Account for	Give reasons for	
Consider	Give your thoughts about	
Assess	Show how important something is	All AS
Comment upon	Give your reasoned opinions on	units
Criticise	Give an opinion, but support it with evidence	but usually in the *later*
Discuss	Give the important arguments, for and against	parts of questions
Evaluate	Discuss the importance of, making some attempt to weight your opinions	

Table 2 Key directive words

A simple method for understanding and interpreting examination questions
Short answer and data response questions

The appendix to this section gives typical OCR AS question papers for each of the three units. You will now find some valuable advice on how you can understand what the questions mean and therefore, how you can be expected to answer them.

Look at the Market System specimen paper on pages 181–184. The early questions are asking you for some

basic knowledge of the unit. For example:

(a) (i) Define the term 'opportunity cost' [2]

If you look at table 2, then 'define' means 'give the exact meaning'. In other words, the question requires you to 'give the exact meaning of the term opportunity cost'. The allocation of two marks to this question indicates that this task requires a short answer of one or possibly two sentences.

So, if you refer back to section 1, you can find the information you need.

Moving on, the next question is:

(a) (ii) With reference to figure 1, explain the trade-offs which are facing the Townley Regional Health Authority [4]

Again, looking at table 2, you will see that 'explain' is in the second block of words. This indicates that the task is that bit more challenging than (a) (i), and requires you to 'give clear reasons or make clear' the trade-offs which are facing the Townley Regional Health Authority. The question also requires you to use figure 1 for this purpose. The four marks further indicate that you should spend at least five minutes on your answer.

So, again, refer back to section 1; then use your knowledge of trade-offs to see from figure 1 that the trade-off is between the provision of dental services and GP services. A good answer would be one which explicitly referred to points A and B on the patient treatment frontier and simply interpolated the trade-offs from the data on the x and y axes.

In this simple way you should be able to know and interpret what you need to do to make an effective response to short answer and data response questions.

Questions where continuous prose is required

Again, look at the specimen question paper for the Market System unit. Part (e) is a typical example of this type of question. Eight marks, almost one fifth of those available, have been allocated to this question. You should try therefore to write for at least a quarter of an hour. If you want to do well, then high marks can be obtained for a good clear answer.

(e) An economist would argue that the market for private dental treatment in Townley is an example of monopolistic competition.

Using the evidence in lines 15–24, discuss the extent to which this market is an example of monopolistic competition. [8]

Let us now take a close look at the question. Again, going back to table 2, you will see that 'discuss' means 'give the important arguments for and against'. This requirement is further supported in the question wording by the addition of 'the extent', indicating that the case study contains only partial evidence that private dentists in Townley operate in a monopolistically competitive market.

Figure 2 shows a simple but effective method that you can use to understand this type of question. Refer back to section 3 for content details.

If you do this then you have the basis for a good, meaningful answer to the question: you will also have a logical structure to follow when writing your answer.

How to impress AS economics examiners

Let us start with a few typical comments that OCR examiners will write on some of the examination answers they read:

'Does not answer the question'

'Too vague'

'Misses point of question'

'No application'

'Commentary not made'

'Ignores second aspect of question'

These comments clearly indicate that the candidates have not done what was expected from them in the question. So, the first way to impress any examiner reading your examination scripts is:

To answer the question

In other words, produce an answer as directed by the question. The information above, in particular the simple method for dissecting examination questions, should help you to write your answer in a clear, well-structured manner as directed by the questions. This point cannot be emphasised too much!

There are various other ways in which you might impress an AS examiner. For example:

◆ *Diagrams* These are very important and a relevant means of economic explanation. Many of the topics you come across in AS Economics can be illustrated by a diagram or by means of an explanation supported by a

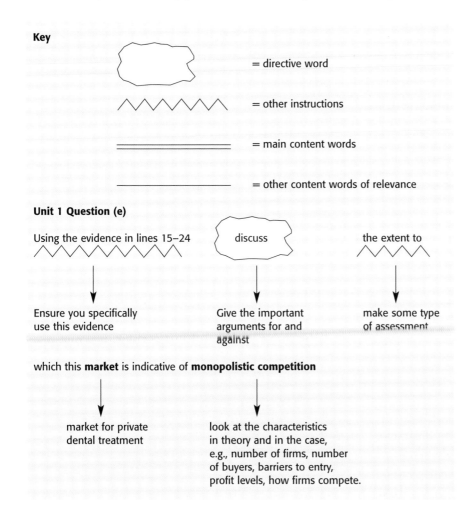

Figure 2 How to dissect a continuous prose question

diagram. You have only to glance at the sections in this book to see this. So, a relevant correctly drawn diagram, used effectively in your answer, will impress an examiner reading your examination script. An example of good technique is shown in figure 3, which is a variation of figure 6.3 in unit 2.

The diagram above shows how the price of theatre tickets will be affected by the introduction of a subsidy. As this diagram indicates, the subsidy will lead to an increase in supply, shifting the supply curve downwards and to the right. The price which theatre goers will have to pay falls from P_1 to P_2 – it does not fall to P_3 as part of the subsidy (that shown between P_3 and P_2) will be retained by the theatre owners to offset the higher costs incurred due to the increase in the number of theatre visits demanded.

♦ *Current issues and problems* One of the reasons for studying AS Economics is to help you understand some of the things that are taking place around you. So, when you get the opportunity, do so! For example, if you are answering a question on the negative externalities associated with environmental pollution, you might refer to a local case which is known to you or something you have seen in a newspaper or magazine. Most of the topics in the syllabus can be supported by additional up-to-date material, not always found in text books.

♦ *Refer to things you have read* It follows that there are instances where it would support your answer if you referred to this source material by name, for example an article, an example from a text book or the views of a particular economist.

Common mistakes made in OCR Economics examinations

In addition to a failure to answer the question, the other main mistakes made by candidates are:

1 A failure to allocate writing time in an appropriate way.

2 Confusion over similar terms.

3 Meaningless, wrongly drawn diagrams or diagrams which add nothing to an answer.

Let us conclude this chapter by looking at each in turn.

1 The time available for each AS examination is relatively short – 1 hr 30 minutes. You must therefore make sure you allocate your writing time in the examination in a meaningful way.

Table 3 shows how you can do this. The following important principles should be applied:

♦ Roughly speaking, allocate your writing time in direct proportion to the marks available.

♦ Do not exceed the time you have allocated for each part.

♦ If you cannot do a particular question, leave it and move on to the next part. (You can always return to it later on in the examination if time permits.)

♦ You will only get marks for the questions you answer – your script, though, will always be marked out of the total marks which are available.

Taking the specimen examination paper for the National and International Economy (see pages 189–91), 1 hr 30 mins is available for this question paper.

You need to spend a few minutes looking at the case study and getting a feel for what the questions mean. Thereafter, allocate your writing time directly in relation to the marks available.

10 minutes (Initial reading)	Scan through the case study. Read the material carefully, highlighting main points; make sure you understand any data and try to pick out basic trends.

	Approx. minutes			
80 mins (Writing)	8	(a)	(i)	6 marks
			(ii)	
			(iii)	
	10	(b)	(i)	8 marks
	15		(ii)	12 marks
	5	(c)	(i)	4 marks
	12		(ii)	10 marks
	25	(d)		20 marks
				60 marks
	1 mark =			$1\frac{1}{3}$ min writing

Try to leave about 5 mins for	Final check; have a go at any parts where it was necessary to move on or any parts where a question could not be answered.

Table 3 A simple method for allocating time in an examination

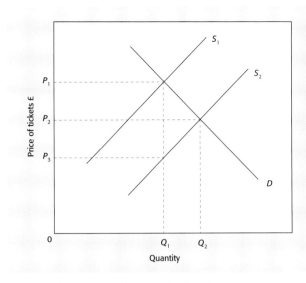

Figure 3 How to use a diagram effectively in your answers
Notes: D – Demand curve for theatre tickets
S₁ – Supply curve of theatre tickets
S₂ – Supply curve after introduction of subsidy

2 A second problem in Economics examinations is that, on occasions, candidates sometimes confuse terms which are similar (in terms of content) or which have similar names (but mean something different). Table 4 contains a few common examples from the AS Economics specification.

3 Finally, a common mistake which candidates often make is in the ways in which they use diagrams in their answers. Common errors are:

Topic	Often confused with
elastic demand	inelastic demand
allocative efficiency	productive efficiency
prices	costs
merit goods	public goods
direct taxation	indirect taxation
external costs/benefits	social costs/benefits
real income	nominal income
rate of interest	exchange rates
fiscal policy measures	monetary policy measures
aggregate demand	aggregate supply
balance of trade	balance of payments
income	wealth

Watch out also that you express formulae correctly – in particular elasticity formulae

Table 4 Common errors over terms and topics in the OCR AS Economics specification

- to label axes incorrectly or not to label them at all;
- to make diagrams too small;
- to draw lines and curves incorrectly, usually through being wrongly sloping;
- to fail to use a diagram in an answer when asked for one to be included;
- to include a diagram when one is not needed and where it does not enhance an answer at all.

Self-assessment task

Three examples of badly drawn/incorrect diagrams are shown in figure 4. How many improvements can you make to them?

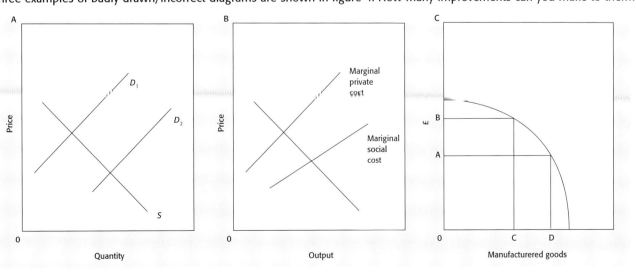

Figure 4 Examples of badly drawn diagrams

Self-assessment task

When you have completed studying each of the three AS units, see if you can do the specimen examination papers which follow on from this section. Do this under examination conditions and in the time allocated.

Remember to think about the matters raised in this section when you are completing this task.

Summary

In this concluding AS section we have established that:

- It is very important for you to be well-organised and to be able to plan ahead if you are to succeed in OCR Economics.

- Revision should be an ongoing process, not just a last-minute activity you carry out just before a written examination.

- OCR's examinations at AS contain a variety of forms of external assessment, with three main types of question.

- Candidates who underperform in examinations have usually not been adequately briefed on the type and style of question.

- A lack of time and an inability to understand the relevance of directive words are the most common causes of underperformance.

Sample examination papers

OCR   2881
Advanced Subsidiary GCE
ECONOMICS

UNIT 1: THE MARKET SYSTEM

Specimen Paper   45 marks

Additional materials:
  Answer paper

TIME 1 hour 30 minutes

INSTRUCTIONS TO CANDIDATES

Write your name, centre number and candidate number in the spaces provided on the answer
paper/answer booklet.

Answer **all** parts of the question.

Write your answers on the separate answer paper provided.

If you use more than one sheet of paper, fasten the sheets together.

INFORMATION FOR CANDIDATES

The number of marks is given in brackets [ ] at the end of each part question.

The quality of your written communication will be assessed in the final part question.

This answer must be written in continuous prose.

1

Answer all parts of this question

Townley Regional Health Authority

All of us at some time in our lives require the services of doctors, dentists and hospitals. Traditionally, in the UK, these services have been provided by the public sector, free of charge to users. Like any sector of the economy though, there is a genuine problem of how to meet the health care needs of the community from the limited resources available. The problem of health care is a very good illustration of what economists mean by the 'economic problem'.   6

The task of allocating resources for health care is carried out by organisations known as Regional Health Authorities. Due to the nature of their funding, there is a maximum quantity of health care that can be provided at any one time. The regional health authority in Townley is faced with just such a problem.   9

Suppose it has to provide just two services to the community, medical services through local doctors (GPs) and dental services through local dental practices. The Production Possibility Frontier in Figure 1 shows some of the trade-offs facing the Townley Regional Health Authority.   12

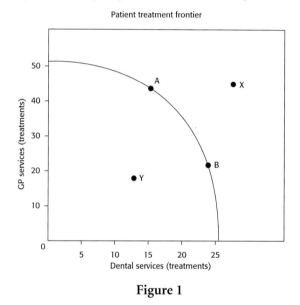

Figure 1

Due to financial pressures and increased demands for its services, the Townley Regional Health Authority is continuously seeking to make a more effective use of its resources.   14

The Molar Dental Practice, like other dentists in Townley, has recently taken the decision to 'opt out' of the control of the Townley Regional Health Authority. It is now one of a large and growing number of private dental practices in the town which treat only private patients who pay the 'full cost' for any treatment they receive. Market research undertaken for the practice shows the estimated demand schedule for the services it provides. This information is shown in Table 1 below.   19

2

Table 1

Estimated Demand Schedule for Treatment Provided by the Molar Dental Practice

Average Price of Treatment	Quantity of Treatment Demanded per month
40	350
35	375
30	400
25	450
20	500
15	600
10	800

Other private dentists in Townley do not charge exactly the same price for treatment as the Molar Dental Practice. However, the market is a very competitive one, with businesses seeking to enhance their reputation in order to attract new patients who are seeking private dental treatment. At present, all private dentists are in a situation where they are able to take on any new patients who are willing to pay the charge for the treatment they receive.   24

(a) **(i)** Define the term 'opportunity cost'.   [2]

   (ii) With reference to Figure 1, explain the trade-offs which are facing the Townley Regional Health Authority.   [4]

   (iii) How can opportunity cost be used to explain the shape of the production possibility frontier?   [2]

   (iv) If the Townley Regional Health Authority makes a more effective use of its resources, how will this affect the production possibility frontier?   [2]

(b) **(i)** Use the data in the table to sketch the demand curve for services of the Molar Dental Practice and explain the shape of this curve.   [4]

   (ii) If the income level of patients falls, use a diagram to explain how this will affect the demand for dental services provided by Molar Dental Practice.   [4]

(c) The 'full cost' of providing dental services consists of some costs which are fixed and other costs which are variable (lines 17–18).

   (i) With aid of examples, explain the difference between fixed and variable costs for the Molar Dental Practice.   [4]

   (ii) If the wages of dental nurses increase, how might this affect the prices charged by the Molar Dental Practice to its patients?   [5]

3

(d) With reference to the data shown in Table 1,

    (i)   Briefly explain how this data might have been collected.   [5]

    (ii) Comment upon its usefulness to the owners of the Molar Dental Practice.   [5]

(e) An economist would argue that the market for private dental treatment in Townley is an example of monopolistic competition.

Using the evidence in lines 15–24, discuss the extent to which this market is an example of monopolistic competition.   [8]

OCR   **2882**
Advanced Subsidiary GCE
ECONOMICS

UNIT 2: MARKET FAILURE AND GOVERNMENT INTERVENTION

Specimen Paper   45 marks

Additional materials:
   Answer paper

TIME 1 hour 30 minutes

INSTRUCTIONS TO CANDIDATES

Write your name, centre number and candidate number in the spaces provided on the answer
paper/answer booklet.

Answer **all** parts of the question.

Write your answers on the separate answer paper provided.

If you use more than one sheet of paper, fasten the sheets together.

INFORMATION FOR CANDIDATES

The number of marks is given in brackets [ ] at the end of each part question.

The quality of your written communication will be assessed in the final part question.

This answer must be written in continuous prose.

11

Answer all parts of this question

The Problem of Pollution

Every day, there are innumerable instances where firms and other organisations pollute their local environment, deliberately in the main but sometimes by accident. The extract below, taken from a national newspaper, reports on a particular case whereby the polluter was successfully prosecuted for the environmental problems caused by a spillage of chemicals into a local river.

Water firm is fined over salmon deaths

A water company was fined £175,000 yesterday for poisoning a salmon river. Severn Trent Water admitted leaking chemicals into the Wye, killing 33,000 young salmon – 98 per cent of the stock in the river.

Cardiff Crown Court heard that the leak was the company's 34th conviction since privatisation in 1990. Judge John Prosser criticised the company for its poor record and described its management as 'very slack indeed'. Mark Bailey, prosecuting for the National Rivers Authority, said that pollution from the Elan Valley water treatment works, at Rhayader, Powys, had 'catastrophic consequences for the river'.

'An estimated 33,000 young salmon were exterminated by this leak, which affected eight kilometres of river', he said. 'It is relatively easy to replace adult salmon, but these young salmon need to be replaced with the fish from the same gene pool. Severn Trent caused this catastrophe through a collection of errors, including bad management and inferior maintenance. The area is one of the most significant salmon fishing areas in England and Wales and this is one of the most significant incidents. The sheer number of fish killed is higher than any other incident.'

Judge Prosser told water company executives sitting in the court that the leak was due to design defects, gross mismanagement and inferior maintenance. The company also claimed it was not responsible for the whole of the pollution.

Incidents such as the one described above are the outcome of a situation whereby the market mechanism has failed to produce the best allocation of resources due to negative externalities. Economists can explain the pollution of the River Wye by Severn Trent Water in terms of the diagram shown in Fig. 1. on the following page.

12

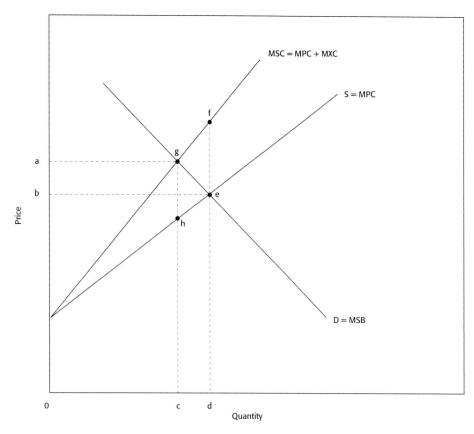

(MXC = marginal external costs; MPC = marginal private costs;
MSC = marginal social costs; MSB = marginal social benefit)

Fig. 1: Private & Social Cost Divergence

[Adaptation: Wilkinson M, Equity, Efficiency and Market Failure, Heinemann Educational, 1997 and Daily Telegraph, 6 August 1996]

13

(a) (i) Describe what is meant by a negative externality. [2]

   (ii) Use the evidence in the newspaper article to show how negative externalities apply to this particular pollution incident. [6]

(b) Use Fig. 1 to answer the following questions and, in each case, assume a competitive market operates with no government intervention.

   (i) What would be the market equilibrium price and output? Explain your answer. [4]

   (ii) What would be the price and output at the social optimum? Explain your answer. [4]

   (iii) What are the consequences for the firm and for its consumers of the differences between price and output levels at the market equilibrium and the social optimum? [6]

(c) (i) Drawing upon the case described in the newspaper article, state the arguments for and against fines as a means of reducing environmental pollution. [6]

   (ii) With the help of Fig. 1, explain how it might be possible to apply a pollution charge or green tax in this particular case. [7]

(d) Suppose the National Rivers Authority decides to consider closing the present Elan Valley water treatment works and recommends its replacement with a new works in a different site. Discuss how an economist might use the cost-benefit approach to determine whether this action should be taken. [10]

14

©OCR 1999
(Oxford, Cambridge and RSA Examinations)

OCR   **2883**
Advanced Subsidiary GCE
ECONOMICS

UNIT 3: THE NATIONAL AND INTERNATIONAL ECONOMY

Specimen Paper   60 marks

Additional materials:
   Answer paper

TIME 1 hour 30 minutes

INSTRUCTIONS TO CANDIDATES

Write your name, centre number and candidate number in the spaces provided on the answer paper/answer booklet.

Answer parts (a) to (c) and **either** d(i) or d(ii).

Write your answers on the separate answer paper provided.

If you use more than one sheet of paper, fasten the sheets together.

INFORMATION FOR CANDIDATES

The number of marks is given in brackets [ ] at the end of each part question.

The quality of your written communication will be assessed in the final part question where there is a choice of question.

This answer must be written in continuous prose.

20

Answer this question

<u>Japan and the UK – A Tale of Two Economies</u>

Japan used to be seen as a strong economy. It consistently enjoyed steady economic growth, low inflation, low unemployment and a surplus on its current account balance until recent years when it was hit by the 'Asian crisis'. Banks and businesses collapsed. Aggregate demand fell and unemployment started to rise. In 1998, the situation grew worse. Output declined, unemployment rose further and confidence fell to a record low level. In an attempt to stimulate the economy out of recession, the Japanese government increased its spending on capital projects, training schemes for the unemployed and support for the housing market. Monetary policy was also eased with the rate of interest being reduced on several occasions.

The Asian crisis subsequently became a global crisis as it spread to Russia and Latin America. The UK government feared it would result in a recession in the UK. In a bid to avoid this, the Bank of England cut interest rates from 7.5% in September 1998 to 6% in January 1999. The government also eased fiscal policy.

Table 1 Key Indicators of the Japanese Economy 1995–1999

Year	% Change in Real GDP	Unemployment %	Inflation %	Current Account Balance ($b)
1995	1.4	3.2	−0.5	114
1996	5.2	3.3	0.0	68
1997	1.4	3.4	1.4	94
1998+	−2.9	4.1	0.2	120
1999+	−0.4	4.6	−0.9	150

Table 2 Key Indicators of the UK Economy 1995–99

Year	% Change in Real GDP	Unemployment %	Inflation %	Current Account Balance ($b)
1995	2.8	8.1	3.4	−3.2
1996	2.6	7.3	2.4	0.1
1997	3.5	5.5	3.1	7.0
1998+	2.5	4.7	3.0	−1.7
1999+	1.0	4.8	1.2	−6.6

Note: + estimates

21

©OCR 1999
(Oxford, Cambridge and RSA Examinations)

(a) The following economic terms are included in the above material:

    (i) Current account balance

    (ii) Recession

    (iii) Fiscal policy

    Describe what each means. [6]

(b) (i) Explain how an economic slowdown in Japan might affect the UK economy. [8]

    (ii) Using the data provided in Tables 1 and 2, compare the economic performance of Japan and the UK for the period shown. [12]

(c) (i) Describe how the unemployment rate in the UK is calculated. [4]

    (ii) Using the information provided in Tables 1 and 2, comment upon the relationship between changes in the rate of unemployment and changes in the rate of inflation. [10]

(d) **Either:**

    (i) Discuss why growth rates may differ between particular economies. [20]

    or

    (ii) Discuss alternative government policies for reducing the rate of inflation in an economy. [20]

22

A2 Unit

Economics in a European context

11 The 'New Europe'

On completion of this section you should be able to:

➤ understand how the 'New Europe' has evolved during the 1990s

➤ understand how the EU is likely to be geographically extended in the future

➤ explain how decisions are made and implemented within the EU

➤ describe the nature of free trade areas, customs unions and economic unions and the differences between them

➤ explain why these forms of integration do not always work in reality as economic theory may suggest

➤ analyse how Europe compares with other major economic forces in the global economy

The origins of the European Union

The origins of European economic integration are largely political and are rooted in the immediate aftermath of the Second World War. With so much of Europe ravaged by the effects of war there was a pressing need for economic reconstruction. The UK participated wholeheartedly in these plans through the US-sponsored Marshall Aid programme and was an important architect of the Organisation for European Economic Co-operation (OEEC), the forerunner of the OECD.

Around the same time other schemes for European co-operation were also being implemented. The most important of these were the formation of a Customs Union between Belgium, Luxembourg and The Netherlands in 1948 and the Schuman Plan for the pooling of the coal and steel industries in Western Europe, which led to the European Coal and Steel Community (ECSC) in 1951. The important point about this alternative route to European unity was that it was to be pursued by economic means. The founders of the ECSC went on to sign the Treaty of Rome in 1957 creating the European Economic Community (EEC). The Treaty of Rome committed the 'Six' to create a Customs Union, involving agreement on a 'common market', a common external tariff against non-members, and with national policies to be replaced by Community policies in certain areas of economic activity (notably agriculture). Britain stood apart from this movement and instead formed the looser European Free Trade Area (EFTA) with Austria, Switzerland, Sweden, Norway, Denmark and Portugal (the 'Seven'). It was to be the former version of unity which was to win the day with

enlargements in 1973, 1981 and 1986 moving the EEC from Six to Nine to Twelve.

The development of economic integration in the 1990s

The 1990s have witnessed an unprecedented momentum in the European integration movement. Following the acceptance of the Delors Report in 1989, moves towards Economic and Monetary Union (EMU) began on 1 January 1990. Alongside, the Single European Market (SEM) was 'completed' on 31 December 1992, leading to greater freedom of movement of goods, services, labour and capital, and in 1993 the Treaty on Economic Union (The Maastricht Treaty) came into effect, committing the member states of the European Union (EU) to the launch of a single currency by January 1999. The European Economic Area (EEA), from 1994, extended the single market to the remaining members of the European Free Trade Area (EFTA). Further enlargement of the EU occurred in 1995 with the accession of Austria, Finland and Sweden. On 1 January 1999, in a blaze of publicity and celebration, the Euro was launched with eleven of the fifteen members of the EU joining a single currency area.

European integration has not been without its problems and challenges in the 1990s nor has it been solely a Western European phenomenon. The early years of the 1990s saw the Exchange Rate Mechanism (ERM) of the European Monetary System (EMS) run into difficulties in a period of currency instability in 1992/3. Major devaluations of sterling, the lira, the French franc, the Irish punt, the Spanish peseta and the Portuguese escudo contributed to the collapse of the EMS. The dramatic events in Central and Eastern Europe Countries (CEEC) in the late 1980s ushered in an era in which the EU could not ignore developments in its own backyard. With the collapse of the Council for Mutual Economic Assistance (Comecon), CEEC began to look for new markets in Western Europe. From an initial fear of cheap CEEC imports the EU has done much to help these countries in their transition to the market economy and to aid their integration with the EU. Poland, Hungary, the former Czechoslovakia and Slovenia formed the Central European Free Trade Area (CEFTA) in 1992 and a series of Europe Agreements have been signed with the EU to promote free trade in a number of 'non-sensitive' goods. By 1993, a set of criteria (the Copenhagen Criteria) had been agreed by which to judge the readiness of former command economies to join the EU. In 1997, the European Commission put forward Agenda 2000, which assessed ten CEECs on the basis of these criteria: the Czech Republic, Estonia, Hungary, Poland and Slovenia have met the criteria and preparations for membership by 2003 have begun. Figure 11.1 shows the changes which have led to the map of Europe being redrawn from that which might appear in a conventional atlas.

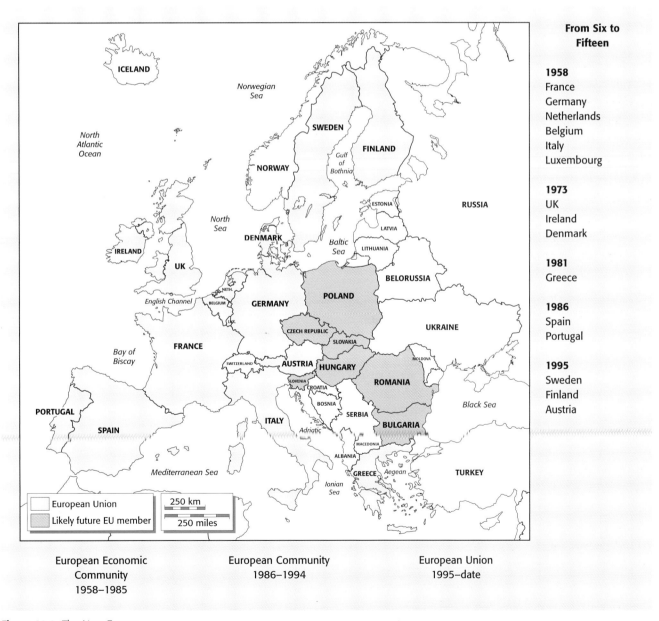

From Six to Fifteen

1958
France
Germany
Netherlands
Belgium
Italy
Luxembourg

1973
UK
Ireland
Denmark

1981
Greece

1986
Spain
Portugal

1995
Sweden
Finland
Austria

European Economic Community 1958–1985

European Community 1986–1994

European Union 1995–date

Figure 11.1 The New Europe

The EU in the global economy
Forty years on from the Treaty of Rome, the EU 15 is the dominant trading bloc in a world economy where multilateral trade has proliferated on a 'regional' rather than global basis. A few general statistics illustrate this dominance:

- With 390m relatively high-income consumers, the EU is the most important consumer market in the world.
- Through trade, the economies of the individual member states are increasingly dependent upon each other.
- The EU had a 40 per cent share of world exports in 1997; its nearest rival, the North America Free Trade Area, consisting of the USA, Canada and Mexico, had 17 per cent.
- The value of the EU's exports was approximately ten times greater than those of Japan and the Asian Tigers, and thirty times greater than for China.

The aim of rest of this unit is to examine the nature and meaning of economic integration and change in both Western and Eastern Europe by applying the economist's 'tool kit' of concepts, theories and techniques which have been built up in the specification.

The meaning and nature of economic integration
What is meant by the term economic integration? Healey defines it as follows:

> Economic integration refers to the merging together of national economies and the blurring of the boundaries that separate economic activity in one nation state from another.
> N. Healey, *The Economics of the New Europe* (Routledge, 1995)

The importance of the boundaries which economic integration seeks to 'blur' is that boundaries reduce the free movement of goods, services and the factors of production between member states (see section 10). The result is a reduction in economic efficiency due to:

Tariffs Tariffs create a barrier to the free movement of goods and services by raising the price of imported goods and services relative to those produced domestically. This increase in the relative price of imports causes a reduction in demand and an increase in domestic supply (see figure 10.1).

Quotas Quotas are physical limits on the quantity of imports and can be thought of as having very much the same effect as a tariff. Their outcome is to restrict the quantity of imports and to force up domestic prices.

Government subsidies Government subsidies are a more subtle form of protectionism but, nevertheless, restrict the free movement of goods and services (see section 6). They enable domestic producers to compete with foreign producers where otherwise such competition would be difficult. This is shown in figure 11.2.

In this diagram UK producers could only produce Q_1 if they were to compete head-to-head with foreign producers at the world price (P_W). Given UK consumers demand quantity Q_3, the difference is made up by foreign imports. If the UK government were to subsidise producers in the UK by s per unit of output, the supply curve would shift to $S_{UK} + s$. UK producers are now able to supply Q_2 at the world price and the subsidy succeeds in reducing imports without raising prices to UK consumers. Once again the protection of the domestic market from international competition is separating economic activity in one nation state from another.

Taxation The tax systems of economies can differ in a number of ways:
(a) The tax base
The tax base refers to what is actually taxed in a country. The UK's tax base differs from that in other EU countries with children's clothing, newspapers and books, for example, being exempt from VAT (see section 6).

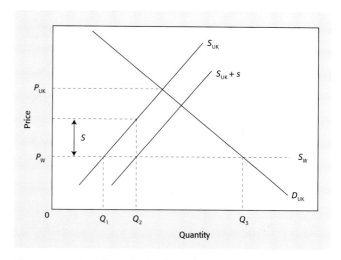

Figure 11.2 The effect of subsidising domestic producers

(b) The tax rate

Even if the tax base were the same in all countries, there may be different rates of taxation depending upon the role taxation plays in governments' fiscal policy (to discourage de-merit goods consumption and internalise negative externalities). UK indirect taxation of alcohol and tobacco is one of the highest in the EU. In the early 1990s excise duty on cigarettes in the UK was twice that in France, the duty on beer was eight times higher than in Germany and the duty on wine fifty times higher than in France. Differences in tax rates can therefore affect the relative prices of goods and services in an economy, which may hinder trade. For example, UK excise duties on wine are almost double the duties levied on beer. By increasing the price of wine relative to that of beer the UK taxation system discourages the consumption of wine. Since most wine is imported into the UK the tax system acts very much like a tariff, altering the terms of trade between countries or, as figure 11.3 shows, reducing the size of the UK market for French producers.

The extent to which variations in indirect tax regimes distort trade and consumption depends upon the way in which taxes are levied. If taxes are levied at the production stage (the so-called *origin* principle), the country with the lowest rates of taxation enjoys an artificial advantage over other countries. Where taxes are levied at the consumption stage, the distortions are removed, yet there needs to be a complex system of refunding taxes on goods exported and taxing imports.

If countries have removed boundaries, such as border controls as part of the integration process, different tax regimes add to the costs of trade.

Differences in taxation regimes can have other important effects on the allocation of resources in addition to the distortions on trade mentioned above. Differences in corporation tax, for example, could affect the location of economic activity as firms seek out low taxation economies and different taxes on incomes and savings distort the free movement of labour and business capital.

Exchange rates Exchange rates impose costs on those firms that trade internationally. Such costs are often termed *transaction costs*. The most obvious example of a transaction cost is the financial cost to firms of exchanging currencies. Transactions costs also include the time spent drawing up contracts or the time and effort spent 'hedging' against currency fluctuations. Such fluctuations in exchange rates also create uncertainty in international transactions, perhaps limiting the volume of trade between countries where individuals and firms are 'risk averse'. In addition some economists have suggested that the argument can be taken one stage further to consider how different macroeconomic policies can add to the boundaries separating economic activity.

Public procurement Public procurement refers to the power that central and local governments have as consumers of goods and services. The size of the public sector varies between economies, but, in the UK, public expenditure on goods and services alone currently accounts for approximately 21 per cent of GNP. In purchasing defence equipment, office equipment and cars or contracting out for waste collection and disposal services central and local governments may give preference to domestic suppliers. This clearly separates economic activity between nation states by closing off important markets to foreign producers.

National qualifications Differences in national qualifications clearly distort the free movement of labour between countries. For

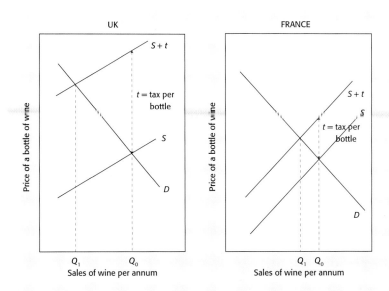

Figure 11.3 The effect on demand of different excise duties

example, if French accountancy qualifications are not recognised in the UK and vice versa, there will be a barrier to the movement of accountants and, to some extent, accountancy firms. Each country's accounting services market will be distinct and separate, resulting in a reduction in potential competition.

Self-assessment task

Non-Tariff Barriers (NTBs) are important obstacles to the free movement of goods, services and factors of production.

(a) Add to the types of NTBs given above using European examples where possible. Divide your list of NTBs into the following two categories:

- ◆ cost increasing barriers;
- ◆ barriers to entry.

(b) How might economic integration seek to eliminate such NTBs?

Levels of integration

Given the large number of boundaries between economies, economic integration is often thought of as a process. Economists analyse integration in terms of stages or levels, ranging from very weak forms of integration to very strong. The different levels of integration do not imply that countries need to move through each stage in sequence. For example, the Treaty of Rome called for the creation of a customs union (a stronger form of integration than a free trade area) from the start and the eventual development of a weak form of common market in its requirement for members to adopt common policies in areas such as agriculture and transport. Some would argue that the launch of the Euro (a Monetary Union) in 1999 has taken place before the EU has fully completed the Single Market or taken any significant steps towards creating an Economic Union. The five levels of integration most commonly used are presented in table 11.1.

Economists also use four terms to distinguish between different types of integration. They are:

1 Market integration Market integration refers to the idea that consumer and producer behaviour is governed by demand and supply conditions in the whole of the geographical area covered by economic integration. It implies that there will be significant flows of goods, services, labour and capital between nations. As such integration deepens price disparities although these will be reduced as a result of competition and trade. Rather than national markets being segmented and fragmented, nations will become part of a larger, single market.

2 Policy integration Policy integration refers to the idea that integration brings about greater co-operation and co-ordination of economic policies between member states. It does not have to mean that economic policies are centralised. For example, the introduction of the Euro has led to the centralisation of monetary policy, with the European Central Bank (ECB) determining Euro area interest rates, but fiscal policy has not been centralised. Instead, national governments conduct their own fiscal policy subject to the constraints of the Stability and Growth Pact which limits a country's budget deficit to 3 per cent of GDP. The EU has developed the notion of subsidiarity to determine whether economic policies require co-operation, co-ordination or centralisation. According to the notion of subsidiarity, economic policies centralised at the EU level are only justified when the policy involves significant externalities or economies of scale. External trade policy is determined centrally in the EU because if each member were to determine its own trade policy there would be important negative externalities on neighbouring economies. The Eurofighter for instance is a joint EU project because of the large economies of scale in the development and production of a modern jet fighter. Competition policy only applies in the case of monopolies, mergers or anti-competitive practices which affect the whole EU market, with national governments pursuing there own competition policy within their own borders.

3 Negative integration This refers to measures designed to remove boundaries and distortions in economic activity between nation states.

4 Positive integration This arises when there is some 'pooling' of decision making or when a centralised institution takes charge of economic policies, as in the case of the ECB.

Level of economic integration	Key characteristics	Comments
Free Trade Area (FTA)	1 Removal of tariffs and quotas on trade between member states. 2 Member states reserve the right to determine their own trade policy towards non-members of the FTA.	*The weakest form of economic integration which only involves negative integration. There is little in the way of market integration as NTBs may distort trade and the FTA may be restricted to a limited range of goods and services. There is a danger that trade may be 'deflected' as imports from non-members enter the FTA via the country with the lowest tariffs and then are re-exported tariff free.*
Customs Union (CU)	3 Removal of tariffs and quotas on trade between member states. 4 Member states agree to a common external tariff on trade with non-members.	*Avoids the problems of trade deflection but goes beyond negative integration since countries must sacrifice some of their economic sovereignty with respect to external trade policy. Only introduces a limited amount of positive and policy integration. Market integration is not developed as NTBs may arise to replace tariffs and quotas.*
Common or Single Market (SM)	5 Removes restrictions on the free movement of labour and capital between member states. 6 Removes NTBs by harmonising product standards, employment laws, taxation policies, competition policies, public procurement policies, state aid to industry, etc. 7 Adoption of common policies in one or more areas.	*By creating the conditions for a genuine single, borderless market, the degree of actual and potential competition is increased. There should be an increase in flows of goods, services and factors of production between member states and a reduction in price disparities. A significant increase in the amount of positive and policy integration occurs.*
Economic Union (EU)	8 Greater degree of harmonisation and co-ordination of economic policies. 9 Some degree of centralisation of economic policies, in particular macroeconomic policies.	*This is a rather vague concept and is really just an extension of the degree of integration found in the SM. There is not much agreement amongst economists of the precise definition of an Economic Union, although most would tend to stress the introduction of a degree of centralisation of economic policy making.*
Monetary Union (MU)	10 Extends macroeconomic policy co-ordination to the monetary field. 11 The degree of monetary union can differ from a system of semi-fixed exchange rates (EMS) to the adoption of a single currency.	*In its strongest form (single currency) MU involves centralised monetary policy. Eliminates exchange rate uncertainty, the transaction costs of dealing in exchanging currencies and gives rise to price transparency increasing trade flows and competition amongst member states. Requires greater co-ordination, harmonisation or centralisation of fiscal policy with respect to the business cycle, taxation and borrowing requirements.*

Table 11.1 The five levels of economic integration

At the time of writing the Eurofighter Typhoon is being developed by a group of European companies, and was intended originally to meet the needs of European air defence during the Cold War. The lead partners are Britain and Germany, with France being notably absent from the consortium. The French government tried unsuccessfully to have its own rather similar Rafale accepted for the role, but when this idea was rejected they pulled out of the project. Rising costs and the end of the Cold War caused the German government in particular to have grave doubts about the project, and the design specification had to be modified in order to reduce costs. The decision to go ahead with the production of this aircraft owes as much to a desire to preserve the European military aircraft industry as it does to considerations of current defence requirements.
Source: Photograph and caption kindly supplied by Dick Barnard.

Self-assessment task

Read the material below and then answer the questions that follow.

The European postal services industry

There has been considerable debate in recent years about the possibility of opening up European postal services to competition. The extract below refers to the prospects for such liberalisation of the European postal services market.

The greatest obstacle to a proper single market in the European Union is surely the existence of state-owned monopolies, like postal services.

European postal services share the obligation of 'universal service', the idea that it should cost the writer no more to send a letter to the most remote address in the land than to the house next door. Those who are sceptical of liberalisation fear that a postal free-for-all, on top of the competition they already face from faxes and e-mail, would make a universal service unaffordable. Hence their determination to keep their 'reserved areas' as legal monopolies.

Like many monopolies, though, Europe's state-owned postal services are often inefficient. Somehow more room must be found for more forms of competition from private sector courier services and other similar firms.

The Commission has proposed a two-stage reform: the immediate liberalisation of all mail that weighs more than 350 grams or is priced at more than five times the standard letter rate; and, from 2001, the liberalisation of 'direct' (junk) and cross-border mail.

	Number of postal staff	Domestic letter traffic, billion	Costs $ billion	Revenues $ billion	Price index for letters up to 100g (EU average = 100)
Germany	342,413	18.32	na	12.25	138
France	289,156	23.87	na	na	105
Italy*	221,534	6.62	5.63	4.13	130
Britain	189,000	16.75	5.83	6.29	54
Spain	65,355	4.06	0.92	0.87	32

A comparison of Europe's postal services in 1994

Notes: *1993 figures

na = data not available

Source: *The Economist*, 15 June 1996 (adapted).

1 With reference to the article, explain how state-owned postal services are obstacles to a 'proper single market'.

2 Explain why the obligation to provide a 'universal service' might be unattractive to private sector firms.

3 Comment upon how the price indices for letters in the table might have been constructed. Use the data to comment upon the relative performance of Europe's postal services.

4 Using economic analysis, assess whether the possible effects of any liberalisation of postal services would be beneficial.

12 The Single European Market and Economic and Monetary Union

On completion of this section you should be able to:

➤ apply the principle of comparative advantage to explain the trade benefits of integration

➤ explain why a customs union might be seen as a form of 'second best'

➤ analyse the static and dynamic effects of integration

➤ analyse the effects of integration on the mobility of labour and capital

➤ understand what is meant by the Single European Market

➤ understand what is meant by Economic and Monetary Union (EMU)

➤ explain why convergence criteria have been necessary to determine likely participation

➤ discuss the respective macro-economic implications for the 'ins' and 'outs'

➤ discuss the likely future progress and prospects of EMU

Economic analysis of integration

In section 10 you learned that free trade, based on comparative advantage, resulted in various benefits to all parties. The European Union, however, represents only a step towards free trade as tariff and non-tariff barriers between the members of the union are abolished but a uniform tariff is imposed against non-members. So, the EU promotes free trade amongst its member states but discriminates in trade with the outside world. What are the economic effects of such discrimination?

The static effects of a customs union

A customs union is one of the levels of integration introduced in the last section. Whilst the EU has begun the process of moving beyond this stage of economic integration, important non-tariff barriers have still to be eliminated. The costs and benefits of European economic integration can still be analysed using the theory of customs unions.

A customs union replaces the individual tariffs of member states with a common tariff against countries outside the union. Economists distinguish between two effects of the formation of a customs union:

◆ trade creation;
◆ trade diversion.

Let us look at each in turn.

1 Trade creation Trade creation refers to the replacement of high-cost domestic production with imports from a more efficient source. The source of imports is from a partner within the customs union. The effect is that countries in the customs union engage in more trade with each other and this gives rise to an increase in economic welfare. Figure 12.1 helps to illustrate this effect. It assumes that the UK is currently outside the EU and that the UK imposes tariffs on imports that raise the prices of goods from EU suppliers from P_{EU} to $P_{EU} + t$ and the goods from suppliers in the rest of the world from P_{ROW} to $P_{ROW} + t$. Both EU

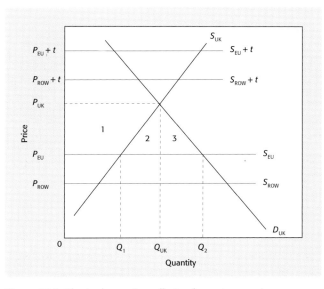

Figure 12.1 The trade creation effects of a customs union

202

suppliers and those from the rest of the world are priced out of the UK market, such that UK producers supply everything UK consumers demand (Q_{UK}) at a price of P_{UK}. When the UK joins the EU it must abolish tariffs on trade with its Union partners. The UK can now import from the EU at a price of P_{EU}. The UK must also adopt the Common External Tariff (CET) of the EU – here we assume that this is equal to the UK's existing tariff. The result is that UK consumers now increase consumption to Q_2. UK producers, however, are forced to reduce their supply to Q_1 at the lower price. The difference between Q_2 and Q_1 is made up by imports from countries in the EU, and in this way trade which previously did not exist is *created*.

What are the economic effects of this creation of trade? UK consumers are clearly much better off, since they consume more at a lower price. The increase in consumer surplus measures this benefit to UK consumers (areas 1 + 2 + 3). Domestic suppliers in the UK have lost out, however. The reduction in producer surplus of area 1 measures this loss. The net gain in economic welfare is represented by areas 2 + 3. You might notice that, although trade creation is a benefit to the UK, this benefit is not as large as if the UK had abolished all tariffs and bought at the world price. Trade creation is a step towards free trade and, therefore, the benefits are similar to those you learnt about in principle in section 10.

2 Trade diversion Trade diversion occurs when joining a customs union causes trade to switch, from a low-cost supplier outside the union to a higher-cost supplier within it. In reality the effect of a customs union will be to both create and *divert* trade, as figure 12.2 shows.

Take the case of the UK's trade in lamb with New Zealand. Before joining the EU, the UK placed a tariff on lamb's meat equal to t. This tariff raised the price of imports of lamb from the EU to $P_{EU} + t$ and from New Zealand to $P_{NZ} + t$. UK consumers consumed Q_2 lamb's meat in total, with Q_1 produced by UK farmers and Q_2Q_1 imported from the lowest-cost supplier (New Zealand). Once in the EU, tariffs on European lamb were abolished but tariffs on New Zealand lamb were replaced by an identical CET. The result was that the price of lamb fell to P_{EU}. Although extra trade is created by this price fall (Q_4Q_3 rather than Q_2Q_1), imports of New Zealand lamb are replaced by imports from Europe. The impact on economic welfare is now much

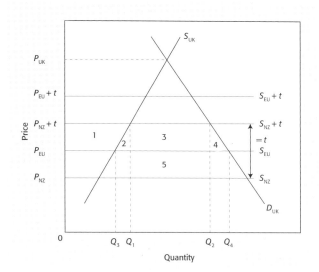

Figure 12.2 Trade creation and trade diversion effects of a customs union

less straightforward than the case of pure trade creation above. Consumers are once again better off, this time gaining an area of consumer surplus equal to 1 + 2 + 3 + 4. UK farmers are worse off, as producer surplus in the UK has fallen by area 1. The impact on the UK government must now be considered, since tariff revenue is lost. This revenue loss is equal to the area 3 + 5. The net result is a change in welfare of areas 2 + 4 minus area 5. The customs union no longer leads to an unambiguous increase in welfare. Whether European economic integration, in the form of a customs union, raises or lowers a country's economic welfare therefore depends upon:

Sheep herded together in a pen are all pregnant and are kept inside until they have had their lambs

◆ how inefficient EU producers are in comparison to world producers (the more inefficient they are, the bigger will be area 5 in figure 12.2);

◆ how price inelastic the demand and supply curves are for the commodities affected by the CET (the more inelastic they both are, the smaller will be areas 2 and 4 in figure 12.2).

Trade creation and trade diversion are obviously responsible for much of the changing pattern of trade of European economies. This has been especially true of agricultural trade. Exports of Australian butter and fruit to the EU have all but been wiped out. Less-developed countries have also suffered badly from the trade diversion caused by the Common Agricultural Policy. Uruguay, Argentina and the Phillipines, for example, have lost valuable markets for beef, wheat and sugar as a result of the variable import levies which protect European agriculture. This can dramatically affect the livelihoods of those engaged in agriculture in developing economies.

Self-assessment task

Trade creation and trade diversion

On the basis of the information given in the tables below decide where production takes place before and after a customs union is formed between countries A and B. Decide which of the situations relates to the trade creation effects of a customs union and which to the trade diversion effects.

Situation 1

Country	Cost of production	Price in home country before customs union (100% tariff)	Where does production take place?	Price in home country after customs union (CET of 100%)	Where does production take place?
A (home country)	?60				
B (customs union partner)	?40				
C (rest of the world)	?34				

Situation 2

Country	Cost of production	Price in home country before customs union (50% tariff)	Where does production take place?	Price in home country after customs union (CET of 50%)	Where does production take place?
A (home country)	?60				
B (customs union partner)	?40				
C (rest of the world)	?34				

Self-assessment task

The changing nature of Italy's external trade

The table below is concerned with Italy's visible and invisible trade with selected countries in 1981 and 1992. It shows that in the period after 1980 Italy became increasingly dependent for its trade on a small number of European countries, all fellow members of the then European Community (EC).

	1981 $ million	%	1992 $ million	%		1981 $ million	%	1992 $ million	%
Imports					*Exports*				
Belgium–Luxembourg	2,825	3.1	9,110	4.8	Belgium–Luxembourg	2,086	2.8	5,919	3.3
France	11,398	12.5	27,199	14.3	France	10,263	13.6	26,038	14.5
Germany	14,265	15.7	40,655	21.3	Germany	11,735	15.6	36,265	20.1
Netherlands	3,773	4.1	11,140	5.8	Netherlands	2,304	3.1	5,589	3.1
Spain	1,119	1.2	6,330	3.3	Spain	1,290	1.7	9,342	5.2
UK	3,540	3.9	10,757	5.6	UK	4,358	5.8	11,741	6.5
USSR (former)	3,073	3.4	5,882	3.1	USSR (former)	1,285	1.7	4,063	2.3
EC (12)	38,519	42.3	110,768	58.1	EC (12)	34,434	45.7	102,997	57.2
EFTA	6,037	6.6	17,047	8.9	EFTA	6,019	8.0	14,708	8.2
Industrial countries[1]	53,440	58.7	144,607	75.8	Industrial countries[1]	47,315	62.8	135,917	75.5

Current account of the balance of payments
Note: [1]Includes the main member states of the EC plus the USA and Japan.

(a) ◆ Compare Italy's trade with EFTA to that with the rest of the EC between 1981 and 1992.

◆ Explain likely reasons for the differences you have observed.

(b) Comment on changes in Italy's current balance with The Netherlands and Spain between 1981 and 1992.

(c) 'In the period after 1980 Italy became increasingly dependent for its trade on a small number of European countries.' Discuss the extent to which the information supports this statement.

The dynamic effects of a customs union

The welfare effects of the European integration are, therefore, ambiguous. They depend upon whether the trade creation effects outweigh those of trade diversion. Economists, however, identify other important economic consequences of integration which occur over a period of time. Such dynamic effects include:

1 Reduced monopoly power

In an enlarged market, with no tariff or non-tariff barriers, there will be an increase in effective competition. Domestic monopolies can no longer abuse their market power in the way described in sections 3 and 5.

2 Other effects of competition

Competition is also likely to result in more innovation and greater levels of research and development. UK consumers, for example, will be faced with enhanced choice of products from which to choose and greater non-price competition. The result will be that demand will increase and firms will be forced to eliminate waste and inefficiencies (so-called *x*-inefficiencies).

3 Economies of scale

Being part of a larger market is also likely to bring the benefits associated with economies of scale. It has often been argued that European firms cannot effectively compete with large American firms, because of their smaller size. The removal of tariff and non-tariff barriers expands the size of the European market. Without economic integration, markets in Europe would be fragmented into small national sub-markets, with competition stunted by the existence of non-tariff barriers even after the formation of a customs union.

In section 3, economies of scale were divided into internal and external economies. The arguments above apply to internal economies. There are also reasons to suggest that European integration could also bring benefits in terms of external economies of scale. The American car industry is much more geographically concentrated than that in Europe. When industries concentrate geographically, cost advantages are likely to result. Witness the benefits in terms of research and development, access to specialist suppliers, skilled labour and the dispersion of knowledge in Silicon Valley in California. Europe has many financial centres (London and Frankfurt being the largest) and would benefit from greater geographical concentration as markets become less fragmented.

4 The costs of economic integration
The above discussion of the dynamic effects of European integration should have set some alarm bells ringing. Surely, all this economic integration is not without its costs?

In fact, many of the dynamic gains also pose potential costs. Greater geographical concentration of industry implies that some regions of Europe will expand as others decline – a booming European 'core' and a 'periphery' which increasingly diverges in terms of output and employment. Adjusting to the changes implied by economic integration could cause severe declines in output and employment in particular regions of the EU. The result could be regional, structural and technological unemployment. Many have argued that Europe lacks the necessary mobility of labour to avoid these costs of integration (see section 5). The search for economies of scale has already seen a number of European-wide mergers in the pharmaceutical and motor industries. To avoid the problems that this would cause, there is a need for an enhanced role for European regional policy.

Rather than integration enhancing competition, it could well lead to greater oligopoly and monopoly power. European steel producers have repeatedly been

found to have engaged in price-fixing cartels. In 1994, Tetra Pak (the major EU supplier of drinks cartons) was deemed to have abused its market dominance by restricting supply, segmenting the EU market, engaging in predatory pricing and forcing an Italian dairy magazine to agree not to carry advertisements for its main competitors. In 1996 six European companies were alleged to have carved up the market for contracts for the supply of district heating pipes across Germany, Denmark and Sweden. Clearly, economic integration implies that competition needs to be policed by a European competition authority if the costs of integration are not to exceed the benefits.

Factor market integration

In terms of the stages of economic integration, the European Union has progressed beyond the stage of a Customs Union. The Treaty of Rome (1957) called for the free movement of not only goods and services but also of the factors of production (labour, business capital and enterprise). The abolition of exchange controls, the Single European Act (SEA) and the movement towards Economic and Monetary Union (EMU) have all helped to create some of the conditions for the free movement of capital and enterprise. The different ways in which national governments treat taxes on savings means that genuine free movement does not really exist, yet much more progress has been made on the free movement of financial capital than on the free movement of labour.

Up until the Single European Act, limited steps had been taken to ensure that labour was freely mobile between member states. A number of important barriers to the free movement of labour in Europe continue to exist. Indeed, it makes little sense to talk about a European labour market. There are big differences in unemployment rates between member states, for example, as shown in figure 12.3 (see also section 7). If labour were truly mobile, such differences would be reduced over time. Negative integration, then, has done little to remove the barriers to the free movement of labour and much more positive integration needs to take place. The problem is that the positive integration measures introduced (or proposed) have led to a great deal of tension in the EU, with past UK governments 'opting out' of measures like the Social Charter (see table 12.1). In the social aspects

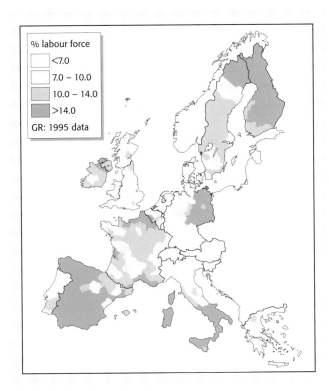

Figure 12.3 Unemployment rates by region, 1996
Source: McDonald and Dearden (1999), *European Economic Integration*, Longman.

of integration, there is very much a 'pick and mix' Europe.

Why is integration of the European labour market important? The main reason is that integrating markets for goods and services makes little sense without labour market integration. The free movement of goods, services and enterprise will create problems in some member states as resources are re-allocated within Europe. Whilst there are benefits to economic integration, as identified above, not all countries or regions will benefit equally and some will lose out (rural areas and those regions in which declining industries are located). Without labour market integration there is a danger that governments will engage in dangerous competition with each other, watering down labour protection laws for example. If employment conditions and social standards are not harmonised, labour will migrate to the country with the lowest rates of income tax or the highest social security provisions – so-called social 'dumping'. More 'laissez faire' economists argue that such competition is desirable, since it will weaken the powers of governments to interfere with market forces and create labour market flexibility in Europe.

1 **Living and working conditions**
'The development of a single European labour market must result in an improvement in the living and working conditions of workers within the EC.'
This provision calls for, amongst other things, a maximum working week.

2 **The right to freedom of movement**
There must be no discrimination between workers on grounds of nationality.

3 **The right to social protection**
'Subject to the arrangements proper to each member state, any citizen of the EC is entitled to adequate social protection.'
A reference to social security or a minimum wage.

4 **The right to freedom of association and collective bargaining**
'Every employer and every worker has the right to belong freely to the professional and trade union organisation of their choice.'

5 **The right to vocational training**
This includes the provision of leave for training.

6 **The right of men and women to equal treatment**

7 **The right to information, consultation and worker participation**

8 **The right to health and safety protection at work**

9 **The protection of children and adolescents**
Establishes a minimum working age of 16 years and entitlement to training in work hours after two years of work.

10 **Disabled persons**
Calls for measures to fully integrate disabled people in working life, including improving accessibility to places of work.

Table 12.1 The main provisions of the Social Charter

Such flexibility and mobility, they argue, is vital if Europe is to make a success of the Euro – an argument we will return to later.

The European Union has taken steps to try to encourage the mobility of labour by:

1 abolishing work permits;
2 improving job information in the EU;
3 allowing entitlement to social security benefits like unemployment benefits to be transferable between member states;
4 allowing workers who cross national frontiers to choose to be taxed in their place of residence to avoid differences in income tax rates acting as a barrier to the free movement of labour;

5 drawing up directives which insisted that national professional and vocational qualifications were acceptable in all EU states;

6 harmonising working conditions, such as paid holidays, maximum working week, minimum paid maternity leave, extending employment rights to part-time workers; and

7 establishing minimum European health and safety standards.

Despite these measures the flow of labour between national labour markets remains low, causing potential problems in the era of a single European currency as we shall discover later in this section.

The Single European Market

The Single European Act (SEA) of 1986 was an attempt to eliminate many of the non-tariff barriers which restricted competition and trade in the European Union. The Act highlighted some 200–300 measures that would create a genuine Single Market in Europe by the end of 1992. There were three guiding principles:

1 Non-discrimination
National regulations, as we discovered earlier, can act as important boundaries separating economic activity in one nation state from that is, another. The principle adopted was that regulations should not discriminate between goods and services produced domestically and those produced elsewhere in the EU.

2 Mutual recognition
Countries in the EU should accept products produced in other countries, despite differences in product standards. Two important cases led to the adoption of this principle. One was the Cassis de Dijon case, involving the French liqueur of that name. Under German law, it did not meet the regulations to be classified as a liqueur, thereby preventing imports into Germany. A successful European Court of Justice (ECJ) ruling established that, if the French classified Cassis as a liqueur so too must the Germans and therefore restricting imports was illegal. A similar case involved the German beer purity laws. These laws effectively stopped imports of foreign-produced beers because they contained chemicals and preservatives. The ECJ rejected the claims of the German government that such beers endangered health. If other countries allowed their

citizens to drink mass-produced beers, so must Germany.

3 Burden of proof
This principle meant that any national restriction based on grounds of health and safety must be proved by scientific evidence if it was to be allowed to continue. The long drawn out case of British beef and its acceptance by other EU members, notably France, is a very good example of this.

The SEA, therefore, implemented measures in four main areas to eliminate non-tariff barriers to trade in the European Union:

1 Removal of frontier controls
Customs checks increase the cost of trading by lengthy formalities and form-filling, raising the cost of imports relative to domestically produced goods. Customs controls were, therefore, abolished between the frontiers of the member states of the EU.

2 Removal of technical barriers
Technical barriers include differences in product regulations and standards and the checking of imports for conformity with national standards. Harmonisation of technical standards has led to cost-savings for European firms and the opening up of national markets to competition. The EU now has the power to over-rule any national legislation which it believes results in the creation of new technical barriers.

3 Opening up public procurement to competition
National and local governments are major buyers of goods and services. They can use this power to favour their domestic firms over other EU companies. The Cecchini Report into the benefits of the Single Market identified public procurement as a major non-tariff barrier in the EU. The SEA proposed that public procurement contracts be opened up to competition from suppliers in other EU states, with the result that public sector contracts are now much more contestable.

4 Removal of fiscal frontiers
As seen earlier, differences in taxation rates amongst the member states can create barriers to the free movement of goods and services and trade. The problem arises with excise duties and rates of VAT (indirect taxes on goods and services). If France has a rate of VAT of 15 per cent and the UK a rate of 17.5 per cent, how are exports to be treated? If French exports are taxed by the French when they are

British lorry heading for central Paris
Source: EST Trucking.

produced and then taxed by the UK authorities when they are sold in the UK, French exports will be more expensive relative to UK-produced goods. The SEA envisaged using the so-called 'destination principle' of taxation. That is, tax should be applied at the rate where the goods are sold. Before the SEA, exports were zero-rated for VAT and excise duties when they crossed borders. The SEA abolished border controls so that UK importers, for example, pay VAT at (say) French rates and then reclaim this VAT from the UK government. It does not get around the form-filling problems but means that UK consumers have an incentive to shop in France to avoid the higher VAT and excise duties in the UK. To reduce these fiscal barriers to trade, European VAT and excise duties need to be brought more closely into line – a process known as tax harmonisation.

Self-assessment task

Read the following material and then answer the questions that follow:

Tax harmonisation in the European Union (EU)

Abolition of trade barriers among the members of a customs union does not necessarily mean that a common market has been completed. A number of obstacles to the smooth operation of competitive markets in goods, services and factors of production still remain. Differences among the tax systems of the members of the customs union are one of the most important of these obstacles and one of the most difficult to reduce. This has been the case in the EU. A genuine 'Single Market' can only exist when tariffs are removed and direct and indirect taxes among the members are brought more closely into line. In other words, in an economic union, tax harmonisation is indispensable, but this does not necessarily imply the complete equalisation of tax rates.

Despite this, progress on tax harmonisation in the EU has been difficult. This is partly because national governments attach great importance to taxation as an instrument of budgetary, social and economic policy. Although some progress has been made in harmonising VAT rates by agreeing maximum and minimum rates, it has been harder to persuade members to end 'zero-rating' of certain items (e.g. newspapers, books and children's clothing in the UK). Harmonisation of excise duties has been even less successful and there remain big differences in duties between member states.

The table shows the differences in the structure of taxation and individual tax rates in selected EU economies in the early 1990s.

	Relative size of tax revenues		Excise duties			Personal income tax rates		Tax on profits
	Total tax revenue as % of GDP	Vat and excise duties as % of GDP	Wine (ECU per hl)	Beer (ECU per hl)	Cigarettes (ECU per 1,000)	Lowest rate (%)	Top rate (%)	Corporation tax rates (%)
UK	36.7	16.7	158	78	118	20	40	33
Netherlands	45.2	11.9	33	20	54	13	60	35
Spain	34.4	9.7	0	4	17	25	56	35
France	43.7	12.3	3	3	55	19	58	42
Ireland	37.2	15.8	279	113	103	29	52	40

Taxation in selected EU member states in the 1990s
Source: T. Hitiris (1994) *European Community Economics* (third edition), Harvester Wheatsheaf (adapted).

1 With reference to the table:
   (a) Give one example of an indirect tax and one example of a direct tax.
   (b) Explain why each country has more than one rate of income tax.
2 Using the information in the table:
   (a) Compare the structure of taxation in the UK with that in France.
   (b) Explain why 'in an economic union, tax harmonisation is indispensable'.
3 Comment on the likely problems of EU tax harmonisation for Spain and Ireland.
4 Discuss how useful the information shown in the table might be to a Japanese multinational company considering where to locate in the EU.

Macroeconomic policy co-ordination and the European Monetary System (EMS)

As we have seen in table 11.1, the weakest form of economic integration is the free trade area, since this does not involve things like common external tariffs, free movement of factors of production, economic policy harmonisation or any centralisation of economic policy making.

It is argued that for member states to take the fullest advantage of a common market, some degree of policy co-ordination and monetary union is necessary. For example, the benefits of a common market may be offset by exchange rate uncertainty and volatility. Policy co-ordination is necessary once economies begin to be integrated. As economies in the European Union become more closely dependent upon each other for trade, one country's macroeconomic policy can have positive and negative spillover effects on other countries in the EU. As shown in table 9.3, when a country expands its economy using fiscal policy it will have to raise interest rates to attract the money markets to fund its budget deficit. Higher interest rates will put upward pressure on its exchange rate. This is the same thing as saying other countries' exchange rates depreciate, stimulating their trade and increasing aggregate demand. Such countries effectively 'free ride' on the fiscal expansion elsewhere in the EU. Similarly a monetary expansion reduces a country's interest rates and its exchange rates, raising the exchange rates of its partners in the EU – their aggregate demand falls and they suffer from the policy decisions made elsewhere in the EU.

If macroeconomic policies are not co-ordinated, then, there is an incentive to wait for others to stimulate demand by fiscal policy and to engage in competitive devaluations against those countries that conduct monetary expansion. The European Economic Community first attempted macroeconomic policy co-ordination by choosing to 'fix' their exchange rates against each other. In 1979, it launched the European Monetary System which had at its heart a semi-fixed exchange rate regime, known as the Exchange Rate Mechanism (ERM). Countries in the ERM agreed to fix their exchange rates within a band of no more than 2.25 per cent (the 'ceiling') and no less than 2.25 per cent (the 'floor') around a central parity against the DM.

Many commentators have argued that the experience of the ERM should act as a warning siren to countries like the UK, contemplating signing up to a single European currency. So, how successful was the ERM? Despite the currency upheavals of the early 1990s, the ERM was a success in achieving external and internal monetary stability. There was a considerable reduction in exchange rate volatility (between 1980 and 1986 sterling had varied by 30 per cent), and member states' inflation rates had converged towards the lowest rate in the EU.

As for sterling's ignominious withdrawal from the ERM in 1993, it is difficult to see with hindsight how the ERM could have been expected to support what most economists agreed was an overvalued currency: the UK had entered the ERM at a time when interest rates needed to be reduced for domestic reasons to improve our international competitiveness. The key feature of the ERM, namely relatively stable exchange rates, had been responsible for its success in achieving inflation convergence but in turn this became the system's enemy. As a consequence, there was a period of intense monetary turbulence in 1992–1993, resulting in sterling and the lira suspending their membership of the ERM, the devaluation of the peseta and the escudo and a forced movement to wider bands of ±15 per cent. At a time of recession in the European economy, the weaknesses of the ERM were clear for all to see.

Economic and Monetary Union (EMU)

The process towards full economic and monetary union was accelerated by the signing of the Maastricht Treaty in December 1991. It is argued that for the full benefits of the single market to be realised there must be both economic and monetary union. These terms were defined earlier in table 11.1 but it is worth recapping on how they have been achieved.

1 Economic Union

   This has meant the creation of a single market in Europe through the dismantling of artificial trade barriers, the development of competition and regional policies, and the co-ordination of macroeconomic policy making.

2 Monetary Union

   This has come to mean a monetary association which results in common inflation and interest rates within Europe. It implies the integration of the financial sectors of the Union, the free movement of capital between member states and the permanent fixing of exchange rates or the creation of a single currency.

   Table 12.2 gives the post-Maastricht timetable for the realisation of EMU. The Treaty also set out the criteria to determine which countries could join. Those meeting the so-called 'Convergence criteria' would join automatically – the UK and Denmark, though, negotiated a special opt-out allowing them to buy time in order to determine their participation.

The benefits of a single currency

1 Reduced transaction costs

   Trade between member states currently requires firms to change currencies: this inevitably incurs costs. Let us take a highly simplistic example. If you were to set out from Manchester with £100 and make a tour of all member countries of the EU, spending nothing in any of them because of free hospitality, but changing the money at each point of arrival, you would emerge from the airport bank on return to Manchester with approximately £26. The foreign exchange markets would have swallowed the rest! On a more serious level, the European Commission has estimated that the savings on transactions costs is 0.5 per cent of the EU's GDP per annum. This results in a resource saving which can be used to raise living standards and employment. Central banks would find that they no longer needed to keep so much foreign exchange

Euro-timetable

June 1989	Delors report on economic and monetary union
July 1990	Stage one, abolition of capital controls
December 1991	Maastricht treaty negotiated
January 1994	Stage two, European Monetary Institute created
December 1995	Euro chosen as name of single currency
May 1998	Euro members chosen, bilateral conversion rates fixed, European Central Bank established
December 1998	Euro conversion rates fixed
January 1999	Stage three, Euro is launched
January 2002	Euro notes and coins introduced
July 2002	National notes and coins withdrawn

Convergence criteria

1 Price stability: a rate of inflation no more than 1.5 per cent above the average of the three best-performing states.

2 Interest rates not more than 2 per cent above the average of the three member states that had the lowest inflation rates over the previous year.

3 The government deficit (that is, the budget deficit) should not exceed 3 per cent of GDP.

4 The public sector debt (that is, the national debt) should not exceed 60 per cent of GDP.

5 Exchange rate movements within the ERM should not exceed their allowed margin of fluctuation for at least two years. Also, there should be no devaluation.

Table 12.2 The countdown to EMU

reserves, releasing resources which could be deployed elsewhere in the economy.

2 Reduced exchange rate uncertainty

   The daily changes in exchange rates, witnessed on the foreign exchange rate markets, introduces an element of risk and uncertainty to trade between nations (see figure 12.4). Businesses 'hedge' against exchange rate risks by purchasing a range of financial instruments like futures, options and swaps. Such purchases would not be necessary under a single currency and again represent a resource saving. Since a single currency eliminates exchange rate fluctuations, it is argued that it will lead to an increase in trade between member states. There are fairly convincing arguments that this was the result of the reduced exchange rate volatility of the 1980s, as a result of the operation of the ERM. Clearly, as European economies become more integrated, this benefit is likely to be significant. The Euro exchange rate will still vary against that of other countries, but this

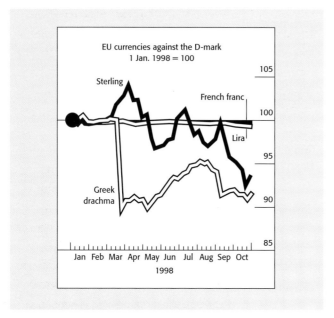

Figure 12.4 Selected currency variations in 1998
Source: Datastream/ICV.

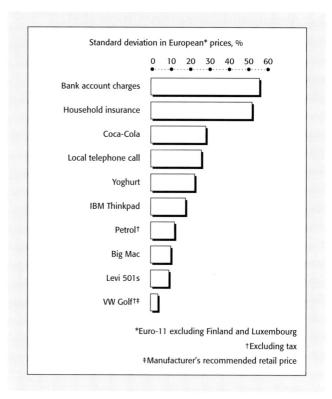

Figure 12.5 Price differentials in Europe in 1998
Source: Leman Brothers.

should not matter as the amount of trade between EU states (intra-EU trade) continues to grow in importance.

3 Price transparency

Once Euro notes and coins are introduced, all prices in 'Euroland' will be expressed in the same currency. Consumers and firms will then be able to compare prices throughout the Euro-area and source the lowest cost supplies (see figure 12.5). At present, exchange rates can 'hide' quite substantial price differences in the EU. This adds to the segmentation of national markets which the single market was designed to erode. Once prices become comparable, competitive forces should reduce prices to the benefit of both EU firms and their final consumers, both in the EU and in international markets.

4 Lower interest rates

Under a system of floating or semi-fixed exchange rates, it is argued that a premium is added to interest rates in order to safeguard against exchange rate movements. Under a single currency such premiums will be eliminated and interest rates should be lower. This, of course, ought to stimulate investment, resulting in greater economic growth and higher living standards.

5 Lower inflation

Governments are prone to manipulate monetary policy for their own short-term advantage. The result,

however, is generally higher inflation. With a single currency, issued by the European Central Bank (ECB), the power of any one member state to expand the growth of the money supply is necessarily constrained. Since the ECB is also independent of political control, acting with an explicit anti-inflation objective, political interference is eliminated and inflation should be lower.

6 Lower unemployment

Some economists have argued that the higher the rate of inflation the more unpredictable it is. Those who believe in the concept of a natural rate of unemployment (NRU) would argue that this will prevent the price mechanism from allocating resources efficiently, such that the NRU will be higher. Figure 12.6 shows how the European economy might be affected by the introduction of the Euro.

The combination of the above effects is a rightward shift of both the AD and AS curves for the EU economy, an increase in GDP and employment and, in the long run, an increase in GDP growth rates, without the consequence of inflation. AD shifts right owing to an increase in trade-related expenditure, and lower costs and greater investment shifts the AS curve to the right.

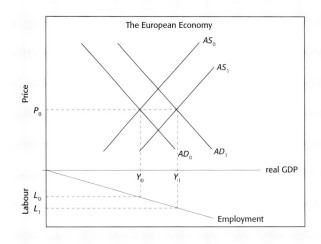

Figure 12.6 The impact of the Euro on the European Economy (optimistic view)

The costs of a single currency

If the introduction of a single currency brings such important economic benefits, why is it that the whole venture, at least from the UK perspective, is so controversial? The controversy is centred around the potential costs of a single currency. These costs are said to include:

1 The loss of economic sovereignty
   As a member of EMU a country loses the power to set its own interest rates and to control the money supply as a result of giving up its national currency. In the short term, governments can use these instruments of economic policy to trade unemployment off against inflation.

2 Coping with asymmetric shocks
   As we have seen, no one economy is the same and they can be subject to different 'shocks' as a result of their different structures and characteristics. The exchange rate allows adjustment to these unique shocks. Without the exchange rate to cushion the blow, unemployment will take the strain, especially in the absence of labour market flexibility. The extent to which the exchange rate is a good adjustment mechanism is debated amongst economists. Constant devaluations are not necessarily desirable for an economy. In addition governments still have fiscal policy with which they could deal with temporary rises in unemployment. Not so, say the Euro-sceptics. A government's ability to run large and persistent deficits is ruled out by EMU's 'Growth and Stability Pact' which fines countries that exceed strict PSBR limits. It may even be the case that these limits reduce the impact of an economy's automatic stabilisers, such that Euro members have more severe business cycles in the single currency area than outside it.

3 Lack of convergence
   If the structure of Euro member economies is so different, then some countries may become permanently poor regions of the EU without any mechanism to adjust. The danger of this happening is increased if the economies in the single currency are not sufficiently converged. For example, if one country is in the boom phase of its business cycle whilst another is in the recession phase, a single interest rate is unlikely to suit either. In 1998 these two extremes were best represented by Ireland and Germany. In joining EMU, the booming Irish economy had to halve its interest rates overnight. In contrast, the sluggish performance of the German economy had led to repeated calls for cuts in the Euro interest rate to stimulate German growth. Since the Euro interest rate must be set to suit 'average' Euro-area monetary conditions, neither country had the interest rate it really needs. To work effectively, then, there is a requirement that 'one monetary policy fits all'.

4 Sensitivity to the Euro interest rate
   If the Euro interest rate has to be raised to combat inflation in the Euro area, some countries may well suffer more than others. This is likely to happen where economies are more sensitive to interest rate changes because of the structure of their borrowing. In the German economy, for example, most borrowing is undertaken at fixed rates and therefore consumers are less affected by changes in short-term interest rates.

5 The theory of optimal currency areas
   The above ideas are captured in an economic theory that attempts to explain what factors make for an 'optimum' currency area. This theory suggests that there are potential costs of a currency union when there are:
   ◆ Different demand shocks
      What happens if one country suffers an increase or decrease in aggregate demand which is unique to that country? In the case of such asymmetric shocks, an optimum currency area requires countries in it to have wage flexibility,

labour mobility or fiscal transfers to adjust to unique changes in demand. They cannot adjust either an interest rate or an exchange rate since they are part of a single currency. Yet each of the above factors is absent in the EU. It has been argued that further integration may increase the likelihood of asymmetric demand shocks by causing greater regional concentration of industries within Europe, as a result of economies of scale and reduced transaction costs. Some evidence of this can be found in the distribution of car production in the EU, which is much less concentrated than that in America. As the single currency leads to more concentration in individual countries they may well become susceptible to industry-specific shocks. This, of course, assumes that industrial concentration does not span national borders.

◆ Different labour market institutions
Germany tends to have relatively centralised wage bargaining whereas the UK has a relatively decentralised system. This means that if two countries are subject to the same demand shock there can be very different outcomes for wages and prices. Countries do not have to have unique industrial structures for a single currency to have significant costs. Centralised bargaining tends to cause unions to take account of their wage increases, whereas a decentralised system causes a 'free rider' effect, whereby individual unions do not take account of their actions on the whole economy because they believe their wages to be insignificant in causing general inflation. If all unions act like this, there is no incentive to moderate wage demands. Highly decentralised systems, however, cause unions to have to think about the effect of pay rises on their own firm so that empirical evidence suggests that the middle ground is the worst in terms of the inflation and unemployment effects of bargaining: this is exactly where the majority of European economies lie.

◆ Different growth rates
If country A grows at 5 per cent per annum and country B at 3 per cent per annum, then

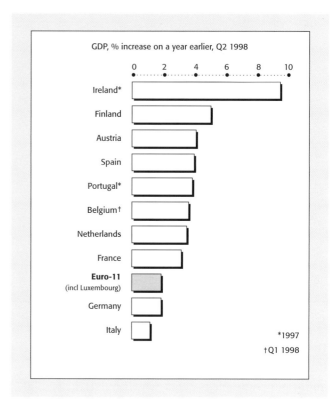

Figure 12.7 European growth rates in 1998
Sources: National Statistics; Eurostat.

country A will tend to run into a trade deficit problem relative to country B. Since in a single currency area there is no exchange rate between the two countries, the only way to cope with this problem is to reduce growth. Some argue that high-growth countries are penalised by a single currency. This implies that for a single currency area to work there must be convergence of growth rates amongst member economies. Figure 12.7 clearly shows that this was not the case for 1997 and 1998.

A way of reconciling the arguments

It would appear that both sides of the argument hold water, at least for certain countries at certain times. One way of resolving the conflicts is to suggest that, the more benefits of a single currency increase and the costs decrease, the more converged and integrated the members of EMU are. This idea is represented in figure 12.8.

The diagram takes the amount of intra-EU trade (as a percentage of GDP) as a measure of convergence and

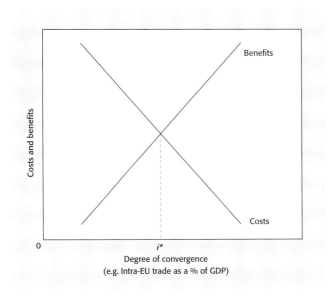

Figure 12.8 The costs and benefits of Euro compared

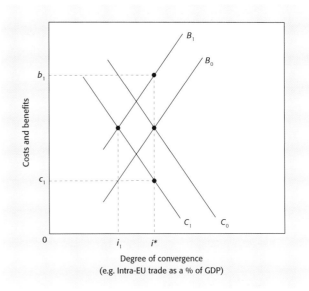

Figure 12.9 The costs and benefits of the Euro: a change in the status quo

integration. The more economies in the single currency area trade with each other (and the more important that trade is as a proportion of their GDP), the more they are likely to benefit from such things as lower transaction costs and price transparency. The 'benefit curve' associated with the Euro, therefore, slopes up from left to right. In addition, the more integrated they are, the less they will be affected by external shocks, or, if they are affected, they will all be affected in a similar fashion – asymmetric shocks will not be significant and therefore economies can live without the need for independent monetary policy. The 'cost curve' slopes down from left to right. To the left of i^*, the costs of the Euro exceed the benefits whilst to the right of i^* the Euro will bring more advantages than disadvantages. Although this theory helps us to understand the issues surrounding the great Euro debate, it is only a theory. Where exactly is this miracle point, i^*, in the real world? Governments and policy makers must make a choice, based on a judgement of whether their economy is sufficiently converged with the rest of Euroland such that the economy as a whole will benefit. Unfortunately economic theory does not give a magic figure for this level of convergence and integration.

Some economists, most notably Professor Nigel Healey, have even suggested that the sheer fact that the EMU now exists has altered the trade-offs. He suggests

that belonging to EMU will actually cause European economies to converge. This means that the benefit curve shifts upwards (to B_1) and the cost curve downwards (to C_1) as indicated in figure 12.9. A country with convergence and integration of i^* will find that having joined EMU benefits exceed costs ($b_1 > c_1$), whereas previously they did not. A country which delays entry into EMU, in the belief that the costs exceed the benefits (it feels itself to be to the left of i^*), might well be making the 'wrong' policy choice – so long as it is between i_1 and i^*, the benefits will indeed exceed the costs once the single currency is actually launched.

The Labour government's position on EMU

On the 27 October 1998, Gordon Brown (Chancellor of the Exchequer) issued a statement to the House of Commons that the UK was not to apply for membership of the single currency in 1999. He also said it was most unlikely that the UK would join in the lifetime of the current Parliament, effectively ruling out membership until 2002 at the earliest.

The Chancellor had commissioned a study into the consequences of EMU. This report was published the same day by the Treasury. What follows is a summary of the main body of that report in which Mr Brown set out five 'tests' for UK membership of the single currency. They were:

Gordon Brown
Source: Popperfoto Reuters.

1 Are business cycles and economic structures compatible so that we and others could live comfortably with Euro interest rates on a permanent basis?

2 If problems emerge, is there sufficient flexibility to deal with them?

3 Would joining EMU create better conditions for firms making long-term decisions to invest in Britain?

4 What impact would entry into EMU have on the competitive position of the UK's financial services industry, particularly the City's wholesale markets?

5 In summary, will joining EMU promote higher growth, stability and a lasting increase in jobs?

Cyclical convergence is central to the Chancellor's view of whether the UK should join a single currency. Table 12.3 summarises the main body of the report.

So, is the UK better being 'out'? This is a very difficult question to answer (see Ins and outs article below). There are certainly like to be potentially large costs from a single currency for the UK. However, it is not clear that the UK will be substantially better off outside the Euro area. Whilst it is probably true that the EU does not meet the conditions for an optimal currency union, the single currency has gone ahead. Outside the EU area, the UK has to choose whether to continue to pursue its own independent interest rate policy or to stabilise its exchange rate against the Euro countries, its main trading partners. If it opts to continue its battle against inflation, the exchange rate could fluctuate widely, damaging British business just as the high pound did in 1999. Alternatively, perhaps Gordon Brown is right to wait and see.

There may be longer-term effects, however, as the new Euro area will involve a combined GDP five times bigger than that in the UK. The Euro area will be very attractive to foreign and domestic European firms, which may wish to locate new investment in the Euro area or relocate to Euroland from the UK. In such a scenario, the UK could become a peripheral part of Europe. This, of course, must be set against the very real risk that the single currency will continue to have problems during its infancy due to a lack of real convergence in the Euro area. Certainly, the Euro has yet to stand any severe tests of its own other than an initial 6% depreciation in its first six months. And that, paradoxically, puts the UK in a disadvantageous position regarding its major trading area.

The importance of convergence

◆ Without convergence, the lack of a domestic monetary policy as a result of EMU could make the UK business cycle more volatile.

   The government would no longer have the power to set its own interest rates. If business cycles are out of synch, Euro interest rates could be at the 'wrong' rate for the UK.

   The lack of an exchange rate to dampen the cycle (appreciations to reduce demand and depreciations to raise it).

The current position

◆ The UK has less spare capacity than other countries (its 'output gap' is smaller).

◆ Interest rates are much higher in the UK (7% compared to 3.3% in Germany and France).

   Using futures contracts the Treasury forecasts that, by 1999, these interest rate differentials are likely to narrow but remain. The euro interest rate will, therefore, be too low for the UK and could risk an inflationary boom emerging or a need to tighten fiscal policy which would be de-stabilising.

Past and future convergence of business cycles

◆ The report concludes that recent history has shown that the UK business cycle has not followed those in the rest of Europe.

◆ In both the 1975–1981 and 1981–1996 cycles the UK had lower and more volatile rates of growth of GDP than Germany and France (1975–81, UK growth was 1% p.a. and standard deviation of growth 2.12%, whereas in France this was 2.4% growth p.a. and s.d. of 1.46).

◆ The UK business cycle is more closely correlated with that in the USA than with either France or Germany.

◆ The report concludes that the reasons for diverging business cycles are unclear: they are partly caused by different policies (financial liberalisation, German reunification) but they also lie in important structural differences between the UK and other EU economies. These differences are likely to remain for some time to come. The UK, therefore, will respond differently to both 'shocks' and interest rate changes and its business cycle will remain divergent. The result will be that a Euro interest rate under EMU is unlikely to be 'right' for the UK.

Important structural differences

◆ The pattern of trade

   The UK has a lower proportion of trade with the EU (52%) than Germany (56%) or France (63%) and a much higher proportion of trade with North America (13% compared to 8%). This might explain why the UK and USA cycles are so related.

◆ The housing market in the UK is much more important than in the rest of the EU. This is because of a greater proportion of owner-occupiers in the UK. This results in:

   Greater house price volatility (almost twice as volatile in the short-term).

   Greater mortgage debt (57% of UK GDP compared to 33% EU average).

   UK households are, therefore, more sensitive to interest rate changes.

◆ UK companies rely more on short-term, variable rate borrowing. UK is the only net exporter of oil

   This means that

   Changes in oil prices are more important for the UK.

   UK is subject to different 'shocks'.

Whilst these difference may well become less significant over time, the report concludes that *the UK needs a period of economic stability to demonstrate that convergence is sustainable*.

Table 12.3 A summary of HM Treasury's five economic tests for EMU

Ins and outs

Perhaps the biggest omission in the Maastricht treaty was the failure to clarify the status of the 'outs' – the countries that decline to take part. (Britain, Denmark and Sweden have chosen to stay out; Greece would love to join but is nowhere near satisfying the Maastricht criteria for membership.) This was not an oversight but a deliberate gap, much in accord with the way Europe's architects have tended to proceed.

The EU's members are pledged to move towards 'ever closer union'. Implicity, the idea is that they will approach this goal (as yet undefined) at about the same speed – so the four countries not taking part in EMU at the outset are expected to join as soon as they can. To have designed a durable relationship between the ins and outs might have encouraged further delay.

It often happens in European politics that if you do not want a contingency to arise, you ignore it, hoping it goes away. Sometimes it does – and this time-honoured approach may also work in the case of EMU's outs. If monetary union is a success, the qualifying outsiders will warm to the idea. But the collapse of the ERM in 1992–93 showed that the head-in-the-sand method is not infallible. If EMU works badly, outsiders such as Britain are likely to become even more reluctant.

There is also the question of EU enlargement. Prospective new members in Eastern Europe may not be ready, or may not choose, to join EMU at the beginning. Indeed, they would be wise to be cautious. Their economies are still struggling with the legacy of socialism. For many years yet they are likely to remain structurally different from their western neighbours, leaving them more exposed to the danger of asymmetric economic shocks. This only adds to the case for lasting arrangements allowing EU countries to opt out of EMU indefinitely.

The main economic problem posed by a permanent division of the EU into EMU and non-EMU countries is that the outs will be seen by the others as cheats. It is easy to imagine circumstances in which the euro will strengthen against other European currencies, putting euro countries at a competitive disadvantage in trade. If this happens (as well it might) at a time of slowing growth in the euro zone and briskly expanding output elsewhere in the EU, the euro-zone governments will be obliged to object.

In due course, therefore, some form of 'monetary co-operation' will probably be required of the outs, if only as a mark of good faith. One possibility would be a revived ERM, albeit a looser arrangement than the one that collapsed. (For instance, governments might promise to limit variations in their real, as opposed to nominal, exchange rates: this would preserve a measure of monetary discretion while ensuring that governments did not use it to pursue a policy of competitive devaluation.) Failing some such accord, the discussion may move to other ways of correcting the 'unfair' advantage of the non-euro countries' depreciated currencies – and that is a discussion that could endanger the EU itself.

A permanent union of ins and outs would also raise a host of day-to-day political difficulties. The outs' great fear – and what eventually may force them into EMU – is that the centre of decision-making for the EU as a whole will move to the committee of euro-zone finance ministers. This seems certain to happen if EMU runs into trouble, and the euro-zone countries adopt remedies such as collective fiscal policy and/or increased harmonisation of taxes and economic regulations. Even if all goes well, though, a dimunution of the outs' political sway seems likely. The ins will surely want to punish the outs, with or without a show of regret. How better to encourage the laggards to change their minds?

Source: The Economist, 2 January 1999.

Self-assessment task

Read the material below and then answer the questions that follow.

The European car industry

The European car industry has undergone significant changes throughout the 1980s and 1990s:

◆ national governments have transferred ownership of most car manufacturing firms to the private sector;

◆ as a result of falling demand and over-capacity in the early 1990s there has been a number of plant closures, mergers, a reduction in the range of models produced and measures taken to raise efficiency;

◆ national quotas on imports of Japanese cars have been gradually reduced and will be removed in 2000 to create a fully open EU market;

◆ there has been significant investment by Japanese producers in car manufacturing plant in the EU.

Despite these changes the European car industry remains a market which is segmented along national lines. It is argued that the benefits of the EU's Single Market programme have not, therefore, materialised in the car market (see extract).

The data below provide an insight into aspects of the characteristics of this market.

Manufacturer	Car registrations February 1999	% change in registrations Feb 1998 – Feb 1999	% of total registrations
VW Group	210700	−9.0	19.13
Fiat Group	143742	1.3	13.05
GM Group	121920	−9.4	11.07
PSA Group	136580	−3.7	12.40
Ford Group	96848	−18.7	8.79
BMW Group	47427	−21.3	4.31
Renault	119173	2.3	10.82
Nissan	27101	−20.6	2.46
Mercedes	50500	24.7	4.58
Mazda	17965	11.3	1.63
Volvo	15843	−17.5	1.44
Others	113749		10.33
Total	1101548	−3.7	100

Summary data on the European car market

Source: just-auto (www.just-auto.com).

Notes: VW Group incorporates VW, Audi, Seat, Skoda. Fiat Group incorporates Fiat, Lancia, Alfa Romeo, others.
GM Group incorporates Opel, Vauxhall, IBC, Saab, others. PSA Group incorporates Peugeot, Citreon.
Ford Group incorporates Ford, Jaguar. BMW Group incorporates BMW, Rover.

	Germany	UK	Spain	Italy	France	Belgium	Netherlands	Austria	Sweden	Total
1996	4,540	1,686	1,942	1,318	3,148	368	145	97	368	13,611

Motor vehicle production in the EU 1996 (thousands of units)
Source: *The European Economy* (David Dyker) Table 15.1.

	1996
Exports	
To rest of Europe	609
To North America	575
To Japan	235
To rest of world	409
Imports	
From rest of Europe	91
From North America	45
From Japan	714
From rest of world	272
Total	
Exports	1828
Imports	1123
Balance	705

EU trade in motor vehicles (thousands of units)
Source: The European Economy (David Dyker) Table 15.2.

	1996
French	56
German	42
UK	11
Italian	44

Market shares of locally owned producers (percentage of total home market)
Source: The European Economy (David Dyker) Table 15.3

	1993	1995
Belgium	116	122
Britain	120	120
France	121	121
Germany	124	128
Ireland	115	112
Italy	100	102
Netherlands	115	121
Portugal	108	108
Spain	108	105

Average price differentials (net of taxes) of same automobile
Source: European Economic Integration (McDonald and Dearden) Table 3.3.

Van Miert drives hard bargain on cars

Once more, EU customers are being denied the fruits of the Union's much-vaunted single market. This time, it is motorists who are suffering.

Price differentials across European markets make it very attractive for bargain-hunting customers from countries such as the UK to look elsewhere in the EU for their cars. But, as recent warnings from acting Competition Commissioner Karel van Miert have underlined, some car companies could be illegally thwarting motorists' attempts to pick up cheaper vehicles abroad.

The root of all evils, according to critics of the European Commission's approach, is the latest 'block exemption' bestowed on the industry by the institution in 1995.

This allows firms to run exclusive dealerships, which means that they can pick and choose who gets a franchise to sell their cars in a particular region. They can grant franchises and they can take them away. They can also decide what dealers pay for their vehicles, and what 'bonuses' and special offers they are awarded for sales. In short, the block exemption means that manufacturers wield enormous power over dealers.

Critics claim it is this which makes it possible for manufacturers to stop dealers from selling their vehicles to foreign customers. They can therefore fragment EU markets and keep prices and profits higher than they would otherwise be.

One of the biggest lobbying battles of recent years is set to erupt over whether this block exemption should be renewed in 2002.

Leading the opposition to the car industry carve-up is European consumer group BEUC, which argues that the block exemption should be outlawed unless it can be shown to work in the interests of car buyers.

'We believe that the exclusive and selective distribution system constitutes a major obstacle to the completion of the single market in cars,' said BEUC's Valerie Thompson. 'It allows manufacturers to continue to segment the market, it restricts competition in the market place and thereby disadvantages consumers, in particular in terms of high prices for cars.'

Unsurprisingly, the European car lobby ACEA claims ending the measure would do EU consumers far more harm than good.

Marc Greven, ACEA's director of legal affairs, said abolishing the block exemption would lead to car supermarkets being set up to replace the trusty old dealer networks. These would not carry the same wide range of cars, big and small, which all major EU marques, from Rover to Renault, offer customers at their showrooms.

Greven questions the benefits of replacing dealerships with vehicle supermarkets, when grocery supermarkets are being accused in some member states of denying consumers choice and charging too much.

He claims that price differentials in the car market are among the lowest in EU industry, at least before vehicle registration taxes are taken into consideration. He also insists that dealers are not deliberately stopping private citizens from striking bargains abroad, although he argues that they are entitled to veto sales to those suspected of reselling vehicles to independent dealers competing with official ones.

Such dealers, warns Greven, have little interest in offering high-quality services to customers in areas such as after-sales back-up and warranty repairs.

Despite the storm of protests from BEUC and others, Van Miert's spokesman defends the Commission's decision to grant the block exemption in the first place.

It was, he argues, bestowed with the best of intentions, with the aim of allowing dealers to compete with each other to get good prices for cars from manufacturers, while allowing customers to drive a hard bargain by playing competing dealers off against each other.

'We thought that opening sales between agreed dealers and direct sales to anyone popping into a dealership was a big step ahead. We thought it more than counterbalanced the extension of a manufacturer's right to run a selective distribution system – ie a dealership network,' he said.

Nor, the spokesman added, did the block exemption give firms carte blanche to manipulate the car market, "Manufacturers infringing the rules automatically lose the protection offered by the regulation. That means its existence does in no way impair the Commission's ability to act against a dealer and indeed a consumer's rights to sue for damages before a national court."

But even though the Commission robustly defends its decision to grant the block exemption in the first place, the industry could face an uphill struggle to get it renewed in 2002.

However, Greven maintains that even the Commission itself does not want to scrap the measure altogether. "No one wants that, least of all the Commission," he insisted. "If you do not get a block exemption, then everyone asks for an individual one. They say, 'can I have this?' or 'can I have that?'. That is the last thing the Commission wants. It does not have the manpower."

At the very least, he predicts, the institution might seek to add car firms to the list of industries covered by a general block exemption which it is currently designing for firms with market shares no greater than 30%.

This proposal, which will lay down the extent to which industries such as brewing and retailing can control their supply chains from manufacture to distribution, is set to enter into force next year.

The key concern, here, warns the car industry, is the uncertainty it would create. No one is sure, it argues, whether member states themselves would apply the 30% criteria or whether it would apply to 30% of the total EU market.

However, Van Miert's aides are warning firms not to take anything for granted. "I, for one, think that the question mark behind a possible renewal of the block exemption is increasing in size every time we find yet another manufacturer ignoring the rules," said one.

Car firms across the length and breadth of the Union employ thousands of workers and wield huge political influence within some member states.

But the Commission's recent actions should have been enough to convince errant companies that they had better clean up their act – and quickly – if the industry as a whole is to continue to enjoy its current privileged status.

Source: Peter Chapman, *European Voice*, 6–11 May 1999.

1 (a) Briefly explain what you consider to be the major determinants of the demand for cars in Europe.

(b) With reference to the data provided describe the structure of the European car market.

2 'Price differentials across European markets make it very attractive for bargain-hunting customers from such as the UK to look elsewhere in the EU for their cars.'

(a) Discuss why price differentials exist in the European car market.

(b) Discuss how the introduction of the Euro is likely to affect prices in the European car market.

3 'Toyota Motor, one of the biggest inward investors in the UK, has warned that the company's European investment strategy might change if the UK stays out of the European monetary union' (*Financial Times*, 30 January 1997).

(a) Explain what factors other than EMU might determine the scale and nature of Toyota's investment strategy.

(b) You have been commissioned to write a report by a firm of economic consultants entitled 'The impact on the UK economy of opting out of EMU'. What economic arguments would you draw upon in this report and how would you assess their relative strengths?

13 The transition economies of Europe

On completion of this section you should be able to:

➤ describe the characteristics of centrally planned economies

➤ explain how and why central planning has failed

➤ analyse how economic reforms have been applied in transition economies

➤ discuss the costs and benefits of economic reforms for transition economies

➤ analyse the economic performance of the former centrally planned economies during transition and how they compare with EU economies

➤ discuss the reasons why some transition economies are expected to join the EU

Introduction

Since 1989 some twenty-eight independent states of Central and Eastern Europe (CEE) and the Commonwealth of Independent States (CIS) have embarked on a journey along the road 'from Marx to the market'. Whilst these states differ markedly in many economic respects (population size, GDP per capita and the structure of the economy), they share one thing in common: a legacy of a planned economic system. For some countries like Russia this legacy is a long one that affected most aspects of economic life: the planning process determined what was produced, how production was organised and the distribution of production (for whom to produce) (see section 1).

The results of the transition to the market have been mixed. This is due, in no small measure, to the enormity and complexity of the task of turning a centrally planned economy (CPE) into a market economy. Whilst economists at the end of the 1990s are beginning to formulate theories of transition, at the beginning of the decade the transition economies, themselves, were stepping out on a path that none before them had trod. Much has been written on how to turn a market economy into a planned economy but, in the early 1990s, no-one had formulated a blueprint for planned economies wishing to move towards a market economy.

In order to understand the complexities and likely problems of transition it is first necessary to understand the legacy of planning which the CEE and CIS states were left with in the late 1980s and early 1990s. This section then goes on to examine the reforms required during transition before considering why the experience of transition has been so varied. Finally, prospects for integrating such economies into the EU are considered.

Characteristics of centrally planned economies (CPEs)

Centrally planned economies can, in principle, avoid many of the problems of the market system outlined in unit 2. Instead of relying on the decentralised decisions of millions of consumers and producers, the government can make allocation decisions which are in the interests of society as a whole. Three priorities can be established:

1 *Self-sufficiency*

In order to be independent of the capitalist economies, socialist economies aim to provide all they require from within.

2 *To allocate resources with minimum use of the price mechanism*

In unit 1 you learned that markets allocate resources through the price mechanism. Prices send out signals and incentives to producers and consumers about relative scarcities. Marx, however, argued that lying behind this allocation device was unequal economic and social power, brought about by the private ownership of the means of production. The socialist economy was, therefore, to be organised along the lines of collective ownership with economic decisions being made centrally by the state. Prices then did not fulfil the same function as in a market economy.

3 Economic growth

Much of the economic history of socialist CPEs is the history of striving for economic growth. Contrary to Marx's theory of the transition towards a socialist economy, most CPEs were actually relatively poor. Their top priority was to catch up with the capitalist world and to overtake it, thereby proving that socialism was superior to capitalism. The arms race and the space race are two examples of this fascination with economic superiority and growth. But there is an opportunity cost involved with economic growth. The bias in the national plan, then, was towards heavy industry and military expenditure.

If these are the objectives of CPEs, how did economic planning attempt to achieve them? To answer this question we need to identify the key characteristics of CPEs. There are four such main characteristics:

1 The absence of property rights

As we have seen, socialism involves public rather than private ownership of the means of production. For many activities public ownership was relatively easy to establish. Governments in Central and Eastern Europe set up State Owned Enterprises (SOEs) responsible to the planners for their output. Small-scale production, agriculture and services were much more difficult to deal with and there were differences between economies in the extent of private ownership of such economic activity.

2 The nature of the planning process

The role of the state in a CPE is to co-ordinate the activities of SOEs. Some enterprises produce output which is used in the production of other goods and services. So, in order to plan economic activity the government needs to employ a technique called *input–output analysis*, which begins by drawing up *material balances* for each industry. Table 13.1 shows a simplified material balance for the coal industry. The left-hand side of the table identifies the sources of supply of coal and the right-hand side the uses of coal. Coal could be used to generate electricity or might be used in the production of steel, as well as being used by households for heating. If, as in the table, the planned uses of coal exceed domestic planned production, the shortfall is made up with imports.

Material balances must, of course, be drawn up for all sectors of the economy: for the extraction of raw materials and their processing, for the energy

Resources (thousands of tonnes)		Uses (thousands of tonnes)	
Domestic production	2,500	Production inputs	
Imports	500	– electricity generation	1,750
		– steel production	1,000
		Final consumption	250
Total	3,000	Total	3,000

Table 13.1 Simplified input–output analysis of the coal industry

industries, for the suppliers of intermediate and capital goods and for the manufacturers of consumer goods. The task is enormous, especially for an advanced economy and likely to result in inefficiency.

3 Limited international trade

Despite the priority of self-sufficiency, all CPEs were engaged in some international trade. Such trade was limited both in its volume and in the number of trading partners. Some 75 per cent of the trade of the former command economies was with other socialist economies. One of the key characteristics of trade was that it was of secondary importance in the plan compared to domestic production. Trade only took place when domestic uses, identified in table 13.1, exceeded domestic production. Unlike in a market economy trade in a CPE cannot be understood using the principles of comparative advantage (see section 10). In addition, little emphasis was placed on exports other than the need to pay for the required volume of imports. Finally, the state held a monopoly over trade through various Foreign Trade Organisations, which planned trade on behalf of industries.

Trade amongst CPEs was conducted under the umbrella of the Council for Mutual Economic Assistance (Comecon). This organisation synchronised the five-year plans of its member economies by drawing up five-year trade agreements according to the 'left-over principle': any shortfalls in domestic output being filled by imports. Some have argued that Comecom was driven by the needs of the Soviet economy. The USSR would import Hungarian buses, Bulgarian forklift trucks, Polish ships and parts for Lada cars in exchange for exports of oil and gas and complete Ladas.

An important point about these trading relationships is that no actual payments ever took place! Prices of imports and exports would be related to world prices with each economy holding an account with Comecon's International Bank for Economic Co-operation (IBEC). When Hungary exported Ikarus buses to the USSR it would be given a credit at the bank in 'trade roubles'. However, if the total value of Hungary's exports exceeded its imports, the surplus at the bank could not be spent because the rouble account was not convertible into the Hungarian forint. Such currency inconvertibility meant that domestic prices bore no relationship to international prices, unlike in a market economy. In addition, there was no incentive for a country to build up a surplus at the IBEC by promoting exports. Exports and imports were really just 'swaps' with other CPEs and exporters had few incentives to control or improve quality.

4 *Undeveloped finance and capital 'markets'*
The financial system of CPEs bore little resemblance to the finance and capital markets found in market economies. As with most other economic activities, banks in CPEs were state owned. There were four parts to the banking 'system': the Central Bank, which was the lender of last resort to the SOEs; an Investment Bank, which was responsible for providing cash to SOEs for the investment agreed in the national plan; various Sectoral Banks which dealt with foreign trade and agriculture, for example; and a Savings Bank which could be used by citizens.

All SOEs had specific accounts with the Central Bank. This meant that the 'money' in the wages account could not be used to buy raw materials and so on. In fact, with such a system of banking it makes little sense to talk of money existing in CPEs. One of the characteristics of money is that it should be acceptable as a means of exchange for goods and services. In CPEs the currency could not fulfil this function, since there were different types of money for different transactions: 'investment money', 'wages money' and 'materials money', for example.

The problems and inefficiencies of planning

How well did central planning work as a means of allocating scarce resources? Steffens once said of communism, 'I have seen the future and it works'. In many respects communism and planning have some astonishing achievements to their credit: in their early days they provided some of the fastest rates of economic growth the world has witnessed; industrialisation in Eastern Europe was achieved without the consequent gross inequalities and mass poverty experienced in the West; it guaranteed full employment and a reasonable standard of living for its citizens. President Kennedy admitted in 1961 that the Soviet Union had achieved parity in space technology; and it was a phenomenal military power, particularly with respect to nuclear weapons.

Despite these achievements there were a number of problems with the planned approach to resource allocation. For example, the differences in collective ownership of the means of production and the lack of property rights created many economic inefficiencies. In the market system private ownership brings rewards and creates incentives. A firm which manages to reduce costs below those of its competitors is able to charge lower prices and is rewarded with higher market share and profits. Incentives are, therefore, created to produce efficiently and to innovate products and production processes. In the socialist economy such incentives are absent. What is the point of a manager of a SOE producing efficiently if there is no reward? What is the point of individual workers increasing their effort if they see no gain to themselves? Some have argued that the dilapidated state of much of the social housing in CEE states is the result of this 'tragedy of the commons'.

The planning process itself caused economic inefficiencies. In order to draw up material balances, planners needed information about the resource requirements of each SOE and their 'capital–output' ratios: that is, the amount of output which could be produced with each unit of capital. Such information was passed on to the planners by the enterprise managers, leading to a 'principal–agent' problem. Enterprise managers are the agents of the planners (the 'principals') responsible for implementing the plan. The managers have more information than the planners and are therefore able to pursue their own interests given this asymmetry of information. The managers of SOEs would put in bids for more inputs than they required and bargain for production targets which were easier to achieve than those proposed by the planners. Incentives and penalties were weakly linked to performance and tended to encourage 'satisficing' behaviour on the part of managers (see section 3). One measure of the resulting inefficiency was that energy use per unit of output was up to four times higher in the CPEs than in the West. Most planned targets were expressed in volume (i.e. numbers of tractors) or weight and production took little account of the quality of what was produced. Soviet agriculture, for example, used more tractors per hectare than Western agriculture yet they frequently broke down. Since the plan for tractor production was expressed as a target for total production, SOEs produced lots of tractors but very few spare parts. This was common in much of industry, which was subject to frequent and long production stoppages.

Incentives for workers were also very crude. In order to raise levels of production in the quest for economic growth, workers were often given bonuses related to the total production of the factory rather than to individual effort. The consequence of this was that individual workers could 'free-ride' off the efforts of others by shirking, for example, or by gaining the benefit of the bonus with minimum effort. As you learned in section 5, free riding gives rise to under-consumption in the case of public goods. In this case, free riding causes low output per worker or productive inefficiency.

CPEs also suffered from a misguided belief in economies of scale. In the former Soviet Union almost two thirds of industrial products were produced by a single SOE. Figure 13.1 illustrates the consequences of such a preference for large-scale production on cost efficiency. The curve LRAC represents the long-run average cost curve for a particular industry, showing economies of scale up to 1,000 units of output, constant returns to scale up to 4,000 units of output and diseconomies of scale thereafter. If the plan target was 6,000 units the cost of production would be C_{cpe}. In a market economy, market demand of 6,000 units could be supplied by six firms each producing 1,000 at a cost per unit of C^*. No individual firm in a market economy would produce more than 4,000 units because of diseconomies of scale, and, therefore, cost per unit would be minimised. The large-scale production favoured by CPEs resulted in cost inefficiencies. This inefficiency, and the monopoly position of firms, has had an important bearing on such businesses during the transition to a market economy, as we shall see later.

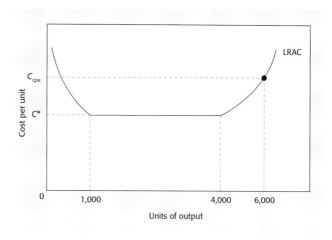

Figure 13.1 The preference for large-scale production in CPEs

Finally, we can argue that the system of administered, as opposed to market determined, prices gave rise to allocative inefficiency (see section 4). In a planned economy prices bear little relationship to costs and consumers have no way of signalling their preferences since excess demand cannot raise the price as in a market system. Instead scarce resources are allocated by queues. Consumers, then, have no way to influence the plan, and the bias towards heavy industry and military goods production in much of Central and Eastern Europe indicates allocative inefficiency.

In short, command economies suffered from numerous problems and inefficiencies: chronic shortages of consumer goods and inherent supply side weaknesses; repressed inflation due to the under-pricing of scarce goods and services; hidden unemployment due to the over-manning of industry and the guarantee of full employment; 'soft' budget constraints caused by the lack of financial control exercised over SOEs.

As these economies began to open up politically (*glasnost*), before the planning system was effectively reformed (*perestroika*), the low level of utility was channelled into political forces for change, culminating in the collapse of both the political and economic systems associated with communism.

The transition to a market economy: reforms and problems

The task of transforming a centrally planned economy into a market economy is enormous. Not only must the foundations of a fully functioning market economy be

225

put in place but the government needs to react to the inevitable problems during transition. If these issues are not complex enough, governments must conduct this transformation lacking any prior experience on which they can draw. Although the major reforms can be identified, there is little guidance on the speed or the sequence in which the reforms should be implemented. Some countries chose to follow the 'shock therapy' approach recommended by some economists. This approach involves extensive privatisation, strict monetary and fiscal policies to reduce inflation and the forces of supply and demand to determining internal market prices and the external exchange rate. Others chose to adopt the 'gradual' approach to transition, arguing that consumers and producers needed time to adapt to the new economic system and that, to maintain public support for the reforms, the pain of transition needed to be softened. The transition to the market is arguably the largest economic experiment which has been conducted in the twentieth century.

The reforms which are needed on the road to the market economy include:

Price liberalisation

The key to microeconomic reform is to allow prices to be determined by supply and demand. By freeing prices from state control former command economies should enjoy benefits in the long term. Figure 13.2 shows the efficiency gains which are likely from such price liberalisation. In a command economy prices bore no relationship to demand and supply. This is represented by a price (P_c) below the market equilibrium (P_m). At this price consumers demand a quantity of Q_2 but the supply is fixed by planners at S_p, with the result that excess demand of $Q_2 - Q_1$ manifests itself as lengthy queues. Price liberalisation causes the price to 'jump' to P_m, encouraging an increase in supply to Q_e in the long run. Producers are better off by the area $P_c P_{meb}$ (the increase in producer surplus) and consumers are better off by the area $P_m P_c + Q_{ae}$ (the increase in consumer surplus). This change in consumer surplus arises because the effective price of the good under the command system was $P_c + Q$ as the price to consumers is raised by the time spent queuing. Similar gains are possible by allowing domestic prices to reflect world prices more closely. Energy was massively under-priced in the CEE and CIS states, with the world price exceeding the plan price by as much as 150 per cent. By liberalising energy prices, gains in economic welfare of up to 10 per cent of GDP could be shown, more than the entire gains from the Single European Market in the EU.

Removal of subsidies

In order to fully realise the gains from price liberalisation the government must also remove the various subsidies to SOEs which kept prices low. As these subsidies are removed prices will 'jump' even further. Some governments, most notably the Russian government, delayed the introduction of such price reforms for fear of the effect of price rises on the real wages of workers. Sensitive prices, such as food, housing and energy, were not fully liberalised. Another fear was that, if prices were liberalised before competition was introduced, the former SOEs might take advantage of their monopoly power and raise prices even further. Some countries, therefore, delayed price liberalisation.

Privatisation

To create a fully functional market economy, SOEs need to be turned into profit-motivated, private sector firms. The privatisation of small-scale SOEs has created few problems – shops, restaurants and bars have largely been handed over to their former managers or, where they could be identified, their former owners. Where those who manage the firm are also its owners and free to make profit, changes can be rapid. Such small-scale privatisation has been the visible sign of transition for

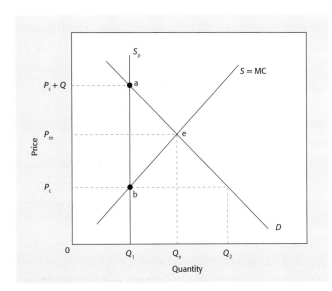

Figure 13.2 The gains from price liberation

many consumers, with a rapid change in the appearance of the 'high street' in terms of window displays and the range of goods and services on offer. Outside the major cities, the typical Central and Eastern European 'restaurant', often part of a large-scale SOE, may still exist, but the growth in fast food outlets and trendy bars is apparent nevertheless. Small-scale privatisation has been an important source of employment generation, much needed as large-scale SOEs shed labour in the quest for greater efficiency.

Large-scale privatisation has been much more of a problem. The key to such privatisation is to ensure that firms respond to the new market signals by seeking opportunities to reduce losses and improve profitability. Incentives need to be put in place so that firms become profit maximisers. In market economies these incentives exist in what is called the market for 'corporate control'. Briefly, firms are owned by shareholders who appoint managers to look after their interests. If shareholders feel that managers are not maximising profits, they can either replace the managers or sell their shares on the stock market. The role of the stock market is crucial. As shareholders sell their shares, prices fall and firms become subject to takeover. Managers are kept on their toes by the threat of takeover and businesses are restructured by the new owners after a takeover. However, during the transition phase active share markets are absent or are only partially developed, causing some governments to delay the privatisation process.

Those governments that have privatised large-scale SOEs have had to think carefully about how to privatise. A number of different ways have been attempted:

1 auctioning them to the highest bidder for cash;
2 issuing privatisation vouchers to the general public and then auctioning the SOEs in return for the vouchers;
3 allowing existing managers, workers and/or foreign companies to buy the SOE;
4 handing over the SOE to managers and/or workers for free.

Private ownership, of whatever kind, is not enough on its own to guarantee success. There is also a need to improve management techniques, especially in the areas of stock and quality control, financial management and marketing. Existing managers, of course, lack such skills

One of the new range of cars from Skoda. After a liaison with Volkswagen the Skoda image changed from one of scorn to well-engineered reliability

and it may take some time for them to be acquired, which has convinced some governments of the need to delay the privatisation process whilst the necessary 'restructuring' takes place. Others have 'imported' the required management techniques by selling (wholly or partially) SOEs to foreign multinational companies, such as the sale by the Czech government of Skoda to the German car giant Volkswagen and the sale of Hungary's largest supermarket chain to Tesco, the UK's biggest grocery retailer. In other words, the type of privatisation during transition is as, if not more, important than the scale of privatisation.

Trade liberalisation

Liberalising prices does not make much sense without trade liberalisation. Since a lot of industry is monopolised by SOEs, liberalising trade can create the competition which might otherwise not exist. However for trade to be liberalised it is necessary for the currency to be convertible into other currencies, at least for transactions involving goods and services (so-called current account convertibility). As we saw in section 12, international trade brings important static and dynamic benefits. By allowing resources to be allocated on the basis of comparative advantage, economic efficiency is improved and there is a spur to greater dynamism in the long run.

In theory, trade liberalisation can be achieved fairly quickly by removing the state monopoly on trade, all tariffs, quotas and non-tariff barriers to trade and by allowing the currency to be convertible. Some temporary protection of domestic industries might, however, be justified, given the inefficient state of many SOEs, the need for the government to raise revenue in the early phase of the transition process and the need to stop the 'monetary overhang' being translated into a big surge in the demand for imports and a consequent deficit on the current account of the balance of payments. But tariffs on imports will cause problems for those industries trying to export since it will increase the cost of their imported inputs.

The transition economies of Central Europe have been in a fortunate position with regard to trade. Geographically close to the European Union, they have been able to find alternative markets for their exports after the collapse of Comecon, unlike Eastern European states and the economies of the CIS. In addition, they have gained tariff-free access to the EU in the form of various Europe Agreements, which have, in some instances, paved the way for potential full membership. Consequently their pattern of trade has undergone a major change and they are becoming more closely integrated with the economies of Western Europe.

Currency convertibility means that the government has to take some view on what sort of exchange rate regime it is going to adopt. Freely floating exchange rates cause problems as the exchange rate will have a tendency to depreciate and this will add to the uncertainty already caused by the transition from one economic system to another. Fixed exchange rate regimes are likely to be difficult for transition economies to support, since they lack the necessary foreign exchange reserves. However, if the exchange rate is fixed at a low enough rate and against the 'right' currency, there is every chance that not much speculation will take place and this will minimise the amount of intervention needed to support the currency. For this reason, most transition economies have opted for a fixed exchange rate regime.

Reform of the financial sector

As we have seen, many of the reforms required as part of the transition process require a fully functioning financial sector. The elements of a typical reform package should include:

1 establishing a Central Bank to control the money supply and interest rates independently of government and to act as a lender of last resort to the commercial banks;

2 creating banking institutions for collecting savings and channelling these savings to former SOEs so that they can invest and re-structure themselves;

3 setting up a framework to supervise and regulate the activities of the financial sector;

4 creating a market in which governments can sell bonds to finance any excess of expenditure over taxation receipts.

Given the nature of the financial system inherited from the years of planning, these reforms are a major task for the governments and one that is likely to take many years to complete. The experience of financial sector reform has been very mixed amongst the former CPEs. In Hungary, for example, the government refused to bail-out banks which had made poor lending decisions, and started to sell them to foreign investors. In addition, there were tough bankruptcy laws ensuring that banks could recover their bad loans. The result has been that, by 1996, almost 50 per cent of Hungarian banks were foreign-owned and their bad debts small. In the Czech Republic, in comparison, almost 50 per cent of loans made by banks are unrecoverable. Here banks remained in state ownership and they were encouraged by the government to finance many of the privatisations of SOEs, creating a conflict of interest. Instead of calling in the bad loans, Czech banks (essentially the owners of the former SOEs) gave them more and more loans. The legal framework tends to favour those who are in debt rather than giving power to the banks to recover their money. Consequently the Czech government has been forced to bail out the banks for fear of a collapse in the financial system and has belatedly begun the process of privatising the banking system.

The costs of transition

Inflation We saw earlier that price liberalisation was likely to result in a big, one-off 'jump' in prices. Why this should then turn into sustained price increases (inflation) is relatively easy to understand. Under a command system shortages meant that consumers are unable to get hold of the goods and services they want. This translates into a lot of spare cash being held by citizens: the economy suffers from a 'monetary overhang'. Once prices are liberalised, this excess demand comes out into the open. Unfortunately, in the short term, production is unable to meet this extra

People standing in a queue to buy milk at a lower price in central Moscow
Source: Popperfoto Reuters.

demand and prices rise dramatically. To prevent real wages falling some former CPE governments allowed SOEs to increase money wages to compensate for the price rises. The result was a wage–price spiral.

Recession and unemployment The early years of transition saw a massive collapse in the recorded output of all the CPEs. For example, Hungarian GDP fell by 12 per cent in 1991 and Georgia suffered four years of recession with output falling by as much as 35–40 per cent per annum. What caused this collapse of output? The short answer is that Comecon collapsed, leading to a big decline in exports for each economy. For example, the world's largest producer of buses, the Hungarian firm Ikarus, saw its exports to Russia fall dramatically, leading to a virtual collapse of its traditional export market. The domestic economy was also dislocated by the collapse of the planning process. Previously, SOEs had relied upon the state to plan both their output and their resource requirements. Suddenly, there were no guarantees that their output would be bought or their inputs would be available. In the worst cases, the economic system almost ground to a halt. Once international trade was liberalised, the market for domestically produced output shrunk as consumers and firms bought from abroad. The consequence of falling output has been a massive rise in unemployment and in addition SOEs have also been shedding labour to

increase efficiency.

Fiscal and monetary problems
The reduction in economic activity had two major consequences for the governments' finances. During the years of planning, money to finance government expenditure was raised mainly through taxing the sales revenues of SOEs and personal incomes. The collapse of output and the consequent reduction in employment meant that the government's income from tax fell dramatically. It also meant that individual enterprises were unable to pay their bills. To prevent the widespread collapse that this might have caused, governments increased their subsidies to enterprises. At the same time, there was upward pressure on government expenditure. Under planning, many social services like transport, housing and even health care were provided by SOEs. Overnight, these social services were taken into central or local government control, increasing government expenditure. Budget deficits, therefore, soared as tax receipts fell and expenditure rose. In the West, budget deficits are usually financed by borrowing from the non-bank private sector through the sale of government bonds. Transition governments cannot do this as they do not have a bond market in which to sell bonds! They must therefore resort to borrowing from abroad (increasing government debt) or simply printing the money. Many governments have financed deficits by turning on the printing presses, thereby fuelling inflation.

A model of the problems of transition The macroeconomic problems for a typical transition economy are represented in the AD/AS diagram shown in figure 13.3.

The employment line underneath the diagram simply represents the relationship between output and employment: that is, extra output requires greater employment of labour. The end of planning effectively dislocated the supply side of the economy, shifting AS_0 left to AS_1. The monetary overhang (the stock of cash set aside by consumers as a result of chronic shortages) led to an initial increase in AD to AD_1 and was fuelled by governments printing money to 'finance' their budget deficits. The consequence was that the falling output (Y_0 to Y_1) coincided with dramatically rising prices (P_0 to

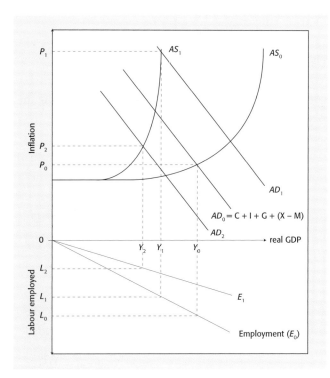

Figure 13.3 Macroeconomic problems in a typical transition economy

P_1) and falling levels of employment (L_0 to L_1). The collapse of Comecon and the surge in the demand for imports began to reduce demand, shifting AD left. Those governments that adopted 'shock therapy' policies began to impose strict fiscal and monetary polices which were aimed at reducing the inflationary pressures, but which only worked by a deflationary shock to the economy (AD_1 to AD_2). At the same time, former SOEs shed labour in order to improve efficiency (E_0 to E_1). Whilst the inflation was curbed (P_1 to P_2), output fell further (Y_1 to Y_2) as did employment (L_1 to L_2).

The diverse performance of transition economies

Despite their shared goal of building a market economy, the former command countries have shown diverse economic performance (see section 7). Table 13.2 shows the record of growth in GDP in all the transition

economies. The sharp decline in the early years of transition, explained above, is clear. There is a major difference, however, in terms of the severity of the recession and the speed of recovery. In general the economies of Central and Eastern Europe appear to have suffered a shorter recession and a more sustained period of recovery. Most CEE economies began to recover in 1994 with Croatia, the Czech Republic, Estonia, Hungary, Lithuania, Poland, Slovakia and Slovenia managing to sustain growth over at least four years. In comparison, only three of the Commonwealth of Independent States (Armenia, Georgia and Kyrgystan) have sustained growth over a four year period and Russia, Turkmenistan and Ukraine only achieved positive growth in 1998. Why has the performance of transition economies been so diverse and why is there such a clear divide between the experiences of the CEE and CIS countries?

Some economists have attempted to explain this diversity in terms of the speed and comprehensiveness of the reform measures implemented. One crude measure of progress might be to look at the size of the new private sector as a proportion of GDP. Countries which have a large private sector might be thought of as making more headway in transforming a command economy into a market economy. As figure 13.4 shows, however, there is a very weak relationship between the size of the private sector and the successfulness of the transition. For example, the private sector in Russia is larger than that in Poland, but this does not associate with strong economic performance over the period.

The European Bank for Reconstruction and Development (EBRD) uses various indices of reform progress in each of the areas we identified above. So countries are ranked on a scale of 1 (very little progress) to 4 (almost complete reform) in terms of large- and small-scale privatisation, price and trade liberalisation, bank reform, legal reforms and so on. Figure 13.5 shows that there is a stronger relationship if these various indices are added together and then related to GDP growth, which has tended to lead some to argue that the shock therapy approach to transition is superior to the gradual approach. But there are still some important

Self-assessment task

Study the information below and then answer the questions which follow.

Eastern Europe – the problems of transition to a market economy

In the move to market-based economies in Central and Eastern Europe, there has been much debate about the speed of transition.

Some economists have recommended that 'shock therapy' is the best way for countries to make this transition. This approach involves extensive privatisation, strict monetary and fiscal policies to reduce inflation, and allowing supply and demand to determine internal market prices and the external exchange rate.

Poland was the first country to apply 'shock therapy' in 1990. Bulgaria followed, although it implemented this approach at a slower rate and with less strict fiscal controls.

The table below shows some aspects of the performance of the economies of Poland and Bulgaria between 1990 and 1997.

	1990	1991	1992	1993	1994	1995	1996	1997
Poland								
GDP (annual % change)	−11.6	−7.6	1.5	4.5	5.2	7.0	6.1	6.9
Budget surplus/deficit (as a % of GDP)	0.7	−3.5	−6.1	−3.4	−2.8	−3.6	−3.1	−4.0
Consumer prices (annual % change)	289.0	60.4	44.3	37.6	29.4	21.6	18.5	14.5
Real wages (annual % change)	−24.4	−0.3	−2.7	−1.5	2.0	n.a.	n.a.	n.a.
Trade balance ($ bn)	5.7	−0.6	−3.0	−4.6	−4.3	−6.2	−12.7	−16.0
Bulgaria								
GDP (annual % change)	−9.1	−11.7	−7.3	−1.5	1.8	2.1	−10.9	−7.4
Budget surplus/deficit (as a % of GDP)	−4.0	−3.5	−6.1	−11.9	−5.8	−6.4	−13.4	−6.3
Consumer prices (annual % change)	72.5	338.9	79.4	63.9	121.9	32.9	311.0	591.5
Real wages (annual % change)	6.9	−39.4	19.2	−11.7	−19.0	n.a.	n.a.	n.a.
Trade balance ($ bn)	−0.4	0.7	−0.5	−1.0	−0.2	−0.3	−0.7	−0.1

1 Compare GDP growth and the trend in consumer prices in Poland and Bulgaria over the period 1990 to 1997.

2 One of the costs of transition to a market economy is that living standards might fall in the short term.

(a) Explain which economic indicator might be used to determine any changes in living standards.

(b) What evidence is there in the table to suggest that, in relative terms, living standards in Bulgaria have been more badly affected than those in Poland?

3 (a) Explain what is likely to happen to prices as price controls are relaxed in a former command economy.

(b) Explain likely reasons why Poland has been more successful than Bulgaria in reducing inflation over the period.

4 Comment upon the effectiveness of the shock therapy approach in the transition to a market economy in Eastern Europe.

	1991	1992	1993	1994	1995	1996	1997	1998
CEE countries								
Albania	−28	−10	11	9	9	9	−8	12
Bulgaria	−12	−7	−2	2	3	−11	−7	3
Croatia	−20	−10	−4	1	2	4	6	6
Czech Republic	−14	−6	−1	3	5	4	1	2
Estonia	−11	−14	−9	−3	3	4	10	6
Macedonia	−12	−21	−8	−4	−2	1	1	5
Hungary	−12	−3	−1	3	2	1	4	5
Latvia	−8	−35	−16	1	−2	3	6	6
Lithuania	−13	−38	−24	1	3	5	6	6
Poland	−7	3	4	5	7	6	7	6
Romania	−13	−9	1	4	7	4	−7	−2
Slovak Republic	−15	−7	−4	5	7	7	7	4
Slovenia	−8	−5	1	5	4	3	3	4
CEE average	−11	4	1	4	5	4	4	4
CIS countries								
Armenia	−11	−52	−15	5	7	6	3	6
Azerbaijan	−1	−23	−23	−21	−8	1	5	7
Belarus	−1	−10	−11	−12	−10	3	10	2
Georgia	−14	−40	−39	−35	2	10	10	10
Kazakhstan	−13	−13	−12	−25	−9	1	2	3
Kyrgystan	−5	−19	−16	−27	1	6	10	6
Moldova	−18	−29	−1	−31	−3	−8	1	1
Russia	−13	−15	−9	−13	−4	−5	0	2
Tajikistan	−7	−29	−11	−22	−13	−4	2	4
Turkmenistan	−5	−5	−10	−20	−10	−8	−25	12
Ukraine	−9	−10	−14	−23	−12	−10	−3	1
Uzbekistan	−1	−11	−2	−4	−1	2	2	2
CIS average	−12	−14	−9	−14	−5	−5	1	2

Table 13.2 The growth of GDP[1] in transition economies 1991–1998
Note: [1] Average annual % change in GDP

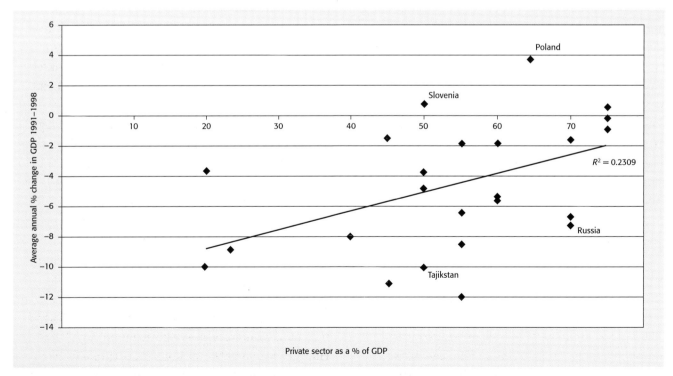

Figure 13.4 Extent of privatisation is weakly associated with successful transition

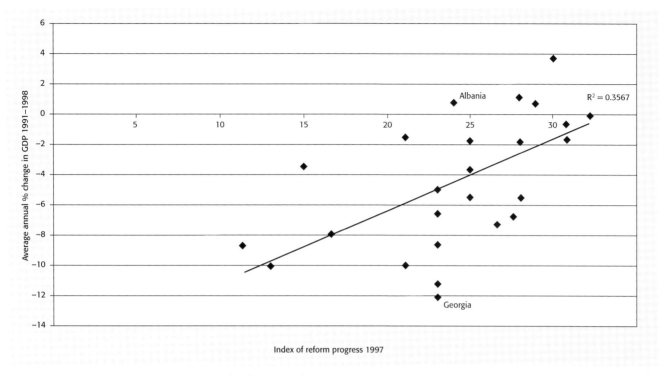

Figure 13.5 Broad-based reforms are associated with successful transition

differences that need to be explained. For example, Albania and Georgia are very similar in terms of the amount of reform each has undertaken but their economic performance (in terms of GDP growth over the period) is markedly different.

Some economists have argued that an important lesson to learn from the experience of the transition economies is that it is the determination of governments to control inflation which is the key to success. Why should this be so? The market system works by sending signals about the relative scarcity of goods, services and factors of production. These signals are sent via the price mechanism through changes in relative prices. When inflation exists there is confusion about whether rising prices are signalling something about the relative scarcity of particular goods and services. The result is that the price mechanism no longer allocates resources efficiently. In section 7 you learned that inflation erodes the international competitiveness of an economy. Both of these costs of inflation are likely to adversely affect economic growth. In countries such as Georgia, inflation averaged over 2000 per cent from 1991 to 1998 and consequently recovery from the initial recession has been difficult. Figure 13.6 shows that this relationship between

inflation and growth is very strong, suggesting that the key to a successful transition is very tight, anti-inflationary fiscal and monetary policies, such as in Poland and Slovakia.

The ability to attract foreign direct investment (FDI) is a further important condition for successful transition in that it allows the transfer of technology and management techniques as well as capital from more advanced market economies. Japanese FDI into Britain, for example, has brought with it management techniques, such as Just-In-Time (JIT), which have spread widely amongst British businesses, improving efficiency. Volkswagen's involvement with Skoda in the Czech Republic may be thought of as important, not only for the dramatic improvements in technology, efficiency and design which have occurred at Skoda, but also because 80 per cent of Skoda's inputs are sourced locally. This has a multiplier effect on the Czech economy as a whole (see section 8). In Hungary, Ford, Suzuki and Audi have set up their own component suppliers which have sourced many of their inputs from domestic suppliers. However, the amount of FDI which transition economies have attracted is not significant. Hungary has attracted the lion's share ($15 billion) in the period 1989–97, yet this is equivalent to only $1,519

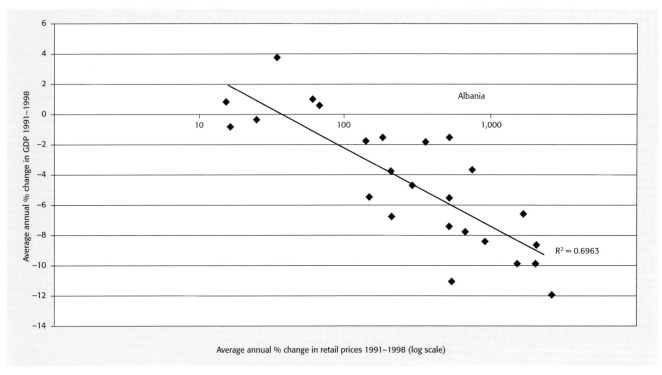

Figure 13.6 Reducing inflation is associated with successful transition

on a per capita basis. Research indicates that there is only a very weak relationship between levels of FDI and success in transition in terms of GDP growth.

So, what other factors may have contributed to the relative success of some transition economies? In section 8 you learned that one of the major determinants of economic growth was improvement in the quality as well as the quantity of the factors of production. In particular, economists have tended to stress the role played by improvements in labour productivity. Productivity data tend to show that economies such as Poland and Slovenia have outperformed other transition economies and this is an important part of their success, with industrial productivity leading the rest of the economy. In Poland, this improvement in labour productivity has taken place alongside falling unemployment, which is a major achievement. In Russia, falling GDP has coincided with constant declines in the productivity of labour as economic theory would suggest. The key question is what has caused this superior productivity performance. FDI may have played a role, but, as we have suggested, the evidence is weak. It would appear that most of the productivity advances have come from small- and medium-sized firms. In economies where such firms were not

swallowed up by the command economy and have survived, the record has been good. It would appear, then, that it is as much the legacy of planning as the actual reforms which matters in terms of a successful transition.

Another determinant of economic growth also introduced in section 8 was investment. Rates of investment have been higher in the CEE countries than in the CIS countries. In addition, these economies have also been much more open to international competition and they have probably benefited from their geographical closeness to, and their ability to integrate with, the EU. In preparation for EU membership economies such as Poland have introduced effective competition and monopoly policies, which have been important in improving levels of efficiency.

Explaining the diverse performance of transition economies is therefore very complex. Clearly, the extent of reforms and macroeconomic stabilisation are important but they do not account for all the variations amongst economies. It may be that a much more general explanation of success is needed in terms of the legacy of planning, political stability and the ability to attract aid and investment.

Integration with the EU: prospects and problems

In the long run the countries of both the EU and the former command economies have much to gain from closer integration. As we saw earlier, integration provides new markets for goods and services and represents an increase in the investment opportunities for firms. The benefits of free trade within the Union are increased, leading to static and dynamic efficiency gains. The larger market is likely to lead to:

1 the ability to benefit from economies of scale;
2 enhanced competition, driving down costs and prices;
3 more product and process innovation;
4 increased levels of investment and the transfer of technology.

The result of such integration should be higher GDP for all countries and an increase in the rate of economic growth.

A number of former command economies have already opened up their markets to trade with the EU. Poland, Hungary, the Czech and Slovak Republics and Slovenia created the Central European Free Trade Area (CEFTA) in 1992 as a way of displaying their willingness to participate in the European integration movement. However, the EU was initially reluctant to follow suit. Whilst it signed agreements with many former command economies, these Europe Agreements (with the Czech and Slovak Republics, Hungary, Poland, Bulgaria and Romania) excluded free trade in 'sensitive' goods, such as agricultural products, iron and steel, textiles, furniture, leather goods and glass. These are the very goods in which former command economies enjoy a comparative advantage – the EU fear was that increased competition from Eastern Europe would adversely affect the poorer regions of the EU.

Despite this, the EU actually enjoys a trade surplus in many of the goods exempted from the free trade agreements. In 1993 it set out three criteria for former command economies to gain full membership of the EU. These so-called Copenhagen criteria were:

1 stability and democracy, with particular protection of the rights of minorities;
2 a fully functioning market economy which would be able to compete with the economies of the EU;
3 the ability to meet the requirements of full membership, including effective competition and monopoly policy, the ability to adopt the rules of the Single European Market and, ultimately, to participate in monetary union.

In 1997, five former command economies (the Czech Republic, Estonia, Hungary, Poland and Slovenia) were deemed to have met, or be close to meeting, these criteria and are expected to gain full membership by around the year 2003. There may, however, be major problems for these and other former command economies in joining the EU, especially in the short term.

The key to success is their ability to compete with the existing economies of the EU. The benefits of membership can only be gained if further radical change takes place. Eastern European firms will have to restructure themselves to gain competitiveness and this is unlikely without bankruptcies, takeovers and mergers and further rationalisation. There could be much structural and technological unemployment as a result of these changes, which may persist in the absence of labour mobility. This labour mobility could take two main forms. Eastern European workers will need to be switched between industries as free trade and competition lead to the decline of sunset industries (occupational mobility). In addition, there may need to be mobility of labour between Eastern European economies and the existing economies of the EU if strains on the EU's regional funds are to be avoided. Despite the fact that the five fast track countries trade mostly with the EU (thereby maximising potential trade creation effects and minimising trade diversion), there are huge gaps between their economies and those of the EU. Poland, for example, has a GDP per capita some 30 per cent of the EU average and has 27 per cent of its population engaged in agriculture, as opposed to 5.3 per cent in the EU.

Such differences create many potential problems for the EU. Since the former command economies are much more dependent on agriculture, full membership is likely to put massive strains on the Common Agricultural Policy (CAP). The high guaranteed prices of the CAP encouraged an increase in the supply of agricultural commodities in the EU, with the consequent food mountains of the 1980s. It has been estimated that accepting Poland, Hungary, the Czech and Slovak Republics would increase the cost of the CAP by as much as 60 per cent. In addition, there will be increases in the cost of the regional and structural funds of the EU as a result of the relatively low GDP per capita of these Eastern European economies. It has been estimated that the combined effect of admitting new members could be to increase the contributions of existing members to the EU Budget by as much as 60 per cent.

The EU has recognised the problems that such enlargement might bring. Agenda 2000 commits it to reforming its common policies and preparing Eastern European countries to meet the criteria for membership. However, reform of the CAP is proving difficult, with member states remaining deeply divided over key parts of the reform plan. Substantial reductions have been proposed for the guaranteed prices for beef and cereals for instance. Although the majority of EU countries support the proposals, nine of the fifteen countries are pressing for hefty compensation to be paid directly to their own farmers. Early signs are that the EU is finding it difficult to cope with the reforms to its common policies which are necessary before more new members can be admitted.

The geographical enlargement of the EU to include some of the transition economies of Central and Eastern Europe raises important economic and political issues. Increased market size will clearly enhance the benefits of integration – there is, though, growing concern about whether it is better to deepen integration amongst existing members or to widen membership by geographical enlargement. What is clear is that deepening integration is far more difficult in an enlarged EU. The outcome may well be a two-tier future structure, with those firmly committed and economically equipped for greater integration to be in the first tier. Just where this might leave the UK is a matter which will affect all UK citizens and have a profound effect upon their economic well-being in the twenty-first century.

Self-assessment tasks

Read the newspaper articles from *European Voice* on the problems of transition and enlargement and then answer the questions that follow. (These articles are indicative of material which will be used in OCR's pre-issued case material for this unit.)

Waving goodbye to the Czech miracle

Humble pie should perhaps become the new Czech national food as the country faces up to severe economic and political challenges.

Times have changed since the mid-1990s, when the Czech Republic sold itself as the example to follow for other central and eastern European countries rushing to embrace the West and achieve the twin objectives of European Union and NATO membership.

The country is now deep in recession, with the trend of negative economic growth in the first nine months of last year likely to be confirmed when the figures for the final quarter are published. They are expected to show that the Czech Republic's gross domestic product fell by 2% during 1998.

Many economists believe that the country will not fare much better this year, with some forecasting feeble growth of just 0.5% while others suggest the figure will be closer to zero.

This poor performance is all the more galling since neighbours Poland and Hungary are posting positive growth figures which can only bolster their bid for EU membership.

For the Czech Republic's Social Democrat government, which has been in power since June 1998, other chickens are also coming home to roost.

Corruption scandals, the latest focused on allegations that Dutch phone company Telsource paid bribes to ensure a stake in national phone company SPT Telecom, have tarnished the republic in the eyes of foreign investors.

Unemployment, which stood at only 4.7% two years ago, has now reached 7.5%, with some economists predicting that it could rise to around 9% by the end of the year. Delayed privatisations and economic reforms, especially in the already bailed-out banking sector, need to be pushed through urgently.

Prime Minister Milos Zeman is attempting to clear up the mess while, justifiably, trying to deflect most of the blame onto his predecessor Vaclav Klaus. "Klaus has left Zeman a time bomb and it is beginning to explode," says Rick Fawn, lecturer in international relations at St Andrews University, Scotland.

Unfortunately for Zeman, blaming his predecessors and long-time rivals is not an ideal recipe for political survival.

Zeman's Social Democrats, the first left-wing party to hold power since the Velvet Revolution a decade ago, rely on the support of Klaus' Civic Democratic Party to retain office in what appears to be an inherently flawed coalition. Even worse, Klaus' stock with the voters appears to be rising as he reaps the benefits from his semi-detached position in the corridors of political power.

Klaus has taken up a largely symbolic post as president of the chamber of deputies (the lower house of parliament) in a direct swap with Zeman. Last month, an opinion poll put his party ahead of the Social Democrats for the first time since the general election.

Even so, the odd couple of Czech politics look destined to stay together for some time to come, largely because there are no other viable options.

In spite of Zeman's forced reliance on the Communist Party to get his budget through the lower house at the start of this month, a long-term alliance between the two is not seen as a realistic prospect, according to Fawn. 'Zeeman's greatest achievement was distancing himself from the Communists,' he says.

Although it gained around 10% of the vote last June and has a youthful – somewhat trendy – following, the Communist Party is still a pariah for many other political parties and voters who recall the purges, state trials and hypocrisy which characterised much of its 40-year rule.

There is speculation about a possible split within the Communist Party between the hardliners who oppose NATO membership and the reformers prepared to accept, but most analysts believe that this would not radically recast the political landscape.

At the other end of the political spectrum, Klaus is reckoned to have offended so many of his possible coalition partners by his brusque behaviour during his term in office from 1992 to 1997 that few would happily contemplate working under him again.

'Such reservations are an important obstacle to creating a right-of-centre coalition', says Jiri Pehe, senior policy adviser to Czech Republic President Vaclav Havel. In any case, Klaus is believed to have his eyes firmly focused on the presidency itself whenever Havel steps down.

New party combinations or a grand coalition to tackle the country's problems are therefore unlikely this year, according to Pehe. As a result, it is Zeman who is likely to bear the burden of administering some painful medicine to the Czech economy.

Analysts warn that he could find himself under attack on two fronts. His attempts to cushion the impact of reform run the risk of both offending foreign investors and failing to fend off criticism from his party's supporters.

The privatisation of the country's banking sector, with the state selling off its majority stake in the two biggest banks (Ceska Sporitelna and Komercni Banka) should be completed by the end of next year. However, the price for restoring the two to health will be high – up to €2 billion, according to ABN AMRO economist Elena Graziadei.

Failure to restructure the financial sector has been identified by the European Commission as one of the Czech Republic's biggest problems. The shake-up has been held up by the mountain of bad loans which banks have accumulated, and fears that fresh problems could be uncovered by any clean-up.

Past privatisations under the Czech voucher system, where every citizen was given a stake in the company being sold off, have left a confused legacy, with ownership unclear in spite of holding companies' attempts to buy up the small stakes. 'Companies coming in would often like to start with green-field sites rather than attempt to tidy up the mess', says Graziadei.

Skoda Auto, which took a different route when it was taken over by German car giant Volkswagen, is a success story, with so many workers being taken on at its Mlada Boleslav plant that it has sparked a mini-boom in local real estate. In spite of the western jokes, Skoda cars outsell all other models combined in the republic.

Some of the industrial monoliths cherished by the former Communist Party also face a painful confrontation with the market economy. Restructuring plans for the steel and coal sectors, engineering company Skoda Pilsen (which specialised in building nuclear reactors for most of the former Soviet bloc) and CKD (whose main unit builds transport equipment) should be prepared this year.

The possible job losses are massive. Initial estimates for the national railway, for example, show that it only needs around one-third of its current workforce of 100,000.

'Many businesses are still kept going on state subsidies', says Fawn. 'Various programmes under Klaus kept people employed. Some of the jobless figures were cooked, with a lot of people taken out of the workforce rechristened under other categories like early retirement.'

Regional and investment packages will accompany the restructuring measures, with Czech government officials promising that the Commission will be consulted before they are put in place. Such consultations are necessary under the competition agreement between the EU and Czech Republic.

More generous tax perks for outside investors have already been outlined. However, some foreign investors such as British brewer Bass are still licking their wounds after the failure of the local competition authority to take a tough line. Brewers Radegast and Krusovice, which were found guilty of tying pubs to restrictive supply agreements, were fined less than €2,000.

Beer, so cherished by the Czechs, offers another, perhaps symbolic, lesson. If the definition of a recession is when pubs close, the Czech Republic has gone one step further. Five breweries, some with 400 years of history behind them, shut their doors last year.

Source: Chris Johnstone, *European Voice*, 28 January–3 February 1999.

Prague forced to face 'cruel truth' in EU warnings

'It is very good when somebody finally tells the cruel truth to those who have been telling us we were number one in central Europe.'

This was the stoical response from Czech Premier Milos Zeman last November after the European Commission published a highly critical report on the republic's progress in preparing for membership of the EU.

While blaming much of the country's poor performance on the previous government of Vaclav Klaus, Zeman's administration decided to take most of the blows on the chin and square up to the tasks set out for it by the Commission.

'We fully agree with the report that we have weaknesses in bank privatisation, the justice sphere, including social justice, corruption and others,' Zeman conceded gracefully.

From being seen as one of the front runners in the race to join the EU, the Czechs fell so far behind by November last year that there was even speculation that they might be relegated to the second wave of applicant countries.

Unlikely though this was, it would have put the Czechs back on the same footing as the Slovaks, still struggling to rid themselves of the pariah status earned by autocratic ruler Vladimir Meciar. Although the Commission complimented the Czech Republic on its progress in making the transition to a functioning market economy, Prague was rapped over the knuckles for failing to cut the cosy links between enterprises and state-owned banks.

This was taken to imply that firms were being kept afloat when any normal commercial bank would have cut the supply of credit months or years earlier. Nor had the Czechs shown 'as sustained a commitment to market reforms' as the best performing applicants: Hungary, Poland and Estonia.

Other problems highlighted by the Commission included the 'inherent weakness of the judiciary' ranging from a lack of trained legal personnel to lengthy delays in dealing with cases. Prague was also reprimanded for the rough treatment meted out to its Roma minority, who face unemployment rates of up to 90% and sporadic racial attacks.

But the Commission reserved its main criticism for a 'worrying slowdown' in the government's progress in adapting national laws to EU rules and standards, a key aspect of its preparations to join the Union.

Its report went to far as to warn that unless the Czechs, along with Slovenia, made up the lost ground, 'it would create a problem for the capacity of these countries to meet their obligations as future members in the medium term'.

While the Czech government had drawn up bold plans for adopting more EU rules and standards, the Commission said these had not yet been put into practice. Prague had, for example, recognised that reform of public administration was a priority but had 'not yet taken the necessary steps to translate the political commitment into concrete action'.

There had, however, been some improvement in the areas of banking and financial services supervision and in setting up bodies to control industrial standards and certification. Prague had also made some headway in bringing animal health and food safety standards close to EU levels.

In their defence, Czech officials point out that the Commission's report covered a 12-month period in which the country's decision-making process was paralysed by instability at the heart of power, with no fewer than three different governments.

This was compounded by the political stalemate caused by the largest centre-right party, Klaus' ODS, splitting into two warring factions. 'Imagine if Helmut Kohl's CDU split in two', said one official.

Some commentators argue that the EU should show more understanding for the Czech situation, given its own experience of the way in which national elections and the fragile coalitions which often follow them interfere with the Union's ability to take decisions quickly.

They point out that the EU itself has just suffered frustrating delays in negotiations on key internal reforms while waiting for the new German government to settle in, and that a change of government was required in the UK before its Union partners would contemplate lifting the beef ban.

In any case, Czech officials promise that the pace of reform in the republic will move up a gear over the next few months, pointing to the medium-term economic strategy which is due to be approved by the end of January and which will set clear deadlines for achieving a range of key policy objectives.

Nevertheless, with the Czech economy struggling to grow at all next year, Zeman faces a host of obstacles as he attempts to deliver on a raft of promises of industry restructurings and bank reforms.

It appears unlikely that he will be in a position to swap stoic acceptance of criticism for pride in genuine achievements by the time the Commission publishes its next progress report in November.

	1998	1999	2000
Real gross domestic product, 1994 prices, % change	−2.5	0.0	+3.0
Real household final capital consumption			
expenditure, 1994 prices, % change	−2.7	−1.1	+2.2
Real total gross fixed capital creation, 1994 prices, % change	−5.3	−1.7	+3.5
Real total industrial production (previous period = 100), % change	2.8	2.0	5.5
Consumer prices (all items, 1994 average = 100), % change	10.7	4.5	5.0
Average nominal wages, whole economy, (CSU series), % change	9.5	6.5	7.0
Money supply, M2 aggregate, end-year, % change			
on previous year end	6.7	5.0	6.5
Trade balance (billions of euro)	−1.98	−1.90	−2.59
Current account balance (billions of euro)	−0.60	−0.78	−1.29

Czech Republic – economic forecasts
Note: January 1999 survey

Source: HSBC Research

Source: Simon Taylor, *European Voice*, 28 January–3 February 1999.

EU companies have little to fear from eastwards expansion

Fears that expanding the Union to take in the five leading applicants for membership from central and eastern Europe could pose a serious threat to investment in existing member states are unfounded, according to a new study on the likely impact of enlargement.

It concludes that expanding the EU to take in Hungary, Poland, the Czech Republic, Slovenia and Estonia would not result in a massive surge in imports from the region or a significant shift in investment from west to east.

According to the study by the Brussels-based think tank CEPS, trade between the EU and the five front-runners has already been almost fully liberalised, because the countries themselves have made major efforts to cut import tariffs.

The report's author Paul Brenton says this means full Union membership for the five will not significantly increase trade flows as most barriers will already have been removed. 'There is no compelling evidence for large increases in trade with the central and east European countries [CEECs]', he told a recent conference.

His report points out that the remaining import tariffs on industrial goods are in the process of being abolished as part of the EU's association agreements with the five countries. This includes products where the price is highly dependent on the cost of labour – which is much lower in the CEEC countries – such as textiles, clothing and shoes. 'Fears of a surge in imports of such products into the EU from the CEECs appear to be without substance', concludes Brenton.

However, some countries are likely to be hit harder by increased competition from the east than others, with Portugal expected to be the worst affected because of its reliance on exports of products such as textiles and shoes which the applicant countries also sell abroad in large quantities.

One key change which will occur in the run-up to enlargement is that accession countries will have to abolish a range of technical barriers to trade such as different product standards, certification requirements, inspections and border controls.

But the report says that it is difficult to assess the precise implications of these changes for trade flows, although it is clear 'those that enter first will benefit at the expense of those left outside', as many of the countries in the region produce and export the same type of goods to the EU.

Brenton also rejects fears that enlargement will prompt companies to invest far more heavily in the applicant countries, at the expense of existing Union member states, to take advantage of the wage costs which are 20–30% lower than EU levels.

He argues that foreign direct investment (FDI) in the five leading contenders is already very close to the usual levels seen in advanced market economies. This is because these countries have completed ambitious programmes of privatisation and market liberalisation, the main factors in attracting foreign funds.

'For the more advanced transition economies, there is no evidence that FDI inflows are comprehensively below their potential level', said Brenton, who argues that foreign investment will therefore not rise above current levels when they join the Union.

His study concludes that the main factor which will determine the inflow of foreign funds in future will be income levels in the applicant countries. In the case of Bulgaria and Romania, which are lagging well behind in making the transition to a market economy, the amount of capital being put into the country could increase if 'suitable conditions for foreign investment are created'.

The report also argues that the risk of companies investing in central and eastern Europe rather than at home are exaggerated. 'Outward FDI to the CEECs has been less than one half of 1% of domestic investment for all the countries considered', it states. 'This clearly suggests that the direct impact of overseas investment in the CEECs on domestic investment in Organisation for Economic Cooperation and Development countries must be very small.'

But the study's findings have been challenged by other economists specialising in enlargement and investment issues.

'It is wrong to say the effect of enlargement on FDI flows would be insignificant', said Ros Lifton, Eastern Europe specialist at HSBC research in London. 'A Japanese or US firm may put a new office in Hungary rather than Germany because of lower wages and the regulatory environment.'

She added that there would always be competition over tax regimes, pointing to the current debate among existing EU member states about eliminating predatory tax policies as evidence of this.

Source: Simon Taylor, *European Voice*, 28 January – 3 February 1999.

1 (a) With reference to the case of the Czech Republic, explain the reforms which have been necessary in the transition from the command economy in Central and Eastern Europe.

  (b) Discuss the problems created by the continued relationship between the state and the banking system in the Czech Republic.

2 (a) Analyse the factors which Volkswagen may have taken into account in its decision to takeover Skoda Auto.

  (b) Discuss the advantages and disadvantages for the Czech economy of such Foreign Direct Investment (FDI).

3 To what extent is the Czech Republic likely to be granted membership of the EU?

4 Discuss the likely impact on the EU and the economies of Central and Eastern Europe of any eastward expansion of the EU.

Glossary

Key words have been identified **when they first occur** in each section of the text.

These key words consist of economic terms and concepts which students should know and which are likely to be used in OCR examination questions and stimulus material, such as case study and data response questions at AS and also at the A2 level. It is good practice for students to incorporate these terms, where appropriate, in examination answers.

This list does not include:

♦ institutions (for example, Bank of England, Competition Commission),

♦ organisations (for example, European Union, OECD),

♦ other specific examples used in the text (for example, Retail Prices Index, Labour Force Survey),

as some of these have changed over time and will change in the future.

It should also be emphasised that this glossary has been produced for guidance only and that some of the terms, particularly those introduced in the sections of units 2 and 3, may be subject to alternative definitions.

Section 1

capital consumption   also known as depreciation, this is the way in which capital is used up and loses value during the production process.

capital goods   man-made aids to production, such as industrial machinery and factories; one of the factors of production.

choice   a consequence of the economic problem, this is the process whereby consumers, producers and governments have to select from various possibilities which are available.

consumption   the process by which goods and services are used to satisfy wants.

developing economy   a country with low living standards compared to the advanced industrial economies of the world.

division of labour   the way in which the production process can be broken down into a series of tasks; the outcome is to increase output when compared to a situation where individuals undertake all tasks.

economic growth   an increase in the productive potential of the economy in real terms and that can be represented by an outward shift of the production possibility curve.

economic problem   the fundamental underpinning of Economics whereby resources are scarce/limited in relation to unlimited wants.

enterprise   the willingness to take risks in order to achieve business success; the management or responsibility for this process is in the hands of an entrepreneur; one of the factors of production.

factor endowment   the underpinning quantity and quality of factors of production available in an economy.

factor mobility   the extent or otherwise that factors of production can be reorganised to produce different goods and services.

investment   the creation of capital goods in the process of production or adding to the stock of real productive assets in an economy.

labour   the human resources available in an economy; one of the factors of production.

land   the natural resources available in an economy; one of the factors of production.

medium of exchange   a function of money that facilitates the process of exchange between individuals, avoiding the need for barter.

money   anything that enables exchange to take place whilst retaining its value, for example coins, notes or physical assets such as gold.

opportunity cost   the amount or cost of any other good or service that could have been obtained instead of any particular good or service; often expressed in terms of the 'next best' alternative.

production   the process of making goods and services.

production frontier   it shows what an economy is capable of producing; it is normally shown in the context of the physical amounts of two particular goods.

production possibility curve   the maximum level of output an economy can achieve when using its existing resources; usually shows the maximum output of one good, given the output of another good.

production transformation curve   as production possibility curve.

resources   anything that contributes or can contribute to production.

reallocation of resources   the process by which resources are transferred from one activity to another.

risk   the uncertainty that entrepreneurs face in the production process.

scale of preference   the ordering of wants in priority order.

scarcity   central to the economic problem whereby there are limited resources and unlimited wants, necessitating choices to be made.

specialisation   the process by which some goods and services are produced rather than others.

wants   anything that anyone might wish to acquire.

Section 2

ceteris paribus   literally means 'other things being equal', it is used as an assumption when looking at how demand or supply changes with a change in the price of a good or service.

complements   pairs of goods for which a rise in the price of one decreases demand for the other.

consumer surplus   the difference between the value a consumer places on all units consumed and the payments needed to be made to actually purchase that commodity; it is represented by the area under the demand curve and above the price line.

cross elasticity of demand   a numerical measure of the responsiveness of demand for one product following a

change in price of a related product; this measure is positive in the case of substitutes and negative for complements.

demand   the quantity of a good or service that purchasers want to buy at various prices.

demand curve   the relationship between the demand for a good or service and its price.

demand schedule   the numerical data which are needed to draw the demand curve for a good or service.

derived demand   a situation whereby the demand for something, for example labour, is dependent on the demand for another final good or service.

disequilibrium   a market situation where demand and supply are not equal.

effective demand   demand that is backed or supported by purchasing power.

elasticity   the responsiveness of demand/supply to a change in another influencing variable.

equilibrium   a situation where under present circumstances there is no tendency for change.

income elasticity of demand   a numerical measure of the responsiveness of demand following a change in income.

inferior goods   goods that have a negative income elasticity of demand, that is, are demanded less as income rises.

labour market   a market where workers and employers are brought together.

market   whenever buyers and sellers get together for the purpose of trade or exchange.

market demand   the total demand for a good or service.

money market   a market where the rate of interest is determined where the demand and supply of money are equated.

normal goods   goods that have a positive income elasticity of demand, that is, are demanded more as income rises.

notional demand   demand not necessarily backed by purchasing power.

perfectly elastic   where price elasticity of demand or supply is infinity, that is, if price rises above a particular price, nothing will be demanded or supplied.

perfectly inelastic   where price elasticity of demand or supply is zero, that is, demand or supply is not at all responsive to a change in price.

price elasticity of demand   a numerical measure of the responsiveness of demand to a change in the price of a particular product.

price elasticity of supply   a numerical measure of the responsiveness of supply to a change in the price of a particular product.

producer surplus   the additional revenue gained by a producer over that represented in the area under the supply curve of a good or service.

rate of interest   the payment that has to be made in order to obtain money or the reward for parting with the money.

sub-market   a particular part or segment of a market.

substitutes   pairs of goods for which a rise in the price of one increases the demand for the other.

supply   the quantity of a good or service that producers are willing to sell at various prices.

supply curve   the relationship between the supply of a good or service in relation to its price.

supply schedule   the numerical data which are needed to draw the supply curve for a good or service.

unitary elasticity   where price elasticity of demand or supply is 1, that is, demand or supply responds exactly proportional to a change in price.

Section 3

abnormal profit   profits earned over normal profits; likely to attract other new firms into that industry; also known as supernormal profit, particularly in perfectly competitive markets.

average fixed costs   total fixed costs of production divided by the quantity produced; decreases as output increases.

average revenue   total revenue divided by the quantity that is sold.

average total costs   total costs (fixed costs and variable costs) divided by the quantity produced.

average variable costs   total variable costs of production divided by the quantity produced; decreases with output but only up to a certain point.

barriers to entry   anything that stops new firms entering a particular market; they tend to be more prevalent as the degree of competition in markets decreases.

collusion   informal action by firm's designed to refrain from competition in their own markets.

concentration ratio   a measure of the extent to which a market is in the hands of a given or particular number of firms.

contestable market   where there are few barriers to entry and where there are potential entrants waiting to join the market if say abnormal profits are being earned.

diminishing returns   as the variable factors used by a firm increase, there will come a point where the returns to the variable units begin to fall.

diseconomies of scale   when the output of the firm increases too rapidly, long-run unit costs start to rise.

economies of scale   the benefits in terms of falling long-run average costs as output expands.

firm   general term used in Economics to denote the basic unit of production and decision making.

fixed costs   costs that are independent of output in the short run.

increasing returns   a situation where a firm's output is rising proportionally faster than its inputs into the production process.

long run   the time period when the firm can alter all of its factor inputs; all factors of production are, therefore, variable in the long run.

managerial objectives   the explanation of the objectives of firms in terms of the specific motivations of their managers; in particular, this can apply where the objective is other than profit maximisation.

marginal cost   the addition to total cost when one more unit of output is produced.

marginal revenue   the addition to total revenue when one more unit of output is sold.

monopolistic competition   a market structure with a large number of competing sellers and few barriers to entry.

monopoly   a market situation with one seller protected by barriers to entry.

non-price competition   any methods by which firms compete, other than through price cutting; typical examples are advertising, quality of product and customer service.

normal profit   included in the costs of production of a firm and just sufficient to keep that firm in operation in that industry.

oligopoly   a market structure with only a few firms; each firm has a sufficiently large share of the market to consider the reaction of others to any price changes it may make.

optimum output   the most efficient level of output represented at the minimum point of the average cost curve.

perfect competition   a benchmark used by economists to compare real-world market structures in which there are a large number of buyers and sellers each acting as price-takers.

price-taker   where a firm is able to sell whatever it produces at the ruling price and where its actions will not influence market prices.

private costs   costs which are directly incurred by the owners of the firm; also used for costs incurred by an individual carrying out a particular activity.

profit   the difference between revenue and costs in the production process.

profit maximisation   the usual objective of the firm in economic theory; it occurs at the output where marginal revenue in all market structures.

sales maximisation   an alternative objective of the firm where output is maximised.

sales revenue maximisation   a situation where a firm is seeking to maximise its revenue from the production process.

satisficing   where the firm's objective is to keep various groups, such as share holders, happy by making sufficient profits; it may also be used as a means of not attracting attention to the firm's business activities.

semi-fixed costs   costs to the firm which possess the characteristics of both fixed and variable costs; an example could be the heating costs of a hotel once it has decided to open its premises for business.

total revenue   the total receipts of a firm from its sales.

variable costs   costs which are directly related to the level of output of a firm.

Section 4

allocative efficiency   this exists where the selling price of a product is equal to its marginal cost of production.

economic efficiency   where an economy is using scarce resources in the most effective way in order to meet the highest level of wants.

Pareto optimality   when it is not possible to make one person better off without making some one clse worse off.

productive efficiency   where production is at the lowest point on the lowest average cost curve.

Section 5

de-merit goods   any good that has negative externalities associated with it; typical examples are passive smoking and drinking excessive alcohol.

equity   fairness (say) in the distribution of income or wealth.

external benefit   a situation where the social benefits exceed the private benefits; this benefit accrues to a third party.

external cost   a situation where the social costs exceed the private costs; this cost is imposed on a third party.

externality   this arises if a third party is affected by the decisions or actions of others.

fairness   see equity.

free rider   the advantage that some consumers receive from the purchase of a commodity by other consumers; it has particular application in the context of public goods.

geographical mobility   the way in which workers are able to move easily and quickly in order to find employment.

information failure   used in the context of merit goods, this refers to a situation where consumers do not have the relevant information or right information with which to make choices.

market failure   any situation where a free market fails to produce the best use of scarce resources.

merit goods   a good, such as health care or education, that has positive externalities associated with it.

negative externality   a situation that occurs when an external cost exists.

non-excludable   a characteristic of public goods whereby it is impossible to stop all from benefiting from the consumption of that good.

non-rival   a characteristic of public goods whereby, as more people consume that good, the benefit to those already consuming it is not diminished.

occupational mobility   the way in which workers are able to move quickly and easily from one type of job or occupation to another.

paternalism   a situation where society knows best and has some right to make a value judgement.

positive externality   a situation that occurs when an external benefit exists.

private benefits   the benefits which accrue to an individual consumer or firm.

public good   a good which possesses the characteristics of non-excludability and non-rivalry; they can be provided by the private sector as well as by the public sector – typical examples are a street light and national defence.

quasi-public goods   goods, such as roads, that are public in nature but that do not fully possess the essential characteristics of public goods.

social benefits   the total benefits arising from a particular action.

social costs   the total costs associated with a particular action.

value judgement   an opinion about the relative merits of a particular situation or set of circumstances that cannot be effectively investigated.

wealth   the accumulated stock of assets.

x-inefficiency   a situation where firms do not have to produce goods at the lowest possible cost.

Section 6

controls   statutory forms of government intervention.

cost–benefit analysis   a technique for assessing the desirability of a particular project, taking into account all of the respective costs and benefits.

financial intervention   the use of taxes and subsidies by the government to influence market outcomes.

government failure   problems of resource allocation that occur as a consequence of government intervention in markets, for example food shortages in a centrally planned economy.

income transfer   a deliberate means of redistributing income by government, for example social security benefits.

in-kind transfer   a free service provided by government but generally funded from tax revenue.

mixed goods   a good or situation where negative externalities and information failure can be recognised.

nationalised industry   a rather dated term for an activity wholly operated by the public sector.

net present value   the outcome of discounting a stream of costs and benefits to a common base date. A positive value indicates that there are valid reasons for a project to go ahead.

privatisation   the sale of a state owned or operated activity to the private sector.

progressive tax   any tax where the revenue collected rises more than proportionally to income, for example income tax.

regressive tax   any tax where the ratio of tax paid in relation to income falls as income rises, for example poll tax, VAT.

regulation   general term used to describe a wide range of measures used by governments to control a market.

shadow price   a price imputed in situations where no market price is available, for example value of time.

social justice   justification on the part of government for the redistribution of income or wealth.

social security benefit   any handout which transfers income to low-income groups or to other disadvantaged groups.

spillover effects   outcomes from market situations where there are external benefits or costs; the market mechanism is unable to take these into account.

subsidy   a payment made by government to consumers or producers that reduces the market price of a good or service.

Section 7

aggregate demand   the total spending on goods and services produced in an economy.

anticipated inflation   a situation where the rate of inflation recorded is broadly in line with that which has been expected or forecast.

balance of payments   a record or overall statement of a country's economic transactions with the rest of the world, usually over a year.

black economy   transactions of goods and services that are not declared and not included in GDP.

capital account   part of the balance of payments showing transfers of capital between a country and the rest of the world.

circular flow of income   a simple model of the process by which income flows around an economy.

current account   the most important part of the balance of payment; it is a record of the trade in goods and services plus investment income and current transfers.

expenditure method   a method of calculating the GDP of an economy by estimating the total value of what is spent in a year.

exports   any goods or services sold to another country.

financial transactions   an important part of the balance of payments relating to capital flows entering or leaving the economy.

fiscal drag   a situation where, due to inflation, the proportion of income collected in taxes rises, and where tax thresholds remain unchanged.

fixed exchange rate   where the price of one currency in terms of another is pre-determined.

floating exchange rate   where the price of one currency in terms of another is determined by market forces.

government spending   spending by central and local government on goods or the provision of services.

Gross Domestic Product   a measure of total output produced in an economy by activities located in that country.

Gross National Product   a measure of total output produced that takes into account the net income of residents from economic activities carried out abroad as well as at home.

hyperinflation   a very high rate of inflation, the outcome of which is that people lose confidence in money.

imports   any good or service bought from another country.

income method   a method of calculating the GDP of an economy by estimating the total incomes earned by the various factors of production.

inflation   a persistent increase in the level of prices in an economy.

international competitiveness   a measure of the relative ranking of an economy compared to the rest of the world.

living standard   the amount of goods and services enjoyed by residents in an economy; often measured in terms of real GDP per head.

managed exchange rate   where the price of one currency in terms of another moves within narrow pre-determined bands.

net errors and omissions   formally known as the balancing item, this is a measure of any discrepancies in the balance of payments of an economy.

nominal GDP   GDP measured in terms of current prices in a given year.

non-marketed goods and services   items not included in GDP due to no financial transaction taking place.

output   the amount which is produced by an industry or service in an economy.

output gap   the shortfall between actual and potential output in an economy.

output method   a method of calculating the GDP of any economy by estimating the total value of what is produced in a year.

potential growth   an increase in the productive capacity in an economy; can be represented by an outward shift of the production possibility curve.

productivity   a measure of the output produced per unit of a factor of production.

ratchet effect   the tendency for import prices to rise as a consequence of a fall in the exchange rate, in turn prompting wage rises.

read GDP   GDP measured in terms of the actual goods and services produced, taking into account any price fluctuations.

shoe leather costs of inflation   the costs of moving money from one asset to another in search of the highest rate of interest at a time when the rate of inflation is rising.

stop–go policy   a short-term tendency for the management of aggregate demand to produce periods of contraction and expansion in the economy.

sustainable economic growth   a growth strategy whereby future needs are not compromised by current growth policies.

transfer payments   any payment made from taxpayers to non-taxpayers, for example welfare payments.

unanticipated inflation   a situation where the rate of inflation exceeds that which had been expected or forecasted.

unemployment   a broad term to describe those willing and able to work but who are unable to obtain a job.

value added   the difference between the final value of sales and the cost of inputs.

Section 8

aggregate supply   the total output of an economy.

consumer spending   the amount spent by individuals on goods and services.

disposable income   personal income which is available to spend, usually total income less direct tax and social security contributions.

expectations   what people expect to happen, for example outcome of external factors which can affect business well-being.

first-round effect   the first stage of the multiplier process.

fiscal policies   the use of taxation and government spending to influence the economy.

hot money   money which is liable to rapid transfer from one country to another.

injection   an autonomous addition to the circular flow of income.

investment expenditure   the process of adding to the stock of productive assets in an economy by private and public sectors.

leakages   an autonomous withdrawal from the circular flow of income.

marginal propensity to consume   the proportion of any increase in income which is spent on consumption.

monetary policies   the use of interest rates or controls on the money supply to influence the economy.

multiplier effect   the process by which any change in spending produces a more extensive effect upon total economic activity.

net expenditure on exports and imports total expenditure on exports less total expenditure on imports.

savings the difference between income and consumption.

supply-side policies any policy that affects the total output of an economy.

Section 9

broad money money held in banks and building societies but which is not immediately accessible.

crowding out where an increase in one form of spending leads to a fall in some other form of spending, for example an increase in aggregate demand through lower taxes could reduce expenditure on investment and exports due to an interest rate rise and a higher exchange rate.

deregulation an aspect of privatisation whereby barriers to entry into a particular market are removed.

government bond a security issued at a face value and that pays a fixed annual rate of interest.

money supply the total amount of money in an economy.

narrow money notes, coins and balance available for normal transactions.

unemployment trap where individuals actually receive more in benefits than when they are actually in a job.

Section 10

absolute advantage where for a given set of resources, one country can produce more of a particular good than another country.

comparative advantage where a country has a lower opportunity cost of production compared with another country.

deindustrialisation a feature of many industrialised economies over the last 30 years or so whereby employment in the industrial sector is declining in importance relative to that in the service sector.

domestic opportunity cost the cost of producing one good relative to another in an economy.

dumping selling goods in an overseas market at below the cost of production.

exchange control setting a legal limit on foreign exchange transactions.

expenditure-dampening policies domestic policies that reduce aggregate demand in order to reduce expenditure on imports.

expenditure-switching policies policies that seek to switch expenditure from imported to domestically produced goods.

free trade a situation where international trade takes place unimpeded by any restrictions, that is, market forces operate to provide the best allocation of resources.

import penetration ratio the proportion of the domestic sales of a product that is met by imports of that product.

infant industry a newly established industry that is unable to compete in the market.

international trade the buying and selling of goods and services across national frontiers.

laissez-faire a policy of non-intervention by governments in the domestic or international economy.

mercantilism the view that economies should aim to be self-sufficient and that there should be a balance of payments surplus for international transactions.

protection any measures or devices that protect an economy or its industries from foreign competition.

quota a physical restriction on imports into an economy.

self-sufficiency a situation whereby all needs in an economy can be met or produced from within.

tariff a tax on imported goods.

Answers to selected self-assessment tasks

Below are some suggested answers to a few of the self-assessment tasks contained in the book. These answers are for guidance – you should appreciate that in some cases other answers are possible. Please ask your teacher for guidance.

Section 1
Choices facing an economy (p.27)

If point p was chosen, then gross investment is less than capital consumption. Net investment is therefore negative. The capital stock in this economy will decline and the production possibilities will diminish. The PPC will therefore shift inwards. Although the present standard of living is high, the future standard of living will be less.

If point q was chosen, gross investment would equal capital consumption. Net investment is therefore zero. The capital stock and production possibilities are unchanged. The PPC maintains its current position. The future standard of living will remain at its present level.

If point r is chosen, gross investment would exceed capital consumption. Net investment is therefore positive and production possibilities will increase in the future. The PPC will shift outwards from the origin. This choice has reduced the standard of living at present as fewer consumer goods have been produced; the benefits will be seen in the future as future generations enjoy a higher standard of living with the increased capital stock accumulated in the present time period.

All the above assumes no other factors affect the position of the PPC.

Section 2
The demand curve (p.31)

1 5,500 PCs
2 £1,930
3 'Ceteris paribus', that is, all other factors, such as income, the price of related products and our attitudes towards PCs, remain the same.

The supply curve (p.36)

1 2,500 PCs
2 £860
3 'Certeris puribus', that is, any other supply-influencing factors, such as the costs associated with supplying the product, the size, structure and nature of the industry or government policy, remain unchanged.
4 Advantages – a very simple representation
Disadvantages – not always easy to read off accurately

Price elasticity of demand (p.45)

1 Branded products in general, such as Coca Cola, are likely to have a relatively low or inelastic price elasticity of demand. Producers try to build up a brand image in order to protect the status of their products. To some though Coca Cola and Pepsi Cola may be seen as substitutes and therefore an increase in the price of one may cause consumers to switch to the other. The broader group of products will have a more elastic price elasticity of demand (soft drinks). Tobacco and fuel though have no close substitutes and are therefore likely to have an inelastic price elasticity of demand.
2 All PED estimates are negative, that is, an increase in price will lead to a fall in demand or vice versa. Mail order ties have the most elastic demand, whilst ties sold from fashion stores have a low inelastic price elasticity of demand. For independent retailers, any reduction in prices is met with an equal increase in demand or vice versa.

Section 3
Firms' costs (p.61)

Wok Stock and Barrel
AFC = £3 per unit
AVC = £3 per unit
ATC = £6 per unit
AR = £8

Abnormal profit £18,000 at capacity output of 9,000 units.

At £6 per unit, revenue would fall to £54,000, which is equal to total costs. Normal profit only would be earned.

Fish and Chips Case Study (p. 69)

1 Low overheads is an alternative term for low fixed costs (for example, low property rental, low capital costs)

2 Price rises will not make a fish and chip shop owner better off because it is implied that there is a high price elasticity of demand for the product. A shop's rivals may not immediately follow suit, compounding the loss of revenue.

3 In a monopoly, the price elasticity of demand would be much lower – the firm could increase prices in order to raise total revenue.

4 Local advertising could shift the demand curve to the right; as the article indicates, though, improving product quality is the most likely way of increasing revenue.

5 Barriers to entry are low because of:
   ◆ low set up costs,
   ◆ low overheads,
   ◆ no particular training required,
   ◆ no special license required.
   although a food hygiene certificate is now required for all staff handling uncooked food.

6 Marginal cost and marginal revenue may not be measurable; cost-plus pricing is therefore used. The owner may have alternative objectives, for example, satisficing as a consequence of limiting the number of openings of his business.

Section 5
Local Hospital Closure Threatened (p. 93)

1 (a) A product that is better for people than they realise (due to lack of information).
  (b) Preventative health care may clearly be better for people than they realise. A lack of consumer information is highly likely. Do consumers know how much they could save by having preventative health care rather than having to be treated later?

2 (a) The best possible use of economic resources. For this, there must be both *productive efficiency* (producing things at minimum cost) and *allocative efficiency* (producing those things most demanded).

  (b) Productive efficiency because it is to do with producing at the lowest cost.

3 (c) Because market economies can result in very unequal distributions of income.
  (b) This relates to concern over the distribution of income.
   The main comment would likely be that this is a strong value judgement about the desirable nature of society. As such, it is beyond the usual range of economic analysis and clearly a normative statement.

4 (a) A range of possible explanations, such as productive inefficiency owing to 'x' inefficiency, allocative inefficiency owing to lack of competitive pressure and prices being set too high.
  (b) It is suggested that there are many economies of scale available in health care provision. This means that health care providers (hospitals) would tend to become very large and may well become local monopolies.
  (c) A range of possibilities here.
   The merit good nature of preventative health care implies that it is likely to be under-provided. Positive externalities if people's health is improved and others benefit (and thus likely to be under-provision).
   Distributional points could be made: unequal incidence of ill health that has to be paid for could be considered as 'unfair'.

5 (a) When a third party is affected by the actions of others. This may be negative (social costs exceed private costs) or positive (social benefits exceed private benefits).
  (b) Most of the externalities mentioned appear to be negative, for example, local unemployment, lower local house prices, adverse affects on local trade. There could be the positive externalities of reduced overall health care costs that implies the possibility of lower taxes and/or more public spending in other areas.

Section 6
Method of government intervention (p.101)

(a) Regulation: the government has used legislation to limit pollution from vehicles. In this case the government regulates the quantity of pollution produced by a vehicle's exhaust emissions. Regulation is used to correct for a market failure owing to negative externalities.

(b) Regulation: the government has used legislation to fix prices. In this case the government fixes the minimum price of labour or the wage rate. Minimum wage rates may be used to redistribute income or to overcome market failure caused by uneven power in the labour market (employers have more power than low-paid workers).

(c) Financial intervention: higher tax rates on petrol are used to discourage consumption of leaded petrol. In this case the government is keen to stop the production of leaded petrol which causes more pollution than unleaded petrol. Thus this type of financial intervention is used to reduce negative externalities.

(d) Financial intervention: free eye tests are the same as a total subsidy. They are used to encourage pensioners to have their eyes tested on a regular basis. This may be to correct a market failure: pensioners are unable to value the importance of frequent eye tests or they may be free for equity reasons.

(e) Regulation: the government uses legislation to impose a minimum standard of driving on the community. This is intended to ensure that all drivers show a minimum competence to drive a vehicle. It corrects for two potential market failures: external costs and imperfect information.

(f) Regulation: legislation is imposed to restrict the purchase of lottery tickets by age. Some people argue that young people are unable to correctly value the costs and benefits of addictive products, such as gambling, and thus need protecting against them. Thus the government is protecting young people against market failure due to imperfect information.

(g) Income transfers: job seekers allowance is a form of transfer of income from tax payers to those seeking work. One reason for this intervention is to protect against loss of income due to unemployment. However, if the individual has large amounts of savings then it is argued that they do not require as much protection against loss of earnings as they have a source of income on which they can draw.

(h) State production: in this case the state is producing education by providing both the building and the staff to run the schools. Alternatively the government could have used financial intervention by providing the finance for the schools to be built privately and staffed by a private education 'company'. The reasons for intervention of this type in education are varied and will include market failure owing to external benefits from education not being valued by private markets. Market failure might also result from imperfect information as both parents and students are unable to correctly value the private costs and benefits of education. Finally government may intervene to produce education for reasons of fairness or equity, measuring that all children have an equal and fair access to education regardless of their parents' income.

Section 7
International comparisons of GDP (pp. 127–128)

(a) GDP is measured in terms of prices in a given base year It is calculated to show actual changes in the quantity of goods and services produced. Can be referred to as real GDP at it is adjusted for inflation.

(b) Germany (30.5 per cent)

(c) UK (15.6 per cent)

(d) A wider range of data including the inflation rate, the trade balance in goods and services, the level and type of investment, the exchange rate and research and development factors. A comparative analysis between the UK and its main trading partners, though, should be handled carefully, as differences in the compilation of statistics between countries might result in the wrong conclusions being drawn.

Section 8
Aggregate demand (pp. 144–145)

1 Various possibilities including:
- the relative decrease in government expenditure over the period;
- no change in the percentage from consumers expenditure from 1990 to 1997;

- an increase in the percentage derived from international trade, particularly imports;
- an increase in the percentage of investment over 1980 to 1990.

2 Again, various explanations of the above could include:
- the impact of privatisation;
- as consumers get richer their propensity to consume often falls;
- a consequence of the close integration of the UK with its EU partners, particularly through the realisation of the Single European Market;
- a period of lower interest rates.

3 For example, the government could:
- increase taxation;
- reduce its own spending;
- increase interest rates;
- cut back on government spending.

Problems include:
- inflationary effects of increasing indirect taxes;
- not always easy to cut back on government spending (central and local), usually unpopular with electors;
- problem of a 'time lag' due to the complex workings of the economy.

Section 9

Effects of policy changes on AD and AS (p. 154)

(a) AD will decrease. In the short run consumers have less disposable income; in the long run workers may react by working harder or by choosing to work less and exist on social benefits. AS can move either way or remain stable.

(b) As (a), except that in the long run pensioners may receive higher pensions, which will then boost AD.

(c) Reduces real incomes and hence AD. May in long run act as a disincentive to work, so reducing AS.

(d) AD gets a direct boost; AS should expand slowly in the long run.

(e) Opposite to (a) above. AD increases in the short run but in the long run AS might decrease as some workers decide to leave the labour force and live off state benefits.

(f) Investment will fall, so in the short run AD decreases. In the long run AS could shift to the left.

Index